AP PSYCHOLOGY
ALL ACCESS

Nancy Fenton, M.A.
AP Psychology Teacher
Adlai E. Stevenson High School
Lincolnshire, Illinois

Jessica Flitter, M.A.
AP Psychology Teacher
Oak Creek High School
Oak Creek, Wisconsin

Research & Education Association
Visit our website: www.rea.com/studycenter

Planet Friendly Publishing
✔ Made in the United States
✔ Printed on Recycled Paper
   Text: 30%   Cover: 10%
Learn more: www.greenedition.org

At REA we're committed to producing books in an Earth-friendly manner and to helping our customers make greener choices.

Manufacturing books in the United States ensures compliance with strict environmental laws and eliminates the need for international freight shipping, a major contributor to global air pollution.

And printing on recycled paper helps minimize our consumption of trees, water and fossil fuels. This book was printed on paper made with **30% post-consumer waste**, and the cover was printed on paper made with **10% post-consumer waste**. According to the Environmental Paper Network's Paper Calculator, by using these innovative papers instead of conventional papers, we achieved the following environmental benefits:

Trees Saved: 36 • Air Emissions Eliminated: 8,793 pounds
Water Saved: 7,011 gallons • Solid Waste Eliminated: 2,582 pounds

Courier Corporation, the manufacturer of this book, owns the Green Edition Trademark.
For more information on our environmental practices, please visit us online at **www.rea.com/green**

Research & Education Association
61 Ethel Road West
Piscataway, New Jersey 08854
E-mail: info@rea.com

AP PSYCHOLOGY ALL ACCESS

Printed in the United States of America

Library of Congress Control Number 2011943704

ISBN-13: 978-0-7386-1026-9
ISBN-10: 0-7386-1026-7

REA® is a registered trademark of
Research & Education Association, Inc.

Contents

Chapter 5: Biological Bases of Behavior 55

Chapter 6: Sensation and Perception 83

Chapter 10: Motivation and Emotion 189

Chapter 11: Developmental Psychology 213

Chapter 12: Personality 247

Chapter 13: Testing and Individual Differences   271

Chapter 14: Abnormal Behavior   289

Chapter 15: Treatment of Abnormal Behavior 315

Chapter 16: Social Psychology 343

About Our Authors

<u>Nancy Fenton</u>, M.A., teaches AP Psychology at Adali E. Stevenson High School in Lincolnshire, Illinois. Ms. Fenton was elected to the APA committee for Teachers of Psychology in Secondary Schools, and appointed to represent high school teachers at the APA Educational Directorate working group for the Coalition for Psychology in Education and Schools. Ms. Fenton was also appointed to the American Psychological Association Review Panel created to review performance indictor submissions which will be used with the National Standards for High School Psychology. She has taught AP Psychology for seven years and has been a reader for the AP Psychology exam since 2008.

<u>Jessica Flitter</u>, M.A., teaches AP Psychology at Oak Creek High School in Oak Creek, Wisconsin. Ms. Flitter has participated in College Board Training Seminars, Enhancing the Teaching of Psychology Conference, and the American Psychology Association and Clark University Institute for High School Psychology Teachers. She has also collaborated with psychology teachers across Wisconsin and Illinois regarding curriculum and teaching methods for Advanced Placement Psychology. Ms. Flitter has taught AP Psychology for seven years.

About Research & Education Association

Founded in 1959, Research & Education Association is dedicated to publishing the finest and most effective educational materials—including software, study guides, and test preps—for students in middle school, high school, college, graduate school, and beyond. Today, REA's wide-ranging catalog is a leading resource for teachers, students, and professionals.

Acknowledgments

REA would like to thank Larry B. Kling, Vice President, Editorial, for supervising development; Pam Weston, Publisher, for setting the quality standards for production integrity and managing the publication to completion; John Paul Cording, Vice President, Technology, for coordinating the design and development of the REA Study Center; Diane Goldschmidt and Michael Reynolds, Managing Editors, for coordinating development of this edition; Claudia Petrilli, Graphic Designer, for interior book design; S4Carlisle Publishing Services for typesetting; and Weymouth Design and Christine Saul for cover design.

Welcome to REA's All Access for AP Psychology

A new, more effective way to prepare for your AP exam.

There are many different ways to prepare for an AP exam. What's best for you depends on how much time you have to study and how comfortable you are with the subject matter. To score your highest, you need a system that can be customized to fit you: your schedule, your learning style, and your current level of knowledge.

This book, and the free online tools that come with it, will help you personalize your AP prep by testing your understanding, pinpointing your weaknesses, and delivering flashcard study materials unique to you.

Let's get started and see how this system works.

How to Use REA's AP All Access

The REA AP All Access system allows you to create a personalized study plan through three simple steps: targeted review of exam content, assessment of your knowledge, and focused study in the topics where you need the most help.

Here's how it works:

Review the Book	Study the topics tested on the AP exam and learn proven strategies that will help you tackle any question you may see on test day.
Test Yourself & Get Feedback	As you review the book, test yourself. Score reports from your free online tests and quizzes give you a fast way to pinpoint what you really know and what you should spend more time studying.
Improve Your Score	Armed with your score reports, you can personalize your study plan. Review the parts of the book where you are weakest, and use the REA Study Center to create your own unique e-flashcards, adding to the 100 free cards included with this book.

Finding Your Weaknesses: The REA Study Center

The best way to personalize your study plan and truly focus on your weaknesses is to get frequent feedback on what you know and what you don't. At the online REA Study Center, you can access three types of assessment: topic-level quizzes, mini-tests, and a full-length practice test. Each of these tools provides true-to-format questions and delivers a detailed score report that follows the topics set by the College Board.

Topic-Level Quizzes

Short, 15-minute online quizzes are available throughout the review and are designed to test your immediate grasp of the topics just covered.

Mini-Tests

Two online mini-tests cover what you've studied in each half of the book. These tests are like the actual AP exam, only shorter, and will help you evaluate your overall understanding of the subject.

Full-Length Practice Test

After you've finished reviewing the book, take our full-length exam to practice under test-day conditions. Available both in this book and online, this test gives you the most complete picture of your strengths and weaknesses. We strongly recommend that you take the online version of the exam for the added benefits of timed testing, automatic scoring, and a detailed score report.

Improving Your Score: e-Flashcards

Once you get your score report, you'll be able to see exactly which topics you need to review. Use this information to create your own flashcards for the areas where you are weak. And, because you will create these flashcards through the REA Study Center, you'll be able to access them from any computer or smartphone.

Not quite sure what to put on your flashcards? Start with the 100 free cards included when you buy this book.

After the Full-Length Practice Test: Crash Course

After finishing this book and taking our full-length practice exam, pick up REA's *Crash Course for AP Psychology*. Use your most recent score reports to identify any areas where you are still weak, and turn to the *Crash Course* for a rapid review presented in a concise outline style.

REA's Suggested 8-Week AP Study Plan

Depending on how much time you have until test day, you can expand or condense our eight-week study plan as you see fit.

To score your highest, use our suggested study plan and customize it to fit your schedule, targeting the areas where you need the most review.

JAN.
9th to 15th

	Review 1-2 hours	**Quiz** 15 minutes	**e-Flashcards** Anytime, anywhere	**Mini-Test** 30 minutes	**Full-Length Practice Test** 2 hours
Week 1	Chapters 1-4	Quiz 1 *(16th)*			
Week 2	Chapters 5-6	Quiz 2	Access your e-flashcards from your computer or smartphone whenever you have a few extra minutes to study. Start with the 100 free cards included when you buy this book. Personalize your prep by creating your own cards for topics where you need extra study.		
Week 3	Chapters 7-8	Quiz 3			
Week 4	Chapters 9-10	Quiz 4		Mini-Test 1 (The Mid-Term)	
Week 5	Chapters 11-12	Quiz 5			
Week 6	Chapters 13-14	Quiz 6			
Week 7	Chapters 15-16	Quiz 7		Mini-Test 2 (The Final)	
Week 8	Review Chapter 2 Strategies				Full-Length Practice Exam (Just like test day)

Need even more review? Pick up a copy of REA's *Crash Course for AP Psychology,* a rapid review presented in a concise outline style. Get more information about the *Crash Course* series at the REA Study Center.

Test-Day Checklist

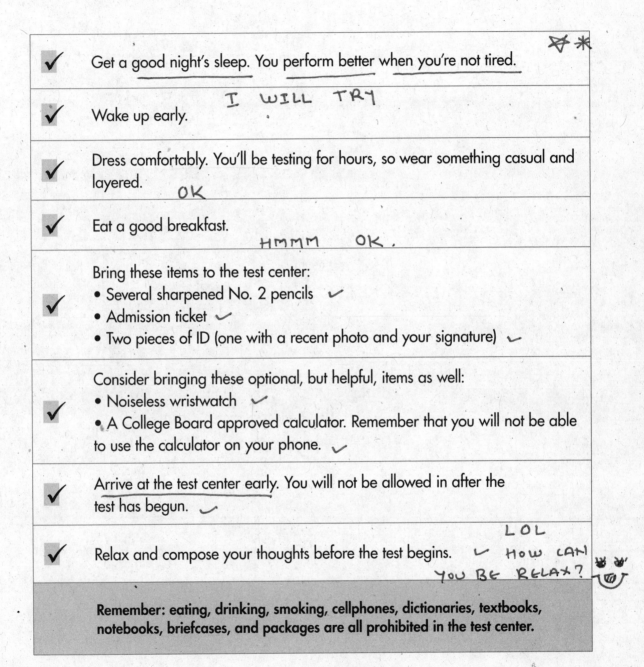

✓	Get a good night's sleep. You perform better when you're not tired.
✓	Wake up early. *I WILL TRY*
✓	Dress comfortably. You'll be testing for hours, so wear something casual and layered. *OK*
✓	Eat a good breakfast. *HMMM OK.*
✓	Bring these items to the test center: • Several sharpened No. 2 pencils ✓ • Admission ticket ✓ • Two pieces of ID (one with a recent photo and your signature) ✓
✓	Consider bringing these optional, but helpful, items as well: • Noiseless wristwatch ✓ • A College Board approved calculator. Remember that you will not be able to use the calculator on your phone. ✓
✓	Arrive at the test center early. You will not be allowed in after the test has begun. ✓
✓	Relax and compose your thoughts before the test begins. ✓ *LOL HOW CAN YOU BE RELAX?*

Remember: eating, drinking, smoking, cellphones, dictionaries, textbooks, notebooks, briefcases, and packages are all prohibited in the test center.

Strategies for the Exam

What Will I See on the AP Psychology Exam?

One May morning, you stroll confidently into the school library where you're scheduled to take the AP Psychology exam. You know your stuff: you paid attention in class, followed your textbook, took plenty of notes, and reviewed your coursework by reading a special test prep guide. You can identify the functions of various parts of the brain, explain Piaget's stages of cognitive development, and describe the pros and cons of different types of research methods. So, how will you show your knowledge on the test?

The Multiple-Choice Section

First off, you'll complete a lengthy multiple-choice section that tests your ability to not just remember facts about the various fields of psychology, but also to apply that knowledge to psychological theories and methods. This section will require you to answer 100 multiple-choice questions in just 70 minutes. Here are the major fields of inquiry covered on the AP Psychology exam:

- History and approaches
- Research methods
- Biological bases of behavior
- Sensation and perception
- States of consciousness
- Learning
- Cognition
- Motivation and emotion

Handwritten margin notes:

Left margin: ensation refers to the rocess of sensing our nvironment trough ouch, taste, sight sound, ne smell. This info is sent to our brains in raw form where rception comes into lay. Perception is the way we interpret hese sensations and Therefore make sense of everything around us.

Right margin (Biological bases of behavior): The physical structure of the body plays an important role in the behaviour of an individual. The most important physical structure for psychologist is the nervous system.

Right margin (Cognition): The mental action or process of acquiring knowled and understanding through and throughout experience and senses.

- Developmental psychology

- Personality

- Testing and individual differences

- Abnormal psychology

- Treatment of psychological disorders

- Social psychology

That's a lot of ideas to cover in just one test, and certainly 100 multiple-choice questions is a lot of items to respond to in a short period of time. But by *working quickly and methodically* you'll have plenty of time to address this section effectively. We'll look at this in greater depth later in this chapter.

The Free-Response Section

After time is called on the multiple-choice section, you'll get a short break before diving into the free-response, or essay, section. This section requires you to produce two written responses in 50 minutes. Like the multiple-choice section, the free-response portion of the exam expects you to be able to *apply your own knowledge to analyze psychological information,* in addition to being able to provide essential facts and definitions.

What's the Score?

Although the scoring process for the AP exam may seem quite complex, it boils down to two simple components: your multiple-choice score plus your free-response scores. The multiple-choice section accounts for two-thirds of your overall score, and is generated by awarding one point toward your "raw score" for each question you answer correctly. The free-response section accounts for the remaining one-third of your total score. Within the free-response section, each question counts equally toward your final score. Trained graders read students' written responses and assign points according to grading rubrics. The number of points you accrue out of the total possible will form your score on the free-response section.

The College Board scores your AP exam on a scale of 1 to 5. Although individual colleges and universities determine what credit or advanced placement, if any, is awarded to students at each score level, these are the assessments typically associated with each numeric score:

5   Extremely well qualified (ACHIEVED)

4   Well qualified

3   Qualified

2   Possibly qualified

1   No recommendation

Section I: Strategies for the Multiple-Choice Section of the Exam

Because the AP exam is a standardized test, each version of the test from year to year must share many similarities in order to be fair. That means that you can always expect certain things to be true about your AP Psychology exam.

Which of the following phrases accurately describes a multiple-choice question on the AP Psychology exam?

(A) always has five choices

(B) may ask you to apply a psychological theory

(C) may ask you to find a wrong idea or group related concepts

(D) more likely to test subject content than the history of psychology

(E) all of the above*

> Did you pick "all of the above"? Good job!

What does this mean for your study plan? You should focus more on the application and interpretation of the various analytical fields of psychology than on the history of psychology and nuts-and-bolts details about different psychological approaches; in fact, about one-third of all multiple-choice questions will require you to apply a psychological theory or approach. Keep in mind, too, that many psychological concepts relate to

---

*Of course, on the actual AP Psychology exam, you won't see any choices featuring "all of the above" or "none of the above." Do, however, watch for "except" questions. We'll cover this kind of item a bit later in this section.

one another. This means that you should consider the connections among ideas and concepts as you study. This will help you prepare for more difficult interpretation questions, and give you a head start on questions that ask you to interpret psychological information. Not sure what this type of question might look like? Let's examine a typical interpretation item:

A teacher gave Ken 20 points too many on a test, but Ken told her about it because he was afraid he might get caught and punished if he did not. Ken is in which of Kohlberg's moral stages?

(A) ~~Concrete operational~~

(B) ~~Formal operational~~

(C) Postconventional

(D) Conventional

(E) Preconventional

> Take a moment to look over the answer choices. Notice that two of them list concepts that are not part of Kohlberg's moral stages, so you can automatically rule these out. Then consider Ken's motivation—to avoid punishment. Which moral stages relate to receiving rewards and avoiding punishment?

Types of Questions

You've already seen a list of the general content areas that you'll encounter on the AP Psychology exam. But how do those different areas translate into questions?

Question Type	Sample Question Stems
Application of Theories and Models	Three-year-old Jeff, who sees lots of cows on the family farm, saw a rhinoceros at the zoo and thought it, too, was a cow. Which of the cognitive processes described by Piaget does this illustrate?
Definition	According to Carl Jung's personality theory, the terms "anima" and "animus" refer to . . .
Example	To better remember the names of the five Great Lakes you might use the acronym HOMES (Huron, Ontario, Michigan, Erie, Superior). This is an example of . . .
Factual	Ivan Pavlov is famous for his research on . . .
Visual Stimulus	Based on the chart, what conclusion can be drawn about the standard deviation of the results of this experiment?

Throughout this book, you will find tips on the features and strategies you can use to answer different types of questions.

Achieving Multiple-Choice Success

It's true that you don't have a lot of time to finish this section of the AP exam. But it's also true that you don't need to get every question right to get a great score. Answering just three-fourths of the questions correctly—along with a good showing on the free-response section—can earn you a score of 4 or 5. That means that not only do you not have to answer every question right, but also that you don't even need to answer every question at all. By *working quickly and methodically,* however, you'll have all the time you'll need. Plan to spend an average of 40 seconds on each multiple-choice question. You may spend less time on questions with simple one- or two-word answers, but find you need a bit longer on those questions with longer, analytical choices. That's okay as long your time balances out to about 40 seconds in the end. Keep in mind, too, that the questions on the AP Psychology exam are arranged roughly in order of difficulty. Expect the first third of this section to be somewhat easier than the middle third, and the last third to be the hardest of all. Working more quickly early in the exam can help you bank time to spend on the more complex items near the end of the section.

You may find it helpful to use a timer or stopwatch for a few questions to help you get a handle on how long 40 seconds feels in a testing situation. If timing is hard for you, set a timer for ten minutes each time you take one of the 15-question online quizzes that accompany this book to help you practice working at speed. Let's look at some other strategies for answering multiple-choice items.

Process of Elimination

You've probably used the process-of-elimination strategy, intentionally or unintentionally, throughout your entire test-taking career. The process of elimination requires you to read each answer choice and consider whether it is the best response to the question given. Because the AP exam typically asks you to find the *best* answer rather than the *only* answer, it's almost always advantageous to read each answer choice. More than one choice may have some grain of truth to it, but one—the right answer—will be the most correct. Let's examine a multiple-choice question and use the process-of-elimination approach:

Which of the following is the most basic need in Maslow's hierarchy of needs?

(A)   Security

(B)   ~~Religion~~

(C)   Nourishment

(D)   ~~Motivation~~

(E)   Self-esteem

> To use the process of elimination, consider each option. Eliminate ideas that are clearly wrong, such as *motivation* and *religion*. Cross out each choice as you eliminate it. Then consider the definitions of the remaining choices. Which *most directly* matches with the fundamental base of Maslow's hierarchy? If you're unsure, you can return to the question later or just guess. You've got a one-third chance of being right. Finally, consider the remaining three options: Which one is the most basic, without which an individual would never be able to fulfill the other needs?

Students often find the most difficult types of questions on the AP exam to be those that ask you to find a statement that is *not* true or to identify an *exception* to a general rule. To answer these questions correctly, you must be sure to carefully read and consider each answer choice, keeping in mind that four of them will be correct and just one wrong. Sometimes, you can find the right answer by picking out the one that just does not fit with the other choices. If four answer choices relate to characteristics associated with schizophrenic disorders, for example, the correct answer choice may well be the one that relates to a characteristic associated with anxiety disorders. Let's take a look at a multiple-choice question of this type.

All of the following choices are advantages of field research EXCEPT:

(A)   "Real people" are studied.

(B)   Reactions of subjects are more natural.

(C)   It has more impact than lab studies.

(D)   Behavior is not influenced by the psychologist.

(E)   An appropriate control is necessarily involved.

> To answer a NOT or EXCEPT question correctly, test each option by asking yourself: *Is this choice true? Does this correctly tell about field research?* Field research allows psychologists to observe people without the constraints of a lab. What benefits does this offer? What benefits of controlled laboratory experiments do researchers give up?

Predicting

Although using the process of elimination certainly helps you consider each answer choice thoroughly, testing each and every answer can be a slow process. To help answer the most questions in the limited time given, you may find it helpful to try to predict the right answer *before* you read the answer choices. For example, you know that the answer to the math problem two-plus-two will always be four. If you saw this multiple-choice item on a math test, you wouldn't need to systemically test each response, but could go straight to the right answer. You can apply a similar technique to even complex items on the AP exam. Brainstorm your own answer to the question before reading the answer choices. Then, pick the answer choice closest to the one you brainstormed. Let's look at how this technique could work on a question on the AP Psychology exam.

Multiple personality is a rare form of which category of psychological disorders?

> You should remember from your studies that another name for multiple-personality disorder is dissociative identity disorder. You can predict that the correct answer will be *dissociative disorder*. Then, scan the answer choices to find the correct one.

(A) Anxiety

(B) Dissociative

(C) Mood

(D) Schizophrenia

(E) Personality

What should you do if you don't see your prediction among the answer choices? Your prediction should have helped you narrow down the choices. You may wish to apply the process of elimination to the remaining options to further home in on the right answer. Then, you can use your knowledge of psychology to make a good guess.

Learning to predict takes some practice. You're probably used to immediately reading all of the answer choices for a question, but in order to predict well, you usually need to avoid doing this. Remember, the test maker doesn't want to make the right answers too obvious, so the wrong answers are intended to sound like appealing choices. You may find it helpful to cover the answer choices to a question as you practice predicting. This will help make sure that you don't sneak a peek at the choices too soon. Let's examine another question to practice predicting in this way. Read the following question and predict an answer.

A person who has greater difficulty hearing high-pitched tones than low-pitched tones probably has which type of deafness?

Think about what you have learned about the sensation of hearing. How do the parts of the ear work together? Which part is most responsible for sending electrical signals to the brain to transfer sounds at different specific tones? You should remember that this function is performed by hair cells in the cochlea, part of the auditory nervous system. From this, you can predict that the answer is *nerve deafness*. Now, scan the answer choices below to find the right one.

(A) nerve deafness

(D) conduction deafness

(B) functional deafness

(E) tone-specific deafness

(C) tonotopic deafness

By predicting the answer before reading the choices, you have not been tempted by the options that sound plausible but are wrong. For example, the wording of this multiple-choice question makes answer choice *D*, tone-specific deafness, seem like a viable pick for the right answer. However, by thinking through the item before being exposed to this choice, you can avoid being misled.

Avoiding Common Errors

Remember, answering questions correctly is always more important than answering every question. Take care to work at a pace that allows you to avoid these common mistakes:

- Missing key words that change the meaning of a question, such as *not, except,* or *least*. You might want to circle these words in your test booklet so you're tuned into them when answering the question.

- Overthinking an item and spending too much time agonizing over the correct response.

- Changing your answer but incompletely erasing your first choice.

Some More Advice

Let's quickly review what you've learned about answering multiple-choice questions effectively on the AP exam. Using these techniques on practice tests will help you become comfortable with them before diving into the real exam, so be sure to apply these ideas as you work through this book.

- Big ideas are more important than minutiae. Focus on learning important psychological concepts, models, and theories instead of memorizing psychologists' names and dates of important experiments.

- You have just about 40 seconds to complete each multiple-choice question. Pacing yourself during practice tests and exercises can help you get used to these time constraints.

- Because there is no guessing penalty, remember that making an educated guess is to your benefit. Remember to use the process of elimination to narrow your choices. You might just guess the correct answer and get another point!

- Instead of spending valuable time pondering narrow distinctions or questioning your first answer, trust yourself to make good guesses most of the time.

- Read the question and think of what your answer would be before reading the answer choices.

- Expect the unexpected. You will see questions that ask you to apply information in various ways, such as picking the wrong idea or interpreting a map, chart, or even a photograph.

Section II: Strategies for the Free-Response Section of the Exam

The AP Psychology exam always contains two free-response questions in its second section. This section always allows you 50 minutes to respond to both of these questions. These questions often provide you with a simple scenario to analyze. Then, the items may ask you to apply several psychological concepts to that scenario, or to describe the steps in a given process. You may be asked to connect definitions to the scenario, or to provide your own examples to enhance your discussion. Students with a deeper understanding on the content tested in the item will normally receive higher scores on these items than students with a superficial knowledge of the content.

Although it's tempting to think of the free-response section as the essay section, that's not exactly correct. Unlike many other AP exams, such as those on History or English, you don't need to write a formal essay with an introduction and conclusion to answer the free-response questions on the AP Psychology exam—unless you receive a rare question that specifically requests one. However, that doesn't mean that you should expect to just make a bulleted list of facts as your written answer to a free-response question. Instead, you'll need to write complete sentences that provide specific information requested in the various parts of a free-response question. Let's examine a typical free-response question.

Kristina and Damon wish to conduct research into psychological dependence on alcohol. Briefly describe how they could use each of the following psychological research methods in their research. Definitions without application do not score.

- Survey

- Case study

- Laboratory observation

- Naturalistic observation

> Many free-response questions begin with a brief scenario. Be sure to relate your responses to this scenario.

> Questions may contain a list of concepts for you to respond to. Others may be broken into section identified by letters. Still others may simply ask you to respond to a question in essay form.

Achieving Free-Response Success

The single most important thing you can do to score well on the free-response section is *answer the questions you are asked.* Seems silly to point that out, doesn't it? But if you've ever written an essay or even a research paper and received a mediocre grade because you didn't fully answer the question asked, or because you wrote about an almost-but-not-quite-right topic, you know how easy it can be to stray off topic or neglect to include all the facts needed in a written response. By answering both of the free-response questions completely, you'll be well on your way to a great score on the AP Psychology exam. Let's look at some strategies to help you do just that.

Organizing Your Time

Although you have 50 minutes to write both free-response items, you may choose to spend as long as you like on each individual question. Before you begin, take a few minutes to make a plan to address the section. Read each question and consider whether one seems especially difficult or easy to you. You can then plan to spend more time addressing the hard item, leaving less time for the simple one.

Remember that you may also answer the questions in any order you wish. You may find it tempting to answer the simpler question first to get it out of the way. However, answering the harder question first is usually a better use of your time. Why? Answering that item first will make you feel less pressed for time, and getting it out of the way will be a relief. You'll be freshest on your first answer, so dealing with the easier item when you're tiring out toward the end of the free-response section will be more manageable. Budgeting your time can come in handy here, too. If you think one question will take you longer to answer, you can plan to spend less time addressing the easier question. Knowing the material for a given item especially well will probably make it take less time for you to write your response. Don't be concerned that you're not spending enough time on a given question if you know that you've written a good, thorough answer. You're being scored on content, not effort!

Prewriting and Outlining

Yes, you have only 25 minutes for each of the two free-response questions on the AP Psychology exam. Yes, that seems like very little time—too little time to waste even a second. Your best strategy is just to jump in and start writing, right? Wrong.

Spending four to six minutes on prewriting will make your written response clearer, more complete, more likely to fully answer the (right) question, and even quicker and easier for you to actually write. That's because creating a simple outline will allow you to organize your thoughts, brainstorm good examples, and reject ideas that don't really work once you think about them. You can use the structure of the free-response question to help build a quick outline. Let's look at another free-response question.

Trace the path that visual information takes on its way to the brain. Describe the roles of the following in your discussion:

- Retina

- Optic nerve

- Optic chiasm

- Thalamus

- Visual cortex

Divide your outline into the same parts as the question stem using the bullet points given. Then write phrases that directly describe the function of each of the listed parts of the eye. Consider whether you need to include the roles of any other structures in order to answer the question fully. You may add those to your outline in the appropriate places or write them to the side and add arrows to help you remember to include them in your response at the appropriate points.

Stick to the Topic

Once you've written a good outline, stick to it! As you write your response, you'll find that most of the hard work is already done, and you can focus on *expressing your ideas clearly, concisely, and completely*. Don't include your own opinions about the subject, and don't include extra information that doesn't help you fully answer the question asked and *only* the question asked. Essay scorers will not award you extra points for adding lots of irrelevant information or giving personal anecdotes.

Remember, too, that the essay scorers know what information has been provided in the stimulus. If a free-response question contains a scenario, don't waste time and effort describing the facts of the scenario unless you are adding your own interpretation. In the first question above, for example, writing *Kristina and Damon are conducting research, so I know that they will consider some different types of observation* will not help your score any. If a question tells you that Erik Erikson was a German-American psychologist who contributed to the development of social psychology in the twentieth century, you do not need to restate Erikson's biography in your response or tell why you think Erikson was important—unless, of course, the question asks you to assess the impact of Erikson's theory on modern psychological understanding of social development. Make your outline short, to the point, and complete, and by following it your response will naturally have the same qualities.

Make It Easy on the Scorers

As you're writing your responses, keep in mind what the AP Readers will see when they sit down to consider your answers weeks from now. Expressing your ideas clearly and succinctly will help them best understand your point and ensure that you get the best possible score. Using your clearest handwriting will also do wonders for your overall score; free-response graders are used to reading poor handwriting, but that doesn't mean they can decipher every scribble you might make. Printing your answers instead of writing them in cursive will make them easier to read, as will leaving a space between lines.

Another good way to point out your answers to scorers is to literally point them out with arrows and labels. Adding labels to each part of your response will help the AP Readers follow your response through the multiple parts of a free-response question, and it can only help your score.

Revision in Three Minutes or Less

Even the best writers make mistakes, especially when writing quickly: skipping or repeating words, misspelling names of people or places, neglecting to include an important point from an outline are all common errors when rushed. Reserving a few minutes at the end of your writing period will allow you to quickly review your responses and make necessary corrections. Adding skipped words or including forgotten information are the two most important edits you can make to your writing, because these will clarify your ideas and so help your score.

Remember that essay graders are not mind readers, so they will only grade what's on the page, not what you thought you were writing. At the same time, remember too that essay graders do not deduct points for wrong information, so you don't need to spend time erasing errors. Just write a sentence at the end of your essay or, if you've skipped lines, on the line below that corrects your mistake.

A Sample Response

After you have read, considered, outlined, planned, written, and revised, what do you have? A thoughtful free-response written answer likely to earn you a good score, that's what. Remember that free-response graders must grade consistently in order for the test to be fair. That means that all AP Readers use a rubric to look for the same ideas to be covered in each answer to the same question. Let's examine how a reader might apply that technique to grading a response.

Trace the path that visual information takes on its way to the brain. Describe the roles of the following in your discussion:

- Retina

- Optic nerve

- Optic chiasm

- Thalamus

- Visual cortex

Visual information, first received by the retina's receptor cells,

passes through a number of different cells and undergoes a number

of transformations before it reaches the brain. Different biological

structures work with the brain to convey other types of sensations.

First, the information passes through the cell layers of the

retina. That is, it is passed through the bipolar and ganglion cell

layers. From the ganglion cells, visual information is carried by

the optic nerve into the central nervous system.

About halfway to the brain, the optic nerve reaches an

intersection called the optic chiasm. Here, some fibers from the

left eye cross over to proceed to the right side of the brain and

vice versa. Some fibers continue up along the side from which

they originate.

> You can jump right into your response on the AP Psychology exam. Readers do not expect to see and do not provide additional points for an introduction, thesis statement, or conclusion unless these parts are specifically requested in the question.

> The question specifically asks for information about vision. The graders will only score statements related to that sensation.

> An AP Reader looks for a clear, concise description that provides accurate information. This student offered just such a description, so this would score a point.

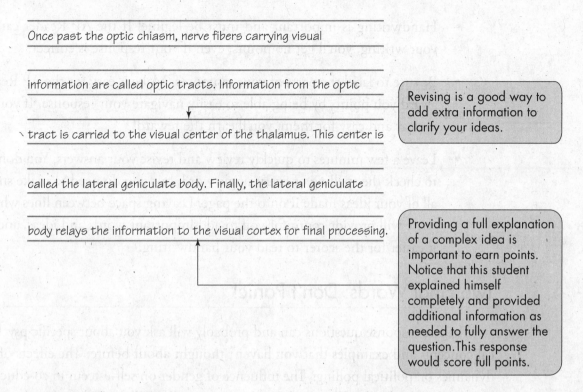

Once past the optic chiasm, nerve fibers carrying visual

information are called optic tracts. Information from the optic

> Revising is a good way to add extra information to clarify your ideas.

tract is carried to the visual center of the thalamus. This center is

called the lateral geniculate body. Finally, the lateral geniculate

body relays the information to the visual cortex for final processing.

> Providing a full explanation of a complex idea is important to earn points. Notice that this student explained himself completely and provided additional information as needed to fully answer the question. This response would score full points.

Some More Advice

What have you learned about the free-response section? Keep these ideas in mind as you prepare for the AP Psychology exam. Becoming comfortable with these techniques will make you feel confident and prepared when you sit down to take the exam in May.

- You don't have to spend the suggested 25 minutes on each question. One question may be very straightforward and you may not need 25 minutes to answer it. If you know it, write your response and move on.

- Consider previewing both free-response questions before starting to write. You can choose to answer the harder question first and leave the easier one for last when you're tired.

- Make a clear and concise outline before you begin writing. This will help you organize your thoughts and speed up the actual writing process.

- Stay on topic and answer the question! Addressing the question fully is the single most important way to earn points on this section.

- Handwriting is important and must be legible! If the AP Reader can't read your writing, you'll get no points, even if your response is correct.

- Be sure to label the parts of your responses. Make it easy for the AP Reader to award you points by being able to easily navigate your response. If you make it clear and easy for them, you'll earn the reward!

- Leave a few minutes to quickly review and revise your answers. You don't need to check the spelling of every single word, but you do need to make sure that all of your ideas made it onto the page. Leaving space between lines while you write will provide room for you to add important words and ideas, and make it easier for the scorer to read your handwriting.

Two Final Words: Don't Panic!

The free-response questions can and probably will ask you about specific psychological concepts and examples that you haven't thought about before: The effects of group dynamics on political polling? The influence of gender on self-esteem in co-educational and single-sex schools? The possibilities are practically endless. Remember that all free-response questions seek to test your knowledge of psychological theories and concepts, not highly specific facts. Applying what you know to these unfamiliar scenarios will help you get a great score, even if you've never thought much about the particular situation given in the question.

History and Approaches

Psychology is the scientific study of the behavior and mental processes of human and nonhuman animals. **Behavior** is defined as any action that may be observed and measured, and **mental processes** include cognitions, sensations, perceptions, and emotions. As a science, psychology seeks to use empirical methods to observe, measure, predict, explain, and positively influence behavior. Some psychologists focus on the biology of behavior and mental processes, such as the influences of nerve cells, genetics, or hormones. Other psychologists study complex social behaviors, such as aggression, attraction, and prejudice. There are many varied approaches to the study of psychology, making it a rich and complex field.

Early Influences on Psychology

Since the beginning of thought, humans have asked psychological questions, such as: How do we experience the world around us? What is the relationship between the way that we experience the world and how our bodies function; for example, why does food lose its flavor when we are sick? How do we learn, and what accounts for differences in behavior and temperament among people?

Greek Philosophy

The science of psychology, like physics, chemistry, and biology, developed from philosophy. Historians trace psychology's beginnings to the philosophers of ancient Greece. Ancient Greek philosophers observed and interpreted their environment and organized their findings, forming the basis for empirical investigation in psychology. These philosophers were the first Europeans to reason that human beings have, in addition to a physical body, an apparatus used for thinking. Philosophers called this thinking apparatus the *psyche* or *mind*. The term *psychology* means literally "the study of the mind" and results from the combination of the Greek root words *psyche* or mind and *logos*, meaning "the study of." Ancient Greek philosophers were the first to debate whether the mind could exist separately from the body in what is referred to as the *mind–body*

innate :- natural
nurture :- care for or encourage the growth or develop
of
asserted :- claim, argue, announce

problem. In what is known as **dualism,** Socrates and his student Plato both believed that the body and the mind were separate and that only the mind survived after death. However, Aristotle suggested that the mind could not be separated from the body, because mind and body were different aspects of the same thing; this is known as **monism.** Greek philosophers also questioned whether thought and behavior were innate or learned through experiences in what is known today as the *nature versus nurture debate.* Socrates and Plato believed that ideas were innate, thus supporting the nature half of the debate. Aristotle asserted that ideas resulted from experience, placing him on the nurture side of the nature versus nurture debate regarding the causes of human behavior. The debate regarding the relative influences of nature and nurture on behavior continues today.

Scientific Revolution

French Philosopher
Rene Descartes

While Greek philosophers examined many of the ideas of modern psychological science, they did so only through the application of thinking and reasoning and without the use of empirical methods. It would be two thousand years before psychological concepts would be examined scientifically. The French philosopher **René Descartes** (1596–1650) was very interested in extending the "mind-body" problem that began with the monism–dualism debate of the ancient Greeks. He firmly believed in dualism and hypothesized that the mind and body communicated through nerves. Descartes reasoned that some ideas were innate and others were derived from experience. Because Descartes combined philosophy and physiology, this is considered an important step in the birth of psychology as a science. **John Locke** (1632–1704), a British philosopher, agreed with Aristotle that ideas were not innate and presented the idea of the mind as a blank slate or **tabula rasa** at birth. This view of a blank slate places Locke on the nurture side of the nature versus nurture debate regarding the causes of human behavior. Locke's view that knowledge should be gained through careful observation and from experimental evidence is known as **empiricism.**

STUDY TIP

Be able to answer questions about the disciplines that led to the creation of psychology. Although modern psychological science has a short history, it has roots in *philosophy* and *physiology* that extend deep into the past.

Historical Perspectives of Scientific Psychology

Birth of Psychology as a Science

Psychological science as a formal discipline began in 1879 with the establishment of the first laboratory devoted entirely to the scientific investigation of psychological phenomena. Since the birth of scientific psychology, the field has evolved, resulting in a variety of historical and contemporary perspectives for explaining behavior and mental processes.

In 1879, physiologist **Wilhelm Wundt** (1832–1920), considered to be the father of psychology, established the first laboratory solely devoted to the scientific study of psychology in Leipzig, Germany. Wundt studied the complex concept of consciousness by dividing the mind into component elements in a perspective later known as *structuralism*. To analyze the mental elements, Wundt used an experimental method called **introspection** that involved having subjects report the contents of their own mind as objectively as possible, usually in relation to stimuli such as light, sound, or odors. The subjects were trained to give elaborate verbal reports that were then analyzed to determine the mental elements the subjects were experiencing.

G. Stanley Hall (1846–1924), who studied for a short time with Wundt in Germany, was influential in the rapid growth of psychology in the United States. Hall opened the first psychology lab in the United States and started the first American psychology journal. Additionally, he helped found the influential American Psychological Association (APA) and served as its first president.

Early Perspectives

Wundt's student, **Edward Titchener**, created the first theoretical perspective in psychology, structuralism, based on Wundt's work. Titchener brought psychology to the United States by starting his own psychology research lab at Cornell University. **Structuralism** concentrated on examining consciousness by breaking it down into its basic components or *structures,* including sensations, images, and feelings. Titchener and Wundt both utilized introspection to have subjects describe their sensations.

The major drawback of structuralism was that it was dependent on the subjective and unreliable process of introspection. The subjective reports of the mind's activities generated by introspection are vulnerable to manipulation by both the subject and the experimenter.

Psychologists today are still concerned with mental activities, but are primarily interested in how these activities influence behavior.

William James (1842–1910), an American psychologist, founded the perspective of functionalism and published the first textbook of psychology, *The Principles of Psychology*. Whereas structuralists were concerned with what the mind was made up of (structures), functionalists examined the evolved purposes (functions) of the elements of consciousness. **Functionalism** is a theoretical perspective inspired by Charles Darwin's theory of natural selection; it focused on discovering the evolved functions of behavior and mental processes that help organisms adapt to a changing environment. William James coined the phrase *stream of consciousness* to describe the way the mind experiences perception and thought as a constant flow of sensation. The largest contribution of functionalism to modern psychology was the addition of research on behaviors, including learning and adaptation to environment. Functionalists were interested in discovering real-world applications for psychology and would influence the development of both applied psychology and behaviorism.

STUDY TIP

Structuralism focuses on the *"what"* of consciousness, while functionalism focuses on the purposes or the *"why"* of consciousness.

Gestalt psychology, like structuralism and functionalism, involved research on consciousness, most frequently on the areas of perception, learning, and problem solving. The word *gestalt* refers to form, or organization, and Gestalt psychologists emphasized the organizational processes, rather than the content of behavior. Gestalt psychology emphasizes the idea that the whole is greater than the sum of its parts. Current cognitive psychologists draw heavily on Gestalt ideas, particularly in relation to questions of vision and information processing.

STUDY TIP

For the Gestalt theory *the whole is greater than the sum of its parts.* For example, when viewing a piece of furniture, a person perceives it as a desk as opposed to a table with four legs.

American Women in Psychology

Although there were considerable obstacles, women played an important role in the development of psychology as a science in the United States. **Mary Whiton Calkins** (1863–1930), a student of William James, developed an important technique for studying memory. Despite being denied the Ph.D. she earned from Harvard because of her gender, Mary Whiton Calkins became the first female president of the American Psychological Association. **Margaret Floy Washburn** (1871–1939), the first woman to formally earn a Ph.D. in psychology, under Edward Titchener, did significant research on animal behavior and greatly influenced the emerging perspective of behaviorism.

Contemporary Perspectives of Psychology

The early perspectives of structuralism and functionalism paved the way for the seven contemporary perspectives we currently use today. Psychologists have developed multiple methods to understand the causes of human behavior. These perspectives are also known as *schools of thought* or *approaches*.

Psychoanalytic/Psychodynamic Perspective

The **psychoanalytic perspective** developed by **Sigmund Freud** (1856–1939) explains that emotional problems and abnormal behavior are the result of unresolved unconscious conflicts. Freud emphasized the impact of early childhood experiences and unconscious sexual and aggressive instincts on behavior. Freud's primary tool for investigation was the case study; he compiled detailed information about patients consisting of both his commentary and the patient's autobiographical material. In order to help his patients, Freud sought out methods to reach the unconscious mind, including dream analysis and free association. Freud believed that individuals needed to be made aware of the problems in their unconscious in order to be able to resolve their issues and become healthy. He developed a comprehensive theory of consciousness, developed techniques that helped many

DIDYOUKNOW?

When Hitler annexed Austria to the Reich in March 1938, Sigmund Freud, a Jew, was considered an enemy of the new Germany. The 82-year-old Freud relocated to London. In 1939, he unsuccessfully tried to obtain visas for his four younger sisters—Dolfi, Mitzi, Rosa and Pauli—who remained in Vienna. Dolfi died of starvation in a Theresienstadt concentration camp. The other three were murdered in the death camps.

patients with their problems, and is credited with the invention of the "talking cure." Freud and his theories have received considerable criticism for being nonscientific, but his influence is undeniable. This continuing influence is apparent in the modern psychodynamic perspective that also focuses on the unconscious and how early childhood experiences influence behavior.

Behaviorist Perspective

The perspective of behaviorism developed in the United States as a response to and criticism of the structuralist and psychoanalytic perspectives prevalent at the time. The **behaviorist perspective** stressed that psychology should involve only the study of behaviors that could be both observed and measured. Psychology according to behaviorists should not study mental processes and consciousness, which was the focus of the dominant perspectives in psychology at that time. Behaviorism was inspired by the work of Nobel Prize-winning physiologist **Ivan Pavlov** (1849–1936) whose research found behaviors were learned through association, leading to the discovery of classical conditioning. The founder of **behaviorism** was **John B. Watson** (1878–1958), who criticized the investigation of consciousness as something that could not be studied objectively and who even denied the existence of the unconscious mind. Watson rejected introspection and believed that psychology should study only observable, measurable behaviors that were the product of stimuli (events in one's environment). Watson's research focused on how classical conditioning worked in humans, especially the development of classically conditioned fears, with his famous study involving "Little Albert." Another major contributor to the field of behaviorism was **B.F. Skinner** (1904–1990) whose work on operant conditioning involved demonstrating how organisms learn voluntary responses. Skinner stressed that reinforcements and punishments influenced future behavior and that free will was an illusion. Behaviorism remains a significant area of study in modern psychology. Behaviorism's emphasis on precise experimentation has been found to have numerous practical applications, including **behavior modification** or the application of learning theory to the control of human behavior.

Humanist Perspective

The **humanist perspective** arose in the 1950s, with a completely different focus than earlier perspectives. According to humanist psychologists, behaviorism concentrated on scientific fact, to the exclusion of human experience, and psychoanalysis concentrated too much on human shortcomings. Humanist psychologists chose to study healthy, creative people rather than mental illness. The two most influential humanist psychologists were

Abraham Maslow and Carl Rogers. **Abraham Maslow** suggested that human beings were basically good and motivated to achieve self-actualization, but that their basic needs had to be met first. **Carl Rogers** also stressed that people are constantly striving to develop to their fullest potential, but that some are prevented from achieving this due to factors in their environment. Humanists, in contrast to behaviorists, emphasized the concept of free will driving individuals to take control of their choices and strive to achieve full human potential.

Cognitive Perspective

Interest in the mind was revived in the 1950s as psychologists realized that behaviorism, while a useful approach, had taught them nothing about mental processes. In contrast to behaviorists, cognitive psychologists discuss the influence of mental processes in determining how humans perceive, understand, communicate, and behave. The **cognitive perspective** is concerned with the processes of thinking and memory, as well as attention, imagery, creativity, problem solving, and language. The cognitive revolution was made possible by technological advances that gave psychologists the power to explore realms that were previously considered too subjective by the dominant behaviorists of the time. Cognitive psychologists began to use computers to simulate human memory, language use, and visual perception.

Biological Perspective

The **biological perspective** focuses on explaining human behaviors, emotions, and mental processes as having physiological causes. Biological psychology covers a wide range of study, including genetics, the nervous system, and the endocrine system. Research in the area of biological psychology may involve dissecting the brain of a human or animal who suffered a behavior disorder, experimenting with drug treatments for mental illness, measuring brain waves during sleep, or investigating the effects of biological factors on eating, aggression, mental illness, or learning. Increasingly, biological research involves the use of brain imaging to determine areas of the brain involved when a person is engaged in a particular behavior or thought.

STUDY TIP

Students often confuse the terms *brain* and *mind,* and consequently the biological and cognitive perspectives. The term *brain* refers to a specific organ in the body, and the term *mind* refers to what the brain does. The biological perspective deals with the brain, and the cognitive perspective focuses on the mind.

Evolutionary Perspective

The **evolutionary perspective** explains social behaviors and mental processes as the product of human adaptation to the environment during the course of evolution. According to **Charles Darwin's** theory of **natural selection**, traits and behaviors exist in humans because these attributes allowed our ancestors to adapt, survive, and reproduce. For instance, evolutionary psychology would explain that aggression is common in humans today because, over thousands of generations, those who were genetically predisposed to defend their territories would have been more successful at producing children than those who did not have the needed traits. Darwin's theories had an enormous impact on the development of psychology and continue to influence the field today.

STUDY TIP

Students often confuse the biological and evolutionary perspectives because they both involve genetics. The key difference is that the evolutionary perspective explains behavior as being the result of gradual changes over extremely long time periods, allowing for species-level survival. The biological perspective explains that an individual's behavior is influenced by the inheritance of specific genes (genetic predisposition) from their biological parents.

Socio-Cultural Perspective

The goal of the **socio-cultural perspective** is to investigate the contribution of diversity and culture to human behavior and mental processes. This perspective emphasizes the impact on behavior of various aspects of individuals' identity and culture such as economic status, ethnicity, age, and gender not previously examined in psychological research.

STUDY TIP

Although the contemporary (modern) theoretical perspectives do not make up a large portion of the exam (2–4 percent), a strong understanding of the various ways psychology explains behavior and mental processes will help you answer questions throughout the AP Psychology Exam.

Modern psychology relies on a variety of theoretical perspectives for explaining human behavior. Each perspective has strengths and weaknesses, and, rather than competing with each other, modern psychology utilizes the approach that is most appropriate for explaining a given situation. Be prepared to examine how each of the seven contemporary perspectives would explain a particular behavior. The following example of test anxiety can be explained according to each perspective.

Table 3.1. Applications of the Seven Contemporary Perspectives

Perspective	Behavior of Test Anxiety
Psychoanalytic/Psychodynamic	Text anxiety serves as a release for unconscious aggression.
Behavioral/Learning	An individual may have learned the behavior of test anxiety by observing siblings who also experienced nervousness in testing situations or through reinforcements and punishments.
Humanistic	Test anxiety results when esteem needs are not met and individuals do not have confidence in their ability to be successful. Test anxiety occurs because individuals are blocked from achieving their goals and becoming the best that they can be.
Cognitive	Negative thoughts about failure result in test anxiety.
Biological/Neurological	Lower levels of the neurotransmitter GABA make an individual more prone to anxiety.
Evolutionary	Anxious behavior leads to human survival because it increases caution and helps individuals to avoid dangerous situations.
Socio-Cultural	Individuals from cultures that value success in school and achievement are more likely to experience test anxiety.

Careers in Psychology

Psychologists work in both practitioner and research capacities and are employed by universities, schools, industries, and governments, and in private practice. As practitioners, psychologists assess individuals through interviews and testing and provide therapy to help cope with stress, adjustment issues, and mental illness. Experimental psychologists conduct experiments in a variety of specialties or subfields consisting of both basic and applied research. **Basic research** involves attempting to answer scientific questions and expand the overall information base of psychology. **Applied research** involves utilizing psychological knowledge to solve real-world problems. The table below provides a description of the main specialties found in psychology.

STUDY TIP

Students often confuse a clinical psychologist with a psychiatrist. Both are concerned with the diagnosis and treatment of psychological problems and disorders. However, a **psychiatrist** has a medical degree and is licensed to prescribe medication or drug treatments.

Table 3.2.   Careers in Psychology

Specialty	Description
Biological/Neuroscience	Investigates the relationship among the body, brain, and nervous system, and behavior and mental processes.
Clinical	Works with the diagnosis, causes, and treatment of mental disorders.
Cognitive	Examines how mental processes, such as thinking, knowing, feeling, and memory operate and affect behavior.
Counseling	Works with people coping with everyday problems, including career decisions, marriage counseling, and social skills training.
Developmental	Studies how people change over time and the developmental stages across the human lifespan.
Educational	Studies theoretical issues related to how people learn and effective teaching practices.
Human Factors	Uses psychological knowledge to increase efficiency between humans and machines.
Industrial/Organizational	Concerned with psychological issues related to the work environment; employee motivation and selection.
Personality	Examines our stable traits and factors that influence temperament. Develops methods of personality assessment.
Psychometrics	Concerned with mathematical or numerical methods of measuring psychological variables by creating valid and reliable tests.
School	Works directly with students who exhibit emotional or learning problems to overcome educational difficulties in a K–12 setting. Creates and implements plans to meet individualized student needs.
Social	Studies the impact of society on individuals and how a person's life and behavior are shaped by interactions with others.

Research Methods

The Scientific Method

As an empirical science, psychology requires verifiable and objective data obtained through the use of the **scientific method** for the development of knowledge. The steps in the scientific method are outlined in the chart below. Psychologists begin the research process by evaluating existing evidence in order to develop a **theory**, or organized explanation for data, gained through empirical processes. The scientific method also requires the development of a testable and falsifiable prediction explaining the relationship between variables known as a **hypothesis**.

To test the hypothesis, the experimenter must clearly define each of the procedures and variables being studied by creating operational definitions. **Operational definitions** state as precisely as possible what each variable means, including how it will be measured. The process of operationally defining variables is critical to the research process because it allows for **replication,** or having future psychologists repeat the exact procedures to obtain the same results. In order to reduce the risk that the results occurred by chance, all conclusions drawn from psychological research must be replicable.

Table 4.1.   Steps of the Scientific Method

1	Theory	Organizing explanations of natural events in order to generate new hypotheses and make predictions or explain behavior.
2	Hypothesis	Generation of a specific prediction designed to test a theory often expressed in the form of an "*if . . . then*" statement.
3	Select method and design study	Utilizing controlled experiments, case studies, psychological tests, surveys, interviews, or naturalistic observation to compile data to increase or decrease support for a hypothesis.
4	Collect and analyze results	Statistically analyze collected data allowing for conclusions to be made regarding the hypothesis.
5	Publication of results	Report findings, usually in a scientific journal where the research will be subject to the critical evaluation of the scientific community.

Research Methods

As a science, psychology seeks to use empirical methods to observe and measure, predict, explain, and positively influence behavior. The descriptive methods relate to the functions of observation and measurement. Correlational studies make predictions, and experiments are designed to explain cause and effect relationships. When psychologists conduct **basic research,** the aim is to answer scientific questions and expand the overall information base of psychology. **Applied research** utilizes descriptive, correlational, and experimental designs to positively influence behavior and solve real-world problems.

Population vs. Sample

When conducting research, the experimenter must first identify a specific population to be studied, i.e., all Americans, all college students, or all female high school soccer players. The **population** includes all members of a group that could be selected for research and to whom the results apply. Because it is difficult or impossible to reach an entire population, psychologists select a **sample**, or small subset of individuals to represent the population.

STUDY TIP

Be able to distinguish the terms *population* and *sample* in an example.

It would be difficult and expensive to give a survey to every female high school soccer player in the United States (population), so researchers select several high school teams in each state (a sample) to represent the population.

Psychologists are concerned with ensuring that the results obtained from the sample are typical of the population, which makes the sample selection process an important part of the research design. Poor sample selection creates problems in generalizing the results to the population referred to as *sampling bias*. **Sampling bias** is any selection method resulting in a sample that is not representative of the population *or* that does not provide all of the members of a population an equal chance to be chosen for the study, which can result in distorted findings. For example, if the hypothesis states that high school students who watch television for more than twenty hours per week will have lower ACT scores than other students, the population would include all high school students that took the ACT. If the sample included only students from public high schools, sampling bias would occur because students who attended private high schools or who were homeschooled were not eligible to be selected for the sample.

Research requires the reduction or elimination of sampling bias by obtaining random and representative samples. **Random samples** are designed so that every member of the population has an equal chance of being chosen for participation in the study. The various methods used to generate a random sample from a population are called **random selection** and can include placing the names of all of the participants in order alphabetically and then choosing every tenth name or by using a computer to generate random numbers for the participants. Random selection is a critical step in the research process because it increases the likelihood that the results of the research can be applied to the larger population. Psychologists also use random selection to increase the chances for obtaining a sample that is **representative** or similar to the population as a whole in regard to variables that might impact the results, such as gender, religious affiliation, income, and ethnicity. Experimenters also use stratified samples for large diverse populations to ensure representativeness. **Stratified samples** are created by dividing the population into subgroups (strata) to create a sample that contains members of each subgroup in the same proportion that exists in the larger population. For example, if the population consists of all of the students taking psychology courses at a particular university and the population is 60 percent female, then the stratified sample would also need to be 60 percent female. In terms of selecting participants for research, it is usually best to have a larger sample size in order to ensure that the subjects are representative of the population as a whole.

Descriptive Methods

Descriptive methods include a variety of research techniques designed to observe and measure behaviors and mental processes. These methods are valuable because they generate a broad viewpoint and indicate specific behaviors that deserve further exploration. The key factor that distinguishes descriptive methods from other research designs is that the experimenter does not manipulate the variables or the behavior of the participants. This means descriptive methods cannot be used to determine cause and effect relationships. The descriptive method of **naturalistic observation** involves carefully and systematically watching human or animal behavior as it occurs in the natural environment. Naturalistic observation allows researchers to determine what organisms actually do in the real world and discover clues as to why they do it. For example, when investigating whether or not students recycle, a researcher utilizing naturalistic observation would carefully watch students and systematically collect data regarding recycling behavior in the lunchroom.

Another descriptive method is the **survey,** whereby individuals are asked to reply to a series of questions or to rate their agreement with various statements. Surveys are designed to discover the beliefs, opinions, and attitudes of a sample in order to draw conclusions about the population. This method is used by consumer psychologists to help retail stores be successful by asking customers to call a toll-free number and answer a series of questions. The survey method is used by clinical psychologists to determine attitudes toward mental illness or the effectiveness of therapeutic methods.

Clinical psychologists and medical researchers utilize the **case study method** to conduct in-depth investigations of individuals or groups. Detailed information for case studies is compiled through the use of observation, interviews, surveys, and testing. This method is especially beneficial when researching rare behaviors or examining a problem or issue relevant to a particular person or group. Educational psychologists assist public school districts by employing the group case study method to identify why students are struggling in a particular subject area by examining test results and data obtained from detailed interviews with students and teachers. A famous example of an individual case study involved the subject referred to as patient H.M. who suffered from memory problems resulting from brain surgery to treat epilepsy. Although the surgery successfully eliminated the epileptic seizures, unfortunately it also resulted in severe and permanent amnesia. Case study research involving patient H.M. has helped psychologists gain a better understanding of how specific brain structures are involved in various memory processes. Case studies are beneficial because they allow for insight into rare behaviors and provide suggestions for further research.

Experimental Method

If researchers want to demonstrate cause and effect regarding a particular behavior, it is necessary to design an experiment. The first step is to randomly select participants from the population. The **participants** or subjects in an experiment consist of the humans or animals participating in the research. Participants in an experiment are exposed to some event, treatment, or condition that is being manipulated by the experimenter; this factor is called the **independent variable (IV).** The observation and measurement of the behavior or mental process of participants in an experiment is called the **dependent variable (DV).** Researchers look for differences between the dependent variable in the control and experimental groups to determine if the IV caused a change. In order to ensure that the experiment can be replicated, both the independent and dependent variables are operationally defined. When using the experimental method, psychologists create either an experimental or a null hypothesis which is a testable and falsifiable prediction. The experimental **hypothesis** is a prediction of the exact outcome in terms of the effects on the DV that are caused by the IV. An experimental hypothesis might involve the prediction that if students listen to music while taking an exam, their test scores will improve. Researchers may also use a **null hypothesis** for the same experiment, which is a prediction that the IV will have no effect on the DV *or* that the findings resulted from chance. The null hypothesis for the previous example would be that listening to music while taking an exam will not improve student test scores *or* that any improvement in test scores would most likely be due to chance and not to the IV. It is always the goal of researchers to reject the null hypothesis, indicating that the IV caused a change in the DV.

STUDY TIP

Be able to identify the independent and dependent variables in a sample experiment.

A simple way to make identification of the variables in an experiment easier is to use the following steps:

1. Find the hypothesis and convert it into an *"if . . . then"* statement.
2. The IV is what comes after the *"if"* in the statement, indicating the cause of the behavior being studied.
3. The DV is what comes after the *"then"* in the statement, indicating the expected effect of the IV.

Example: Stephanie believes that walking briskly during passing periods will result in increased participation by students during class.

1. If students walk briskly during passing periods, then they will be more motivated in class.
2. "If . . . walk briskly" becomes the IV.
3. Then . . . "more motivated in class" becomes the DV.

In an experiment participants are placed into either a control group or an experimental group. The participants in the **experimental group (experimental condition)** receive the IV, but participants in the **control group (control condition)** are not exposed to the IV; they function as a comparison for evaluating the effectiveness of the factor being studied. By controlling all other variables, researchers work to ensure that the only difference between the two groups in the experiment is the presence of the IV. Any difference present other than the IV between the experimental or control group participants that might have an effect on the DV is considered to be a **confounding variable.** Researchers eliminate or control possible confounding variables because they prevent the researcher from being able to draw cause and effect conclusions.

STUDY TIP

Be able to differentiate between control within an experiment and the control group.

- Researchers exert *control* within an experiment by eliminating all differences between the two groups other than the IV. Experimenters control conditions by using such methods as obtaining a random sample, using random assignment, and standardizing procedures.
- The *control group* is the condition or subjects within the experiment that do not receive the IV; they will be used for comparison with the experimental group to determine if there is a cause and effect relationship.

Random assignment ensures that each participant has an equal chance of being assigned to either the experimental or control group. The process of random assignment is required in order to determine cause and effect and eliminate confounding variables. In contrast to the experimental method, **quasi-experimental** research does not include random assignment. In quasi-experiments, the difference between the experimental and control groups has been previously determined, because the variable being studied has already taken effect. In quasi-experiments researchers exert very little control and, as a result, cannot make cause and effect conclusions. Quasi-experimental designs are used because they may be more convenient, and they allow for the investigation of phenomena that participants could not be randomly assigned to experience because it would be unethical. For example, if researchers were interested in observing how poverty impacts success in school, a quasi-experimental design would be used, because it would be unethical or impossible to randomly assign participants to live in poverty.

STUDY TIP

Be able to distinguish between the terms *random selection of a random sample* and *random assignment*.

- *Random selection* involves choosing a *random sample* in which each member of the population has an equal chance of being selected for the sample.
- *Random assignment* involves placing participants into either the experimental or control group by chance and is required in order to determine if there is a cause and effect relationship.

Research Bias

Experimenter (researcher) bias is the tendency for researchers to unknowingly influence the results of an experiment. Because the researchers are aware of the hypothesis, they may unintentionally treat participants in a manner that confirms their predictions. **Participant bias** occurs when subjects know that they are being watched or recognizes what the experimenter is investigating. Potential hints or indications of what is being studied that might be discovered by participants are known as **demand characteristics** and can result is distorted findings.

Researchers may control for participant bias and demand characteristics by deceiving subjects in the control group with a fake treatment called a **placebo.** The classic example of a placebo involves giving members of the control group in a drug experiment a pill containing an inert substance (sugar pill), rather than the actual drug that is given to participants in the experimental group. The **placebo effect** occurs when a physical or psychological treatment that has no active ingredient produces an effect because the person receiving it believes that it will. Researchers control for the confounding variable created by the placebo effect by not letting subjects know whether they are receiving the actual treatment or a placebo. If subjects do not know whether they are receiving the drug (IV) or the placebo, the experiment is called a **single blind study** and controls for demand characteristics and the placebo effect. In a **double blind study** both the experimenter and the subjects are unaware of who has received the treatment (IV). Double blind studies eliminate both experimenter and participant bias.

STUDY TIP

Be able to identify the participants, variables, and groups within a sample experiment.

A researcher investigating the effects of listening to music while studying on test performance randomly assigns high school student participants to a music group or a quiet group while preparing for the test. The researcher subsequently compares the two groups' test scores using inferential statistics and concludes that $p = .05$.

- The *participants* in this study are high school students.
- The *independent variable* in this study is listening to music.
- The *dependent variable* in this study is test performance.
- The *control group* in this study consists of students randomly assigned to the quiet group for studying.
- The *experimental group* in this study consists of students randomly assigned to listen to music while studying.

Correlational Method

Correlational studies allow researchers to determine whether a relationship exists between two variables. Although correlational research cannot determine cause and effect, these studies illustrate the strength and direction of the relationship between variables, allowing for prediction.

The data used in the correlational method is collected through other research designs, such as surveys, interviews, and case studies. Even very strong correlations cannot be perceived as cause and effect relationships because it is possible that both variables are in fact caused by another additional factor in what is referred to as the **third-variable problem**. Variables may be found to be correlated either positively, or negatively. A **positive (direct) correlation** means that, as one variable increases, so does the second variable *or,* as one variable decreases, so does the other. In a positive correlation, both variables move in the same direction. For instance, the statement that the taller a person is, the larger his or her shoe size will be, indicates a positive correlation. This could also be stated as the shorter a person is, the smaller the shoe size will be. A **negative (inverse) correlation** means that high scores on one variable will be paired with low scores on the other variable. For example, if the data indicate that as age increases, eyesight deteriorates, this would be a negative correlation. In some cases, two variables are not related to each other at all, resulting in a **non-correlation**. Psychologists would be interested in examining data to determine if there is a correlation between playing violent video games and increased aggression in children. If children who played more violent video games were more aggressive, a positive correlation would exist between the two variables. Sometimes individuals identify an **illusory correlation**, an incorrect perception that two variables are related *or* an overestimation about the strength of the relationship.

STUDY TIP

Be able to identify the direction of correlations.

- *Positive correlations identify a relationship between two variables that "go together."*

Positive Correlations

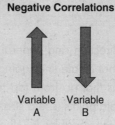

Variable A   Variable B   OR   Variable A   Variable B

- *Negative correlations identify a relationship between two variables that "go in opposite directions."*

Negative Correlations

Variable A   Variable B

In addition to the direction of the relationship, correlational research determines the strength of the relationship between the variables through the use of a statistical concept known as a **correlation coefficient**. The most common example is the Pearson correlation coefficient represented by the letter r and ranging from -1.0 to $+1.0$. Higher values represent stronger relationships, or, put another way, the greater the number, the stronger the two variables are related either positively or negatively. For example, a correlation of $-.73$ is just as strong as a correlation of $+.73$; they differ only in the direction of the relationship. A correlation of -1.0 indicates a perfect negative correlation or a situation in which every time one variable increases, the other variable decreases. A correlation of $+1.0$ indicates a perfect positive correlation or a situation in which every time one variable increases, the other variable increases. Most correlations involving human behavior are not perfectly positive ($+1.0$) or negative (-1.0) correlations. For example, the variables of class attendance and exam scores are positively correlated. Students that have better attendance are more likely to have higher exam scores. Of course, there will be some students who might not have good attendance, but still do well on exams, resulting in a correlation between the variables of attendance and exam scores that is positive but not perfect. A correlation coefficient of 0 indicates that no relationship exists between the variables, and values closer to zero indicate weaker correlations.

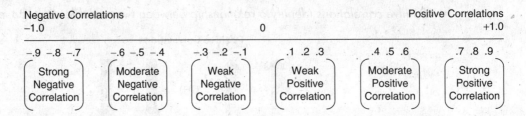

The correlation between two or more variables is illustrated on a graph called a **scatterplot (scattergram).** Positive correlations create scatterplots where the data forms a curve or line going up and negative correlations create curves on a scatterplot that go down.

STUDY TIP

Be able to identify the direction and general strength of a correlation based on looking at a scatterplot. Scatterplots that create lines going from bottom to top (A and D) represent positive correlations, and patterns that go from top to bottom (B) represent negative correlations. The closer the collection of data points is to a straight line, the stronger the correlation (D). If there is no relationship between the variables (C), the points on the scatterplot do not create a pattern in either direction.

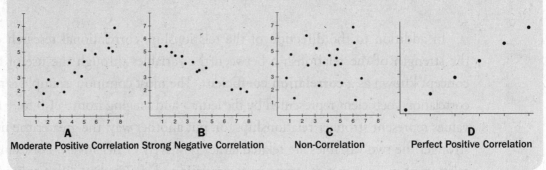

Advantages and Limitations of Research Methods

Based on the hypothesis and ethical concerns involved, psychologists choose from a variety of scientific methods to conduct research. If the goal of the research is to observe and measure behaviors and mental processes, researchers will select descriptive methods. Descriptive methods include naturalistic observation, surveys, and case studies. On the other hand, when psychologists are interested in predicting or explaining behaviors and mental processes, they will select either correlational or experimental methods. Descriptive, correlational, and experimental methods each have separate advantages and limitations.

STUDY TIP

Be able to describe each of the various research methods, including the advantages and limitations of each.

Table 4.2. Advantages and Limitations of Research Methods

Research Method	Purpose	Advantages and Limitations
Naturalistic Observation	Describe—designed to observe and measure	**Naturalistic Observation Advantages** • Allows researchers to observe behavior as it would occur in the real world **Naturalistic Observation Limitations** • Researcher cannot determine cause and effect. • Presence of the researcher may result in the participants altering their behaviors. • Observations made by researchers are subjective.
Survey	Describe—designed to observe and measure	**Survey Advantages** • Researchers can generate large amounts of data for comparison quickly and inexpensively. **Survey Limitations** • Researcher cannot determine cause and effect. • Difficulty in obtaining a random and representative sample • Data may be inaccurate due to intentional lying or inconsistencies between what participants say and what they do. • Data may be inaccurate, due to *social desirability bias* or the tendency for participants to not answer personal questions honestly in order to present themselves in a positive way. • Data may be inaccurate due to the wording of survey questions.
Case Study	Describe—designed to observe and measure	**Case Study Advantages** • Useful for examining rare behaviors in detail • Provide a starting point for developing hypotheses **Case Study Limitations** • Researcher cannot determine cause and effect. • Results are vulnerable to experimenter bias. • Sample size is too small to generalize results to the larger population. • Participants may quit at any time, thus ending the study.

(continued)

Table 4.2. (Continued)

Research Method	Purpose	Advantages and Limitations
Correlation	Predict—designed to describe a relationship	**Correlation Advantages** • Tests the strength of a relationship and allows for predictions to be made regarding two variables • Builds on existing knowledge gained through descriptive methods • Generates predictions for further experimental research **Correlation Limitations** • Researcher cannot determine cause and effect. • Difficulty in obtaining a random and representative sample
Experiment	Explain—designed to determine cause and effect	**Experiment Advantages** • Only method that can determine cause and effect **Experiment Limitations** • Confounding variables weaken cause and effect explanations. • Difficulty in obtaining a representative sample

Statistics

Psychologists use statistics both to describe the findings they collect and to make conclusions about behavior by converting the results into mathematical data. In order to be prepared for statistics on the AP Psychology Exam, be prepared to describe the purposes of descriptive and inferential statistics, interpret statistical significance, determine the strength and direction of correlations, and calculate measures of central tendency and simple standard deviations.

Levels of Measurement

Data collected from research falls into four types of measurement with varying levels of precision in terms of statistics. The four types in order from least to most precise are nominal, ordinal, interval, and ratio. A mnemonic to remember the four types of measurement is the French word for the color black (*noir*); the first letter of each of the four types of measurement spell the word *noir*.

Table 4.3.   Types of Measurement

	Description	Examples	Limitations

Nominal Data	Data categorized to represent names or characteristics.	• Gender
		  Female (1)
		  Male (2)
		• Diagnosis
		  Depression (1)
		  Schizophrenia (2)
		  Bipolar (3)
			Nominal data will only provide a label and does not have any mathematical properties. Nominal data cannot be rank ordered or averaged; it can only be classified.

Ordinal Data	Data that indicates rank order.	• Finishing the football season in first place, second place, etc. • Subjects rate level of anxiety on a scale of 1–5.	Ordinal data does not indicate exact intervals and cannot be averaged. Numbers or variables can be seen only as more or less than others in the set.
Interval Data	Data that indicates the order in which figures can be ranked, as well as providing equal distances (intervals) between items. Equal spaces between points on a scale make it possible to know how much one score is greater than or less than another.	• Standardized tests for personality, anxiety, and IQ often use interval scales.	Interval scales do not have a true zero, or, in other words, a score of zero has meaning and does not represent absence of a score.
Ratio Data	Data that indicates equal intervals and the presence of a *true zero* (zero stands for a complete absence of what is being measured)	• Weight is ratio data because there is a true zero and ratios can be calculated. Ten pounds is twice as heavy as 5 pounds.	Ratio data is the most precise and allows for the best statistical analysis.

Descriptive Statistics

Descriptive statistics are used to illustrate data and include tables, graphs, charts, correlations, measures of central tendency, and variance. One specialized type of descriptive data in table form is a frequency distribution. **Frequency distributions** are tables that contain data about how often certain scores occur or how many subjects fit into each category; they are often used for nominal data. If a frequency distribution is displayed as a specialized type of bar graph, it is called a **frequency histogram,** and if the data is presented as a specific style of line graph, it is called a **frequency polygon.**

Measures of **central tendency** consist of various statistical procedures that describe the typical or central score within a data set. There are three main ways to measure central tendency: mean, median, and mode. The **mean** is the arithmetic average of a set of scores, and it is determined by computing the sum of all the scores and dividing the sum by the total number of scores in the distribution. The mean is the most commonly used measure of central tendency, but it is also the statistic most affected by extreme scores, known as outliers. The **median** is the score that falls in the exact middle of the distribution; half the scores fall above the median and half the scores fall below it. If a given data set contains an equal number of data points, the median is the average of the two middle scores. The main advantage of the median is that it is not sensitive to extreme scores or outliers. The **mode** is the most frequently occurring score. A distribution is considered **bimodal** if there are two separate scores that appear most frequently and **multimodal** if three or more scores occur most often.

STUDY TIP

Be able to compute measures of central tendency and variance for a simple series of scores.

Example
Sample Distribution: 37, 5, 3, 4, 6, 4, 5, 8

The first step is to place the distribution in numerical order: 3, 4, 4, 5, 5, 6, 8, 37

Measures of Central Tendency
- The *mode* is 4 and 5, because both numbers are the most frequent, resulting in a bimodal distribution.
- The *median* is 5. This distribution has an equal number of data points. To determine the median, compute the average between the two middle scores of 5 and 5.
- The *mean* is 9. The mean is the sum of all of the data points in this distribution, divided by eight, which is the total number of scores in the distribution.

In this example, the median is the most useful measure of central tendency because the mean is distorted by one extreme score (37).

Measures of Variability
- The *range* is 34, or the difference between the highest score (37) and the lowest score (3).
- The *standard deviation* is the $\sqrt{114}$ or 10.67.

Descriptive statistics also include measures of **variability** that indicate how much individual scores differ from each other and the average. The simplest measure of variability is the **range**, or the distance or spread between the highest and lowest scores in the distribution. Another measure of variability, **standard deviation,** is a mathematical representation of how far on average each of the individual scores in a data set varies from the mean. In other words, the standard deviation is the average distance of each score from the mean. The steps for computing and interpreting standard deviations are presented in the table below.

Figure 4.1. Computing the Standard Deviation

1. Determine the mean for the distribution.

2. Determine the distance of each individual score from the mean.

3. Square each score that was found in step two.

4. Add all of the scores found in step three together.

5. Divide this number by the total number of scores in the distribution.

   Note: The result of step of five is a statistic called the *variance*.

6. The square root of the total from step five is the standard deviation.
   • Larger standard deviations indicate that scores are spread out farther from the mean.
   • Smaller standard deviations indicate that scores are located closer to the mean.
   • A standard deviation of 0 indicates that all scores in a distribution are equal.

Normal Distribution

If the mean, median, and mode are all equal and located at the center of the distribution, the result is a **normal distribution (curve)** that forms a symmetrical bell curve. Many psychological characteristics, such as IQ or test scores, create normal distributions with predictable percentages of scores that fall between specific standard deviations. In a normal distribution, approximately 68 percent of scores fall within one standard deviation of the mean, 95 percent of scores fall within two standard deviations of the mean, and 99 percent of scores fall within three standard deviations of the mean.

Extreme Scores—Skewed Distributions

Not all data sets create normal distributions that form symmetrical bell curves. When most of the scores in a distribution land on one side of the scale or the other, they are considered skewed.

Skewed distributions are not symmetrical and are characterized by a "tail" on one end of the scale or on the other end. If a distribution is **positively skewed (right skewed),** most of the scores will be low and the tail of the distribution will be pointing toward the right or positive side of the number line. If a distribution is **negatively skewed (left skewed)**, most of the scores will be high and the tail of the distribution will be pointing to the left or the negative portion of the number line.

Figure 4.2.   Positively and Negatively Skewed Distributions

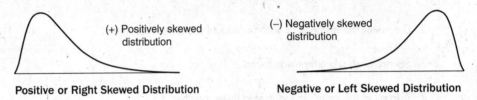

(+) Positively skewed distribution

(−) Negatively skewed distribution

Positive or Right Skewed Distribution   **Negative or Left Skewed Distribution**

Inferential Statistics

When conducting an experiment, the researcher virtually always measures behavior in a sample (a representative subset) of people drawn from a larger population (such as all Americans or all college students). The scores for a particular sample can be summarized by using descriptive statistics. However, psychologists are rarely interested in only the data obtained from the sample. Researchers are more interested in what the data indicates for the population. For example, if the results of an experiment indicate that individuals in a sample who talked on a cell phone while driving a simulator were more likely to have accidents, would this be true for the population? Because most research is conducted with a sample that is much smaller than the population it represents, psychologists utilize inferential statistics to make inferences about the population.

Inferential statistics indicate whether or not results based on the sample are significant enough to be applied to the larger population or if the results were most likely caused by chance. Researchers evaluate the differences in the dependent variable between the control and experimental groups to determine if the difference is a result of the independent variable and not coincidence. Inferential statistics take into account the size and quality of the sample, as well as how large a difference exists between the dependent variables in the control and experimental groups. If a difference in the dependent variable between the control and experimental groups is **statistically significant,** it simply means that the results were *not likely* to have happened by chance. Statistical significance indicates a high probability that the independent variable caused the change in the dependent variable, allowing the researcher to reject the null hypothesis.

In order to understand statistical significance, keep in mind that any difference between two means (in an experiment) could have happened by chance. Researchers use a variety of inferential statistics to determine statistical significance that include chi square tests, t-tests, and analyses of variance (ANOVAs) to generate a probability value (p). A *probability value (p)* is an inferential statistic that indicates how likely it is that the difference between the control and experimental groups was caused by chance and not the independent variable. In order for the results to be considered statistically significant, the *p* value must be ≤.05. If the results indicate that *p* = .05, the researcher believes that there was a 95 percent likelihood that the results were not due to chance. In other words, the researcher is 95 percent certain that the independent variable was responsible for the change in the dependent variable. It is important to note that a *p* value can never be zero because it is impossible to be 100 percent certain that the hypothesis is correct and that chance was not involved in any way. Generally the lower the *p* value, the more significant the results are and the less likely they were caused by chance.

STUDY TIP

Statistical significance refers to the likelihood that the results of an experiment are not due to *chance*. It does *not* refer to how important the results are. Any strong definition of statistical significance must refer to chance.

Ethics in Research

Because psychological research involves humans and animals, psychologists must consider the ethical implications of the research design. Careless methods can potentially cause significant physical or psychological harm, and psychologists have developed guidelines to protect participants.

Human Participants

The United States government requires that every institution receiving federal support establish an Institutional Review Board (IRB) to evaluate and approve all research studies. Many other professional organizations, including the American Psychological Association (APA), have also created ethical guidelines for the protection of participants. Any research involving humans must receive prior approval from an IRB to ensure that participants are protected from physical and emotional harm and that all ethical guidelines are met. IRB's carefully review all proposed studies and evaluate the potential harm caused against the potential benefits that would result from a study.

Table 4.4. Ethical Guidelines for the Protection of Research Subjects

Ethical Consideration	Definition	Researcher or Participant Rights and Responsibilities
Physical or Emotional Harm	Participants cannot be exposed to severe physical or emotional harm.	• Studies involving even *minimal* physical pain or emotional distress must be approved by an IRB board. • Participants must be informed prior to the start of the experiment if any short-term stress or discomfort might occur.
Informed Consent	Participants must know that they are involved in research and participate voluntarily.	• Participants must be informed about the purpose, time commitment, and procedures of the experiment. • Participants must be told that they can withdraw from the experiment at any time (*voluntary participation— no coercion*). • Participants must be informed about the potential benefits and risks associated with the research. • Participants must be informed if they will be paid for participation.
Confidentiality	Participants' privacy must be protected.	• Researchers must disguise the identity and actions of the participants when presenting findings. • Researchers must obtain permission to record the voices of participants.
Deception	Research practice that involves misinforming participants regarding the true nature of the study.	• Researchers *cannot deceive* participants without prior approval from the IRB. • Researchers *cannot deceive* participants by providing false statements about their training. • Researchers *cannot deceive* the public by falsifying data (*falsification*). • Researchers *cannot deceive* participants by failing to warn them about potential pain or stress that may be associated with the research. • Researchers *can deceive* participants about the hypothesis if the IRB determines benefits outweigh the drawbacks. • Researchers *can deceive* participants if the IRB determines there is basic or applied research value.
Debrief	Researchers must fully explain the details of the research and inform participants if any deception was involved; this must be done immediately after the research ends.	• Participants must be told whom to contact if they have questions in the future regarding the experiment.

Nonhuman Subjects

Psychology also involves the study of nonhuman animals, and these experiments have often provided the basis for psychological theories and treatment. The controversy over animal rights occurs when animals are exposed to treatments that might be harmful to humans. The American Psychological Association (APA) has created ethical guidelines for the protection of animals in research. These guidelines include using only legally obtained animals, complying with all federal and state regulations, and providing humane housing and care procedures. Prior to the use of animals in any study, it must be demonstrated to an IRB that the research has scientific value, especially if the animals will be harmed or subjected to pain in the process. If an animal's life needs to be terminated, this must be handled in a humane manner.

Bias in Research

Interpreting psychological research involves thinking critically about the various types of bias that can distort findings. Bias involves how either consciously or unconsciously our attitudes, behaviors, and expectations can influence research outcomes. Different types of bias can influence how researchers design and evaluate a study and how participants behave. The various types of bias important in psychological research are explained in Table 4.5.

Table 4.5. Common Types of Bias in Research Design

	Definition	Prevention Strategy	Example
Hindsight Bias	Tendency to believe we could have predicted the outcome of an event after it already happened	Awareness of this bias and the use of the scientific method	After taking the AP Psychology Exam and seeing the questions, Garrett announces that he knew all along that the free-response question would be about statistics.
Confirmation Bias	Tendency to selectively attend to information that is consistent with our viewpoint and ignore or minimize information that challenges our beliefs	Researchers seek evidence that might disprove their hypothesis. Researchers publish their results for critical evaluation by the scientific community.	Erica and Jenny both read the same article about the use of animals in experimental research. Erica believes it is inhumane to use animals in research and notices only facts that back up her beliefs. Jenny believes animal testing is valuable and notices only statements that support her claim. Both Erica and Jenny are exhibiting confirmation bias.
Overconfidence Bias	Tendency to overestimate how correct our predictions and beliefs about ideas actually are	Psychologists test their hypotheses with controlled experiments.	Students are often overconfident when editing their own papers. When they submit a paper to be proofread by their teacher, they do not expect that any mistakes will be found. After receiving the returned paper, they are surprised by how many spelling or grammar mistakes were actually made.
Experimenter Bias	Tendency for researchers to unknowingly influence the results in an experiment	Double-blind studies prevent researchers from knowing which subjects are receiving the treatment.	Clever Hans, a famous horse, was known for his amazing ability to respond to mathematical equations by tapping his hoof. Through careful observation, it was found that his owner was unintentionally cuing the horse through body language. Similarly, researchers may unknowingly provide signals that will impact participant behavior.
Social Desirability Bias	Tendency for subjects to not answer personal questions honestly in order to create/depict themselves in a positive way	Participants can be given a social desirability assessment that will correct for this bias.	Arthur is completing a survey about his driving behavior and indicates that he never speeds and never fails to come to a complete stop at a stop sign, even though he knows this is not true. Arthur answers incorrectly because he wants to be perceived positively by others.

Time for a quiz

- Review strategies in Chapter 2
- Take Quiz 1 at the REA Study Center
  (www.rea.com/studycenter)

Biological Bases of Behavior

Biological psychology can be traced to the beginnings of psychology because it has its roots in physiology. The field of biological psychology, also called *neuroscience*, focuses on how genes, the nervous system, and the endocrine system influence behaviors and mental processes. Technological advances have allowed biological psychologists to provide a more complete understanding of what occurs on a physiological level during a psychological experience such as thinking or memory.

Heredity, Environment, and Evolution

An important aspect of the study of psychology is the interplay among genetic, environmental, and evolutionary influences. Complex human traits such as intelligence, aggression, altruism, and personality are influenced by all of these factors. Psychologists attempt to determine how an individual's level of aggression is impacted by inheritance and exposure to violence, as well as why aggressive tendencies were naturally selected.

Biologists and psychologists are both interested in the various influences of nature and nurture on human traits. Biologists study physical traits such as height and eye color or susceptibility to diseases such as cancer. In contrast, psychologists are interested in behavioral traits and psychological illnesses. Behavioral traits include aggression, intelligence, and personality; psychological illnesses include anxiety, schizophrenia, and depression. The scientific discipline of **behavioral genetics** attempts to integrate the influences of heredity, environment, and evolution in terms of their effect on human behavior.

Heredity

Psychologists are interested in the study of heredity or how the traits of parents are transmitted biologically to offspring. The nucleus of each human cell contains forty-six **chromosomes,** twenty-three donated by each parent. Chromosomes which determine gender are **X and Y chromosomes**. One X chromosome is donated by the mother, and either an X or Y chromosome is donated by the father. An XX individual is female; an XY person is male. Each chromosome contains **genes,** which are made of a chain-like molecule called *deoxyribonucleic acid* (**DNA).** Each individual gene can be either dominant or recessive. A dominant gene takes precedence over a recessive gene for that particular trait. For the gene that determines eye color in humans, brown is the dominant gene and blue is the recessive gene. If either parent donates a dominant gene for eye color, the child will have brown eyes. If both parents donate recessive genes for eye color, the child will have blue eyes. A Punnett square can be used to predict the outcome of various traits. The **genotype** is the genetic makeup for a trait in an individual which may or may not be expressed, while the observable characteristics of genes are referred to as the **phenotype.** Regarding the eye color example above, the genotype for a particular individual might be one dominant brown gene and one recessive blue gene (Bb). The observable phenotype for this person would be brown eyes because of the presence of a dominant gene. Psychologists study behavioral traits which can involve just one gene, such as the chromosomal disorders listed in Table 5.1, but also study traits that involve the complex interaction of many genes. Thus, there is no one specific gene that determines intelligence, personality, or mental illness.

Environment

What makes us who we are—genes or the environment? Genes obviously affect expressed traits, as previously discussed, but environmental influences need further investigation. Psychologists address the relative contributions of genes and environment regarding particular behaviors in what is known as the **nature versus nurture** debate. The term **nature** specifically references influences on behavior that are genetic or biological. The term **nurture** involves the influence of environmental factors on behavior such as family, culture, interactions with others, education, wealth, etc. Most psychologists now agree that both nature and nurture interact to influence behavior. Nature sets the possibilities for behavior, while nurture determines how those possibilities will be realized. The influence of the nature nurture interaction is illustrated when an individual with limited intellectual capability succeeds because of the environmental influences of additional resources and education. Stern (1956) likened the process to a rubber band: Inherited traits are represented by a rubber band. The environment determines how much the rubber band "stretches."

Table 5.1. Chromosomal Disorders

Disorder	Gene/Damage	Symptoms
Colorblindness	Recessive gene on the X chromosome	Lack of cones necessary to see color
Down Syndrome	Additional chromosome present on the 21st pair	Cognitive disability Distinctive facial features
Phenylketonuria (PKU)	Recessive gene resulting in the inability to process a specific amino acid leading to a buildup of toxins in the nervous system	Cognitive disability resulting from serious permanent brain damage *Note:* Early detection and dietary restrictions prevent brain damage.
Fragile X Syndrome	Mutation of an X chromosome gene occurring on a weak "fragile" area, resulting in the inability to produce a specific protein required for normal brain development	Cognitive disability Distinctive facial features
Tay-Sachs Syndrome	Recessive gene resulting in a lack of a specific protein needed to break down chemicals in the nervous system	Progressive and fatal nerve damage
Huntington's Disease	Defect on a specific dominant gene resulting in a portion of the DNA repeating more than it should	Progressive and fatal nerve damage Impaired behavioral and mental functioning
Turner Syndrome	Females with only one X sex chromosome (X)	Short stature Webbed neck Alters physical and sexual development Normal intelligence
Klinefelter's Syndrome	Males with an additional X sex chromosome (XXY)	Lack of secondary sex characteristics Lower levels of testosterone Excessive shyness and reserved personality

Evolution

Charles Darwin's theory of evolution explains that gradual change in the expression of particular genes over time occurred because traits that allowed our ancestors to survive were passed on to successive generations. Psychologists study genetics to determine how the inheritance of a particular gene leads to differences in human behavior, but they also evaluate why particular behaviors were naturally selected for survival value. Psychologists studying the social custom of marriage would consider how evolution might have influenced this behavior. The prevalence of marriage rituals in human society according to evolutionary psychology indicates that this behavior was naturally selected because it maximized the chances that children would survive, possibly because two parents were better than one in providing protection to vulnerable children.

Twin and Adoption Studies

Psychologists evaluate how much of a particular trait or behavior is based on nature versus nurture by determining the amount of heritability. **Heritability** is a mathematical measure that indicates the amount of variation among individuals that is related to genes. A measure of heritability is an estimate and applies only to the population as a whole and not to individuals. The concept of heritability is expressed as a numerical value ranging from 0 to 1.0 and can be translated into a percentage. For example, if heritability for a particular trait is found to be .6, then the results suggest that 60 percent of the variation among individuals within a population for that trait is caused by genetic influences and 40 percent of the differences are related to factors in the environment. An example of a trait with high levels of heritability is height. If a given population is not deprived of health care and nutrition, most of the differences among the individuals regarding height will be due to differences in their genes.

Behavior geneticists study the expression of behavioral traits in individuals by using twin and adoption studies to investigate the influences of nature and nurture and determine heritability estimates. Schizophrenia, intelligence, and alcoholism have all been studied in this manner, with some support for a significant level of heritability in each of these traits. **Twin studies** involve comparisons of identical and fraternal twins or comparisons of identical twins who were raised apart for differences in the expression of traits. Identical or **monozygotic twins** share 100 percent of the same genes, because they developed from a single fertilized egg. Fraternal or **dizygotic twins** share 50 percent of the same genes because they developed from two separate fertilized eggs and are no more genetically similar to each other than to their other siblings. Twin studies have

DID YOU KNOW?

Have you ever heard of Carl Erich Correns, Erich Tschermak von Seysenegg, or Hugo de Vries? Most likely not, as their research findings in heredity came thirty-four years too late. In 1854, Gregor Mendel discovered the basic principles of heredity and laid the foundation for modern genetics through his work with the edible pea in his monastery's garden. Although published, his findings were not well known. It wasn't until 1900 when botanists Correns, von Seysenegg, and de Vries independently arrived at similar results that they found both the data and the general theory had been published by Mendel thirty-four years earlier.

determined that monozygotic twins who have identical genes and are raised in the same home have a greater likelihood of developing schizophrenia than dizygotic twins or siblings. This result allows researchers to conclude that genetics has a significant influence on whether or not an individual develops schizophrenia. Studies of monozygotic twins raised apart are especially useful in separating the contributions of heredity and environment on behavior. These individuals share 100 percent of the same genes but were raised in different homes; therefore, any trait similarities cannot be explained by having been raised in the same environment and are instead due to genetics. Traits shared by monozygotic twins raised apart are considered to have high heritability, and traits that they differ on are considered to have low heritability. Thomas Bouchard at the University of Minnesota began the famous study of identical twins raised apart in 1979, called the *Minnesota Twin Study*, which continues today. The Minnesota Twin Study found that monozygotic twins raised apart had remarkable similarities in behavioral traits, including intelligence, personality, interests, fears, and talents.

Another method to determine the relative amount of influence nature and nurture have on a particular trait is the use of adoption studies. **Adoption studies** involve examining individuals who were adopted to determine if they are more similar to their biological parents or adoptive parents. Traits adopted children share more with their biological parents are considered to be higher in heritability, and traits adoptive children share with the parents who raised them are considered to be influenced more by the environment. Numerous studies have shown that adopted children are more similar to their biological parents in terms of intelligence, personality, and susceptibility to specific mental illnesses. The influence of nurture can be seen in adoption studies because children are more similar to the parents who raised them in regard to their morals, religious affiliation, and attitudes.

The Nervous System

The human nervous system manages and directs all the voluntary and involuntary actions that we make, as well as our thoughts. The organization of the nervous system as a whole includes several major divisions, neural cells, and the brain. In order to understand this complex system, psychologists find it helpful to recognize the major divisions and basic building blocks that enable the body to control and regulate thoughts and behavior.

Divisions of the Nervous System

There are two main divisions to the human nervous system: the central nervous system (CNS) and the peripheral nervous system (PNS). The **central nervous system** is made up of neural cells and nerves in the brain and spinal cord. The **peripheral nervous system** includes all the neural cells and nerves outside of the spinal cord and skull and carries information to and from the CNS through motor and sensory neurons. The peripheral nervous system is divided into the somatic nervous system and the autonomic nervous system. The **somatic nervous** system consists of the nerves that carry information from the sensory receptors to the CNS, as well as nerves that send information from the CNS to regulate voluntary control of skeletal muscles. For example, the somatic nervous system controls the coordination of muscle movements needed to pick up this book. The **autonomic nervous system consists** of nerves that control automatic functions by integrating the CNS with bodily organs and glands. While reading this book the autonomic nervous system controls involuntary muscles that regulate heart rate, breathing, pupil dilation, digestion, etc.

Figure 5.1. The Human Nervous System

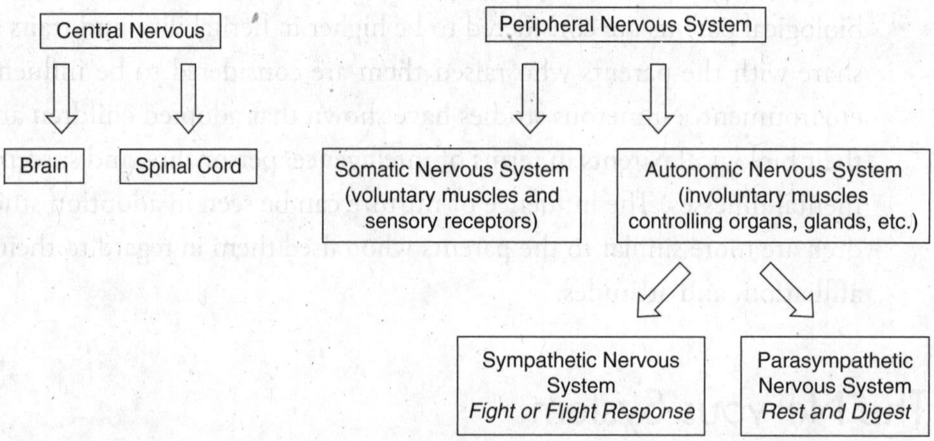

The autonomic nervous system is further divided to include the parasympathetic and sympathetic nervous systems. The **parasympathetic nervous system** acts to increase the body's stored energy. During this period of *rest and digest,* all body systems slow down, with the exception of digestion. The **sympathetic nervous system** acts in emergencies. During this *fight or flight response,* all bodily systems are aroused except for digestion. For example, if while studying, you were suddenly confronted by a grizzly bear, your sympathetic nervous system would increase your heart rate, dilate your pupils, release adrenaline, and increase your breathing. The sympathetic nervous system has prepared your body for a confrontation with the bear or to run away very quickly (remember to take your REA book with you). After reaching the safety of the library, you sit down and resume studying. At this time the parasympathetic nervous system will calm your body by returning your heart rate and breathing to normal. Both sympathetic and parasympathetic branches have the common goal of maintaining **homeostasis,** or the equilibrium which allows the body's internal condition to stay constant.

STUDY TIP

Be able to differentiate between the sympathetic and parasympathetic nervous systems.

- Sympathetic Nervous System—*Fight or Flight Response*
- Parasympathetic Nervous System—*Rest and Digest Response*

Neuron

The nervous system is made up of specialized cells. The most significant of these are the neural cells, or **neurons,** responsible for communication throughout the nervous system. It is estimated that the number of neurons in the human brain exceeds 100 billion. Most neurons are located in the brain, forming an intricate interconnected communication system that allows individual neurons to send and receive messages with one another.

Figure 5.2.   Structure of a Typical Neuron

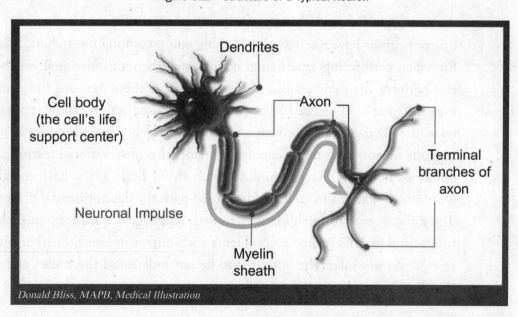

Donald Bliss, MAPB, Medical Illustration

Source: Courtesy of the National Institutes of Health

The major types of neurons within the human body include afferent, efferent, and interneurons. **Afferent neurons (sensory neurons)** transfer information from the sense organs to the brain for analysis. **Efferent neurons (motor neurons)** transfer information from the brain and spinal cord to the muscles, organs, and glands of the body. Efferent neurons are responsible for both voluntary movements, such as walking, and involuntary movements, such as breathing and digestion. Communication between afferent and efferent neurons is facilitated by the most abundant type of neurons—**interneurons**—located in the brain and spinal cord.

STUDY TIP

Be able to distinguish between the three major types of neurons. Utilize the acronym MESA to recall the multiple names for neurons.

- M = Motor neurons
- E = Efferent neurons ⎤ Motor neurons are also called *efferent* neurons.

- S = Sensory neurons
- A = Afferent neurons ⎦ Sensory neurons are also called *afferent* neurons.

For example, as Claudia sits down for dinner, she bangs her toe on *la mesa* (the Spanish word for table), and sensory or afferent neurons send a message to interneurons in her spinal cord, which then transmits this information to her brain (not a spinal reflex). Claudia's brain will then interpret the sensation as pain and send a message to her motor neurons via interneurons, instructing her hand to rub her toe.

Although there are a variety of specialized types of neurons, the recently discovered mirror neurons have received considerable interest among researchers. **Mirror neurons** fire when performing a particular action *and* when an individual watches somebody else perform the same action. It is believed that these neurons fire because one can imagine what it would be like to perform this same action. These specialized neurons were first discovered in monkeys and have been identified in humans as well. Research suggests mirror neurons are involved in empathy, observational learning, and reading emotions in others. Recent findings with fMRI brain scans have revealed problems with mirror neurons in children diagnosed with the developmental disorder of autism. The difficulties autistic children have with language acquisition, empathy, and social interaction may be related to problems with mirror neurons. Further investigation of mirror neurons offers the potential to better understand the causes and symptoms of this disorder.

STUDY TIP

Although neurons vary in shape, size, and specific function, they all share the same general features. Be able to identify the location and function of the various components of a neuron presented in the Table 5.2.

Table 5.2.   Neuron Location and Function

Neuron	Location	Function
Cell body (Soma)	Center of the neuron	Contains the nucleus and produces energy for the neuron
Nucleus	Center of the cell body	Contains the genetic information of the neuron in the form of DNA
Dendrites	Branches extending from the cell body	Receives chemical messages via neurotransmitters from other neurons and transports them to the cell body of the neuron
Axon	A long tube-like extension attached to the cell body	Sends the electrical message (action potential) away from the cell body of the neuron
Myelin sheath	Insulating layer of fat cells surrounding the axon of the neuron	Fatty substance produced by the glial cells that provides insulation and increases the speed of the electrical message (action potential) *Note:* Deterioration of the myelin sheath leads to the loss of muscle control associated with the neurological disease *multiple sclerosis* (MS).
Nodes of Ranvier	Regularly spaced gaps in the myelin sheath along the axon	Enables ion exchange resulting in the electrical message (action potential) jumping across gaps in what is called *saltatory conduction*
Terminal buttons (terminal buds/ axon terminal)	Small knoblike structures at the end of an axon	Contains neurotransmitters in vesicles (sacs) to be released across the synapse
Synaptic vesicles	Tiny sacs located in the terminal buttons	Responsible for storing neurotransmitters
Synapse (synaptic cleft/gap)	Extremely narrow space between the terminal button of the sending neuron and the receptor site of the receiving dendrite	Location of neurotransmission No physical contact between neurons
Receptor site	Ends of the dendrites on the postsynaptic neuron	Areas on the dendrite that receive neurotransmitters to initiate cell firing Receptor sites are specifically designed for particular neurotransmitters

Glial Cells

Neurons are not the only cells in the nervous system. The nervous system also contains glial cells, which are more abundant and outnumber neurons by approximately 10 to 1. **Glial cells** (glia) are brain cells that provide nourishment, protection, and insulation for neurons. These supportive brain cells also protect the brain from toxins and produce the myelin sheath coating the axons of many neurons resulting in faster transmission of messages. Recent research has also suggested that glial cells may contribute significantly to memory formation and the experience of chronic pain.

Neurotransmission

Neurons are able to communicate with each other through the transformation of chemical and electrical energy. The electrical message that travels down the axon stimulates the release of chemical messengers, called **neurotransmitters,** from the synaptic vesicles located inside the terminal buttons. The chemical message crosses the synapse where the neurotransmitters bind with the dendrites of the receiving neuron at specific receptor sites. Neurotransmitters generate postsynaptic potentials or changes in the membrane of the postsynaptic neuron. Postsynaptic potentials can be either **excitatory postsynaptic potentials (EPSPs)** that make the receiving neuron more likely to fire or **inhibitory postsynaptic potentials (IPSPs)** that make the receiving neuron less likely to fire. The total amount of EPSPs that an individual neuron receives from other neurons must be greater than the total amount of IPSPs it receives in order for the neuron to fire. The amount of excitatory neurotransmitters must also reach a specific minimum level or **threshold** to fire. If a neuron's threshold is met, the cell fires, but if the minimum threshold is not reached, the cell does not fire. The firing of the action potential works on the **all-or-none principle**, either firing at 100 percent strength or not at all. After a nerve cell is stimulated enough to reach threshold, a brief electrical charge, called an **action potential,** travels down the axon, section by section, to the terminal buttons where neurotransmitters are released into the synapse.

STUDY TIP

Be able to differentiate between the *chemical* and *electrical* processes involved in neural communication.

- Dendrites receive *chemical* messages in the form of neurotransmitters that are sent to the cell body.
- Axons send *electrical* signals in the form of the action potential away from the cell body.

Neural Impulses

When neurons fire, the process involves an electrical message traveling down the axon, resulting in the release of neurotransmitters into the synapse. An electrical message, referred to as an **action potential,** moves down the axon section by section as channels (gates) along the axon open, allowing for the exchange of ions. **Neural impulses,** or a series of successive action potentials traveling down the axon, are amazingly fast. In fact, all of the steps from when threshold is reached until repolarization is complete occur in about one millisecond or 1/1000 of a second.

STUDY TIP

Be able to describe the various steps and terminology involved when a neuron fires including the important ions and changes in electrical charge that occur during depolarization and repolarization. The steps involved in the firing of a neuron or neural impulse are listed in Table 5.3.

Table 5.3. Steps of a Neural Impulse

Resting Potential (Polarization)	While the neuron is waiting for a message, the fluid filled interior of the axon has a negative charge (–70 millivolts) and the fluid exterior has a positive charge.
	Charged particles or *ions* are located on the inside or outside of the axon membrane.
	• Sodium (Na^+) ions are on the outside.
	• Potassium (K^+) ions are on the inside.
Threshold	When the neuron is stimulated by pressure, heat, light, or chemical messages, the electrical charge inside the axon can reach a tipping point (slightly more positive than resting potential) known as the *threshold*. If the stimulation is below the threshold (tipping point), the neuron will not fire.
All or None Principle	Once threshold has been reached, the neuron fires completely, regardless of how strong the stimulus was.
Action Potential (Depolarization)	Depolarization occurs during the action potential when the interior of the axon changes to a less negative or slightly positive charge. The firing process of the neuron begins when the axon allows certain ions through its semi-permeable membrane, making the interior of the axon become less negative.
	• Sodium (Na^+) ions move to the inside of the axon.
	• Potassium (K^+) ions move to the outside of the axon.
Repolarization	During this period the sodium-potassium pump returns the ions to their original positions in the cell, reestablishing the resting potential.
Refractory Period	While repolarization is occurring, the neuron cannot fire because it is resetting itself to its original resting potential state.

Neurotransmitters

When the action potential reaches the end of the axon known as the terminal button, there is a release of **neurotransmitters,** or chemical messengers, into the synaptic gap. Neurotransmitters are sent from the presynaptic terminal button to the postsynaptic dendrite. These chemicals fit like a key into a lock within the **receptor sites** located

Figure 5.3. Neurons in the Brain

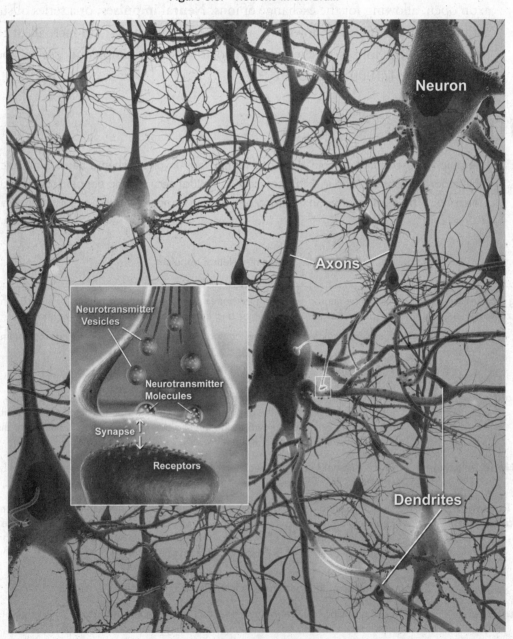

Source: Courtesy of the National Institute on Aging/National Institutes of Health

on the dendrites and activate an action potential in the receiving neuron. There are several specific neurotransmitters to be aware of for the AP Psychology exam which are presented in Table 5.4.

Table 5.4. Neurotransmitters

	Function	Lack	Excess
Dopamine	Pleasure, reward, voluntary movement, learning, and attention. Certain dopamine pathways are involved in drug addiction.	Parkinson's Disease	Schizophrenia
Acetylcholine	Memory and movement	Alzheimer's Disease Paralysis	Muscle convulsions
Serotonin	Mood, appetite, and sleep	Depression Eating disorders Sleep disorders Aggression	
Norepinephrine	Mood and sleep	Depression	Anxiety
Glutamate	Memory and learning. Major excitatory neurotransmitter.		Migraines and seizures
GABA	Relaxation and sleep. Major inhibitory neurotransmitter.	Anxiety disorders, seizures, and insomnia	
Endorphins	Inhibits pain signals and regulates pleasure	Lower pain thresholds. Use of heroin and other opiates leads to decreased production of endorphins.	Higher pain thresholds Runner's high

Clearing the Synapse and the Influence of Drugs

Once a neurotransmitter has been released and has activated the next cell, any excess must be removed from the synapse. Neurotransmitters can be reabsorbed by the presynaptic neuron in a process called **reuptake,** or broken down by enzymes within the synapse. Psychoactive drugs impact neurotransmission and include both medications and drugs of abuse that either work as agonists or antagonists. **Agonist** drugs work by either blocking reuptake or mimicking the natural neurotransmitters by fitting into receptor sites on the postsynaptic neuron. **Selective Serotonin Reuptake Inhibitors (SSRIs),** such as *Prozac,* a drug used to treat depression, function as agonists by delaying the reuptake of serotonin, allowing the neurotransmitter more opportunity to stimulate the postsynaptic neuron. Anti-anxiety medications such as *Xanax* are agonists because the drug molecules fit into receptor sites for the inhibitory neurotransmitter GABA and excite the cell. Drugs referred to as **antagonists,** work by occupying the receptor sites on the postsynaptic neuron and block the impact of neurotransmitters. Individuals with schizophrenia have too much dopamine, and antipsychotic medications act as dopamine antagonists to block the receptor sites and prevent cell excitement.

Figure 5.4. The Effect of SSRIs on Neurotransmission

Normal

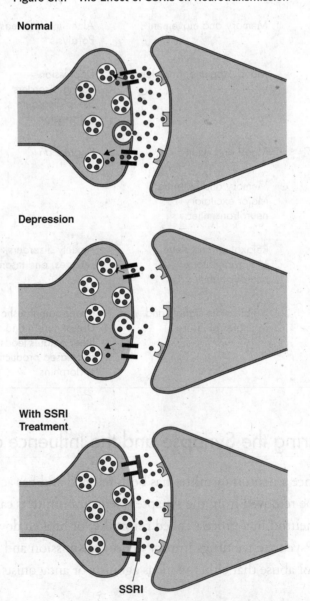

Depression

With SSRI Treatment

SSRI

The Central Nervous System

The **central nervous system** consists of two major components—the spinal cord and the brain—which are responsible for coordinating, storing, and determining the response to information received from the peripheral nervous system. Both the brain and spinal cord are composed of gray and white matter. The vulnerable and critical structures that comprise the central nervous system are protected by bone, cerebrospinal fluid, the blood-brain barrier, and a three-layer membrane system. The most obvious line of defense for the brain and spinal cord are the skull and spinal column that provide a physical barrier. Both structures are also bathed in **cerebrospinal fluid** (CSF), which surrounds the brain and spinal cord and circulates through the **ventricles** or cavities found in the brain. Cerebrospinal fluid protects the central nervous system by providing additional cushion and removing toxins. The **blood–brain barrier**, a network of tightly packed cells in the walls of capillaries, prevents many harmful substances, including poisons from entering the brain. The blood–brain barrier was discovered by researchers when blue dye was inserted into the bloodstream of an animal, and was visible within all of the tissues of the body except the brain and spinal cord. When developing medications to treat neurological diseases, researchers must be certain a drug can cross the blood–brain barrier to have an effect on neurotransmission. All drugs of abuse, such as alcohol and cocaine, are capable of crossing the blood–brain barrier. The final level of protection for the central nervous system involves three connected layers, called the **meninges**. The three layers of meninges are the pia mater, arachnoid mater, and dura mater.

Spinal Cord

The main purposes of the **spinal cord** are breathing, movement, and reacting to pain signals. Resembling an information superhighway, the spinal cord provides the pathway for information between the brain and the body by coordinating sensory and motor responses through interneurons. **Spinal reflexes** are unlearned responses that happen without communication with the brain, including the knee jerk and withdrawal reflexes. The spinal reflex involves a quick circuit starting with a sensory neuron sending a message to the spinal cord, where interneurons within the spinal cord communicate to motor neurons that carry the message out to the muscles, ending in a movement. Reflexes happen very quickly because the spinal cord sends a message along a motor nerve directing a motor response, while simultaneously sending the original sensory message along to the brain. Spinal reflexes most likely evolved because they allowed an individual to respond rapidly by automatically reacting to potentially dangerous stimuli.

STUDY TIP

Be able to explain the steps in a spinal reflex. An example of a spinal reflex is the withdrawal (flexor) reflex that is activated by a painful stimulus such as a sharp object, heat, or electrical shock.

Rory touched a hot stove and quickly removed his hand. This withdrawal reflex can be explained in five simple steps.

1. *Sensory receptors* located in Rory's hand are stimulated by a hot stove.
2. *Afferent (sensory) neurons* send a pain signal to Rory's spinal cord.
3. *Interneurons (association neurons)* in Rory's spinal cord communicate a message to his efferent neurons.
4. *Efferent (motor) neurons* send a signal for movement to Rory's muscles.
5. *Effector muscles* in Rory's hand are instructed by the efferent neurons to move his hand away from the hot stove.

Brain Structure and Function

The human brain consists of three major divisions: the hindbrain, the midbrain, and the forebrain. Situated at the base of the brain, the **hindbrain,** often referred to as the "primitive" part of the brain, coordinates basic bodily functions and is composed of the cerebellum, pons, and medulla. Located above the hindbrain, the **midbrain** is very small in humans and coordinates simple movements with sensory information. The **forebrain** is the sophisticated part of the human brain and includes the cerebral cortex and the subcortical structures of the cerebrum, including the limbic system. It is the well-developed forebrain that allows for the complex thoughts and behaviors unique to humans. The specialized functions of each of the main parts of the brain are described in Table 5.5.

Table 5.5.   Brain Specialization

Hindbrain			
	Location	**Function(s)**	**Helpful Hint**
Brainstem	Base of the brain at the top of the spinal cord	• Automatic survival functions • Sends and receives information	Severe damage to the brainstem would result in death.
Cerebellum	Behind the brainstem underneath the brain	• Balance and coordination • Fine motor movements • Procedural memory	Cerebellum literally means "little brain" and looks like a miniature brain attached to the brainstem.

(continued)

Table 5.5. *(continued)*

Hindbrain

	Location	Function(s)	Helpful Hint
Pons	Above the medulla on the brainstem	• Sleep and arousal • Dreams • Facial expressions	Imagine the pons as a pillow (sleep) located at the top of the bed (brainstem).
Medulla (Medulla Oblongata)	Below the pons on the brainstem	• Survival functions (heartbeat, breathing, and digestion) • Reflexes (sneezing, coughing, vomiting, and swallowing)	"I ♡ my medulla!"

Midbrain

	Location	Function(s)	Helpful Hint
Reticular Activating System (*Reticular Formation* and connections)	Network of nerves running vertically through the brainstem and extending to the thalamus	• Arousal to stimuli • Sleep • Attentiveness • Filters incoming stimuli and relays important information to the thalamus	Damage to the reticular formation results in a coma.
Basal Ganglia (Including the *striatum* and *substantia nigra*)	Midbrain and forebrain	• Smooth voluntary body movements	Cell damage to dopamine producing neurons in the basal ganglia disrupts movement for individuals with Parkinson's disease.

Forebrain

	Location	Function(s)	Helpful Hint
Thalamus	Two connected egg shaped structures located at the top of the brainstem	• Filters and relays sensory information *except for smell* to the appropriate parts of the cerebral cortex • For example, the thalamus would sort information by sending visual signals to the occipital lobes and sound information to the temporal lobes.	Think of the thalamus as the banker in Monopoly that manages all of the money (incoming sensory information) and distributes the money to the players (specific brain areas responsible for that type of information).

(continued)

Table 5.5. (*continued*)

Forebrain			
	Location	**Function(s)**	**Helpful Hint**
Limbic System	Bagel shaped group of structures between the brainstem and the cerebral cortex	• Learning • Memory • Emotion • Basic drives	The main structures of the limbic system include the hippocampus, amygdala, and hypothalamus.
Hippocampus	Limbic system structure surrounding the thalamus	• Explicit memory formation • Learning	Imagine the hippocampus as a college campus where students make a lot of memories and learn a lot of things.
Amygdala	Limbic system structure at the end of each arm of the hippocampus	• Emotions (especially fear and aggression)	Imagine scary hands/fingers located at the end of each arm of the hippocampus. This hint helps identify the amygdala's function (fear and aggression) and location (almond shaped structures at the end of each arm of the hippocampus).
Hypothalamus	Limbic system structure below the thalamus	• Maintenance functions (eating, drinking, body temperature, and sex) • Controls the autonomic nervous system • Controls the endocrine system by influencing the pituitary gland	To help identify four of the significant hypothalamus functions, think of the four Fs: Fighting, Fleeing, Feeding, and Fornicating.
Nucleus Accumbens	Region of the forebrain near the limbic system	• Pleasure or reward circuit • Associated with drug dependency	The nucleus accumbens is rich in dopamine, which is associated with pleasure.
Suprachiasmatic nucleus	Small region within the hypothalamus	• Regulation of circadian rhythm • Regulation of sleep cycle	The suprachiasmatic nucleus controls the pineal gland.
Corpus Callosum	Bundle of neurons connecting the two cerebral hemispheres	• Relays information between the two hemispheres	Think of the corpus *callosum calling* the other hemisphere to communicate messages.

Cerebral Cortex and Lobes

The largest area of the brain, the **cerebrum,** refers to all parts of the brain except for the brainstem and cerebellum and is comprised of two separate layers. The internal layer of the cerebrum is made up of the axons of neurons and glial cells and is called *white matter.* The one-fourth-inch thick wrinkled outer layer is called the **cerebral cortex** and is made up of the cell bodies of neurons called gray matter. The cerebral cortex is responsible for sophisticated thinking and learning in humans. Any portion of the cerebral cortex that is not devoted to motor or sensory functions is known as an **association area.**

STUDY TIP

Be able to differentiate among the cerebrum, cerebral cortex, and the cerebellum.

- *Cerebrum* is the Latin word for "brain" and consists of most of the forebrain.
- Cerebral cortex is the outermost layer of the cerebrum responsible for higher-level thinking.
- Cerebellum is the brain region located behind the brainstem known for coordination and balance.

The rather large cerebral cortex (cortex) in humans, which would be approximately the size of a newspaper if it were stretched out flat, is folded upon itself to fit within the skull. The ridges along the surface of the cortex are referred to as **gyri,** and the valleys on the surface are called **sulci.** The two halves of the brain are referred to as the *left and right hemispheres.* Especially deep or pronounced grooves on the cerebral cortex in each hemisphere are called **fissures.** Several deep fissures divide the cerebral cortex into four regions or lobes: the **frontal lobes** (located behind the forehead), the **parietal lobes** (located directly behind the frontal lobes), the **temporal lobes** (located above the ears), and the **occipital lobes** (located at the back of the cortex). The specialized functions of each of the lobes and their corresponding brain parts are described in Table 5.6.

Figure 5.5. Side View of the Brain

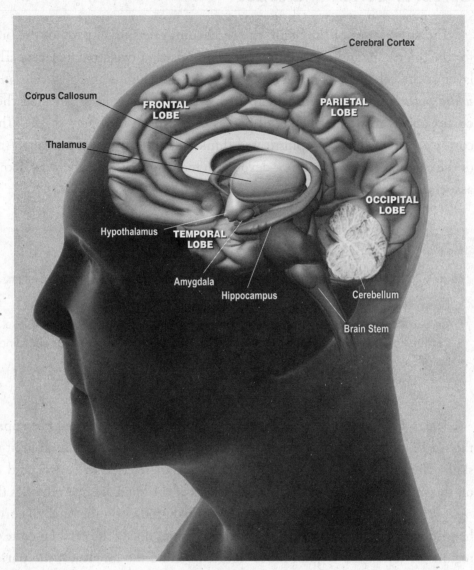

Source: Courtesy of the National Institute on Aging/National Institutes of Health

Table 5.6.   Lobe Specialization

Lobe	Function	Specific Area	Location	Function
Frontal Lobes	• Higher-level thinking • Reasoning • Planning • Judgment • Impulse control	**Prefrontal Cortex**	Association area located in front of the motor strip in the frontal lobes	• Controls conscious thoughts and actions • Working memory • Short-term and long-term planning
		Broca's Area	Front of the *left* frontal lobe	• Controls the facial muscle movements required for the speech production
		Primary Motor Cortex	Rear of the frontal lobes, parallel to the sensory cortex *Note:* Extending from ear to ear like a headband	• Controls voluntary movement • Left motor cortex controls movement on the right side of the body • Right motor cortex controls movement on the left side of the body
		Motor Homunculus	Symbolic representation of the motor cortex *Note:* This is not a brain area.	• Distorted figure that represents proportion of brain area dedicated to each body part in relationship to movement • More cortical tissue is devoted to highly controlled body parts
Parietal Lobes	• Receives sensory information about the somatic senses of touch, pain, and temperature • Spatial abilities	**Primary Somato-sensory cortex** (sensory cortex)	Front of parietal lobes, parallel to the motor cortex *Note:* Extending from ear to ear like a headband	• Sensory input is received for touch and body position • Left sensory cortex controls sensation for the right side of the body • Right sensory cortex controls sensation for the left side of the body
		Sensory Homunculus	Symbolic representation of the sensory cortex *Note:* this is not a brain area.	• Distorted figure that represents proportion of brain area dedicated to each body part in relationship to sensitivity of stimuli • More cortical tissue is devoted to highly sensitive body parts.

(continued)

Table 5.6. *(continued)*

Lobe	Function	Specific Area	Location	Function
Occipital Lobes	• Visual processing	**Primary Visual Cortex**	Bottom area of the occipital lobes	• Information from the left visual field goes to the right side of each eye and is interpreted by the right visual cortex. • Information from the right visual field goes to the left side of each eye and is interpreted by the left visual cortex.
Temporal Lobes	• Auditory processing (hearing) • Olfaction (smell) • Recognition of faces	**Primary Auditory Cortex** **Wernicke's Area**	Upper area of the temporal lobes Top of the *left* temporal lobe	• Processes most auditory information from the opposite ear. • Responsible for language comprehension • Creates meaningful statements.

Plasticity

Although distinctions among these regions are convenient for describing the structure of the cortex, brain functions tend not to be restricted to any particular lobe. One of the most amazing abilities of the human brain is the capacity it has for adaptation or plasticity. **Plasticity** allows the brain to be able to repair itself after damage; for example, if a particular area in the brain is damaged, nearby areas can learn to assume the functions of the regions that were destroyed by developing new connections between dendrites.

Brain Hemisphere Specialization

Consisting of two generally symmetrical halves or hemispheres, the cerebral cortex is responsible for controlling sophisticated cognitive tasks, including logic, memory, language, consciousness, and learning. The two cerebral hemispheres are connected by a large bundle of nerve fibers, called the **corpus callosum**, that facilitates communication between the two hemispheres. Specific functions controlled by each half of the cerebral cortex have been identified in what is referred to as **lateralization** or **hemispheric specialization**. The left hemisphere receives sensory information and controls movement for the right side of the body, and the right hemisphere receives sensory information and controls movement for the left side of the body, which is called *contralateral control.* In most, but not all, individuals, much of the ability to produce and understand language resides in the left hemisphere. Additionally, some evidence indicates that the left hemisphere is more involved in logic, problem solving, mathematical reasoning, and positive emotions and that the right hemisphere is better at recognizing faces, spatial tasks, and creativity.

Much of what we know about lateralization was discovered through work with split-brain patients. Split-brain patients are individuals whose corpus callosum was severed to treat severe epilepsy that did not respond to medications or other treatments. Work by Nobel Prize-winning neuroscientist **Roger Sperry** and researcher **Michael Gazzaniga** with split-brain patients illustrated the differences in lateralization, especially regarding language. Split-brain patients do not display differences in intelligence or personality, but the lateralized functions of each hemisphere can be observed in specific laboratory experiments. During these experiments the split-brain patient focuses on a center point as pictures or words are flashed to either their left or right visual fields. If a word is flashed to the left visual field (received by the right side of each eye), this information is sent by the optic nerve to the right hemisphere. Normally this information would then cross the corpus callosum to the left hemisphere where language exists. Because these connections have been cut in a split-brain patient, the individual will be unable to say the word aloud. However, the nerves of the right motor cortex cross under the medulla and will allow the split-brain to use his or her left hand to select the object that was viewed. If a word is flashed to the right visual field, the split-brain will receive the word in the left hemisphere and be able to pronounce the word because the left hemisphere is in charge of language.

Aphasia

Aphasia is a neurological condition in which brain damage from disease or injury to the portions of the brain responsible for language produces difficulties in communication. **Broca's aphasia,** resulting from damage to Broca's area in the left frontal lobe, results in problems with speech production, including pronunciation, speaking, writing, and coordinating the facial muscle movements required for speech. Broca's aphasia was discovered by the French physician **Paul Broca** who performed an autopsy on a patient who had developed a language problem and discovered a lesion in the patient's frontal lobe. **Wernicke's aphasia** occurs as a result of damage to Wernicke's area in the left temporal lobe; it is named for the German physician **Carl Wernicke** who discovered the region. Damage to this area results in difficulties in language comprehension and individuals with this condition have problems understanding language in others and/or producing meaningful speech.

Methods of Studying the Brain

Early brain research typically involved reviewing case studies of individuals who had suffered brain damage. Advances in biological psychology have been developing rapidly due to the technological improvements achieved with modern brain scanning equipment which allow for noninvasive examination of both healthy and damaged brains. Psychologists use four main techniques to study the brain's functions: accidents, lesions, direct stimulation, and brain imaging.

Accidents

Many important findings have been discovered through observing behavioral changes in individuals who have suffered brain damage, such as war, accident, and stroke victims. Important insights into the interactions between the limbic system and frontal lobes were discovered by studying the changes in behavior evident in one of psychology's most famous case studies, Phineas Gage. Phineas Gage was a railroad foreman in the late nineteenth century who was injured in an explosion. The explosion resulted in a thirteen-pound metal rod (tamping iron) being forced through his head. The rod entered through his left cheek, then behind his left eye, and exited at the top of his skull, severing the connections between his frontal lobes and limbic system. Amazingly, Gage survived the accident with his intellect intact and regained most of his prior physical health. However, the dramatic difference in his personality attracted attention. Prior to the accident Gage was an employee valued for his leadership and was respected by the workers for whom he was responsible, but after the accident he became hostile, profane, and aggressive. The tragic consequences suffered by Gage provided psychologists with an opportunity to examine how the frontal lobes regulate emotion and the ability to plan future events.

Lesions and Stimulation

Psychologists use the techniques of lesioning and direct stimulation to study the brain's functions. Lesioning involves the removal of a portion of an organism's brain. Researchers perform lesions and observe the behavioral changes to determine the function of specific areas of the brain. For example, removing the lateral portion of the hypothalamus in a rat will cause the animal to stop eating. Removing the ventromedial portion of the hypothalamus will cause the animal to lose its appetite. This research method is often used on humans to remove and stop the spread of brain tumors. Research based on the evaluation of patients with lesions has helped scientists localize brain regions responsible for memory, learning, speech, and other functions. Direct stimulation is the opposite of lesioning. Instead of removing a portion of the brain, researchers electrically stimulate the brain. As with lesioning, direct stimulation is often used on animal subjects. For example, stimulating the amygdala in mice will result in an aggressive reaction. Neurosurgeon Wilder Penfield stimulated the brains of fully conscious patients undergoing brain surgery to map the cerebral cortex of the brain, especially the primary motor cortex. The use of electrical stimulation to map the brain has helped surgeons understand the potential results of removing specific areas of the brain during tumor removal.

Brain Imaging

A variety of brain imaging techniques available today enable psychologists to look inside the human brain to identify either the structure or function of various brain parts. Several contemporary brain imaging techniques are described in Table 5.7.

Table 5.7.   Brain Imaging Techniques.

Scan	Definition	Purpose	Advantages/Disadvantages
EEG	Electroencephalogram measures electrical activity of the neurons below the electrodes placed on the scalp. The EEG is often used to show brain wave patterns of electrical activity during sleep stages and seizures.	Only function	**Advantages** • Noninvasive method of study • Abnormal patterns indicate neurological disorders. **Disadvantages** • Difficult to determine which specific brain areas are producing the electrical activity
PET	Positron emission tomography involves the injection of a small harmless amount of radioactive material such as glucose (sugar) into the bloodstream. The PET scan indicates areas of the brain active during cognitive tasks by tracking the specific structures using the radioactive material as fuel, resulting in a color coded image.	Only function	**Advantages** • Allows investigation of mental illness, and neurological problems including Alzheimer's disease, and epilepsy • Allows investigation of specific types of neurotransmitters and drugs **Disadvantages** • Exposure to low levels of radioactive material • Difficult to pinpoint the exact location of brain activity

(continued)

Table 5.7. (*continued*)

Scan	Definition	Purpose	Advantages/Disadvantages
CT (CAT)	Computerized axial tomography creates advanced and specific X-rays of the brain. When the individual is in the machine the X-ray tube rotates around the body taking a series of X-rays. The CT scan is often used to locate tumors and brain damage resulting from blood clots or strokes.	Only structure	**Advantages** • Can view large brain abnormalities • Significantly more sensitive than traditional X-ray imaging **Disadvantages** • Involves radiation • Incapable of locating small brain abnormalities
MRI	The magnetic resonance imaging technique uses strong magnetic fields that cause different molecules to vibrate at different frequencies, which produces detailed images of slices of brain tissue.	Only structure	**Advantages** • Generates images of brain structures with greater clarity than the CT scan • No exposure to radiation or radioactive materials **Disadvantages** • Cannot be used on an individual with a metallic implant including a pacemaker or surgical pin • Individual is required to remain still for an extended period of time in a confined space
fMRI	The functional magnetic resonance imaging technique uses magnetic fields to produce images of the brain and tracks real-time brain activity by measuring blood flow carrying oxygen to active brain tissues.	Structure and function	**Advantages** • No exposure to radioactive materials like during a PET scan, allowing researchers to conduct multiple scans on the same individual • Ability to pinpoint and track mental processes that occur over seconds as opposed to minutes, such as thinking about an object **Disadvantages** • Cannot be used on an individual with a metallic implant including a pacemaker or surgical pin • Although no harmful consequences have been identified, the long-term impact of exposure to powerful magnets is unknown.

The Endocrine System

The **endocrine system** consists of ductless glands which secrete **hormones** or chemical messengers into the bloodstream. The endocrine system uses these hormones to control and coordinate functions including growth, metabolism, reproduction, and stress responses. See Table 5.8. Transported by the bloodstream throughout the body, hormones are capable of influencing behavior in a slow fashion over minutes, hours, or weeks, instead of the nervous system's fast milliseconds. Though hormones circulate throughout the bloodstream, only certain types of cells respond to each hormone in the same way neurotransmitters fit into only certain receptor sites. The central nervous system exerts control over the endocrine system through the activity of the **hypothalamus**, a forebrain structure that releases hormones that trigger action by the pituitary gland. Once stimulated by the hypothalamus, the **pituitary gland** or master gland, manages the release of hormones by other endocrine system organs and glands.

Table 5.8.   Endocrine System Basics

Gland/Location	Hormone	Function	Dysregulation
Pituitary Gland "Master gland" Forebrain structure below the hypothalamus	• Growth • Prolactin • Oxytocin storage • Various hormones that stimulate other glands	The pituitary gland regulates growth, breast milk production, childbirth, and bonding, and communicates to other glands to release hormones.	Extremes in height
Pineal Gland Forebrain structure	• Melatonin	The pineal gland regulates seasonal and sleep cycles. Melatonin concentrations fluctuate daily with higher levels at night causing drowsiness.	Seasonal Affective Disorder (SAD)
Thyroid and Parathyroid Glands Throat	• Thyroxin • Calcitonin • Parathyroid	The thyroid controls metabolism or the rate at which glucose is converted into energy. Together these glands regulate calcium levels in the blood.	Hypothyroidism (underactive gland) Hyperthyroidism (overactive gland)

(continued)

Table 5.8. (*continued*)

Gland/Location	Hormone	Function	Dysregulation
Adrenal Glands Above kidneys	• Cortisol • Epinephrine (Adrenaline) • Norepinephrine (Noradrenaline)	The adrenal glands are controlled by the sympathetic nervous system's fight or flight response which increases heart rate, blood pressure, and glucose levels to respond to a threat.	Excessive sympathetic nervous system activity can compromise the immune system.
Pancreas Close to the stomach	• Insulin • Glucagon	The pancreas regulates sugar metabolism.	Diabetes Low blood sugar
Gonads Testes Ovaries	• Androgens including testosterone • Estrogen • Progesterone	The gonads allow for sexual reproduction.	Reproductive difficulties Higher levels of testosterone are correlated with increased aggression.

Sensation and Perception

What does one know about his or her world? Since the beginning of scientific psychology, psychologists have been interested in understanding sensation and perception and how these two interconnected processes relate to cognition and behavior. **Psychophysics**, a branch of psychology started by German scientist **Gustav Fechner**, studies how physical stimuli (sensations) translate to psychological experiences (perceptions). **Sensation** involves an organism's experience of sensory stimuli and knowledge about the surrounding world based on information received via sensory organs. Psychophysicists investigate the human senses, including vision, audition (hearing), gustation (taste), olfaction (smell), somatic (touch, temperature, pain), vestibular, and kinesthetic. Each sense has specific receptor cells located in the sense organs which transform physical stimuli into neural impulses in a process known as **transduction**. The complementary process to sensation is **perception**, which involves the interpretation of sensations in the brain. Perception includes the cognitive processes of receiving, encoding, storing, and organizing sensations.

STUDY TIP

Be able to distinguish between the processes of sensation and perception.

Thresholds

How intense does a stimulus have to be to produce a sensation? Psychophysicists have answered this question with **absolute thresholds**, or the minimum intensity of stimulation needed for detection 50 percent of the time. For example, an experimenter attempting to find a subject's absolute threshold for sound may walk away from the individual with a ticking watch. As soon as the subject cannot reliably hear the watch 50 percent of the time, the experimenter has determined that subject's approximate absolute threshold for sound.

A **subliminal stimulus** is a weak stimulus presented below threshold that cannot be consciously registered. Research has questioned if very weak or quick stimuli below one's level of consciousness can be perceived; this is known as **subliminal perception**. Although subliminal commands to change behaviors have not been confirmed, there is some evidence that subliminal stimuli may have a subtle influence on behavior, but the influence is neither strong nor long lasting. Any claims by advertisers that subliminal messages can change complex behaviors such as ending addictions or learning a new language are *not* supported by scientific evidence.

The word *approximate* is important when discussing absolute thresholds. An individual's absolute threshold is not constant. The level of attention, motivation, experience, and expectation of an individual can impact the detection of stimuli under different circumstances. **Signal detection theory** predicts when an individual will decide if a stimulus is present or not based on the signal's intensity and the individual's motivation. Psychologists use signal detection theory to evaluate how accurately participants perceive faint stimuli under a variety of conditions. The participants indicate if the stimulus was either present or absent, and the researcher assesses if the decision was correct. For example, Siggy is waiting for an important text message from his girlfriend letting him know when to meet at the movie theater. According to the signal detection theory, various psychological factors, including Siggy's level of attention, motivation, and expectations, will impact whether or not he detects the incoming text message. There are four possible outcomes for Siggy in this situation based on the signal detection theory described in Table 6.1.

Table 6.1.   Signal Detection Theory

		Signal (Text message)	
		Present	**Absent**
Response (Checking your phone)	**Yes**	**Hit**	**False Alarm**
		Siggy checked the phone, and there was a text message.	Siggy checked the phone, and there was not a text message.
	No	**Miss**	**Correct Rejection**
		Siggy did not check the phone, and there was a text message.	Siggy did not check the phone, and there was not a text message.

In addition to the absolute threshold, the lowest detection possible, psychophysicists are interested in the sensitivity to differences between stimuli. The smallest difference between stimuli that can be detected is known as the **just noticeable difference (JND)** or **difference threshold**. The just noticeable difference can be determined when the stimulus has changed in intensity enough for the subject to be able to detect the change. For example, a student would establish the JND for weight when they have removed enough books from their backpack to notice that it became lighter. The JND can also be detected when a student notices that his or her backpack is heavier than a friend's backpack.

Weber's law, based on the work of psychophysicist **Ernst Weber** (1795–1878), is a formula for determining the just noticeable difference. Weber's law states that the minimum amount of change needed to create a just noticeable difference is a constant percentage of the original stimulus. This means that larger stimuli require greater increases in intensity for a difference to be noticed. Each type of stimuli, such as sound or light, has a different constant percentage known as the Weber constant (K). Weber's constant (K) for detecting differences in weight is .02. To compute the size of the stimulus needed for a difference to be detected, one must multiply the intensity of the stimulus by Weber's constant (K). For example, in order to compute the JND for a fifty-pound backpack, one must multiply 50 (the size or intensity of the stimulus) by .02 (Weber's constant for weight), which equals 1. The result is that the JND for a fifty-pound backpack is 1 pound. In this example, any weight added to or removed from the original fifty-pound backpack that is greater than one pound will be detected by the subject. However, any weight below one pound will not be recognized. Weber's law is effective for predicting the JND for most senses over a wide range of intensities, but it does not work as well for extremes.

STUDY TIP

Be able to distinguish between absolute and difference thresholds.

- If Ernie wants to determine his *absolute threshold* for tasting salt, he would begin by tasting French fries that are not salted and slowly add salt until he can taste the salt. The smallest amount of salt he can detect 50 percent of the time is his approximate absolute threshold.

- If Ernie wants to determine his *difference threshold* for tasting salt, he would add more salt to his French fries until he reached the smallest difference in saltiness that he could detect 50 percent of the time.

Sensory Mechanisms

Experimental psychologists investigate the various ways that sensation and perception interact for each of the senses, as well as a variety of unusual sensory phenomena, to provide the basis for both basic and applied research. This research allows for a greater understanding of how humans understand and interact with their world, potentially allowing for improvements in the treatment of sensory disorders and other applied research.

Sensory Adaption

When receptor cells are constantly stimulated, **sensory adaptation**, or a loss of sensitivity to stimuli, can occur. For example, the pressure of a cell phone in one's pocket may disappear after several minutes. Sensory adaptation occurs for all of your senses: sight, sound, touch, smell, and taste. Evolutionary psychologists explain sensory adaptation as a behavior that was naturally selected because it enabled our ancestors to survive. It would have been important for early humans to notice changes in their environment, such as an approaching predator versus repetitive nonthreatening stimuli. By ignoring repetitive stimuli, one is able to focus attention on the potentially more important novel stimuli in the environment.

Sensory Transduction

The process of sensation begins with **transduction**, or the transformation of energy received from environmental stimuli by specialized receptor cells in sensory organs into neural messages. Different types of specialized receptor cells are found in each of the sense organs, and the stimuli received from the environment vary according to each sense. For example, the incoming stimuli for vision would be visible light waves entering the eye, and the stimuli for the hearing sense would be incoming sound waves. Specialized receptor cells for each sense transduce or translate the incoming physical stimuli into neural messages in the form of action potentials traveling along sensory (afferent) neurons to the brain for interpretation (perception).

The process of sensation involves the following general steps:

1. Sensory stimuli are received from the environment via the sense organs.

2. Physical or chemical energy stimuli are converted (transduced) by specialized receptor cells into neural messages. Think of the receptor cells as translators converting the incoming messages into a language that the brain understands.

3. Neural impulses carrying sensory information travel to the brain and arrive in the thalamus, which then forwards the messages to the area of the cortex responsible for that particular sense. For example, visual information is sent through the thalamus to the primary visual cortex in the occipital lobes, and touch information is sent through the thalamus to the somatosensory cortex located at the back of the parietal lobes. A notable exception is the sense of olfaction (smell) that does *not* travel through the thalamus.

4. The brain interprets the incoming stimuli in a process known as perception that happens in the specific primary sensory area designated for each sense, as well as in the frontal lobes.

STUDY TIP

Be able to describe the process of transduction, beginning in the specialized receptor cells in each of the sensory organs and the specific pathway that the information takes to the brain. This process is listed for each sense in Table 6.2.

Table 6.2.   Transduction in the Senses

Sense	Sense Organ	Stimuli	Specialized Receptor Cells	Pathway to the Brain
Vision	Eye	Light waves	Photoreceptor cells: rods and cones located in the retina	The neural message travels from bipolar cells to ganglion cells whose axons form the optic nerve that transports information through the thalamus to the visual cortex in the occipital lobes.
Audition (Hearing)	Ear	Sound waves	Cilia (hair cells) located on the basilar membrane of the cochlea	The neural message travels along the auditory nerve through the thalamus to the auditory cortex located in the temporal lobes.
Gustation (Taste)	Tongue	Molecules dissolved in saliva on the tongue	Taste receptor cells in the taste buds located in the papillae	The neural message travels along a cranial nerve through the thalamus to the cortex.

(continued)

Table 6.2. (*continued*)

Sense	Sense Organ	Stimuli	Specialized Receptor Cells	Pathway to the Brain
Olfaction (Smell)	Nose	Molecules dissolved in the mucous membranes of the nose	Olfactory receptor cells that communicate to the olfactory bulb	The neural message travels along the olfactory bulb to olfactory areas located in the temporal lobes that pass the information on to the limbic system. *Note:* Olfactory information does not travel through the thalamus.
Somatic (Touch)	Skin	Pressure on skin based on intensity of stimuli	Pressure receptor cells located in the skin	The neural message travels along cranial or spinal nerves through the thalamus to the somatosensory cortex at the front of the parietal lobes.
Temperature	Skin	Temperature changes in stimuli	Warm and cold receptor cells located in the skin	The neural message travels along a spinal nerve through the thalamus to the somatosensory cortex at the front of the parietal lobes. *Note:* Temperature can interact with touch sensations.
Pain	Skin	Tissue injury or damage	Pain receptors located in the skin	The neural message travels along a spinal nerve through the thalamus to the somatosensory cortex of the parietal lobes.
Vestibular	Ear	Changes in body position and gravity	Cilia (hair cells) in the semicircular canals	The neural message travels along the auditory nerve to several brain regions, including the cerebellum.
Kinesthetic	Joints, tendons, and muscles	Muscle contractions	Receptor cells (proprioceptors) located in joints and muscles	The neural message travels along a spinal nerve through the thalamus to the somatosensory cortex in the parietal lobes.

Vision

Researchers have made significant strides in explaining the complicated process of how a visual sensation becomes a perception within the brain. The entire process begins with a single light wave that travels through the sense organ of the eye and is translated by specialized receptor cells to be transported to the brain where color is perceived. Vision is one of the senses that is best understood by psychologists and is an especially important concept for students to focus on while preparing for the AP Psychology exam.

Visual Stimuli: Light Waves

For humans, visible light includes only a limited portion of the **electromagnetic spectrum**. Other animals can see infrared light, which consists of longer wavelengths than humans can see, or ultraviolet light, which consists of shorter wavelengths of light than humans are capable of perceiving. Light waves from the visual spectrum for humans can be described in terms of three physical properties and their equivalent psychological properties: the wavelength determines hue, the amplitude (intensity) determines brightness, and the purity determines saturation. The **hue** or color that humans perceive is determined by the wavelength of the light, or the distance between successive peaks in light waves. An easy mnemonic that can be used to remember how different wavelengths are associated with specific colors is ROYGBIV: red, orange, yellow, green, blue, indigo, and violet. Different colors correspond to different wavelengths of light, with red having the longest wavelengths and violet having the shortest. The **brightness** humans perceive is related to the amplitude (intensity) or height of each light wave. Bright colors have greater amplitude (taller waves) and dull colors have smaller amplitude (shorter waves). The **purity** of a wave determines the level of saturation. For example, if all of the light waves entering the eye contain only one wavelength, this high level of purity would result in a perception of a highly saturated color.

Visual Sense Organ: The Eye

The front of the eye is covered by the **cornea;** the outer transparent coating that protects the eye's interior and focuses incoming light. Light entering the eye passes through an opening called the **pupil**, the dark circle at the center of the eye. The colored portion of the eye, called the **iris,** is a ring of muscles that controls the size of the pupil allowing various degrees of light to enter the eye. See Figure 6.1 for a diagram of the eye.

Figure 6.1. Anatomy of the Eye

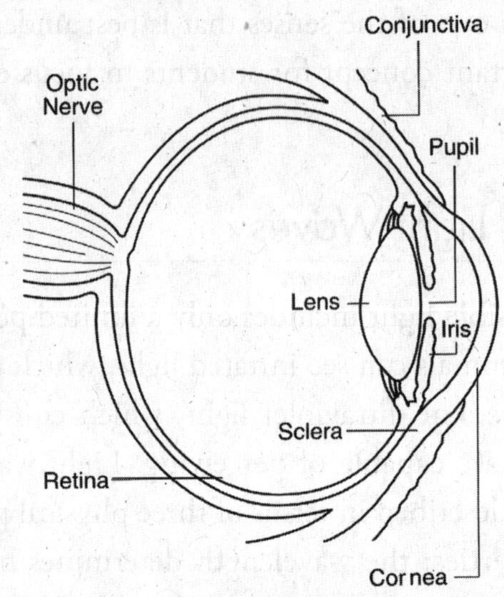

Source: Courtesy of the National Eye
Institute/National Institutes of Health

Just beneath the cornea is the **lens,** a transparent tissue that further focuses the sensory information in the form of light waves on the retina. The **retina** is a photosensitive layer of receptor cells located at the back of the eye where transduction for vision occurs. The lens is adjustable and changes shape, either flattening or curving in a process called **accommodation.** Both the cornea and the lens focus incoming light rays onto the retina, creating an upside-down image. This image initiates a series of nerve impulses that travel to the brain for interpretation. A visual impairment such as myopia (nearsightedness) occurs when the eyeball is longer than normal and the lens focuses the image in front of the retina, resulting in reduced acuity or sharpness of vision for far-away objects. Hyperopia (farsightedness) occurs when the eyeball is shorter than normal and the lens focuses the image behind the retina, resulting in decreased acuity or sharpness of vision for close objects.

The retina contains over 120 million **photoreceptors,** the specialized receptor cells responsible for sensing light waves and converting them into neural messages. Two types of photoreceptors are present in the retina, cones and rods, each with specialized functions. The nearly six million **cones** in the human retina are responsible for detecting color and detail and are most effective in daylight. There are three different types of cones that respond to long, medium, and short wavelengths. These wavelengths are often referred to as red, green, or blue, and the combined wavelengths that stimulate these cones generate the color of any image. Cones are mainly located in the **fovea,** a small central region of the retina where visual acuity is the sharpest. **Visual acuity** involves clarity and the ability to notice fine details in images. When an individual stares at an object that is straight ahead, the image will be focused on the cone-filled fovea, enabling the individual to clearly view the object, including the fine details. In addition to cones, there are also about 120 million rod cells in the eye, primarily concentrated on the outer edge or periphery of the retina. **Rods** are very sensitive under low light conditions such as nighttime, but do not provide as much acuity or detail and cannot see color. Although rods are not sensitive to color, they are significantly more sensitive to light, which means that they are the photoreceptors used to see at nighttime or in dim lighting. When an individual notices an object in his or her peripheral vision, the object will appear as a shape lacking detail because only rods along the outer edge of the retina were activated. The processes by which rods and cones increase or decrease in sensitivity to light are called *light* and *dark adaptation.* Both of these processes require chemical changes in the photoreceptors cells in order to improve visual acuity under different lighting conditions. **Dark adaptation** involves chemical changes in the rods and cones to allow for an increase in sensitivity to light during dark conditions. **Light adaptation** involves a decrease in responsiveness to light during very bright conditions. Both of these processes take time, and, for that reason, entering or exiting a dark movie theater on a bright sunny day will require a period of time before vision adjusts.

Transduction of light wave energy into neural messages occurs in the rods and cones that are connected by specialized **bipolar cells** to the ganglion cells at the front of the retina. **Ganglion cells**, whose axons form the **optic nerve**, then carry the neural impulse to the brain for analysis. It is important to note that the rods and cones are located at the back of the retina, and bipolar and ganglion cells are located in front of the rods and cones. Where the optic nerve leaves the eye, there are no photoreceptors, and this area is known as the **optic disk.** Due to the lack of photoreceptors in the optic disk, a **blind spot**, or gap within the field of vision, exists within each eye. However, individuals are unaware of this blind spot because the brain fills in the gap with information provided by the other eye or the surrounding visual field. After the neural impulse leaves the eye, a part of the optic nerve from each eye crosses through the **optic chiasm** to the opposite hemisphere of the brain. Information from the right visual field (taken in by the left side of each eye) will travel to the left hemisphere of the brain, and information from the left visual field (taken in by the right side of each eye) will travel to the right hemisphere of the brain.

STUDY TIP

Be able to describe the process of sensation from when light waves enter the eye until the information reaches the brain.

1. Light waves are bent and focused by the cornea.
2. The focused light waves then travel through the pupil controlled by the surrounding iris.
3. The lens further bends the light waves and focuses them on the retina, which is located along the back of the eye.
4. Rods or cones at the back of the retina convert light waves into neural signals in the process of transduction.
5. Biopolar cells collect neural signals from the rods and cones and transfer the messages to the ganglion cells.
6. Ganglion cells organize the neural signals, and their axons converge to form the optic nerve.
7. The optic nerve carries the neural signals to the primary visual cortex located in the occipital lobes via the thalamus, where perception occurs.

From the optic chiasm, information is transmitted to the thalamus where it will be relayed to the primary visual cortex located in the occipital lobes to be processed. **David Hubel** and **Torsten Wiesel** won the Nobel Prize for the discovery of feature detectors in the visual cortex. Hubel and Wiesel investigated how specific neurons in the brains of cats reacted when black and white geometric drawings were presented to the visual fields of the animals. The results showed that neurons were specialized to respond to only certain features or aspects of an image. For example, specific neurons reacted only to straight edges, while other neurons reacted only to curved lines. This led to the discovery of **feature detectors**, or specialized neurons in the brain, that are each responsive to particular elements of an image, including straight lines, edges, curves, angles, and direction. Feature detector cells allow for the identification of a figure by combining information from many cells. The firing of multiple feature detector cells in the brain results in the rapid interpretation of sensations because the basic features (elements) of a visual image are processed simultaneously in what is known as **parallel processing**.

Perception in the brain results from two distinct processes—bottom-up and top-down processing. **Bottom-up processing** involves assembling the basic elements of a stimulus in the brain to form a complete perception. The visual system in the brain uses bottom-up processing by creating perceptions based on input from feature detectors. **Top-down processing** occurs when the brain utilizes a person's memories, expectations, and experiences to influence what is perceived. Perceptions are formed in part by actual stimuli from the environment (bottom-up) and the individual's expectations (top-down).

STUDY TIP

Feature detectors are located in the brain, *not* the eye, and are involved in perception, not sensation.

Color Vision

All the objects in our environment absorb and reflect light waves and what we perceive in terms of color is created only by the light waves which are being reflected. A blueberry is perceived as the color blue because the object absorbs all wavelengths except blue wavelengths, which are reflected. The perception of color (blue) is not the product of the object (blueberry), but rather the brain's perception of light waves (energy) that have been reflected by an object.

Furthermore, the perception of color is produced based on one of two different mixing processes involving either absorbing (removal) or adding wavelengths. Differences in the physical makeup of objects impacts the amount of absorption and reflection of light waves that occurs. **Subtractive color mixing** involves the removal of wavelengths through absorption. For example, paint has pigments (chemicals) that absorb wavelengths. When artists mix blue and red paints, the result is purple. When artists mix all of the subtractive primary colors of paint (red, blue, and yellow), each of the pigments absorb each other's wavelengths and the perceived color is black or a lack of any reflected light. **Additive color mixing** involves the addition of light waves to produce color. For example, when stage lighting designers mix red and green light, the result is yellow. When all of the additive primary colors of light (red, green, and blue) are mixed together, the resulting color is white or the reflection of all colors of light.

Experimentation has supported two major theories of color vision: the trichromatic theory and the opponent-process theory. The **trichromatic theory (Young–Helmholtz)** of color vision states that there are three types of color photoreceptors (cones) in the retina of each eye that are most sensitive to red, green, or blue wavelengths. According to this theory all the colors of the visible spectrum can be perceived by combining these three reflected wavelengths. For example, the perception of the color yellow is created in the brain because cones sensitive to red and green wavelengths (red and green cones) were stimulated.

The visual impairment of **color blindness**, which can be related to damaged or missing cones, almost never involves the complete absence of the perception of color and would be more correctly described as color deficiency. Individuals who are completely colorblind and lack all three cone types are extremely rare. These individuals do not perceive any color and instead view the world in terms of black, white, and gray. The most common type of partial color blindness is red–green, whereby an individual lacks either red or green cones, resulting in the perception of red and green as the same color. Genes regulating the perception of color are located on the X chromosome, making partial color blindness a sex-linked trait, more common in males, who have only one X chromosome.

A second theory to explain color vision, the **opponent-process theory**, states that there are three pairs of opponent neurons that work together. One half of the opponent pair is inhibited by the other half of the pair that is activated. The complementary pairs are red–green, blue–yellow, and white–black. For example, when the red–green opponent neuron is excited by the color red, the color green will be inhibited. Unlike the trichromatic theory, the opponent-process theory offers an explanation for the phenomenon of afterimages. **Negative afterimages** are misperceptions in which an image appears in the opposite color than the one that was viewed after the visual stimulus is removed. For example, if a person stares at an image of a green, black, and yellow flag for an extended period of time and then looks at a white piece of paper, a lingering image of the flag will remain. However, the afterimage will appear in the colors opposite the ones that were originally seen. In the flag example, the green becomes red, the black becomes white, and the yellow becomes blue. This phenomenon can be explained by the opponent-process theory which states that the red–green opponent neurons become fatigued for green when staring at the green on the flag for an extended amount of time and the shifting of one's eyes to the white paper allows the red to be stimulated in order to have the perception of the color red in the afterimage.

Although the opponent-process theory was presented initially as an alternative to the tri-chromatic theory, modern evidence indicates that neither approach explains the perception of color completely. The current theory for color vision, the **dual-process theory**, combines elements of both the trichromatic and opponent-process theories to describe the perception of color as a two-step process. Color perception begins in the cones of the retina where different combinations of activity in red, green, and blue cones combine to produce neural signals indicating color. The second step occurs further along in the visual system when information received from the cones (trichromatic theory) is translated by an opponent process and sent to the brain to be interpreted.

Audition (Hearing)

The sense of hearing, referred to as *audition* by psychologists, is a complex process that involves the transduction of energy in the form of sound waves into neural messages that can be interpreted by the brain. Audition, like vision, is well understood by psychologists and is an especially important concept for students to focus on while preparing for the AP Psychology exam.

Auditory Stimuli: Sound Waves

The sense of audition, or hearing, results from sound waves created by vibrating objects being converted into neural messages. Sound waves, like light waves, have three physical dimensions and equivalent psychological properties: the frequency determines pitch, the amplitude (intensity) determines loudness, and the purity determines timbre. The psychological property of **pitch** or the highness or lowness of a sound is determined by the frequency of the sound wave. **Frequency** is how many complete wavelengths pass a specific point within a second. A **wavelength** is the distance between the peak of one wave and the peak of the next wave. Sounds with higher frequencies have shorter wavelengths that are tightly packed together, resulting in a high pitch. Sounds with lower frequencies have longer wavelengths that are spread out, resulting in a low pitch. Just as humans can detect only a small portion of the electromagnetic spectrum, humans can detect sound waves only within a narrow range of frequencies. The psychological property of **loudness** is determined by the **amplitude** or height of each sound wave. (See Table 6.3.) The psychological property of **timbre** refers to the purity of the sound. Pure tones are possible in laboratory experiments but difficult to find in the natural world. Most natural sounds contain several different sound waves at many different frequencies, resulting in different timbres.

Table 6.3. Sound Wave Properties

Physical Property of Sound Wave	Psychological Property of Sound	Measurement	Wave Property	Wave Property
Frequency	Pitch	Hertz	Longer wavelengths or low frequencies create lower pitched sounds.	Shorter wavelengths or high frequencies create higher pitched sounds.
Amplitude	Loudness	Decibels	Higher amplitude or tall waves create louder sounds.	Lower amplitudes or short waves create softer sounds.

STUDY TIP

Be prepared to identify the properties of both a light and a sound wave.

Auditory Sense Organ: The Ear

The ear is divided into three sections—the outer, middle, and inner ear (see Figure 6.2). The **outer ear** consists of the pinna, auditory canal, and tympanic membrane, which all function to funnel sound waves further into the ear. Sound waves first enter the outer visible portion of the ear, called the **pinna**, and then move down the **auditory canal** (ear canal) to the **tympanic membrane** (eardrum) that vibrates in response to the funneled sound waves.

Figure 6.2. Anatomy of the Ear

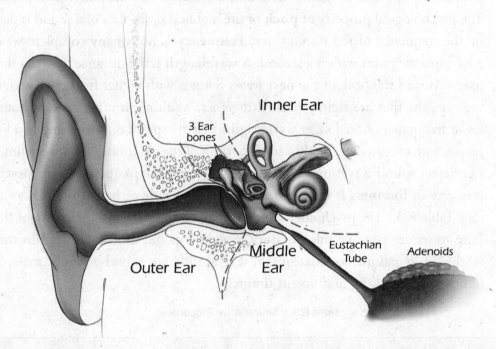

Source: Courtesy of the National Institutes of Health

The **middle ear**, consisting of an area between the tympanic membrane and the cochlea, contains the three smallest bones in the body, known as the **ossicles**, which help amplify the sound waves traveling to the inner ear. The ossicles consist of the malleus (hammer), incus (anvil), and stapes (stirrup), and their function is to amplify the vibrations received from the tympanic membrane and focus them onto the oval window, a membrane covering the opening to the inner ear.

The **inner ear** contains two sense organs: one concerned with hearing (cochlea) and one concerned with balance (semicircular canals). The **cochlea** is a fluid-filled and coiled tube where sound waves are converted into neural impulses in a process called **transduction**. When vibrations transmitted to the oval window occur, the pressure causes waves in the fluid of the cochlea to move the **basilar membrane** that runs down the center of the cochlea. The sound waves cause the cilia (hair cells) located on the basilar membrane and organ of Corti to bend, initiating the process of transduction. The neural message that begins with the specialized receptor cells for audition, the cilia of the basilar membrane, is carried via the auditory nerve to the thalamus. After reaching the thalamus, the message will be routed to the auditory cortex in the temporal lobes where the message will be processed.

Hearing Theories and Sound Localization

The process of transduction that occurs in the cilia of the basilar membrane involves translating information about sound wave frequencies into neural messages in order for the brain to perceive pitch. The perception of pitch, similar to color vision, involves the integration of more than one theory to provide a more complete description of the process of pitch. The Helmholtz **place theory** states that we perceive a range of pitches because sound waves activate hair cells in different locations (places) along the basilar membrane. High frequency sounds travel short distances, activating the area of the basilar membrane at the beginning of the cochlea, while low frequency sounds travel longer distances, activating areas closer to the end of the cochlea. Place theory explains the perception of high-pitched sounds well, but does not accurately represent low-pitched sounds. Very low frequency sound waves cause consistent vibration along the entire basilar membrane, so that no particular area (place) is more stimulated than another.

The **frequency theory** suggests that the basilar membrane vibrates at the same frequency as the sound wave. This vibration results in a neural impulse traveling to the brain at the same frequency as the sound wave, allowing the brain to perceive sound. A sound wave of 200 hertz would excite hair cells along the basilar membrane to fire at a frequency of 200 times per second. This in turn would cause neural impulses to travel up the auditory nerve at a rate (frequency) of 200 times per second, allowing the brain to interpret a specific pitch. High frequency sounds activate more neural impulses, while low frequency sounds activate fewer neural impulses. However, one major problem with this theory is that neurons cannot fire more than 1,000 times per second; therefore, any sounds above 1,000 hertz require the activity of multiple neurons working together in a process known as the **volley theory**. The place theory best explains high-pitched sounds, and the frequency theory best explains low-pitched sounds. Combined, the frequency, pitch, and volley theories provide the most complete explanation of the wide range of pitch that humans are capable of detecting.

Sound localization involves interpretation by the brain of sound waves entering both ears in order to determine the direction the sound is coming from. This is possible because the sound waves arrive at one ear faster than they reach the other ear, and this information about timing is then interpreted by the brain. Sounds that originate from directly above, below, in front of, or behind a person are the most difficult to locate because they reach each ear at the same time and with the same intensity. In order to determine the location of these sounds, humans also utilize their sense of vision or move their heads to cause the message to arrive at the ears at different times.

Deafness

Individuals with hearing loss typically suffer from one of two types of hearing impairments, known as conduction deafness or sensorineural (nerve) deafness. Hearing impairments may result from various causes, provide different types of hearing loss, and be treated in different ways.

Conduction deafness is the result of problems with funneling and amplifying sound waves to the inner ear. Damage to the eardrum or the bones of the middle ear that prevent the transmission of sound waves are typical causes of this type of hearing loss. A person suffering from conduction deafness will have equal difficulty hearing both high and low pitched sounds. The sounds have simply become softer. There are a variety of treatments for conduction deafness, depending on its cause, including medication, surgery, or the use of a hearing aid that will amplify the sound waves to the cochlea for the damaged area in the ear.

Sensorineural (nerve) deafness is the result of damage to the aspects of the auditory system related to the transduction of sound waves or the transmission of neural messages. Damage to the cochlea, cilia (or hair cells) on the basilar membrane, or the auditory nerve can all result in sensorineural deafness. Damage resulting in sensorineural deafness is typically the result of damage to the cilia or hair cells caused by prolonged exposure to loud noise, aging, or disease. A person suffering from sensorineural deafness will often have a much harder time hearing high-pitched sounds than low ones. The cilia near the oval window are responsible for high-pitched tones and are exposed to all sounds entering the ear, whereas the cilia near the end of the cochlea are exposed only to low pitches. Therefore, the cilia for high-pitched tones, located at the beginning of the cochlea, are more susceptible to damage. A hearing aid may be helpful to individuals who have damage to the cilia by stimulating nearby hair cells.

It is important to note that because destroyed hair cells do not regenerate, sensorineural deafness involves permanent damage. Researchers are presently working on methods to restore or repair these cells, but currently severe sensorineural deafness is treated with a cochlear implant. A **cochlear implant** is an electronic device that converts sound waves into electrical signals and works by taking over the function of the hair cells, directly stimulating the auditory nerve.

STUDY TIP

Be prepared to explain the difference between conduction deafness and nerve deafness.

The Chemical Senses

The chemical senses of taste and smell respond to chemical molecules dissolved in liquid (taste), or that are found in the air (smell). The chemical senses serve two purposes: (1) identification of molecules safe to consume and (2) identification and rejection of molecules that are dangerous.

Gustation (Taste)

Transduction for the chemical sense of gustation or taste occurs when molecules mix with saliva or fluid in the mouth. **Taste receptor cells** are mostly located within taste buds and are not visible to the human eye. Taste buds are clustered in small bumps, known as papillae, that are visible along the surface of the tongue. There are also receptors for taste located at the back of the throat and along the roof of the mouth. Researchers have identified five basic tastes, including sweet, sour, bitter, salty, and umami. Umami, the most recently discovered taste, is a flavor enhancer associated with glutamate and often described as meaty or savory.

Considerable variation exists between individuals in terms of how sensitive they are to various tastes, and this sensitivity is mostly determined by genetics. Both humans and other animals prefer sweet and salty tastes to sour or bitter ones. Psychologists believe that these preferences evolved to help humans and animals more easily identify nutritious foods and avoid those that are rotten or poisonous. Taste receptors regenerate every one or two weeks, but overall responsiveness to taste declines with age or because of certain activities like smoking or drinking alcohol.

Olfaction (Smell)

Our sense of smell, referred to by psychologists as olfaction, results from chemicals in the air (odorants) entering the nostrils and sweeping upward to dissolve in mucous membranes containing **olfactory receptor cells**. The specialized receptor cells for olfaction are hair cells, or cilia. Researchers have been unable to identify specific basic smells, as they have for taste. It appears there are at least 350 different specialized receptors cells involved in olfaction. The axons of the olfactory receptors travel to the olfactory bulb, located below the frontal lobe. Unlike all the other senses, olfaction does not travel through the thalamus on the way to the brain, but instead makes direct contact with the olfactory areas of the temporal lobes that pass the information to the limbic system. Contact with the limbic system structures, including the hippocampus and amygdala, create the strong emotional responses and memories associated with smell.

Sensory Interaction

Sensory interaction involves one sense affecting another. An example of sensory interaction is the perception of flavor as the combination of smell and taste. This interaction is evident when an individual has a cold and a reduced ability to smell influences the perception of taste. Temperature and texture, as well as other sensations such as the burning associated with certain spices, can also impact flavor.

Synesthesia is a phenomenon occurring in some individuals in which stimulation of one sensory system generates unexplained sensations in another sensory system. For example, some people with synesthesia hear colors or taste shapes. Experimental findings suggest that approximately one in 2,000 individuals have regular experiences with synesthesia and that potentially one in 300 people have some experiences with the phenomenon. This unusual condition is investigated by psychologists to help better understand sensory systems and sensory interaction.

Touch

Touch is considered a somatic sense (body sense) because the specialized receptor cells responsible for transduction are spread throughout the body. Transduction for the sensation of touch occurs when these specialized receptor cells located in the skin respond to physical pressure, temperature, or chemicals. Skin, the organ covering the entire body, contains various specialized **touch receptor cells** responsible for different functions such as *pressure, cold, warmth,* and *pain*. Although a large variety of receptor cells have been identified, the specific type of receptor cell and its corresponding sensation is unclear. The sense of touch is perceived in the brain by contralateral organization. Sensations received on the left side of the body are perceived by the somatosensory cortex in the right hemisphere of the brain and sensations received on the right side of the body are perceived by the somatosensory cortex of the left hemisphere of the brain. Additionally, areas of the body that are more sensitive to touch are represented by greater surface area along the somatosensory cortex.

Pain

Pain has special significance as an information sense because it signals that something is terribly wrong with the body and allows organisms the opportunity to reduce potential damage. Although pain is an unpleasant experience, it is critical for survival because it generates a rapid response designed to reduce or prevent damage from occurring to tissues. Pain receptors responsible for transmitting pain messages to the brain are located throughout the body and follow one of two main pathways. The fast pathway involves small nerves which carry sharp pain messages. The slow pathway involves large nerves that carry dull pain messages that persist after the initial injury.

The perception of pain is complicated because it involves both physical, as well as psychological, factors. Melzack and Wall proposed the gate control theory as an explanation for how the perception of pain can be managed or controlled. The **gate control theory** is based on the idea that pain signals traveling to the brain via the spinal cord pass through a series of invisible gates. These gates can open to allow pain signals to travel to the brain or close to block pain signals. There are two ways the gates can be closed to reduce the perception of pain. First, additional sensory information traveling up the spinal cord may close the gate and prevent the passage of pain messages. This occurs when you rub the area around an injury, and the rubbing sensations temporarily block the gate and prevent or reduce the transmission of pain signals. Second, the brain may send signals down the spinal cord, closing the gate and preventing additional pain messages from traveling to the brain. Factors such as the release of endorphins, distraction, emotion, and visual input all impact how much or how little pain is perceived.

The Body Senses

The **vestibular sense**, also known as equilibrium, helps us keep our balance by providing information about changes in body position in relation to gravity. Transduction for the vestibular sense takes place in specialized receptor cells, called *cilia*, located in the semicircular canals of the inner ear. Information from these specialized cells regarding head position is sent to the brain via the auditory nerve where perception happens. Overstimulation of the vestibular system can cause one to feel dizzy. **Kinesthesis** is the sense that provides information about the location of body parts in relation to one another. The specialized receptor cells for kinesthesis are called *proprioceptors* and are located in the joints and muscles of the body. The proprioceptors transduce sensory information for kinesthesis to be sent to the brain for interpretation.

Perceptual Processes

After sensations are transduced, the complementary process of perception occurs in the brain. The process of **perception** involves interpreting and assigning meaning to the sensations that have been received. Perceptions are formed through a combination of both bottom-up and top-down processing. **Bottom-up processing** occurs when the brain builds a perception based on data received from sensory organs. **Top-down processing** occurs when the brain fills in any missing aspects with information from experience, motives, and contextual cues. The result is that the perceptions we create regarding the world we live in are based on both the actual sensory information we receive and our own thoughts and expectations.

Perceptual Set

Perceptions are very subjective in nature because they are based on personal assumptions and interpretations. This is why two people looking at the exact same scene can form completely different perceptions. The perceptions individuals create may be based on **schemas** or mental frameworks that organize past experiences in order to make faster or more accurate perceptions. For example, an individual may have a schema for UFOs that includes saucer-shaped objects in the sky. Schemas can help form a **perceptual set**, or the predisposition to interpret an event or stimulus in a particular way based on beliefs, emotions, or previous experiences. When an individual who has recently viewed a science-fiction movie unexpectedly views an ambiguous round object in the sky, that person will be predisposed to perceive the object as a UFO because of previous experiences, schemas, and perceptual set.

An individual's culture can also influence the perceptions created. The impact of cultural interpretations is apparent with the *Müller-Lyer illusion* shown in Figure 6.3. The vertical line on the left appears longer than the one on the right. However, if the two lines are measured, it is clear that they are equivalent in length. One theory suggests that individuals who live in a world filled with square buildings are more likely to incorrectly estimate the length of the lines because of their experience with corners on buildings. Research has indicated that individuals who live in societies without buildings with right angles, such as some rural African groups, are not as susceptible to this illusion. Cultural experience has played a critical role in creating a perceptual set in both circumstances.

Figure 6.3.   The Müller-Lyer Illusion

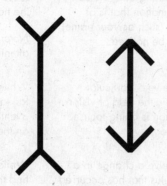

Parapsychology

Perception without sensation is known as **extrasensory perception (ESP)**, and the study of this phenomenon is called **parapsychology** and is not supported by scientific research. Despite the lack of empirical evidence, many Americans believe that parapsychological phenomena, such as telepathy (mind reading), precognition (predicting the future), and clairvoyance (the awareness of remote events), occur. The main problems with research in this area include providing a scientific theory of how these processes might work, successfully demonstrating psychic abilities under controlled lab conditions, and replicating findings.

Attention

Selective attention involves making choices regarding which stimuli to focus on and which to ignore. An example of selective attention is the **Stroop effect**, in which an individual is presented with a list of words for different colors (blue, red, green) that are printed in different colors of ink. For example, the word *red* would be printed in blue ink. Researchers ask participants to state the color of the ink, as opposed to reading the word. The task is made difficult because the word *red* is printed in green ink and, therefore, there is a strong tendency to want to read the word *red* and this is a strain on attention. There are a variety of additional psychological concepts that can be related to attention and have been included in Table 6.4.

Table 6.4. Attention

Attention	Definition	Example
Cocktail Party Effect	Ability to focus attention on one voice while ignoring other noises. However, information that is of special interest (such as your name) will most likely be noticed.	During lunch in the cafeteria you are able to focus on your friend's voice, while ignoring the noise around you. *Note:* Your name can quickly grab your attention.
Inattentional Blindness	Failure to perceive a particular stimulus that is in the field of vision because attention is being focused somewhere else	While watching the football game, you may fail to notice the cheerleader fall because your attention was focused on the football players on the field.
Change blindness	Failure to perceive a change in a particular stimulus that has occurred after there has been a disruption in the field of vision	While playing a game in which you have to find the difference between two very similar pictures you look back and forth from one picture to the other and disrupt your visual field. This disruption results in a failure to notice the difference between the pictures.
Visual Capture	Tendency to focus primarily on information from the sense of vision if conflicting information from other senses is being received	While viewing a movie in a theater, the actors are seen moving their lips, but the sound is actually coming from speakers located behind the individual in the theater. The brain perceives the sound as originating from the mouths of the actors on the screen because vision dominates hearing.

Gestalt Principles

The word *gestalt* refers to form, or organization, and Gestalt psychologists began much of the research involving perception. Gestalt psychology emphasizes the whole and the idea that the whole is greater than the sum of its parts. Early Gestalt psychologists, including Max Wertheimer, explored the development of Gestalt principles to explain how humans organized their perceptual experiences. Perceptual research on vision and information processing begun by Gestalt psychologists continues today in the field of cognitive psychology. Gestalt principles for grouping and organizing perceptions are explained in Table 6.5.

STUDY TIP

Be able to apply the Gestalt principles to a specific example.

Table 6.5. Gestalt Principles

Principle	Definition	Example
Figure-Ground	When individuals view an object in the visual field, they perceive the object (figure) as being separate and important and pay less attention to the area surrounding it (ground) or the background.	The band director stands out as the figure in his black suit against the band members dressed in white and blue behind him.
Proximity	Objects, events, or individuals that are physically close to each other are perceived as a group.	The members of the band carrying instruments are perceived to be one group because they are standing close together in formation.
Similarity	Objects, events, or individuals that are alike are perceived to belong to the same group.	All the members of the band carrying wind instruments such as flutes and clarinets are perceived to be one group and band members playing horn instruments such as trumpets or trombones are perceived to be a different group.
Continuity	Objects, events, or individuals that create a smooth ongoing shape or pattern are perceived as a group.	The final formation created by the marching band involves the students forming an interconnected "O" and "C" for Olive Creek High School. Even though the two letters overlap one another, the audience still perceives an ongoing O and C shape.
Connectedness	Objects, events, or individuals that are linked together by another element are perceived as a group.	Two groups of cheerleaders holding up either side of a large banner for the home team football players to run through are viewed as one group because they are linked together by the banner.
Closure	Tendency to fill in missing portions of incomplete figures or other stimuli to form a group in the form of a completed whole.	Even if members of the marching band are not physically touching each other, the audience can fill in the gaps to recognize that the band members are in a group formation that spells the school name.

Depth Perception Cues

Humans live in a three-dimensional world. To play catch or drive a car, we need to be able to perceive depth. **Depth perception** is the awareness of our 3-D world and the distance between us and other objects. Researchers Eleanor Gibson and Richard Walk created an apparatus called the **visual cliff** designed to examine if depth perception existed in newborn animals and infants who have just learned to crawl. The visual cliff consists of a glass-topped table that creates the illusion of a drop-off on one side. The infant is placed on the table at the shallow end and encouraged by their mother to cross the perceived cliff, but most infants refuse to do this, indicating that they can perceive depth. This finding suggests that the perception of depth in humans might be innate. However, it is impossible to determine if infants have learned to judge depth before they are able to crawl, so the visual cliff cannot conclusively prove that depth perception is innate in humans and not learned. Gibson and Walk also tested newborn animals on the visual cliff, including kittens, chickens, and a goat, all of which can move independently very soon after birth. The findings showed that these animals would also not cross the visual cliff, providing further evidence that depth perception may be innate.

Depth can be perceived using either one or both eyes in what is known as monocular and binocular depth cues (see Table 6.6). Perceptual cues for distance that involve only one eye are called **monocular cues** and are related to how objects are positioned in the environment. While there are numerous monocular cues for depth, there are also two specific cues for determining distance that require two eyes, called **binocular cues**. The two binocular cues for depth are retinal or binocular disparity and convergence. Monocular and binocular cues allow individuals to perceive the distance of objects by determining if the objects are either closer or farther away.

Table 6.6.   Depth Perception Cues

Name of Cue	Type of Cue	Definition	
		Cue provided when the object is perceived as being closer	Cue provided when the object is perceived as being farther away
Retinal (Binocular) Disparity	Binocular	There is a larger difference between the separate images provided by each eye when viewing objects that are closer.	There is a smaller difference between the separate images provided by each eye when viewing objects that are farther away.

(continued)

Table 6.6. *(continued)*

Name of Cue	Type of Cue	Cue provided when the object is perceived as being closer	Cue provided when the object is perceived as being farther away
Convergence	Binocular	More muscle strain is associated with the inward turn of the eyeballs when looking at objects that are closer.	Less muscle strain is associated with the inward turn of the eyeballs when looking at objects that are farther away.
Relative Size *Note:* Assumes size constancy.	Monocular	Objects that are larger compared to others in the visual field are closer.	Objects that are smaller compared to others in the visual field are farther away.
Interposition (Overlap)	Monocular	Objects that block the view of another object are closer.	Objects being blocked by another object are farther away.
Relative Clarity *Note:* Atmospheric changes can include dust, fog, clouds, and precipitation.	Monocular	Objects that appear clear within the atmosphere are closer.	Objects that appear blurry within the atmosphere are farther away.
Texture Gradient	Monocular	Objects that have a detailed, distinct texture are closer.	Objects that have a less detailed, indistinct texture are farther away.
Motion Parallax	Monocular	Objects that are moving in the opposite direction as the observer and appear to be moving faster are closer.	Objects that are moving in the same direction as the observer and appear to be moving slower are farther away.
Linear Perspective *Note:* Not to be confused with the binocular cue of convergence	Monocular	Objects located away from the point where two parallel lines converge (meet) are closer.	Objects located near the point where two parallel lines converge (meet) are farther away.
Relative Brightness	Monocular	Objects that appear bright and reflect a greater amount of light are closer.	Object that appear dull and are shadowed are farther away.
Relative Height *Note:* This cue does not refer to the height of the object, but rather its location within the visual field.	Monocular	Objects located lower in the visual field are closer.	Objects located higher in the visual field are farther away.

STUDY TIP

Be able to differentiate between the two binocular cues of convergence and linear perspective.

Motion

In addition to the perception of distance or depth, our brains are also capable of identifying motion. Feature detectors in the visual cortex are dedicated to the perception of motion in addition to the lines, curves, and color that make up objects. Psychologists study motion by analyzing both experience and perceptual illusions. The **stroboscopic effect (illusion)** is the perception of movement by the brain when a series of images that change slightly are presented in rapid sequence. A movie uses the stroboscopic effect to quickly present a series of still images, creating the illusion of movement and action. The **phi phenomenon** discovered by Gestalt psychologist Max Wertheimer is an illusion of movement created when a group of stationary lights placed in a row turn on and off in rapid sequence. The result is the perception by the brain of a single light moving across space. An example of the phi phenomenon occurs when viewing an electronic sign that shows a message that appears to be running smoothly across the screen. Your high school may have signs of this type with messages announcing important events or achievements. This is an illusion of movement because the sign really consists of a series of lights rapidly firing sequentially.

Perceptual Constancy

The world around us is constantly changing, but we are able to recognize objects that are familiar to us despite continuous changes in their position, distance, or illumination. Without this ability to recognize objects and individuals as remaining the same, the world would be very confusing. The ability to hold onto the perception of an object despite continuous change is known as **perceptual constancy**. Four specific types of perceptual constancy are explained in Table 6.7.

Table 6.7. **Perceptual Constancy**

Constancy	Definition	Example
Size Constancy	Objects are perceived as being the same size, despite the fact that the image on the retina may increase or decrease.	A dog is perceived as remaining the same size despite the distance it is away from you. The farther away from you the dog is, the smaller the image on your retina will be. However, you realize that the dog did not shrink in size.
Shape Constancy	Objects are perceived as being the same shape, despite the fact that the image on the retina may involve a change in angle or orientation.	Bracelets are perceived as keeping their circular shape, despite the angle the objects are viewed from when placed on a table.
Brightness Constancy	Objects that are black, white, or gray are perceived as being the same in terms of brightness, despite the fact that illumination may change.	Blacktop pavement is perceived as black in sunlight or shade because you know it is black.
Color Constancy	Objects are perceived as being the same color, despite the fact that the amount of reflection may change.	A red stop sign is perceived as red, despite different amounts of light being able to reflect off the object, such as in early morning or late afternoon (or a cloudy or sunny day).

Time for a quiz
- Review strategies in Chapter 2
- Take Quiz 2 at the REA Study Center
  (www.rea.com/studycenter)

States of Consciousness

Consciousness refers to the state of being responsive to events and stimuli in the environment, as well as being mindful of internal thoughts such as feelings, memories, and beliefs. Therefore, consciousness is unique to each individual and continually fluctuates. William James was one of the first psychologists to examine the nature of consciousness. James, who published the first psychology textbook, *Principles of Psychology*, spoke of a **stream of consciousness** in which consciousness was a continuous and constantly changing flow of feelings, sensations, and thoughts.

STUDY TIP

Be able to differentiate among the different levels of consciousness.

The multiple terms associated with the study of consciousness can be very confusing. Some terms are specifically associated with the various theories proposed by psychoanalyst Sigmund Freud and others are used more broadly. Freud's theory proposed that awareness in the mind involves three levels: conscious, preconscious, and unconscious. Terms that are associated with Freud's theory are listed in Table 7.1.

Table 7.1. Freud's Theory of Consciousness

Level	Definition
Conscious	The part of the mind that is currently active and responsive to events and stimuli in the environment and is aware of internal thoughts.
Preconscious	The part of the mind located between the conscious and unconscious that contains thoughts, feelings, knowledge, and memories that an individual is aware of but not currently thinking about.
Unconscious	The part of the mind that contains thoughts, wishes, memories, and feelings that an individual is not aware of and cannot bring into conscious awareness. Freud believed that this area of the mind was filled mainly with unacceptable sexual or aggressive thoughts and wishes. *Note:* Sometimes the word *subconscious* is used to refer to both the preconscious and unconscious parts of the mind.

Psychologists are interested in studying a wide range of experiences within consciousness including wakefulness, sleeping, dreaming, hypnosis, meditation, and the effects of psychoactive drugs. Psychologists today often refer to consciousness in the same terms as Freud did, but other terminology is also used frequently. Table 7.2 lists common terms associated with the study of consciousness.

Table 7.2. Consciousness Terminology

Conscious or consciousness	The state of awareness that occurs when the mind is active and responsive to events and stimuli in the environment and is aware of internal thoughts. Most commonly consciousness refers to the normal awake state, but it can include altered states of consciousness.
Altered state of consciousness	The state of awareness or experience that departs from the normal subjective experience of the world and mind. Altered states may include sleep, dreams, hypnosis, meditation, and drug-induced states.
Divided consciousness	The ability to focus awareness on more than one item at a time.
Unconsciousness	The state in which an individual has no sense of who he or she is and is not experiencing thought or responding to the environment. Individuals in a coma or under the influence of anesthesia are in a state of unconsciousness.
Nonconscious	Physiological processes that the mind controls that an individual is not mindful of, such as the regulation of breathing, heart rate, and hormone levels.

Biological Rhythms

Humans and animals have regular biological rhythms, which are physiological and behavioral changes that occur in predictable patterns controlled by an internal clock. A **circadian rhythm** refers to a specific type of biological rhythm in which a predictable pattern occurs in the fluctuations of hormones, blood pressure, temperature, and wakefulness over a twenty-four-hour period. Body temperature, for example, rises and falls throughout the twenty-four-hour period, with an individual's body temperature reaching the lowest point during sleep. This daily pattern of temperature change is connected to feelings of alertness and influences behavior because individuals are the most alert when their body temperature is the highest.

The most researched circadian rhythm in humans is the daily cycle for sleep and wakefulness and appears to be controlled by both an internal clock and external factors. Although the circadian rhythm for sleep and wakefulness is roughly twenty-four hours, individual differences exist in terms of the timing of the sleep–wake cycle. Some individuals, called morning people, wake up earlier and fall asleep earlier, while others, referred to as night owls, typically stay up later and find it more difficult to wake up early. These variations individuals experience are a result of biological differences in their circadian rhythms and not voluntary choice. Located in a region of the hypothalamus, the **suprachiasmatic nucleus (SCN)** is the area of the brain most associated with the sleep–wake cycle. The SCN manages the sleep–wake cycle by sending messages to the pineal gland influencing the release of melatonin. **Melatonin** is a hormone that results in drowsiness when released into the bloodstream. When the SCN receives information from the retina regarding the presence of light, it instructs the pineal gland to decrease the production of melatonin, leading to wakefulness. When the SCN receives information regarding a decrease in the amount of light, it will instruct the pineal gland to release melatonin, resulting in drowsiness. In addition to light, other external factors, such as alarm clocks, seasonal changes, disease, aging, and travel, can impact an individual's circadian rhythm. Changes in these external factors can disrupt the sleep–wake cycle and lead to problems sleeping while the circadian rhythm adjusts. Jet lag, which results when individuals travel across different time zones, is an excellent example of how the circadian rhythm can be disrupted. Research suggests that the best way to reset the biological clock in this circumstance is through exposure to bright light.

STUDY TIP

Increased levels of melatonin in the bloodstream lead to drowsiness.

Sleep Cycle

Sleep involves a state of consciousness during which the brain passes through a series of distinct stages. Psychologists can measure these stages by monitoring changes in patterns of electrical activity in the brain through the use of an **electroencephalogram (EEG).** When an individual is awake and alert, the dominant EEG brain-wave pattern includes **beta waves,** which have low amplitude (height) and high frequency. During very relaxed states, including the period leading up to sleep, the dominant EEG brain-wave pattern includes **alpha waves,** which have a higher amplitude (height), lower frequency, and more regular pattern than beta waves. After individuals are asleep, the electrical pattern of brain waves, measured by the EEG, changes in a predictable way as the person passes through the entire sleep cycle. A **sleep cycle** involves four stages of non-rapid eye movement sleep (NREM) and one stage of rapid eye movement (REM). Approximately every ninety minutes individuals pass through the entire cycle of four NREM stages and the REM stage.

Table 7.3 indicates the brain wave activity measured with an EEG associated with each stage of sleep.

Table 7.3 Brain Wave Activity Associated with Sleep

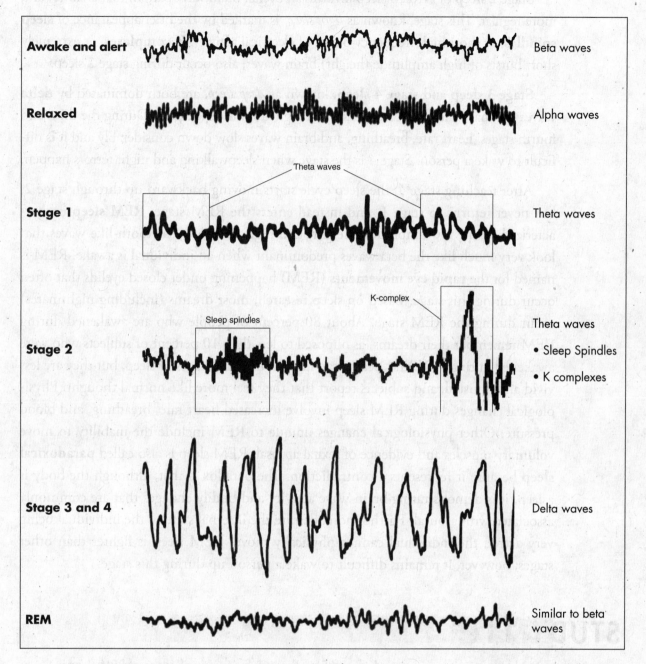

Stage 1 sleep of NREM sleep represents the very short transition period between wakefulness and sleep during which alpha waves are replaced by even slower **theta waves.** During this stage the person is drifting along the edge of consciousness and can be easily awakened. Stage 1 of NREM sleep is referred to as a **hypnagogic state** and may include brief dreamlike hallucinations or sudden movements called *hypnic jerks*.

Stage 2 sleep of NREM sleep involves an overall brain wave pattern that is slower and more regular. This stage, known as *light sleep*, is marked by the brief appearance of **sleep spindles,** or short high frequency bursts of electrical activity. **K complexes**, or extremely short bursts of high amplitude (height) brain waves, also occur during stage 2 sleep.

Stage 3 sleep and **stage 4 sleep**, known as *deep sleep*, are both dominated by **delta waves** that have the lowest frequency and high amplitude (height). During the third and fourth stages, heart rate, breathing, and brain waves slow down considerably and it is difficult to wake a person. Stage 4 is the stage when sleepwalking and night terrors happen.

After reaching stage 4, the sleep cycle starts moving backward up through stage 2, but never returns to stage 1, and instead enters the REM stage. **REM sleep** is characterized by the low amplitude (height) and high frequency sawtooth-like waves that look very much like the beta waves predominant when an individual is awake. REM is named for the **rapid eye movements (REM)** happening under closed eyelids that often occur during this stage. Based on sleep research, most dreams (including nightmares) occur during the REM stage. About 80 percent of people who are awakened during REM remember their dreams, as opposed to less than 10 percent of subjects who were awakened during NREM. Dreams can happen in other stages of sleep, but they are less vivid and unusual, and subjects report that they feel more like normal thought. Physiological changes during REM sleep involve increased heart rate, breathing, and blood pressure. Other physiological changes unique to REM include the inability to move voluntary muscles and evidence of sexual arousal. REM sleep is also called **paradoxical sleep** because it represents a contradiction. The paradox is that, although the body is asleep, it is demonstrating brain-wave activity and bodily changes that are commonly associated with arousal. Furthermore, despite the internal state of the individual being very active, the individual cannot physically move. REM sleep is lighter than other stages; however, it remains difficult to wake a person up during this stage.

STUDY TIP

Be able to provide evidence, such as REM rebound, for the significance of REM sleep.

Psychologists have deprived subjects of REM sleep to study the importance of this unique stage. Using an EEG machine, psychologists wake participants up as they enter REM sleep. When the REM-deprived subjects are allowed to sleep again, individuals enter into REM sleep very soon after they fall asleep and experience more REM time overall in what is called **REM rebound**. Compared to control participants, REM-deprived participants had greater problems concentrating and remembering.

The entire sleep cycle, from stages 1 through 4 followed by 3, 2, REM, lasts approximately ninety minutes and is repeated four to six times during an average eight-hour period of sleep. Throughout the night the length of each sleep stage varies within the sleep cycle. As each cycle of sleep is repeated, the REM stage becomes longer. The first REM stage happens during the last five to ten minutes of the first sleep cycle, and each subsequent REM stage will become longer. Many people wake up during their last stage of REM sleep, when they may be having a dream lasting half an hour or more. The developmental process of aging leads to differences in the amount of sleep individuals require. Infants spend more time than anyone in REM sleep and require more sleep overall than any other group. As an individual ages, the overall need for sleep and REM decreases.

STUDY TIP

The average sleep cycle lasts approximately ninety minutes and is repeated four to six times per night. Throughout the night the amount of time spent in the REM stage increases and the amount of time spent in stage 4 decreases. See Figure 7.1.

Figure 7.1 Typical Sleep Patterns

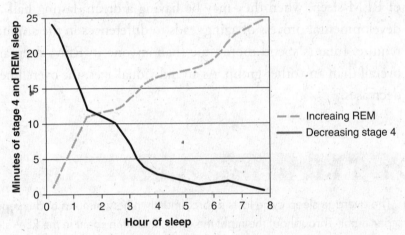

(a) The pattern and stages of sleep experienced during a typical night

(b) A typical sleep pattern with increasing REM sleep and decreasing Stage 4 sleep

Sleep Deprivation and Functions of Sleep

Although a few individuals have stayed awake for up to ten days, most people find the need to sleep to be one of the most overpowering urges they have ever experienced. Sleep deprivation studies provide psychologists with an opportunity to better understand the importance of sleep and how deprivation affects physical and cognitive processes. Long-term extreme sleep deprivation has been associated with the development of psychotic symptoms, including hallucinations and delusions in some individuals. The effects of chronic sleep deprivation have been demonstrated to reduce attention levels, especially for repetitive tasks, reduce reaction time, increase negative emotions, reduce immunity, and increase weight gain. Most sleep-deprived individuals begin to take **microsleeps**, or naps, that last only a few seconds. Individuals are often not aware that they are having these short lapses in consciousness which can be very dangerous because they may lead to car accidents.

What is the purpose of sleep? Several different theories have been proposed regarding the reason that sleep evolved. One theory regarding the function of sleep is that this behavior simply served to keep humans and animals out of harm's way and allow for the conservation of energy. By sleeping, animals preserve energy and are prevented from wandering around in the dark when predators are active. For example, because humans do not see very well in the dark, sleeping may have been naturally selected because it aided their chances of survival. Another theory for sleep's function is that it gives the body a chance to rest and repair itself. Also, because of the fact that growth hormones are released mainly during sleep stages 3 and 4, it is possible that sleep plays a critical role in the growth process. Finally, recent research has demonstrated that sleep may be necessary in order for the brain to consolidate new memories and for learning to occur. Individuals who slept not long after learning new material were better able to retain and retrieve the information they learned. Furthermore, participants who slept after learning were more successful at evaluating the information they learned, resulting in the ability to make more innovative connections. Participants in the study who did not sleep after exposure to the new material did not have as much success. In variations of this study, it was discovered that, regardless of the time of day during which the experiment was done, participants who slept were better able to recall the new information.

STUDY TIP

Be able to identify various theories that explain the purpose of sleep.

Sleep Disorders

Large numbers of individuals suffer from sleep-related disorders that may result in too little sleep, causing difficulties, including an increased risk of accidents, reduced immunity, and irritability. Psychologists have identified a wide variety of sleep-related problems, some of which are very common and others that are quite rare.

STUDY TIP

Be able to identify common sleep disorders and typical methods of treatment for each sleep disorder.

The most common sleep disorder is **insomnia**, or the chronic inability to fall asleep or stay asleep. The consequences for individuals with insomnia are often fatigue, memory problems, and reduced immunity. An occasional difficulty in falling asleep, often due to anticipation of an exciting event or a worry, is normal and does not constitute insomnia as a diagnosis. Insomnia may be caused by stress, pain, breathing difficulties, disruption of the sleep pattern, changing to working the night shift, alcohol, or sleeping pills. Sleeping pills, which individuals take initially to treat their insomnia, can actually add to the problem. Short-term use of sleeping pills causes a reduction in the amount of both REM sleep and deep sleep that are associated with reparative body functions. Long-term use of sleeping pills can lead to addiction, and the individual will require larger doses in order for the sleeping pills to be effective. Insomnia can often be treated with nondrug methods, including establishing regular sleep patterns, relaxation techniques, and diet and exercise changes.

Sleep apnea is a sleep disorder in which the person suffers from momentary cessations of breathing that last about ten seconds until the person briefly wakes up, begins breathing, and falls back asleep. This condition severely disrupts sleep, resulting in the physical and cognitive difficulties associated with a lack of sufficient sleep. Often the only sign is heavy snoring, and victims may be unaware of why they feel fatigued the next day. Incidences of sleep apnea increase for individuals who are overweight or use depressant drugs, including alcohol. Treatments include weight management, medications, and surgery. Sometimes sleep apnea is treated by having the person sleep while wearing a special device called a continuous positive airway pressure (CPAP) machine. The CPAP mask fits over the nose and forces continuous airflow, preventing the cessations of breathing that disturb sleep.

Narcolepsy is a rare sleep disorder characterized by chronic sleep attacks. An individual with narcolepsy may fall asleep suddenly at any time, in any place, and often at inappropriate times. The sleep attacks result in the person falling immediately into REM sleep, which is accompanied by muscle paralysis, but after a few minutes the narcoleptic patient will wake up. The exact cause of this syndrome is not known, but it does appear to be genetic. Narcolepsy can be managed through the use of medications, including both stimulants and antidepressants, and controlled naps.

Sleepwalking, or **somnambulism**, affects between 1 and 5 percent of the population. Somnambulism happens more frequently in children, males, and individuals who have suffered from enuresis (bedwetting) or who have a family history of the condition. Usually sleepwalking disappears by the time the sleepwalker reaches adolescence. Sleepwalking often happens early in the night and when the person is in deep sleep. Generally, a single sleepwalking episode lasts between fifteen and thirty minutes, and the sleepwalker has no memory of the incident. The individual's eyes are usually open while sleepwalking, sometimes making it difficult for family members to determine if the person is awake and drowsy or sleepwalking. This sleep disorder is not related to the acting out of a dream. In REM, when most dreaming happens, a person's muscles are paralyzed, which would make sleepwalking impossible.

Night terrors (sleep terrors) are characterized by the individual abruptly awakening while experiencing increased physiological responses, such as faster heart rate and rapid breathing. The individual may also appear terror stricken or confused or may cry or scream. This sleep disorder is more common in children and happens early in the night during deep sleep (NREM). Individuals experiencing a night terror are difficult to wake because night terrors typically happen during the deep sleep of stage 3 or 4 and those experiencing them do not remember what happened.

Many investigators also consider **nightmares** to be sleep disorders. A nightmare is a dream associated with fear or dread, and, although everyone dreams, nightmares are not terribly common. They are, however, slightly more common among young children. Nightmares tend to happen during REM sleep and the individual has an excellent recollection of the bad dream.

STUDY TIP

Be able to differentiate between a nightmare and a night terror. Nightmares are bad dreams that occur during REM sleep, and individuals can remember them. Night terrors occur during stage 4 sleep, and, when the individual awakens, they are extremely frightened and do not recall the event.

Dreaming

Dreams have long been a source of fascination for scientists and non-scientists alike. For thousands of years, different cultures have investigated how dreams might be spiritual experiences, insights into the wishes of the dreamer, or even signify supernatural powers. People love to talk about their most memorable dreams, and the content and the meaning of dreams is a frequent theme in literature, music, and film. There is tremendous variation in terms of how often people dream and how vivid and memorable their dreams are. The purposes of dreams have been extensively examined from psychoanalytic, cognitive, and biological perspectives. One way to investigate dreams is to have participants sleep in a lab and then wake them up when they have entered REM sleep (based on measurements from an EEG and the presence of rapid eye movement). After the research participants are awakened from REM sleep, researchers ask them if they were dreaming and if so to describe the experience. **Daydreams** are not like the fantasies of sleep. A daydream is a fantasy an individual creates while awake, controlled by waking consciousness, in order to conjure up images that are gratifying. Hence, daydreams are usually closely related to reality and are logical and coherent. While daydreaming, the dreamer willfully controls his or her thoughts and recognizes that he or she is fantasizing. In some sleeping dreams called **lucid dreams**, people not only realize that they are dreaming, but act to change and control them. Many cultures teach people to increase their rate of lucid dreaming; however, many psychologists find this concept controversial.

The question of why we dream can be approached in a variety of ways. **Sigmund Freud** was the first major psychologist to consider dreams meaningful; he even referred to them as the royal road to the unconscious. Freud believed that dreams provide the clearest example of unconscious processes at work and published his findings in his famous book, *The Interpretation of Dreams*. According to psychoanalytic theory, the psychological energy a person consciously uses is shifted to the unconscious portion of the brain while a person is asleep. The content of dreams is then dependent on the emotions which have been aroused that day. According to Freud, these emotions are linked to primary sexual and aggressive drives, as well as repressed memories of these drives. While studying children, Freud found that most dreams had to do with **wish fulfillment**. For example, a child who wanted a particular toy might dream that he or she would get it. However, adults' motives are not so clear. Though most adults reported that their dreams were nonsense, Freud believed he observed two types of interrelated content in those dreams. The **manifest content** is the information about the dream that the dreamer can remember and report afterward. Beneath the manifest content lurks the **latent content**, the unconscious desires causing the dream. These latent (hidden) desires are usually related to sexual or aggressive drives. Freud thought that these desires were too painful to recognize during waking hours and, thus, entered dreams. However, even in dreams, unconscious wishes remain hidden and are indirectly expressed. A few common Freudian dream symbols are parents as emperors, empresses, kings, and queens; children (siblings) as small animals; birth as water; and death as a journey. In this way, unconscious wishes are communicated in code. The problem is to determine what a particular person's code means. Freud's analysis of dreams was more of an art, and not a science. No scientific method for proving or disproving Freudian dream theory exists.

STUDY TIP

Remember that *latent* means *hidden*. According to Freud's dream theory, the latent content of a dream is the *hidden* meaning. According to Tolman's theory, latent learning involves learning that remains *hidden* until it is needed.

According to the **information-processing theory**, a cognitive approach, dreams are methods that the mind uses to sort out the events of the day and place them into memory. It is known that REM sleep, for example, is positively correlated with memory retention. In experiments, if participants are awakened during REM, their recall of information is much worse than the recall of participants who were able to receive a restful night of sleep. It is believed that REM sleep may play a critical role in the ability of the brain to consolidate memory. Cognitive psychologists also suggest that the dreaming associated with REM is involved in the process of placing and organizing thoughts into long-term memory.

The purpose of dreams has also been examined from the biological perspective. McCarley and Hobson proposed the **activation–synthesis model**, which states that dreams are merely the result of the forebrain attempting to interpret the stimulation it is receiving during sleep. According to this theory, signals from the brainstem, especially the pons, are reaching areas of the cortex in charge of vision, hearing, and memory, and the forebrain is working to create meaning from these limited messages, resulting in what we experience as dreams. Other biological theories suggest that dreams occur because some activation during the long period of sleep is needed to create and maintain neural connections.

Hypnosis

Hypnosis was first popularized in the late eighteenth century by a Viennese physician named Anton Mesmer, and the method was used for some time by Freud in an attempt to reach the unconscious. **Hypnosis** is considered by some psychologists to be an altered state of consciousness that utilizes the power of suggestion. Hypnotized subjects experience a relaxed mental state and lack the ongoing "stream of consciousness" which occurs in most waking states. Psychologists agree that hypnosis is not a form of sleep because hypnotic subjects' EEG activity indicates that they are in an awake and active state. However, there is disagreement among psychologists regarding whether or not hypnosis is, in fact, a distinct state of consciousness. Subjects under hypnosis are generally believed to be in a state of high **suggestibility**; they more readily accept instruction and information from the hypnotist, even sometimes bizarre instructions. Suggestibility varies among individuals, and, in general, children are more suggestible than adults, and individuals who are more daydream- or fantasy-prone may have higher levels of suggestibility. **Posthypnotic suggestion** refers to the idea that statements made by a hypnotist, while a person is hypnotized, will be able to influence the person's behavior later. **Posthypnotic amnesia** refers to the phenomenon of individuals not being able to remember what transpired while they were hypnotized. Dramatic claims related to posthypnotic suggestion and posthypnotic amnesia are not supported by research. Additionally, the use of hypnosis as a tool to improve memory or recall the past is not effective. One area of hypnosis which has shown promise is the area of **hypnotic analgesia** or the reduction or elimination of pain through hypnosis. Some rare individuals can be hypnotized to the point that they can undergo surgery without anesthesia, but for most individuals hypnosis can only mildly reduce pain. The effectiveness of hypnosis for other areas of treatment remains controversial, but, according to the American Psychological Association, some success has been found using hypnotherapy for the treatment of insomnia, hypertension, habit modification, smoking, overeating, etc. Potential therapeutic uses of this technique, as well as the specific way that the phenomenon of hypnosis works, are the subject of continued debate in the field of psychology.

There are two main theories for how hypnosis works. One theory proposed by **Ernest Hilgard** states that hypnosis is a state of **dissociation** or divided consciousness when awareness splits into two distinct states that happen concurrently. According to Hilgard, one of the two states of consciousness reacts to the suggestions of the hypnotist, while the other, from the background, monitors behavior and processes information not available to the part of the mind responding to the hypnotist. This part of consciousness that is monitoring from the background is called the **hidden observer**. According to this theory, the state of dissociation created by hypnosis is merely an exaggerated form of how we often find our consciousness split during everyday life. An example of everyday hypnosis is the frightening realization that sometimes people can drive home from school or work and have no real memory of the experience. Another theory often proposed by skeptics is that hypnosis is a social phenomenon. This theory, advocated by many theorists including Nicholas Spanos, states that individuals are *not* in an alerted state of consciousness, but that they are also *not* faking it. According to the **social phenomenon theory**, individuals who are hypnotized are simply playing a role that they have become caught up in, and the behavior they demonstrate is a result of doing what is expected of them in their role. Advocates of the social phenomenon theory contend that hypnosis is not an alerted state of consciousness because hypnotic phenomena are not unique to hypnosis and no significant differences in brain activity have been found for hypnosis, distinguishing it as a truly separate state.

Meditation

Another altered state of consciousness is **meditation**, in which an individual achieves a relaxed and tranquil state through physical and mental exercises. Meditation requires intense concentration and is designed to rid the mind of daily concerns and thoughts and achieve a state of complete relaxation. Meditation is often associated with Eastern religions, but it is widespread in Western religions, too. Meditation exercises often involve having the individual sit or kneel in a comfortable position in a quiet and simple setting, to prevent distractions. The person who is meditating then concentrates or focuses on a particular object or idea. In general, the idea is to concentrate one's attention and block out everyday thoughts. During meditation individuals undergo physiological changes: heart rate slows, blood pressure decreases, and oxygen consumption is reduced. EEG readings of individuals who meditate on a regular basis show greater levels of alpha waves associated with relaxation when compared to control subjects who are told to simply sit quietly. Many people use meditation to help control anxiety and stress, and it has been useful in treating certain illnesses worsened by stress, such as asthma. Part of the interest in meditation was spurred by **biofeedback**, a system whereby people learn how to exert voluntary control over involuntary functions, such as their heart rate or brain waves, by using equipment to monitor how their physiological state responds to both stress and relaxation. After gaining experience with the monitoring equipment, individuals learn to notice when they are becoming tense and choose to relax instead.

Psychoactive Drugs

Psychopharmacology is the scientific study of how drugs impact physical, cognitive, and behavioral functioning by interacting with the nervous system. **Psychoactive** or **psychotropic drugs** produce changes in consciousness affecting thought, mood, and perception. Some psychoactive drugs, such as cannabis, cocaine, heroin, and ecstasy, are **illicit** or illegal. Many medications prescribed by doctors are also psychoactive, including antidepressants, sedatives, antipsychotics, mood stabilizers, and pain relievers. Caffeine is a very commonly used psychoactive drug contained in familiar beverages such as coffee, tea, soda, and energy drinks. Psychoactive drugs, including all drugs of abuse, are able to impact the nervous system by crossing the blood–brain barrier and entering the brain. Psychopharmacology involves treating neurological disorders by developing medications that are also capable of crossing the blood–brain barrier to have an effect on neurotransmission.

Psychoactive drugs impact neurotransmission by acting as either agonists or antagonists. **Agonist** drugs work by either blocking reuptake or mimicking the natural neurotransmitters by fitting into receptor sites on postsynaptic neurons. Cocaine, for example, works in part by blocking the reuptake of the pleasure-inducing neurotransmitter dopamine, allowing it to remain in the synapse longer, increasing transmission. Drugs referred to as **antagonists** work by occupying the receptor sites on the postsynaptic neuron and blocking the delivery of neurotransmitters. Antipsychotic medications are antagonist psychoactive drugs that reduce the symptoms of hallucinations and delusions by preventing the transmission of excess dopamine.

Substance Dependence

Drug addiction results in serious physical, social, emotional, and economic costs for individuals and their families. Furthermore, many individuals with mental illnesses also struggle with addiction. Because of the wide-ranging impact of drug use, this topic represents a significant area of focus for both research and clinical practice in psychology. Psychologists distinguish between *substance abuse* and *substance dependence,* both of which involve dysfunctional behavior. A diagnosis of **substance abuse** involves individuals continuing to use a drug despite negative physical or social consequences. These consequences may include problems maintaining their responsibilities at work, home, or school. **Substance dependence**, also known as addiction, is a diagnosis that involves continued drug use despite significant negative physical and social consequences; it is also characterized by both physical dependence (withdrawal and tolerance) and psychological dependence (intense cravings for the drug). **Physical dependence** results in physiological withdrawal symptoms. **Withdrawal** refers to the unpleasant physical symptoms that result if the addict stops taking the drug associated with substance dependence. Withdrawal symptoms vary depending on the drug and often include cold sweats, vomiting, convulsions, hallucinations, depressed mood, and anxiety. Substance dependence also involves the development of **tolerance**, a condition in which an individual will need to take greater amounts or stronger versions of a drug in order to achieve the same psychotropic effect. **Psychological dependence** is characterized by intense cravings created by the reinforcing properties of the drug.

STUDY TIP

Be able to differentiate between tolerance and withdrawal.

There are several main categories of psychoactive drugs: depressants, opiates, stimulants, and hallucinogens. Each of these categories of drugs affect the central nervous system in different ways, resulting in variations in what the drug user experiences, the amount of time it takes for tolerance to develop, withdrawal symptoms, and addictive potential.

Depressants

Depressants lead to muscle relaxation, sleep, and inhibition of the cognitive centers in the brain. Because their primary effects are relaxation and drowsiness, depressants have also been called *downers*. Depressant drugs are associated with symptoms such as poor coordination, slurred speech, and drowsiness. Examples of depressant drugs include anxiolytics or anti-anxiety medication and alcohol. The most commonly prescribed anxiolytics include benzodiazepines, such as Xanax and Valium, which replaced barbiturates, which had more significant negative side effects. The most abused depressant drug is alcohol, whose effects on the nervous system are extremely powerful. Once certain levels of alcohol cross the blood–brain barrier, the nervous system slows down and behavior is altered in relationship to the area of the brain affected. Examples of alcohol related impairments include loss of motor coordination related to the cerebellum, trouble making memories related to the hippocampus and poor judgment, emotional control, and decision making related to the frontal lobes. If the hindbrain, especially the medulla, is severely slowed down by alcohol, death due to overdose will result as breathing or circulation stops. Many depressants, including alcohol, are highly addictive, and people who stop taking them may suffer withdrawal symptoms and convulsions.

STUDY TIP

Alcohol is an example of a depressant because it slows down the nervous system.

Opiates or **narcotics** are a specific type of depressant that comes from an opium poppy plant that produce euphoria, pain reduction, and an insensitivity to stimuli in the environment. Opiates are extremely addictive, both physically and psychologically. Examples of opiates include morphine, heroin, and codeine. The human brain produces its own natural opiates, called **endorphins**, that can relieve pain. Opiate drugs work as endorphin agonists because they are chemically similar and are able to activate endorphin receptor sites relieving pain. The continued use of opiates reduces the body's natural production of endorphins, causing withdrawal symptoms that lead the user to take more of the drug. **Heroin** addiction is extremely powerful. One of the most effective treatments is for addicts to use a synthetic type of opiate called *methadone*. This drug works by eliminating withdrawal symptoms without creating a "high" or the pleasurable aspects of heroin. Treatment plans involving methadone are controversial, but have been effective in reducing addiction.

Stimulants

Stimulants counteract fatigue and produce mood upswings. By increasing the activity of the nervous system, they promote physiological activity and alertness. Examples of stimulants include caffeine, nicotine, amphetamines, and cocaine. When stimulants are abused, symptoms such as insomnia, loss of appetite, aggression, paranoia, nervousness, and argumentativeness may appear. Chronic abusers may also develop hallucinations and psychotic reactions. **Cocaine**, a very powerful stimulant, produces a euphoric "high" lasting approximately ten to thirty minutes, followed by a crash characterized by cravings and withdrawal. An incredibly dangerous type of stimulant, **methamphetamine**, commonly called crystal meth, results in longer lasting and more intense feelings of euphoria. Crystal meth is powerfully addictive, both physically and psychologically, and is associated with violence, rapid physical deterioration, psychotic behavior, and crime. Another illicit stimulant drug is ecstasy or MDMA, a synthetically created drug that has hallucinogenic properties.

STUDY TIP

Be able to provide examples of stimulants, including everyday examples such as caffeine and nicotine.

Hallucinogens

Hallucinogenic or psychedelic drugs, needless to say, cause hallucinations, delusions, or unusual perceptions. These illusions include auditory and visual hallucinations and sometimes *synesthesia*, a phenomenon in which stimulation of one sensory system generates unexplained sensations in another sensory system. For example, many **LSD** (lysergic acid diethylamide) users report that music seems "colored," that the sounds they hear are actually accompanied by colored lights floating before their eyes. Common psychedelics include LSD, MDMA (ecstasy), psilocybin, and marijuana. The psychoactive drug **marijuana**, derived from the cannabis plant, contains the active ingredient of **THC** (tetrahydrocannabinol) and is characterized as a mild hallucinogen. The THC in marijuana works on the receptor sites of multiple neurotransmitters, including GABA and dopamine. Hallucinogenic drugs vary greatly as to how strongly they affect cognition (thought processes), emotion, and perception. They may produce pleasurable or depressive emotions and a sense of detachment from the body. Abusing hallucinogens can result in panic attacks and disorientation, and long-term abuse may contribute to psychoses.

Learning

Psychologists define **learning** as an enduring or relatively permanent change in an organism caused by experience or influences in the environment. Behaviors that are caused by factors such as fatigue, intoxication, or illness are not considered to be the result of learning because they are not long-lasting or permanent. Changes in an organism due to normal growth, aging or genetics are also not the result of learning because they were not caused by experience or environmental influences. Much of the understanding of how learning works was discovered by behaviorists. Early **behaviorists,** including John B. Watson and B.F. Skinner, stressed that psychology should include only the investigation of observable and measurable behavior. Although the study of learning is typically associated with the perspective of behaviorism, learning is also influenced by biological, cognitive, and social factors. Psychology involves the identification and investigation of a variety of types of learning that include classical conditioning, operant conditioning, observational learning, and the impact of cognition and biology on learning.

STUDY TIP

Be able to identify the stimulus and response relationship between the environment and an organism involved in learning.

Any factor in the environment that causes a reaction is known as a **stimulus,** and any reaction by an organism which is either voluntary or involuntary is called a **response.**

Classical Conditioning

Historically, the psychological study of learning began in **Ivan Pavlov's** laboratory in Russia in the late nineteenth century. Pavlov was initially studying what he called the salivation reflex or the involuntary behavior of salivating in response to meat powder placed in the mouths of dogs. While conducting research, a problem occurred, as the dogs began to salivate before the meat powder was placed in their mouth in response to the sight or sound of the experimenter. The dogs were anticipating the arrival of the meat powder. Based on this observation, Pavlov began the investigation of how organisms learn by association. In 1904 Pavlov was awarded the Nobel Prize in medicine and physiology for his investigation into what is now known as classical conditioning. **Classical conditioning (Pavlovian conditioning)** is a type of learning involving pairing a previously neutral stimulus with an unlearned stimulus to generate a learned response.

Classical conditioning is based on involuntary responses that include reflexes. A *reflex* is an automatic, unlearned response that does not involve experience or conscious effort.

STUDY TIP

Psychologists study a variety of types of learning, often referred to as *conditioning*.

Pavlov's Classic Experiment

Ivan Pavlov developed a method to study classical conditioning in dogs by constructing an apparatus that would allow for a controlled experiment. The dog was placed into the device which consisted of a harness to hold the animal securely behind a screen that would obstruct the animal's view. This obstruction was necessary to prevent the dog from seeing the researcher approaching with the food. Pavlov then surgically inserted a tube into the cheek of the animal in order to collect the saliva that would serve as a measurable response.

During the first stage of the controlled experiment, Pavlov used the natural or unlearned stimulus–response pattern in which meat powder placed in the dog's mouth resulted in salivation. During the second stage of the experiment, Pavlov repeatedly paired the ringing of a bell, which will not naturally cause a dog to salivate, with the presentation of meat powder to the dog. After multiple pairings, the final stage of the experiment involved presenting the bell alone in order to demonstrate the learned response of the dog salivating to the once neutral stimulus of the bell without the presence of the meat powder. In addition to the bell, Pavlov replicated his findings with a variety of different stimuli, including tuning forks, metronomes, and a light. Through this controlled experimentation on dogs, Pavlov was able to identify the steps involved in classical conditioning, as well as to define specific terminology related to the process.

STUDY TIP

Be able to define and apply terms related to classical conditioning to both Pavlov's classic experiment and real world situations. Each of the terms and how they specifically relate to Pavlov's research, as well as a real-world example, are outlined in Table 8.1.

Table 8.1.   Classical Conditioning—Basic Terminology

Classical Conditioning Term	Definition	Pavlov's Experiment Application	Real-World Application
Unconditioned Stimulus (UCS)	Factor in the environment that causes an unlearned reaction including physiological reflexes.	Meat Powder	Chemotherapy drug
Unconditioned Response (UCR)	Unlearned reaction caused by an unconditioned stimulus.	Salivation (to the meat powder)	Nausea (to the chemotherapy drug)
Neutral Stimulus (NS)	Factor in the environment that does not cause the reaction being studied prior to acquisition.	Bell (prior to acquisition)	Waiting room of hospital (prior to acquisition)
Conditioned Stimulus (CS)	Factor in the environment that causes a learned reaction due to having been paired with the unconditioned stimulus.	Bell (after being paired with the meat powder)	Waiting room of hospital (after being paired with the chemotherapy drug)
Conditioned Response (CR)	Learned reaction caused by a conditioned stimulus that is the same or similar to the unconditioned response.	Salivation (to the bell)	Nausea (to the waiting room)

STUDY TIP

The NS will become the CS after multiple pairings.

The UCR and CR will be identical or very similar and will both be an involuntary reaction, which is often an emotion or reflex with a corresponding physiological response.

The process of classical conditioning happens in three stages. Before classical conditioning can occur, an unconditioned stimulus will result in an unconditioned response. This pairing provides the basis for learning through classical conditioning. The neutral stimulus, which will become the conditioned stimulus, is neutral at this time and does not produce any reflexive response. During the second stage, the neutral stimulus is repeatedly paired with the unconditioned stimulus until it becomes the conditioned stimulus. In the final stage of classical conditioning, the conditioned stimulus will produce a conditioned response without the presence of the unconditioned stimulus. The three stages of classical conditioning are identified and applied to Pavlov's classic experiment in Table 8.2.

Table 8.2. Three Stages of Classical Conditioning in Pavlov's Classic Experiment

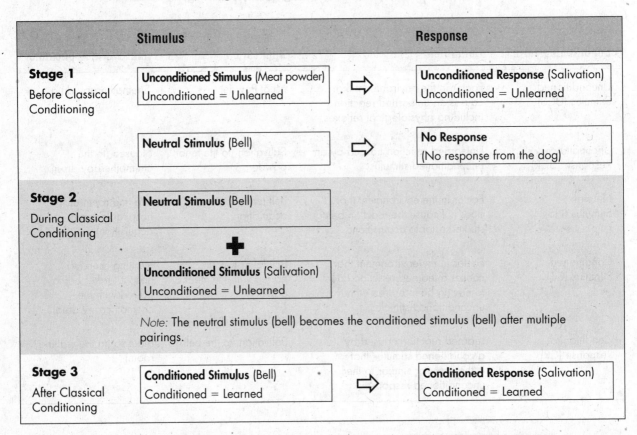

During his research Ivan Pavlov discovered that the effectiveness of classical conditioning related to a variety of factors, including the frequency (number of times) of the pairings and the timing of when each stimulus was presented. Pavlov discovered that responses would be strengthened if the NS and UCS were paired together more often. Although there are a variety of procedures for presenting stimuli in classical conditioning, research has determined that introducing the NS (which will become the CS) immediately before the UCS will result in the most effective learning. In addition, the amount of time between presenting the NS and UCS is most effective if the interval is between half a second and a few seconds. Several different procedures for pairing stimuli and their application to Pavlov's research are listed in Table 8.3.

Table 8.3. Procedures for Pairing Stimuli

Type of Conditioning	Definition	Application to Pavlov's Experiment
Delayed Conditioning (Forward Conditioning)	A procedure in which the CS is introduced and remains present before the UCS is introduced. *Note:* This method is considered an effective technique for conditioning and works best if the UCS is introduced quickly after the CS is presented.	The bell (CS) is introduced and remains present for a short period before the food (UCS) is introduced.
Trace Conditioning (Forward Conditioning)	A procedure in which the CS is introduced and stopped before the UCS is introduced. The presentation of the two stimuli is divided by an interval of time.	The bell (CS) is introduced and removed. After a period of time the food (UCS) is introduced.
Simultaneous Conditioning	A procedure in which the CS and UCS are introduced at the same time.	The bell (CS) and food (UCS) are introduced at the same time.
Backward Conditioning	A procedure in which the UCS is presented before the NS. *Note:* This method is not considered an effective method of conditioning.	The food (UCS) is presented before the bell (NS).

STUDY TIP

Be able to identify how frequency and timing can impact the strength of a classically conditioned response.

- Repeated pairings (frequency) of the CS and UCS increases the strength of the learned response.
- Presenting the CS before the UCS (timing) increases the strength of the learned response.
- Providing a short separation in time between the presentation of the CS and UCS increases the strength of the learned response.

In addition to determining the stimulus–response pattern and the procedure of pairing stimuli involved in classical conditioning, Pavlov identified additional key phenomena. These classical conditioning processes can help explain aspects of both human and animal learning and behavior. Remember that although these terms can be associated with other types of learning, when applied to classical conditioning, the processes will always involve involuntary behaviors. Each key phenomenon related to classical conditioning is explained in Table 8.4.

Table 8.4.   Classical Conditioning Phenomena

Phenomenon	Definition	Pavlov's Experiment Application	Real-World Application
Acquisition	Initial process of learning that involves pairing of the neutral stimulus (NS) with the unconditioned stimulus (UCS) so that the conditioned stimulus (CS) causes a conditioned response (CR)	A dog learns to salivate to a bell by pairing a bell (NS) with meat powder (UCS).	A song (NS) is played frequently when Colette is out with her boyfriend (UCS) whom she loves. Now when she hears the song (CS), it causes her to have positive emotions (CR).
Generalization	Learned response (CR) to stimuli that are similar to the conditioned stimulus (CS)	A dog may learn to respond to a metronome or tuning fork because they sound similar to a bell (CS).	Colette experiences positive emotions (CR) when listening to *any* similar song (CS).
Discrimination	Learned response (CR) to stimuli that are different than the conditioned stimulus (CS)	A dog may learn to respond to a bell (CS) but not a metronome.	Colette experiences positive emotions (CR) when listening to *only* the specific song (CS) that she heard with her boyfriend.
Extinction	When the conditioned stimulus (CS) no longer creates a conditioned response (CR). The elimination or weakening of a learned response occurs because the UCS and CS were no longer paired.	The bell (CS) no longer causes the dog to salivate (CR) because the bell (CS) was presented several times without being paired with the meat powder (UCS).	Colette no longer responds with positive emotions (CR) to the specific song (CS) because, for several months after they broke up, the specific song (CS) was not paired with her boyfriend (UCS).
Spontaneous Recovery	The reappearance of an extinguished conditioned response (CR) after a delay	The dog spontaneously salivates (CR) due to the presentation of a bell (CS) after the learned response had been extinguished for several day.	Colette spontaneously responds with positive emotions (CR) to the specific song (CS) that was played on the radio one year after her breakup with the boyfriend.
Reconditioning	After extinction, the rapid relearning of a conditioned response (CR) because of the conditioned stimulus (CS) being paired with the unconditioned stimulus (UCS). This process illustrates that extinction involves weakening and not the complete elimination of the CR.	After extinction, the dog will rapidly relearn to salivate (CR) because the bell (CS) was paired again with the meat powder (UCS).	After Colette and her boyfriend break up and her reaction to the song becomes extinct, Colette will be able to rapidly relearn the experience of positive emotions (CR) when the couple gets back together. This process is fast because the song (CS) will once again be paired with her boyfriend (UCS) when they are dating.

(continued)

Table 8.4. *(continued)*

Phenomenon	Definition	Pavlov's Experiment Application	Real-World Application
Higher-Order Conditioning (Second-Order Conditioning)	Turning a second neutral stimulus (new NS) into a conditioned stimulus (new CS) by pairing it with the conditioned stimulus (original CS) that was already established. Eventually the CR will be produced without the new CS having been paired with the UCS.	A light (new NS) becomes a new CS by pairing it with the bell (original CS). Eventually the light will produce salivation (CR) even though the light was never paired with the meat powder (UCS).	Colette is at work (new NS) and hears the song (original CS). Eventually her workplace (new CS) produces positive emotions (CR), even though her workplace was never paired with her boyfriend (UCS).

STUDY TIP

Be able to explain the data generated by experiments in learning including classical conditioning phenomena. The graph below shows the rate of learning (y axis) in relation to time (x axis). The response rate strengthens over time during the acquisition phase when the UCS is paired with the CS. When the CS is presented alone, extinction begins and the response rate drops. After a delay, the extinguished CR reappears in what is known as spontaneous recovery, and the response rate is strengthened once again, but will begin to weaken with extinction.

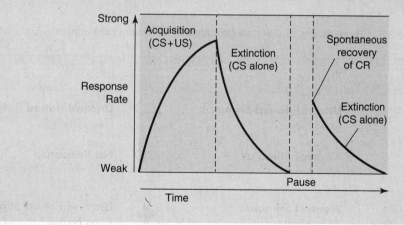

Watson's Experiment

John B. Watson, the father of American behaviorism, and his assistant Rosalie Rayner demonstrated how classical conditioning could be used in humans to create a learned fear response. In an ethically debatable experiment according to current standards, a nine-month-old boy named Albert was taught to fear white furry objects. In order to create fear in Little Albert, Watson needed to pair a neutral stimulus (white rat) with an unconditioned stimulus that would cause an involuntary fear response. What are babies naturally afraid of? Watson chose to use a loud noise as his unconditioned stimulus. Little Albert was allowed to play with a white rat, and then Watson would make a loud noise by hitting a hammer to a pipe whenever the child reached for the white rat. Poor Little Albert was very frightened by the loud noise, and his involuntary fear response was observable when he cried. Conditioning occurred after limited pairings of the loud noise and white rat. Eventually the white rat alone would cause a learned reaction of fear which was visible to the researchers when Little Albert cried. Further research found that Little Albert not only feared the rat, but similar stimuli as well, including a rabbit, a dog, sealskin coat, Santa Claus mask, and even Watson's white hair. See Table 8.5. Little Albert had **generalized** his fear of the white, furry rat to include all white, furry items in his environment. The closer the item resembled the white rat, the more likely the item produced fear.

STUDY TIP

Be able to identify the elements of classical conditioning that John B. Watson used to condition fear in Little Albert.

Table 8.5.   Three Stages of Classical Conditioning in Watson's Experiment—Little Albert

	Stimulus		Response
Stage 1 Before Classical Conditioning	**Unconditioned Stimulus** (Loud Noise)	⇨	**Unconditioned Response** (Fear/Crying)
	Neutral Stimulus (White Rat)	⇨	**No Response** (No reflexive response from Little Albert)
Stage 2 During Classical Conditioning	**Neutral Stimulus** (White Rat)	✚	**Unconditioned Stimulus** (Loud Noise)
	Note: The neutral stimulus (white rat) becomes the conditioned stimulus (white rat) after multiple pairings.		
Stage 3 After Classical Conditioning	**Condition Stimulus** (White Rat)	⇨	**Conditioned Response** (Fear/Crying)
	Stimulus Generalization (White, Furry Items)	⇨	**Conditioned Response** (Fear/Crying)

Counterconditioning

John B. Watson's experiments with Little Albert proved that fears could be learned through classical conditioning. Psychologist **Mary Cover Jones** would later use the same principles to remove a fear in what would become the first example of behavior therapy known as *counterconditioning*. In **counterconditioning,** unconditioned stimuli that create involuntary feelings of pleasant emotions are paired with the anxiety-producing object or event until it no longer produces fear. Mary Cover Jones worked with a young patient named Little Peter who was afraid of rabbits. A positive stimulus (cookie or piece of candy) was paired with the rabbit each time the rabbit was placed closer to the boy, until Little Peter was no longer fearful of rabbits. Counterconditioning is only one of many methods of behavioral modification based on behavioral research.

Operant Conditioning

Early behaviorists investigated both classical and operant conditioning, and these two types of learning share some common terminology. However, the two methods of learning also differ in key ways. In classical conditioning, learning results from the pairing of two stimuli that create a new involuntary response. In operant conditioning, learning results from an action that is under the subject's control and is not a reflexive or involuntary behavior. The learner is very active and operates on his or her environment through voluntary responses which are influenced by consequences that follow the behavior. On the other hand, in classical conditioning the learner is very passive and the pairing of stimuli must occur before the new involuntary reaction.

STUDY TIP

Be able to compare and contrast classical and operant conditioning.

- *Compare:* Classical and operant conditioning are both studied by behaviorists and share common terminology such as *acquisition, generalization, discrimination,* and *extinction.*

- *Contrast:* Classical conditioning involves involuntary responses that occur from the pairing of stimuli. Operant conditioning involves voluntary spontaneous behaviors that are guided by consequences.

Thorndike and Instrumental Learning

Research conducted by American psychologist **Edward L. Thorndike** in the late 1800s formed the basis for understanding learned voluntary behaviors. Thorndike constructed what he called a puzzle box to investigate how animals learn. A **puzzle box** consists of a small cage with a lever that can be pressed to release a latch and free the animal. Thorndike placed hungry cats inside the puzzle box with the tempting reinforcement of fish just outside the cage for the cat to see. In an attempt to escape the puzzle box to get to the food, the cat would try a variety of random movements until finally it accidently hit the lever and opened the door of the cage. After the cat escaped, Thorndike repeatedly placed the animal back into the puzzle box and timed how long it took for the cat to escape. With each subsequent trial the cat made fewer mistakes until it eventually learned to step on the lever and release the cage door immediately.

Based on observations from his experiments with puzzle boxes, Thorndike developed the theory of **instrumental learning** to explain how individuals learn voluntary goal-directed behaviors. Thorndike formulated his **law of effect,** which states that a voluntary behavior followed by a positive outcome would be repeated and a voluntary behavior followed by failure would not be repeated. The law of effect was demonstrated by the cats in the puzzle box because actions that were failures and did not lead to escape were less likely to be repeated and actions that resulted in escaping and reaching the food were likely to be repeated. The failures and successes experienced by the animal determined the future actions.

B.F. Skinner and Operant Conditioning

An important American behaviorist, **B.F. Skinner**, did research in the 1930s on learning voluntary behaviors based on Thorndike's law of effect. Skinner referred to Thorndike's instrumental learning as **operant conditioning**, because this type of learning involves voluntary, goal-directed behavior that is under the organism's control (as opposed to being reflexive). As a strict behaviorist, Skinner believed that psychology should study only observable and measurable behaviors and not cognition or consciousness. Although he recognized that cognitions, beliefs, and expectations impacted behavior, he felt that there was no method available to study them scientifically. In operant conditioning a particular behavior is increased or decreased in frequency based on the consequence that follows. If a voluntary action is reinforced, the organism will be more likely to repeat the behavior, and, if a voluntary action is punished, the organism will be less likely to repeat the behavior.

Skinner conducted much of his research on animal learning by using a device he invented, called an operant chamber, more commonly referred to as a Skinner box. A **Skinner box (operant chamber)** is a small apparatus that studies operant behavior in animals by providing a controlled environment. Consequences are presented and observable responses are recorded automatically. While there are different variations of a Skinner box, key components typically include an electrified floor to administer shocks and a lever to press or a key (colored disc) to peck for the administration of a consequence. When a hungry animal is placed inside the Skinner box, it will eventually hit the lever, resulting in either reinforcement (food or removal of shock) or punishment (shock or removal of food). Each action of the animal could then be observed and recorded as evidence of learning. Skinner devised a variety of experimental conditions using the operant chamber (Skinner box) to determine the effects of reinforcement and punishment on future behavior and discover learning terminology, including acquisition, extinction, generalization, and discrimination relate to operant behavior. See Table 8.6.

Table 8.6.   Operant Conditioning Phenomena

Phenomenon	Definition	Real-World Application
Acquisition	Initial stage of learning when an organism receives a consequence (reinforcement or punishment) after a voluntary behavior that influences future behavior	Suzy learns to beg for candy from her parents at the store because her parents gave her candy (reinforcement) when she begged the last time.
Generalization	Tendency of an organism to voluntarily respond to a stimulus that is similar to the original stimulus	Suzy chooses to beg for candy from her parents in places other than the store, including the bank and on vacation in an attempt to gain candy (reinforcement).
Discrimination	Tendency of an organism to voluntarily respond to only the stimulus that was reinforced	Suzy learns that begging for candy from her parents only results in receiving candy (reinforcement) when she is at the store and not at other locations.
Extinction	Tendency for a voluntary response to decrease or disappear when reinforcement is no longer provided	Suzy does not beg for candy from her parents at the store anymore because her parents stopped giving her candy and ignored her (removal of previous reinforcement).

Reinforcements

In operant conditioning the term **reinforcer** refers to any stimulus that increases the chance that a particular voluntary behavior will be repeated in the future. **Reinforcement** refers to a procedure involving the addition or removal of stimuli known as reinforcers to increase a voluntary behavior. Operant conditioning identifies both primary and secondary reinforcers. **Primary reinforcers** are stimuli that increase the likelihood that an organism will repeat a particular behavior because they fulfill a biological need. Primary reinforcers, including food, water, air, shelter, sleep, and pain removal, are naturally reinforcing and do not require learning. Although primary reinforcers are powerful because they satisfy basic needs, they may not work all the time. If an individual or animal is not hungry or not feeling well, a primary reinforcer such as food may not be as effective. **Secondary reinforcers** are stimuli that are associated with primary reinforcers. Money is an example of a secondary reinforcer because it is not naturally reinforcing. Individuals learn to associate money with the ability to purchase primary reinforcers such as food or clothing. Other secondary reinforcers include praise, success, or grades. Using secondary reinforcers to influence behavior is complicated by the fact that what constitutes a reinforcing stimulus varies among individuals. While money or bonuses might be the most effective reinforcer for some employees, others might prefer recognition or praise.

Psychologists today utilize operant conditioning and reinforcers for behavior modification. **Behavior modification** involves techniques designed to change unwanted behaviors and increase the frequency of positive behaviors. Money belongs to a special class of secondary reinforcers called **tokens** that can be accumulated and exchanged for other reinforcers. In fact, environments in which people are rewarded with objects or points that can then be traded in for primary reinforcers are called **token economies.** Token economies have been successful at changing behaviors in institutional settings, including schools, prisons, and mental hospitals.

Operant conditioning identifies two separate types of reinforcement that increase the frequency of behaviors. **Positive reinforcement** involves the procedure of adding a desirable stimulus after the behavior to increase the likelihood of the behavior occurring in the future. For example, after Luke makes his bed, he receives a piece of candy that will increase the likelihood that he will make his bed in the future. In Skinner's experiment a rat would be positively reinforced with a food pellet after pressing a bar and that would make the rat more likely to press the bar again in the future. The **Premack principle** explains that it is possible to use a behavior which is preferred by an individual to increase the likelihood that a behavior that is not as preferred will occur. According to the Premack principle, for students who like listening to music more than studying, the more preferred behavior of listening to music could be used to increase the less desirable behavior of studying. **Negative reinforcement** involves removing an undesirable stimulus after the behavior to increase the likelihood of the behavior happening again in the future. For example, after Molly buckles her seatbelt, the loud buzzing noise is removed, which will increase the likelihood that she will buckle her seatbelt the next time she enters the car. In Skinner's experiment, a rat would be negatively reinforced with the removal of an electric shock after the animal pressed the bar, and that would make the rat more likely to press the bar again in the future. In both positive and negative reinforcement, the use of a reinforcer will increase the frequency of the behavior it follows.

STUDY TIP

Negative reinforcement is *not* punishment; it is the removal of something unpleasant or an escape from an unwanted condition.

Punishment

Punishment is a procedure in operant conditioning involving the addition or removal of stimuli to decrease a voluntary behavior. Operant conditioning identifies two types of punishment that can decrease behavior. **Positive punishment** involves adding an undesirable (aversive) stimulus, also known as a punisher, after the behavior to decrease the likelihood of the behavior occurring in the future. For example, after Leo eats an entire box of ⊖reo cookies, he gets sick, which will decrease the likelihood that he will eat an entire box of cookies in the future. In Skinner's experiment, a rat would be positively punished with the addition of an electric shock after the animal pressed the bar, and that would make the rat less likely to press the bar again in the future. **Negative punishment** involves removing a desirable stimulus after the behavior to decrease the likelihood of the behavior occurring in the future. For example, Amy uses her cell phone in class, and the teacher takes the cell phone away, which will decrease the likelihood that she will use her phone in class again. In Skinner's experiment a rat would be negatively punished with the removal of food after the animal pressed the bar, and that would make the rat less likely to press the bar again in the future. In both positive and negative punishment, the likelihood of the organism repeating the voluntary behavior is reduced. See Table 8.7.

Table 8.7. Four Types of Operant Consequences

	Desirable Stimulus	Undesirable (Aversive) Stimulus
Positive (Add)	**Positive Reinforcement** After a voluntary response, a *desirable stimulus is added* to increase the likelihood of the behavior occurring again. *Randy cuts the grass and receives $10. The addition of money (desirable stimulus) leads Randy to want to cut the grass more often.*	**Positive Punishment** After a voluntary response, an *undesirable (aversive) stimulus is added* to decrease the behavior. *Paul stays out late and, therefore, has to do more chores. The addition of chores (undesirable or aversive stimulus) leads Paul to not want to stay out late again.*
Negative (Remove)	**Negative Punishment** After a voluntary response, a *desirable stimulus is removed* to decrease the behavior. *Patricia cheats on her psychology test and her parents take away her car keys. The removal of her car keys (desirable stimulus) leads Patricia to not cheat again.*	**Negative Reinforcement** After a voluntary response, an *undesirable (aversive) stimulus is removed* to increase the behavior. *Rachel picks up the clothes on her bedroom floor and her mother stops nagging. The removal of nagging (undesirable or aversive stimulus) leads Rachel to pick up the clothes on her bedroom floor more often.*

In order for punishment to be effective, the addition of aversive stimuli (positive punishment) or the removal of pleasant stimuli (negative punishment) needs to be significant enough to discourage the reoccurrence of the behavior. In addition, punishment must be imposed immediately and consistently in order for the individual to associate the behavior with the consequence. Although punishment can be a quick and effective way to change behavior, punishment must be used with caution because of the many drawbacks that exist with this method of learning. One major problem with punishment is that although it may stop an undesirable behavior, it does not teach an alternative response. Additionally, the use of punishment may create anger, fear or hostility in the individual who receives it, preventing the effective learning of alternative behaviors. Individuals who are punished may learn simply to hide the behavior when they believe that they are likely to be caught and punished and not eliminate the undesired response. For example, if cell phones are not allowed in the hallway, students may hide their phones when they see a teacher nearby. In terms of effectiveness, reinforcement is preferred by psychologists over punishment as a method of instituting behavioral change.

STUDY TIP

In regard to conditioning, the terms *positive* and *negative* are not related to emotions, but indicate the addition or subtraction of stimuli that will ultimately increase or decrease the chance that an organism will repeat a particular behavior.

Escape and Avoidance Conditioning

Aversive stimuli are any factors that are negative or unpleasant and often result in avoidance or escape behaviors. The application of aversive stimuli is involved in two specific types of learning—escape and avoidance conditioning. **Escape conditioning** occurs when an organism learns that a particular voluntary behavior will result in the removal of an unwanted or aversive stimulus (negative reinforcement). This type of learning can be studied in animals using a shuttle box. The **shuttle box** is a device used to study operant conditioning in animals that has two chambers connected by a doorway that can be opened or closed by the researcher. During experiments on escape conditioning, the floor of one chamber of the shuttle box is electrified. The animal eventually learns to avoid (escape) the shock by moving to the other chamber. The voluntary behavior of the animal is negatively reinforced to repeat the behavior of running to the other chamber after a shock appears because it results in the removal of pain. In this case the animal has learned how to end the unwanted stimulus and escape a bad situation. A child who does not like to clean their room may learn to escape from having to do this chore by whining. If the child whines and the parent removes the responsibility of cleaning the room (negative reinforcement), this will increase the likelihood that whining behavior will reappear in the future. **Avoidance conditioning** happens when an organism learns that a particular voluntary behavior prevents an unwanted or aversive stimulus from being introduced in the first place. In order to study avoidance conditioning with a shuttle box, a light or sound appears before the floor of one chamber of the shuttle box is electrified and the animal learns to run to the other chamber in order to avoid receiving any shocks. Avoidance conditioning involves both classical and operant conditioning procedures. The first step in avoidance conditioning involves classically conditioning the animal to associate the appearance of the light with painful shocks. The UCS is the shock and the UCR is pain. Through repeated pairings, the animal learns that the CS of the light indicates that the UCS of a shock will happen next. The second step in avoidance conditioning involves the animal learning the voluntary response of running to the other chamber through negative reinforcement, an operant conditioning procedure. Avoidance conditioning can explain why phobias persist because, although they may be created by classical conditioning, they are maintained by the operant behavior of avoiding the feared stimuli.

Shaping and Chaining

Animal behaviors can be created through shaping or chaining, two methods of operant conditioning. In **shaping,** a series of responses are taught by reinforcing closer and closer approximations of a behavior. For example, teaching a dog a complex behavior like fetching a ball requires the process of shaping. At first, the trainer may positively reinforce the dog with a treat for just approaching the ball. Next, the reinforcement may depend on approaching and picking up the ball. Finally, a treat may be given if the dog returns the ball to the trainer. The dog's behavior was shaped gradually until the complete desired response was produced. **Chaining** is a method for teaching a series of behaviors where each response cues the next response. The process of chaining begins with positively reinforcing each individual behavior in the series and ends with the use of positive reinforcement only after the entire series of behaviors is completed. Dog trainers use chaining to teach a series of behaviors necessary to perform a trick. For example, the dog is trained to fetch, then sit next to the trainer, and finally to release the ball. At first, positive reinforcement is given after each individual behavior, including fetching, sitting, and releasing the ball. However, after the process of chaining, the positive reinforcement is given only when the dog completes the entire series of behaviors. If chaining is successful, the dog will be able to execute all three behaviors after hearing only one command.

Schedules of Reinforcement: Controlling Behavior

Psychologists are interested in how often reinforcements should be presented in order to ensure learning and maintain the behavior over time. Experimenters sometimes use a **continuous reinforcement schedule** by reinforcing the desired response every time it is presented. Continuous reinforcement is the fastest way to learn an association between the behavior and the reinforcer, and is effective in terms of producing a steady, high rate of behavior. In addition, the learned response is rapidly extinguished if reinforcements are stopped. **Partial reinforcement schedules,** on the other hand, involve reinforcement of the desired behavior only some of the time and create behaviors that are less likely to become extinct. See Table 8.8.

The type of the schedule of reinforcement used for learning has a significant effect on the rate of response and must be carefully considered in any discussion or explanation of operant behavior. Schedules of reinforcement are either ratio or interval and either fixed or variable. *Interval schedules* vary the frequency of reinforcement according to time intervals, such as minutes, hours, days, or months, while the number of responses an organism makes is irrelevant. On the other hand, in *ratio schedules,* reinforcement is given based on the number of responses, while the amount of time between responses is irrelevant. In both these schedules, reinforcement can be delivered on either a regular basis, called a *fixed schedule,* or randomly, on a *variable schedule.* The combination of these schedules results in four basic types of partial reinforcement schedules.

STUDY TIP

Be able to identify four types of partial reinforcement schedules. A simple way to identify which type of reinforcement schedule is being presented is to break apart the example using the following steps.

1. Determine if the reinforcement is given after a *fixed* (set) or *variable* (changing) schedule.

2. Determine if the reinforcement is given after a *ratio* (number of correct behaviors) or *interval* (time period that has passed usually dealing with the clock or calendar) schedule.

Table 8.8.   Partial Reinforcement Schedules

Response	Definition	Example(s)	Result
Fixed-ratio	Reinforcement is given after a *set number of correct behaviors* have occurred.	• A customer receives a free beverage (reinforcement) at a local coffee house after every five purchases (set number of behaviors). • A worker is paid (reinforcement) after 10 fruit baskets are filled (set number of behaviors).	This schedule creates high response rates with short pauses after reinforcement is presented. The faster a subject responds, the more reinforcements they will receive.
Variable-ratio	Reinforcement is given after a *changing number of correct behaviors* have occurred. For instance, sometimes the organism receives reinforcement after 5 desired behaviors and sometimes after 10 desired behaviors.	• A gambler receives a payout (reinforcement) after a varying number of lever pulls (changing number of behaviors) on a slot machine. • A salesperson makes a sale (reinforcement) after contacting a varying number of customers (changing number of behaviors).	This schedule produces the highest rate of performance and a steady response rate with few pauses because the subject does not know how many behaviors are required before reinforcement will occur again.

(continued)

Table 8.8. *(continued)*

Response	Definition	Example(s)	Result
Fixed-interval	Reinforcement is given for the first correct response after a *set period of time* has occurred. Responses made during the interval or set time period are not reinforced; only after the interval is over will reinforcement be available.	• A salaried employee is paid (reinforcement) after two weeks (set period of time) has passed. • Students are allowed to leave the classroom (reinforcement) at the end of the 50-minute class period (set period of time).	This schedule creates low response rates until just prior to the delivery of the reinforcement because the subject has learned when to expect reinforcement.
Variable-interval	Reinforcement is given for the first correct response after a *changing period of time* has occurred.	• A fisherman catches a fish (reinforcement) after varying amounts of time waiting for the line to pull (changing period of time).	This schedule creates a moderate and consistent response rate because the subject does not know how long it will be before reinforcement occurs.

STUDY TIP

Be able to interpret the typical response patterns generated by various partial reinforcement schedules. The following are conclusions from the graph below:

- Ratio schedules produce the greatest amount of responses.

- Interval schedules require more time for learning to occur.

- Fixed schedules produce the least consistent amount of responses which results in a scallop-like pattern on the graph.

- Variable schedules produce the most consistent amount of responses which results in a pattern that creates a straight line on the graph.

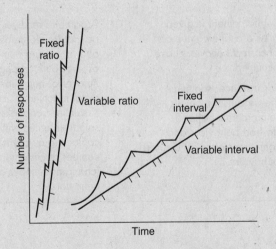

Superstitious Behavior

When B.F. Skinner left multiple pigeons alone in a Skinner box and scheduled for food to be delivered every fifteen seconds, regardless of the behavior of the animals, he noticed that the pigeons began to display unusual behaviors. Some birds began turning in circles, others started pecking randomly at a particular wall, and some began to move their bodies in unusual ways. Although the pigeons received the reinforcements purely by coincidence, they had learned to associate the arrival of food with whatever behavior they were doing just prior to the delivery of the reinforcement and continued to repeat that action in order to receive reinforcement. Skinner called this behavior displayed by the animals *superstitious* and noted that the voluntary actions taken by each of the animals was unique and was the result of coincidental operant conditioning. The development of superstitious behaviors through operant conditioning is not unique to animals in a Skinner box; many people are superstitious and develop rituals designed to prevent bad luck, or bring about good fortune. For example, one time before Jeff's band played in front of a live audience, they shared a pizza. The performance went well, and now Jeff and other members of the band always eat pizza before live performances in an effort to maintain good luck.

DIDYOUKNOW?

Some professional athletes are well known for their unique superstitious rituals. NBA player Jason Terry goes to bed the night before a game wearing the shorts of the next day's opposing team. Tennis player Serena Williams makes sure to bounce the tennis ball five times before her first serve and two times before her second. And the superstitions of an influential player like Michael Jordan can bring about change to the way a game is played, or, at least, how its players dress. Jordan believed his baby-blue mesh shorts brought so much good luck as he led the North Carolina Tarheels to the NCAA championship in 1982 that he continued to wear those shorts under his Chicago Bulls uniform. In order to cover up his lucky shorts, Jordan began wearing longer shorts, which inspired a change in the uniform style of the NBA.

Cognitive Influences on Learning

As psychology changed during the 1950s to incorporate the study of mental processes, cognitive psychologists began investigating the role of cognition or mental activity on learning. Although they recognized the importance of classical and operant conditioning, these two processes did not present a complete picture of human and animal learning. Learning is impacted by cognitive factors that include attention, memory, creativity, and imagery. Important contributions to the understanding of learning were made by cognitive and Gestalt psychologists, including Robert Rescorla, Edward Tolman, Wolfgang Kohler, and Martin Seligman.

Contingency Model of Learning

Pavlovian classical conditioning is based on the **contiguity model,** which states that, when events are placed together close in time or space, learning results. For example, after repeated pairings of the bell and food presented close together in time, the dog would be conditioned to salivate at the presentation of the bell. Pavlov's theory was extended by **Robert Rescorla's** contingency model of learning. The **contingency model** of classical conditioning states that one stimulus reliably predicts the arrival of the second stimulus for learning to result. The bell is dependent on the food, and, therefore, one predicts the other. Stimuli that are more consistently paired are more predictable and, therefore, generate stronger responses. According to Rescorla, cognitive expectations about contingencies guide learning. Both the contiguity and contingency models can also be applied to operant conditioning, because, in order for the consequence to be effective, it needs to be imposed immediately and consistently. As explained by the contiguity model, a delay in the delivery of the reinforcer or punishment can result in a failure of the organism to associate the consequence with the undesired behavior. According to the *contingency model* of operant conditioning, a voluntary behavior needs to reliably predict the consequence in order for the organism to learn.

Latent Learning

Cognitive psychologist **Edward Tolman** was one of the first to investigate the role of cognitive processes in operant conditioning, challenging the viewpoint of strict behaviorists like B.F. Skinner. Tolman agreed with Rescorla that learning was not merely a stimulus–response connection, but that cognitions and expectations within this association resulted in a learned behavior. Tolman explored the thinking process that occurred between the stimulus–response patterns in animals by recording how long it took the rats to master a maze under three different conditions over seventeen days of trials. In this experiment, learning was operationally defined as a decrease in the number of errors or wrong turns made by the rats in each attempt to complete the maze. Rats in each of the three conditions demonstrated increases in learning, but differed in their rates of improvement. See Table 8.9.

Table 8.9. Tolman's Latent Learning Experiment

Group	Condition	Results
Group 1	Rats were not given reinforcement when they reached the end of the maze.	This group had the lowest rate of learning compared to the other groups of rats because they made the most errors.
Group 2	Rats were given reinforcement in the form of food every time they reached the end of the maze.	This group rapidly decreased the number of errors, demonstrating that learning took place.
Group 3	Rats were not given reinforcement at the end of the maze for the first 10 days, but were then reinforced for the final 7 days of the trials.	This group made a similar number of errors as group 1 during the first 10 days of the trial, but made a dramatic improvement by making much fewer errors after day 11 which demonstrated learning took place.

The results from group three indicated that the rats did learn the maze, but lacked the motivation to complete the task quickly. In fact, the rats in the final group showed fewer errors in the last few days of the trials than the rats that received the food reinforcer consistently in each trial. Tolman referred to this as latent learning. **Latent learning** involves an organism mastering a new behavior without effort, awareness, or reinforcement, and this behavior is not demonstrated unless a need or reinforcement is presented. The word *latent* refers to something that is hidden, so, in the case of latent learning, the behavior the organism has mastered remains hidden until there is a need to perform. Tolman also believed that the rapid increase in learning displayed in the third group indicated that the animals were able to create a mental picture of the maze or spatial concept of how the environment of the maze looked; he referred to this as a **cognitive map.**

STUDY TIP

Be able to interpret the typical response patterns generated by the three different conditions within Tolman's latent learning experiment.

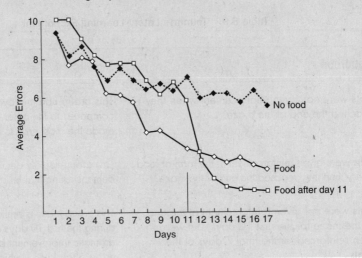

Insight Learning

Insight is the "Aha!" experience people have when a solution to a problem unexpectedly becomes clear. Gestalt psychologists thought of insight as the sudden perception of relationships between multiple parts of a problem. **Wolfgang Kohler** investigated insight learning by presenting chimps with a problem of attaining a banana that was just outside their reach and supplying the animals with various objects to use as potential tools. In one example, sticks were provided in the cage as possible tools for the chimps to use in order to reach the banana. At first the chimps would try to reach the banana with their hands, sit for a while, and then suddenly connect the sticks together to reach their prize. Insight learning happened for the chimps when they suddenly realized the solution as opposed to the gradual pairings associated with operant conditioning. Therefore, Tolman determined a cognitive component must be involved with insight learning.

Learned Helplessness

Cognitive psychologists investigate the phenomenon that results if the learner cannot determine which behaviors lead to reinforcement or punishment. In other words, if there is no contingency between the stimulus and the behavior of the organism, they may choose to give up trying anything; this is known as *learned helplessness*. **Martin Seligman** defined **learned helplessness** as the loss of motivation and failure to attempt to escape from unpleasant stimuli, which happens if individuals perceive that they are not able to exert control over their environment. Seligman observed learned helpless by accident when working with dogs. First the dogs were classically conditioned to associate a light or tone with an electric shock that they were unable to stop. After this initial learning occurred, the dogs were placed in a shuttle box, an apparatus that allows the dog to escape the electrified chamber by jumping over a low barrier. When the dogs were placed in the shuttle box and the floor became electrified, they would cry and passively endure the pain rather than jump to the safety of the other side of the shuttle box. The escape learning that is normally acquired easily by animals was not visible, leading Seligman to hypothesize that the dogs had learned from the prior conditioning that the shocks were unavoidable, and, therefore, they did not attempt to escape. Seligman's cognitive theory of learned helplessness explains that the behavior of the dogs was influenced by the expectation that any behavior they attempted would not improve their situation.

Observational Learning

Observational learning involves how organisms develop new skills, knowledge, and behaviors by watching other organisms perform and imitating these behaviors. This concept can be used to train animals by allowing them to watch another animal of the same species perform the desired action. **Social learning** was studied extensively by **Albert Bandura**, who emphasized that observational learning was the result of modeling. **Modeling** consists of observing another organism and imitating the behavior. When accompanied by positive reinforcement, modeling is an efficient technique for learning the social roles that are expected of a person in different situations. Bandura described four important processes involved in modeling. The effectiveness of modeling depends on the learner paying attention to the model, remembering the behavior, being able to physically reproduce the behavior, and motivational factors such as the presence of reinforcement. Observational learning is very powerful in families, for example, between siblings. Little children often surprise their parents by displaying behavior that they gained from watching and imitating older siblings, for example, applying makeup or using swear words. Bandura and colleagues demonstrated the effects of observational learning in the classic Bobo doll experiment. Children were placed in an experimental room to play with several different toys, including a Bobo doll or inflatable toy that could be knocked over. Next, an adult enters the room and, after an extended period of time, displays novel violent behaviors toward the Bobo doll, including tossing the doll around or striking it with a hammer. Later, when the children who observed the adult were allowed to play alone with the toys, they were more likely to model the novel aggressive acts that they observed in the models than were the children in the control group who did not observe the adult being aggressive.

Biological Predispositions and Constraints

Learning happens in part due to the organism recognizing stimulus–response patterns, but it is also dependent on the particular stimulus the animal is biologically predisposed to notice. The evolutionary approach suggests that each species has evolved biological predispositions that enable them to learn behaviors that elevate the likelihood of their survival. This biological predisposition of different organisms to learn certain behaviors by pairing particular stimuli over others is called **biological preparedness**. Humans, for example, are more likely to develop phobias of objects and situations that would have posed danger in the past to our ancestors, such as confined places, heights, darkness, snakes, and spiders. Human phobias to nonthreatening objects and events such as flowers, daylight, or music are extremely rare.

According to traditional behaviorist theory, all animals learn in a similar way, and any stimulus can become a conditioned stimulus. **John Garcia** was one of the first researchers to question this theory and investigate how biology can influence learning and how learning varies by species. Garcia found evidence for **biological constraints** or limitations set by biology regarding what an animal is capable of learning. His studies showed that rats could make connections to smell-related stimuli more easily than visual stimuli such as a light. Because rats have an excellent sense of smell and weaker vision, they are more likely to respond to odors during classical conditioning. The difficulty rats have in making connections to visual stimuli is due to biological constraints. Garcia expanded his research with rats to include a variety of experimental conditions that included different stimuli, such as taste and sound, in order to determine which stimuli pairings would be the most likely to result in learning. Garcia discovered that not all stimuli cause similar results when paired together. Taste stimuli worked well when paired with stimuli associated with nausea. However, attempts to pair auditory stimuli to cause nausea in the rats were not as successful. Instead, auditory stimuli worked well for creating an association with pain. Unlike what behavioral theory at the time suggested, certain organisms make learned associations with some types of stimuli more easily than with some other stimuli. The rate and strength of conditioning is dependent on whether or not the conditioned stimulus can create a natural association for the organism.

STUDY TIP

Be able to describe how biological preparedness and biological constraints can impact an organism's ability to learn.

While biological preparedness influences the types of associations best learned by a particular animal, biological constraints are limitations imposed by biology on a species in terms of what they are capable of learning. For example, humans are the only organisms capable of language (biological preparedness), but humans are not capable of breathing under water and cannot learn that skill (biological constraint).

Conditioned Taste Aversions

Humans are biologically predisposed to learn certain behaviors more easily than others through classical conditioning. An example of such a behavior is the conditioned taste aversion. **Taste aversions** involve an organism learning to avoid a particular food item or liquid after it becomes associated with nausea. For example, if an individual were to eat a piece of pizza (the potential CS) just prior to becoming infected with a flu virus (UCS) which makes them sick (UCR), the individual may become nauseous (CR) when considering eating pizza in the future. Taste aversions may have had an evolutionary value because they allowed individuals the ability to associate sickness with foods eaten prior to illness and learn to avoid potentially dangerous foods.

Taste aversions were first studied by **John Garcia** and colleagues when it was noticed that rats who had received radiation treatment in their cage were avoiding their water bottles. The rats had learned to avoid the water because it had been associated with getting sick from the radiation. The UCS was the radiation and the UCR was nausea. Garcia discovered that the CS (water) needed to be paired with the UCS (radiation) only one time for learning to result. This finding, which would become known as the Garcia effect, was stunning because it showed that the association between the water and nausea could be made even though the sick feeling did not result for many hours after the exposure to the water. This contradicted the existing behavior theory that learning required the UCS and CS to be presented close together in time. Taste aversions, unlike other classically conditioned behaviors, are unusual because they typically require only one pairing for learning, and the CS does not need to be presented immediately before the UCS.

John Garcia and others applied psychological research regarding taste aversions to assist ranchers having problems with coyote attacks on their herds. Researchers placed poisoned sheep in areas near ranches where coyotes had been spotted. The coyotes that ate the sheep became sick and developed a learned taste aversion to sheep. This research has been replicated in other situations and provides a method of controlling predators that does not involve killing animals.

Instinctive Drift

Instinctive drift is the tendency for animals to abandon learned behaviors and replace them with ones that are instinctive or innate. For example, when trainers attempt to condition raccoons to pick up coins and place them in a container, eventually the animals fall back on their natural instincts and instead rub the coins together and dip them in and out of the container. The raccoons continue to perform this action even though it is not reinforced because it is an innate behavior that raccoons use in the wild to wash their food. Instinctive drift provides further evidence that what organisms are capable of learning is strongly influenced by biology.

STUDY TIP

Be able to identify the key researchers and associated experiments for various types of learning. See Table 8.10.

Table 8.10. Important Figures in Learning Theory

Contributor	Learning Theory	Experiment or Concept
Ivan Pavlov	Classical Conditioning	Nobel Prize-winning researcher who identified the key components of classical conditioning using dogs
John B. Watson	Classical Conditioning	American psychologist and father of behaviorism that demonstrated how fears can be created using classical conditioning. He created a fear of white rats in Little Albert
John Garcia	Classical Conditioning	Conducted research regarding conditioned taste aversions as an exception to the rules of classical conditioning
Edward Thorndike	Instrumental Learning	Conducted research on instrumental learning by observing the law of effect in cats as they learned how to escape from puzzle boxes

(continued)

Table 8.10. *(continued)*

Contributor	Learning Theory	Experiment or Concept
B.F. Skinner	Operant Conditioning	Important American behaviorist and creator of the operant chamber (Skinner box) for studying operant learning concepts in animals
Robert Rescorla	Cognitive Processes	Developed the contingency model of learning and added a cognitive component to classical conditioning based on prediction and expectations
Edward Tolman	Cognitive Processes	Conducted research on how cognition impacts learning in animals and developed the concepts of latent learning and cognitive maps
Wolfgang Kohler	Cognitive Processes	Gestalt psychologist who conducted research on insight learning with chimps
Martin Seligman	Cognitive Processes	Cognitive psychologist that investigated learned helplessness in animals and theorized about how this concept contributes to depression
Albert Bandura	Cognitive Processes	Important social cognitive psychologist who conducted research on social learning, modeling, and observational learning of aggressive behavior with the Bobo doll experiment

Time for a quiz
- Review strategies in Chapter 2
- Take Quiz 3 at the REA Study Center
  (www.rea.com/studycenter)

Cognition

Psychology involves the scientific study of the behavior and mental processes of human and nonhuman animals. The term **cognition** refers to the mental processes portion of the study of psychology and can be translated simply to mean thinking. The term *thinking* alone, however, does not do justice to the complex and varied processes that comprise cognition. Cognitive psychologists investigate the wide range of processes that make up thinking, including perception, memory, attention, reasoning, language, and problem solving. Cognitive neuroscientists take the study of thought even further to determine the neural processes and brain regions responsible for various types of cognitions. This chapter on cognition addresses four of the largest and most integrated areas of cognitive research: memory, language, thinking, and problem solving.

Memory

Memory is the cognitive process that allows individuals to retain knowledge of information and events and is the result of three processes: encoding, storage, and retrieval. Cognitive psychologists investigating memory examine the process in terms of **information processing** or how information travels through the nervous system including perception, memory creation, reasoning, and formulating responses. Information processing theorists have presented a variety of stage models to explain human cognition, but the theory that has received the most attention is the Atkinson and Shiffrin information-processing model of memory.

The three stage **information-processing model of memory** developed by Atkinson and Shiffrin describes memory as a sequential process moving through three distinct stages: sensory memory, short-term memory, and long-term memory. A visual representation of this model is represented in Figure 9.1. Information flows from one stage to the next as it is encoded, stored, and retrieved. The original concept of short-term memory within this model has been expanded by Alan Baddeley and renamed *working memory* and consists of additional components. Within the **working memory model** there is a *central executive* that controls and directs attention through a *visuospatial sketchpad* (visual picture) and *phonological loop* (verbal rehearsal). Items must go through the working memory to get to long-term storage and must return to working memory to be consciously recalled.

Figure 9.1. Atkinson and Shiffrin's Three-Stage Information-Processing Model of Memory

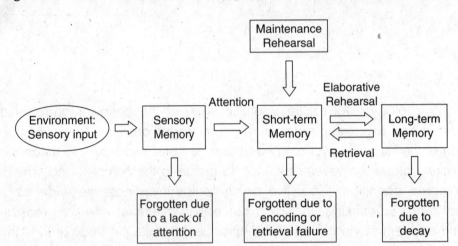

Encoding

During the process of **encoding**, information is combined, organized, and placed into memory. If information received from the environment does not get placed into memory or if it is not attended to, it will not move past this stage and is referred to as **encoding failure**. Encoding of information happens both automatically and as the result of conscious effort by the individual. **Automatic processing** involves carrying out mental activity quickly and without effort. **Effortful processing**, on the other hand, requires attention and generally results in longer-lasting memories. **Selective attention** processes play a significant role in determining what information is transferred from sensory memory to short-term memory or from short-term into long-term memory. If information is not very important or interesting, the individual is less likely to pay attention or engage in effortful processing, and the result will be either encoding failure or problems with retrieval. One example of the effect attention can have on information being processed is the cocktail-party effect. The **cocktail-party effect** is the ability we possess to focus our attention on one voice while ignoring any other noises that are happening, yet still be aware enough to pick up relevant information like our name. Information that is not being attended to that is happening in the background most likely is not being processed and will not be available for retrieval later.

Craik and Lockhart's **levels-of-processing model of memory** states that the attention given to the process of encoding will impact future recall. Deeper levels of processing as opposed to shallow levels of processing create more durable memories that can be recalled easier. In order to create deeper memories, one must either enrich the encoding process through rehearsal or choose a more effective type of encoding. **Rehearsal** involves the deliberate, conscious repetition of information. The most effective rehearsal involves the use of elaboration by making as many connections between the new material and what is already known as possible. **Elaborative rehearsal** that utilizes connections to previously learned material provides better retention rates than **maintenance rehearsal** that involves merely repeating information. Examples of maintenance rehearsal include repeating a phone number as one is dialing or stating a fact in one's head over and over until the start of the test. When you study for a test by explaining the vocabulary to yourself in your own words and create original examples, you are using elaborative rehearsal, which is more effective because it involves deeper processing. A particularly effective type of elaborative rehearsal is the **self-reference effect** or the tendency for an individual to have improved recall for information that personally relates to their life. In one study, participants were given a list of adjectives to memorize. Half of the participants were instructed to also rate the list of adjectives in terms of how much each word related to them and half merely memorized the list. The individuals that evaluated the adjectives for personal relevance remembered more words overall because they were personally meaningful, thus demonstrating the self-reference effect.

STUDY TIP

The self-reference effect states that information that is encoded along with a personal connection will be easier to recall. With this in mind, it is important to connect the psychology terms you are learning to personal examples while studying the material. Try to imagine a time when the cocktail-party effect applied to you personally. For example, while talking to a friend at a dance, you were unaware of the noise going on around you, but when you heard your name called as the winner of a prize, you immediately paid attention.

There are also three types of encoding that can impact the ability to retrieve memories at a later date. The method that we use to encode information affects how well we remember the information later. The three types of encoding are visual, acoustic, and semantic (meaning). Craik and Tulving conducted an experiment that examined which type of encoding—visual, acoustic, or semantic—would result in the best recall. Participants in the experiment were shown words they would need to remember followed by one of three types of questions. They were either asked if the word was written in capitals, rhymed with another word, or was a type of some item. The results indicated that the amount of recall was related to the type of encoding that was used. Words that were shallowly encoded with **visual** memory (written in capitals) had low recall. Words that were intermediately encoded with **acoustic** memory (rhymes with . . .) had better recall. Words that were deeply encoded with **semantic** memory (type of . . .) had the best recall. Semantic encoding, or the processing of meaning, provides the strongest results for memory retention.

STUDY TIP

Be careful to not confuse visual encoding and visual imagery.

- *Visual encoding* refers to how the memory system processes what we experience in terms of a visual image. Whereas, *visual imagery* refers to the mental picture that has been created in one's mind. Visual encoding does not provide deep processing for better recall, while visual imagery does.
- For example, when visually encoding the word *elephant* you would be looking at the individual letters on the screen. However, when you use visual imagery, there is a picture of a four-legged animal in your mind that represents an elephant.

Storage

Individuals use three different mental stages to build their memories: sensory memory, short-term memory, and long-term memory. (See Table 9.1.) Psychologists believe that memory starts at the stage known as **sensory memory**, sometimes called the *sensory register,* where a very short-lived recording of sensory information occurs. George Sperling investigated sensory memory by presenting participants with a grid containing twelve letters for a limited amount of time. Participants were instructed to recall as many letters as they could after the image disappeared. Most participants were able to report about four letters, but Sperling hypothesized that they actually saw more letters, but their perception of the other letters faded while they were reporting what they saw. Sperling used a system of tones to direct participants' ability to recall. If the participant heard a high tone, they were instructed to report what they had seen on the top row, if they heard a medium tone they were instructed to report what they had seen on the middle row, and a low pitched tone indicated that they should report what they had seen on the bottom row. The tone was presented *after* the letters were removed so the participants were no longer looking at the actual letters but instead had to rely on the visual trace that remained. Sperling analyzed the recall of the participants and found that the visual sensory store could hold a large amount of information, but only for a very limited time before fading or being passed along to the next stage of memory. Furthermore, sensory memory contains two main types of memories—iconic and echoic. **Iconic memory** (visual sensory store) is the retention of a brief visual image for a fraction of a second so that a person can keep track of an experience from moment to moment. **Echoic memory** (auditory sensory store) is the storage of a brief auditory stimulation for a few seconds. Sensory memory is capable of absorbing enormous amounts of information, but most of it disappears very quickly, either by entering short-term memory or because of a lack of attention. Cognitive psychologists believe that the purpose of sensory memory is to collect potential data about the world and hold onto the material briefly for processing to take place.

Table 9.1. Comparison of the Three Stages of Memory

Stage	Duration	Capacity
Sensory Memory	Seconds	Limitless
Short-term Memory	10 to 30 seconds	Seven, plus or minus two
Long-term Memory	Limitless	Limitless

STUDY TIP

Iconic memory is *not* the same as eidetic imagery. Iconic memory happens in sensory memory and involves the retention of a fleeting visual image. On the other hand, eidetic imagery refers to a visual mental image that remains for a longer period of time (minutes to months). Eidetic imagery is what is actually meant by a photographic memory and is a rare ability that occurs more often in children.

If the individual is not distracted and the information is meaningful, it will then be passed from sensory memory to the second stage known as **short-term memory,** which is also called working memory, because it allows information to be stored long enough to solve problems. Short-term memory is the information storage a person would use to remember a phone number long enough to make a call. Researchers Peterson and Peterson discovered just how quickly a short-term memory fades. Participants were provided with a group of three-consonants to remember such as KDF. After performing a distraction task, participants were asked to recall the original group of letters. Without rehearsal, subjects could retain the information for only approximately ten to thirty seconds. More specific information about the limits of the capacity of short-term memory was discovered by **George Miller**. In general, people can remember seven items at a time, give or take a few, which is one reason why phone numbers are seven digits long. George Miller said that 7 was the magic number for short-term memory capacity and that individuals could retain **7 items plus or minus 2** (5 to 9 items if you want to be more direct than Miller). Even a short interruption will destroy all the information in the short-term store, and in general most short-term memory will fade in a matter of seconds unless extra effort is applied to transfer the information to long-term memory. The process of **rehearsal** allows items in short-term memory to be retained and facilitates the transfer of material from short-term to long-term memory. In most cases, the amount of time allocated for rehearsal is a significant variable relating to how well material is retained. Rehearsal can also be helped by the process of chunking. Short-term memory can store only about seven items; however, some items are larger than others. **Chunking** or grouping related items into meaningful units can increase the amount of material that can be held in short-term memory. This process is used when combining the numbers 4–1–4 into a single area code or the words *American Psychological Association* into the acronym *APA*. Chess masters can memorize entire boards in a few seconds by mentally grouping pieces on the board according to location, function, and so on.

Long-term memory is the third stage of memory and is considered to be a generally permanent storage capable of containing a limitless amount of information. The limitless nature of long-term memory ultimately cannot be proven, but evidence is provided by individuals who possess remarkable levels of memory.

Long-term memory storage is very complex and involves multiple brain areas. Individuals with different types of amnesia have specific problems related to long-term memory based on where the injury occurred. From these case studies, psychologists have been able to divide long-term memory into several different types of memory. Major categories of long-term memory include explicit and implicit memories. Explicit memories (declarative) may either be semantic or episodic, and implicit memories (nondeclarative) include priming, conditioned reflexes, and procedural memories. See Figure 9.2.

Figure 9.2.   Different Kinds of Memory

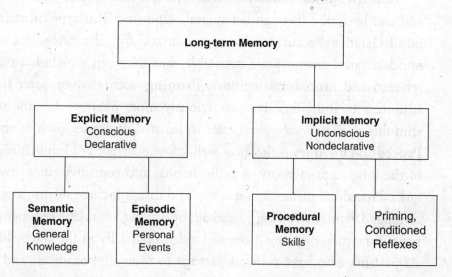

Explicit (declarative) memory can be consciously recalled when requested and sometimes becomes disrupted because of age or amnesia. This type of memory will include conversations, facts and events, and everything we normally think of as memory. Specifically there are two types of explicit memory—semantic and episodic—that are both processed in the hippocampus. **Semantic memory**, a type of explicit memory, contains general knowledge or facts, including grammar, words, dates, and theories. **Episodic memory**, also a type of explicit memory, consists of personal experiences and events tied to particular times and places. Think of episodic memories as episodes in the story of your life. Examples of episodic memories would include what happened at the first high school dance you attended or the day you graduated from high school. In general, episodic memories are more easily distorted and forgotten than semantic memories. A **flashbulb memory** is a specific type of episodic memory that involves an especially detailed remembrance of an event that is highly personal and intensely emotional. They are called flashbulb memories because it feels like a camera flash went off preserving the memory in photographic detail. Subsequent research has revealed that although memories for significant events are recalled in greater detail than everyday occurrences, they are not as photographic in quality as was once believed. The better recall for flashbulb events is due in part to the fact that emotionally significant events seem to be encoded more strongly by the brain and because we continually retrieve and rehearse these memories as a result of their significance to us personally.

STUDY TIP

Flashbulb memories are strong emotional experiences that often lead to memories that are clear and long-lasting. Examples of flashbulb memories include natural disasters, deaths of notable importance, and significant celebrations.

Implicit (nondeclarative) memory is created indirectly, without conscious effort and can be tested through behavioral responses. This type of memory is considered nondeclarative because it occurs automatically. The categories within implicit or nondeclarative memory are debatable, but they often include priming, conditioned reflexes, and procedural memory. **Priming** occurs when, after being exposed to a stimulus, an individual is unconsciously more likely to be able to recall that same stimulus. *Conditioned reflexes* refer to learned responses such as emotional reactions. **Procedural memory** is the most well-known category of implicit memory and consists of the long-term memory of skills, habits, and cognitive rules involved in particular tasks. Procedural memories for how to do things include solving a puzzle, riding a bike, singing, dancing, throwing a baseball, or driving a car. Unlike other types of memories, procedural memories are processed at least partially in the cerebellum. Certain amnesia patients who have suffered damage to their hippocampus and cannot remember conversations for more than a few minutes or recognize new people no matter how many times they meet, can learn to solve puzzles faster and faster with practice. These patients will protest that they have never seen the puzzle before each time the psychologist brings it, yet they solve it more and more quickly each time. Although their ability to form new episodic and semantic memories has been destroyed due to damage to their hippocampus, they are still able to learn new procedural memories because their cerebellum was unaffected.

STUDY TIP

Semantic (explicit) memories begin with "I remember that . . ."

- Paris is the capital of France.
- my middle name is Diana.
- psychology is the scientific study of the behavior and mental processes of human and nonhuman animals.

Episodic (explicit) memories begin with "I remember this time when . . ."

- I won first place in an art contest.
- I first drove a car.
- my sister smacked me in the face with a bottle.

Procedural (implicit) memories begin with "I remember how to . . ."

- snowboard.
- change a tire.
- do a cartwheel.

Cognitive Processing

Imagine that you are an expert piano player. If you sit down with a new piece, you will play it easily, giving little thought to where each note lies on the keyboard, where your hands are, or how you are moving your fingers. On the other hand, if you are a novice, you may struggle to find each individual note. The experienced pianist is using **automatic (unconscious) processing;** interpreting music takes little effort and almost no conscious awareness of completing the activity. The novice, on the other hand, is using **controlled (conscious) processing;** a conscious decision is being made regarding how and when to play the correct note. Interestingly, if the novice who is utilizing controlled processing is interrupted, the pianist can easily find the correct place again. This is because controlled processing requires a great deal of attention. The automatic-processing expert, if distracted, will have a harder time finding the place because that person is not paying as much attention to the task. Automatic processing, though faster than controlled processing, is best left to tasks that are less important to survival or that are unlikely to go wrong.

Several models of how thinking or processing of memory and learning occur have been presented, often based on analogies between the human mind and computers. One important concept based on how computers work is that of serial versus parallel processing. In **serial processing,** the problem is solved one step at a time and uses the solution of one problem as input for the next problem in much the same way that computers work. In **parallel processing,** many different independent problems are solved all at once. Saul Sternberg theorized that retrieving information from short-term memory involves serial processing, while searches through long-term memory take place in parallel. Serial searches are practical for short-term memory's seven items, but to search the entirety of long-term memory by serial means is impractical. It would simply take too long. Parallel processing takes up much more memory than serial processing, but it is also much faster. At present, computer scientists are trying to program their machines for parallel processing, something the brain already uses effectively in terms of the processes of perception and retrieval of information from long-term memory.

Cognitive psychologists have often wondered just how the process of storage in long-term memory happens. Several theories have attempted to describe the organization of long-term memory, including semantic networks and the connectionist or parallel distributed processing (PDP) model. The **semantic network model** suggests that memories are stored as words connected to associations. For example, the word *psychology* can activate several different associations such as class, job, AP Psychology exam, review, etc. Each of those associations also has additional associations which can be activated. The time it takes for retrieval reflects the spreading of activation within this large network that can be visualized as a spider web. While this theory provides a great mental representation, it is important to note that it is only an illustration and not an actual brain structure.

The **connectionist** or **parallel distributed processing model** suggests that encoding of memories happens through the building of connections and that retrieval occurs through the spreading of activation within this large network. Memories are not localized and detached from one another allowing them to be recalled one at a time. For example, when Steven first started learning to play guitar he learned specific skills such as how to position his fingers, how to use the guitar pick on the strings, how to read music, etc. Over time, these skills form a network of information that creates a more general understanding of how the guitar works. Neurons are closely connected with one another sending and receiving messages from thousands of different cells. This integrated system of communication is known as a **neural network**. The process in which neural networks function is known as **parallel processing** and involves the activity of a combination of many neurons firing in multiple brain regions at once, rather than individually, in order for the brain to be faster and more efficient.

Retrieval

Once information is ready to enter long-term memory, it must be encoded and stored so that it can be retrieved. **Retrieval** or the recovery of information from memory storage can either occur rapidly with little to no effort or require attention. The first type of retrieval is effortless and often occurs when new information is similar to data that has been previously stored. Word recognition is an example of this type of retrieval. When new information is not similar to previously stored data, memory takes more effort. For example, seeing a familiar face does not guarantee that we will remember the person's name. The new visual information of a face is not close enough and, therefore, does not match the verbal name stored in memory. Information retrieval seems to happen in stages. In response to a trivia question, some people can answer effortlessly, others will require a few clues, and some can say immediately that they do not know the answer. Each of the individuals in the previous example is at a different stage in the process of retrieval. If an individual is struggling to retrieve information, a clue might help them to have complete retrieval.

The process of retrieval can be tested using the methods of recall and recognition. **Recall** is the ability to retrieve information or experiences from memory consciously without clues. The AP Psychology free-response questions require recall. There are no hints to help retrieval beyond the question itself. On the other hand, **recognition** is the ability to remember information consciously through the use of previously learned material. The AP Psychology multiple-choice section utilizes recognition. Each question is followed by a list of five possible answers which can help to trigger a memory for the answer.

Retrieval can be aided by specific methods and also hindered, due to the inability of stored material to be easily retrieved. When items are presented as a list, the location of a particular item on the list can affect how easily it is remembered, based on what is known as the serial position effect. The **serial position effect** states that if we are presented with a list, we will remember best the items at the beginning and the end, and recall for items presented in the middle will be the worst. Sometimes this phenomenon is broken up into two separate concepts and the ability to recall the items presented early in the list is called the **primacy effect,** and the ability to recall the items at the end of the list is called the **recency effect**.

Forgetting, or the inability to retrieve information that has been successfully stored in long term memory, is called **retrieval failure**. An example of retrieval failure familiar to most people is the **tip-of-the-tongue phenomenon** which happens when we cannot locate the desired word in the memory even though we are sure we know it. When we experience this retrieval problem, we have the sense that what we are looking for is just beyond our reach. When something is on the tip-of-the-tongue, individuals use a variety of methods to try and unblock the memory, often by using information from their environment or attempting to trigger other existing memories. Typically the person having trouble remembering a word or name begins by guessing words that are similar to the target. Words that sound like the target word, start with the same letter, have the same number of syllables, or have a similar meaning come to mind. The more a person can narrow down the semantic (meaning) and phonetic (sound) characteristics of a word, the easier recall will be. Interestingly, the person will almost always instantly recognize the word if it is mentioned by someone. There are a variety of retrieval cues or factors in the environment that assist memory recall and several of these are listed in Table 9.2.

Table 9.2. Memory Retrieval Cues

Retrieval Cue	Definition	Example
Priming	Memory retrieval is aided for an individual if he or she has been exposed to a stimulus previously. This prior exposure or priming will make it more likely that the person will recall that same or a similar stimulus later. *Note:* Priming is also a type of implicit memory.	Researchers show subjects a series of incomplete pictures in which each subsequent picture is more finished until finally the complete drawing is visible. If the subjects are then shown the same series of drawings several weeks later, they will identify the completed picture much earlier than the first time. This result is due to the effects of priming because particular aspects of the stimuli triggered an association with the completed drawing.
Mood-congruent	Memory retrieval is aided if an individual is in the same emotional state (mood) when the person is trying to remember something as when he or she first encoded the information.	Individuals who are in a good mood are better able to recall pleasant events, and individuals who are in a sad or angry mood are more likely to recall negative events.
Context-dependent	Memory retrieval is aided when an individual is in an external environment similar to the one where the material was originally encoded.	Before you leave for school, you realize there is no more milk, and you decide that you will stop and get some on your way home. By the time you finish with your busy day, you forget all about picking up the milk. However, once you walk into the kitchen, the context or environment triggers the memory, and you realize you did not pick up the milk.
State-dependent	Memory retrieval is aided if the individual is in the same physical and mental state as when the information was encoded.	An individual who learns material under the influence of caffeine may recall that same information better when under the influence of caffeine again. *Note:* The entire process of memory (encoding and retrieval) works better when a person is not under the influence.

Forgetting

An important early memory researcher, **Hermann Ebbinghaus** is notable for his work on forgetting. Ebbinghaus studied how much individuals forgot over time and what types of techniques could be utilized to reduce forgetting. The research method he used involved creating long lists of what he called **nonsense syllables**, combinations of three letters that did not create words or evoke associations. Ebbinghaus personally memorized lists of nonsense syllables and then carefully tested himself on recall after intervals of several minutes to many days and recorded the total amount remembered. The result of this research was the identification of what he called the **forgetting curve** or the *graphed representation* of how much information was lost over time. According to Ebbinghaus, the greatest rate of forgetting occurs within the first day after learning. After the initial steep drop-off in recall, the forgetting curve levels off and no more learning is lost. The research also indicated that the speed at which information was forgotten was related to how effectively the material was encoded in the first place. Both the amount of time spent on rehearsal and the depth of processing impact how rapidly information is forgotten. Equally important, Ebbinghaus also recognized that although a great deal of the information initially learned is forgotten, the process of **relearning** the same material would happen in less time than it took to memorize the material in the first place.

The process of **overlearning** or continuing to rehearse material after you have mastered it has been shown to reduce the amount of forgetting and help individuals hold on to material over longer periods of time. For example, when a football team executes a play perfectly the first time in practice, they still continue to rehearse so that the skill becomes automatic. The same is true for studying for exams; after you know the material, you should continue to rehearse so the information will remain in your memory longer in order to do well on the test, your finals, and the AP Psychology exam.

STUDY TIP

To combat the effect of forgetting, Ebbinghaus suggested **spaced practice** or distributed practice. The best way to overcome the forgetting curve is to break up the time you spend studying over several days. In other words, research suggests that if you want to hold onto what you learned longer, spread out your studying and do a little bit each night rather than one long cramming session or **massed practice**.

Brain Damage and Forgetting

Serious problems with memory encoding and retrieval can result from damage to the brain due to degenerative diseases, physical injury, infection, or tumor growth. An example of a degenerative brain disorder that impacts memory is **Alzheimer's disease**, which causes memory loss due to the deterioration of neurons producing acetylcholine. The specific type of memory impairment that occurs in an individual is related to the area of the brain that is affected. Injury to the hippocampus will lead to problems with encoding new explicit memories (semantic or episodic). Because the cerebellum is involved in both procedural memory and fine motor control, when it is damaged, the result is often a loss of memories related to movement or certain conditioned reflexes including the eye blink reflex and emotional reactions. If the amygdala is damaged, it results in the disruption of the ability to encode and retrieve the emotional aspects of memory. Individuals who suffer injuries to their frontal lobes or prefrontal cortex often have problems with recalling episodic memories and determining the order in which events occurred. Evidence from both studies on animals and evaluation of behavioral changes in people who have suffered brain damage reveal that memory is a complex process involving numerous brain regions.

DID YOU KNOW?

Alzheimer's disease is named after Dr. Alois Alzheimer who, in 1906, studied the brain of a woman who had died of an unusual mental illness. This woman suffered from memory loss, language problems, and unpredictable behavior. Upon examination, Dr. Alzheimer found in the woman's brain many abnormal clumps (called amyloid plaques) and tangled bundles of fibers (called neurofibrillary tangles). Plaques and tangles in the brain are two of the main features of Alzheimer's disease, with the third being the loss of connections between the neurons in the brain. Today, roughly 5.1 million Americans may have Alzheimer's disease.

Repression

Some forgetting is due to motivated forgetting, or the desire to forget events or material that we find upsetting. If thinking about something that has happened to us is stressful or embarrassing, we may try to put it out of our mind because thinking about it is painful. **Suppression** is the term used by Sigmund Freud for motivated forgetting if the individual is conscious of his or her efforts to block painful memories or unacceptable wishes. Sigmund Freud used the term **repression** to refer to unconscious motivated forgetting of upsetting memories or unacceptable urges and desires. According to Freud, both suppression and repression are important defense mechanisms or methods that individuals utilize to reduce stress and anxiety by forgetting their unacceptable thoughts and desires either consciously or unconsciously.

Amnesia

Most of the time when we think of amnesia, what comes to mind is the memory loss that results from injury or illness, but there is also a particular type of amnesia experienced by all individuals known as *infantile amnesia*. **Infantile amnesia** refers to the fact that individuals cannot remember their early childhood years, or at least accurately, ranging from infancy until about age 5. Neuroscientists suggest that individuals do not have explicit memories from the early years of life because the hippocampus is not mature enough for the memories to be transferred into long-term memory. There are two general types of amnesia involving limited or total memory loss that is either temporary or permanent as the result of biological damage (amnestic disorder) or psychological factors (motivated forgetting). Biological factors resulting in amnestic disorders include damage to brain areas related to memory formation or retrieval due to physical injury, tumor, stroke, or disease.

There are also two subtypes of amnestic amnesia—retrograde and anterograde. **Retrograde amnesia** involves the inability to remember events or information that was stored before the illness or injury that resulted in amnesia. An athlete that suffers a concussion and does not remember the events just prior to getting hurt has suffered retrograde amnesia.

In contrast, **anterograde amnesia** involves the inability to retain memories for events after the injury or disease that resulted in amnesia. An athlete who suffers a concussion and does not remember being examined by the trainer after the injury, but remembers everything that happened before he or she was hurt is experiencing anterograde amnesia. A famous case study of permanent anterograde amnesia involves a man, referred to in scientific journals as patient H.M., who developed temporal anterograde amnesia as a result of a surgery that he underwent in an attempt to treat his epilepsy. During surgery part of his hippocampus, a brain structure buried deep within the temporal lobe, was removed. Although the surgery was successful in treating the epilepsy, the devastating result for this patient was that he would be permanently unable to create new memories. However, scientists have learned a great deal about the biological processes related to memory by studying this patient as a case study. Because patient H.M. could recall items that were placed in his memory before the surgery, scientists were able to determine that the hippocampus is not involved in the storage of long-term memory, but instead was responsible for the transfer of new explicit memories into long-term memory. Scientists were also able to determine that implicit memories are not stored in the hippocampus because these types of memories are unaffected in individuals with hippocampus damage. Testing proved that these individuals retained conditioned responses and that they were capable of learning new motor skills.

STUDY TIP

Be able to differentiate between the two types of amnestic amnesia.

- The prefix "antero" means after, and individuals with anterograde amnesia cannot make memories after the injury or onset of the disease that caused the amnesia.
- The prefix "retro" means before or old, and the term *retro* is associated with old-school music or clothing from the past. Individuals with retrograde amnesia cannot remember what happened before the injury or onset of the disease that caused the amnesia.

Decay

Are memories destroyed, or do they merely fade away? The **decay theory** suggests that memories disappear with time if they are not retrieved. Psychologists relate the decay of memories to muscles weakening over time if they are not exercised. This hypothesis is strengthened by studies showing that neural activity progressively weakens if the connections are not used.

STUDY TIP

To help remember the multiple reasons that people forget information, think of a boy named Brad who is very forgetful. Each letter in his name stands for a different way information can be forgotten. BRAD = **B**rain damage, **R**epression, **A**mnesia, and **D**ecay.

Inteference

Forgetting can also be due to the activities a person engages in during the time between learning and the test of retention. The **interference theory** states that forgetting occurs because two memories are in conflict with one another. Memories are not lost because they have disappeared, but because the brain cannot find them in the clutter of competing alternative responses. In **proactive interference**, previously learned information interferes with the ability to recall a new memory. Anthony experiences proactive interference when he has trouble remembering the new plays his college basketball coach is trying to teach him because he keeps thinking of his high school basketball plays. **Retroactive interference** happens when recently learned information prevents the recall of old memories. Although Rita is a baseball fan, she has a hard time remembering last year's World Series champion team because all she can think of is this season's winner, which is retroactive interference.

STUDY TIP

Be able to differentiate between the two types of interference.

- For proactive interference old information gets in the way of new information and prevents the recall of new information.
- For retroactive interference new information gets in the way of old information and prevents the recall of old information.

Memory Construction

How accurate is our memory for past events? Do you remember what your third-period teacher was wearing yesterday? If you were asked ten minutes later, could you describe the person who stopped you at the mall to ask directions? Maybe, but how accurate would you be? What if the person you were asked to describe was a bank robber or a criminal who fled the scene of a crime? Often witnesses to crimes are very confident about their ability to identify criminals in lineups or give descriptions to the police, but controlled research demonstrates that we do not have as good of a memory as we believe we do. Problems with eyewitness recall have serious social and legal implications because inaccurate witness memory has led to the false imprisonment of innocent people and the acquittal of guilty suspects. Elizabeth Loftus studied the constructive nature of memory or how memory can be affected by the existing knowledge we have about similar events and how information we receive from other sources can become unknowingly added into our original memory. Loftus also investigated how the inaccuracy of human memory affects eyewitness testimony. Contrary to what many people believe, our minds do not work like video recorders that we can simply play back in order to view our memories exactly as they happened.

Elizabeth Loftus demonstrated that memory is not as accurate as we believe it is and that eyewitness testimony is unreliable because false memories or confabulations can be created easily through suggestion. A **confabulation** or false memory is generated when a person's actual memory becomes distorted because the person unconsciously adds or removes information received from other sources. Elizabeth Loftus demonstrated how confabulations can be created using the **misinformation effect** in which researchers give participants subtle misleading information cues that causes them to alter their memories by adding the false information to their recollections. The participants in Loftus's research watched a video of a car crash and were then asked to say how fast they believed the cars were going. Some of the subjects were asked the question, "How fast were the cars going when they *hit* each other?" and some of the participants were asked the more leading question, "How fast were the cars going when they *smashed* into each other?" The subtle difference of replacing the word *hit* with *smashed* had dramatic results. Participants who heard the word *smashed* in the question estimated the speed of the cars to be significantly faster than those who were asked the same question using the word *hit*. These results show that the way a question is worded can alter a person's memory. This finding has significant implications for how suspects and witnesses should be interviewed by the police and members of the court system. Research on memory indicates eyewitness testimony alone should not be sufficient in criminal cases and that other evidence should be required.

As a result of the constructive nature of memory, individuals may also have difficulty recalling the origin (source) of where a particular memory was acquired, despite having a strong recollection of the actual detail about the memory itself, known as **source amnesia**. Ultimately, our brains are better at storing and retrieving facts and events than determining where that information came from (source). If your friend tells you a joke that you actually told them a week ago, they are demonstrating source amnesia. Your friend remembers the information in the form of the joke, but did not recall the source of the information, which was you.

Brain and Memory

Where are memories created and stored in the brain? Cognitive and biological psychologists continue to debate whether the process of memory is something that is spread out across many areas of the brain or more localized to one specific region. The physiology of how memories are encoded, stored, and retrieved, as well as the locations for the storage of various types of memories, is extremely complex. Evidence from both animal research and case studies of humans who have suffered brain damage to specific regions has revealed that although some regions are specialized for certain aspects of the memory process, memory itself is not located in only one area in particular. It is known for example that the hippocampus is very involved in the process of encoding new explicit memories and transferring them to long-term memory, but that it is not responsible for memory storage. Numerous areas of the brain, including the prefrontal cortex, medial temporal lobe, amygdala, hippocampus, and cerebellum, have all been shown to have specific functions that relate to memory encoding, storage, and retrieval.

Psychologist Karl Lashley contributed to the understanding of the biological aspects of memory through research on where memory is stored in rats. Lashley taught rats to solve a maze and then lesioned (destroyed) a specific area in their brains before having them attempt the maze again. He found that although learning was briefly interrupted, the rats were ultimately able to complete the maze, suggesting that the area of the cortex that was removed was not where the memory of the maze was stored. Lashley's research provides evidence that memory does not reside in one specific place within the brain, but that memory is in fact spread across many areas of the brain. Lashley began the search for the *memory trace* or the specific physical changes that occur in the brain when a memory is created, which he called the *engram*. Neuroscientists continue today to search for the memory trace, and, although the exact physiological changes that occur when a memory is encoded are still unknown, there is much support for long-term potentiation. According to the theory of **long-term potentiation,** repeated stimulation of neural networks strengthens the connections between neurons and results in the formation of new synapses leading to learning and memory creation.

Memory Improvement

Mnemonic strategies are techniques that are usually effortful, though sometimes automatic, designed to assist in the process of memory. Often these strategies include elaboration by creating connections with other material. The use of **imagery** or creating a mental picture for items or events to be memorized is especially helpful and can be incorporated into a variety of other mnemonic strategies. Imagery is particularly effective if the mental picture that is created is dramatic or unusual. Two mnemonic strategies that depend heavily on the power of imagery are the method of loci and the peg-word system. The **method of loci** involves associating the information that needs to be memorized with a series of locations typically in a familiar place through the use of vivid imagery. Another efficient method for memorizing lists of items in order involves using the **peg-word mnemonic system.** This method requires that the person first memorize a series of words (pegs) connected to numbers. Typical peg-word number combinations are: one is a bun, two is a shoe, three is a tree, four is a door, etc. In order to memorize a list, each new term is associated with the peg-word through the use of imagery. The peg-word system offers the additional benefit of allowing you to be able to go immediately to the part of the list that you are searching for, such as identifying the fifth item on the list without having to list the first four.

Language

Language is a form of communication consisting of symbols that can be arranged to derive meaning. In spoken language, sounds represent objects and ideas, while sign language uses hand motions for communication. Languages enable individuals to explore actual or potential relationships between parts of the environment. Though most animals communicate, psychologists vigorously debate whether or not they use language. Both chimps and dolphins have been studied, yet the best candidate for the possession of language is the honeybee. When bees return to their hives, they perform complicated dances which may tell other bees where to find honey. However, for reasons described below, most psychologists believe language is unique to humans.

Basic Units of Language

Spoken language is made up of three basic units or ways of conveying meaning: phonemes, morphemes, and grammar. **Phonemes** are the smallest units of sound in a language and are the first sounds infants make. English has forty-five phonemes, including single letters such as *f* and *g* and combinations of letters such as the *th* in the word "think." The Japanese language has fewer phonemes and some languages have more. Other languages also involve phonemes that do not exist in English. The Kung tribe of Africa uses a sort of clicking sound in their language, represented by an exclamation point. One of the most difficult aspects of learning another language, especially as an adult, is learning how to pronounce correctly new phonemes associated with the second language. **Morphemes** are the smallest units of meaning in a language that result from combinations of phonemes. In English, morphemes can be whole words (i.e., rain, dog) or prefixes (i.e., *dis-, ante-)* and suffixes (i.e., *-ing, -ed).* There are more than 100,000 morphemes in the English language, and this list does not even begin to exhaust all of the possible combinations of the forty-five phonemes.

Grammar consists of the rules that define how a language is used so that people speaking the same language understand each other. The broad overall term *grammar* contains two separate parts: semantics and syntax. **Semantics** is the part of grammar that relates to the meanings of words and their combinations. After constructing meaningful words out of morphemes, a person learning a language would need to be able to create understandable combinations of words. An understanding of semantics is necessary to be truly fluent in a language because understanding a statement may involve more than simply combining the definitions of each of the words involved. **Syntax** is the part of grammar that refers to the system of rules within a language regarding the order of how words can be arranged. Syntax varies among languages; for example, in English it is typical for the adjective to precede the noun "the blue sky," but in Spanish the adjective follows the noun "el cielo azul," reflecting a difference in syntax.

Language Acquisition

Babies are capable of learning their native language or even more than one language effortlessly, quickly, and without any direct instruction (no worksheets or flashcards required). Language acquisition, also called language development, is the process by which children learn to communicate.

Language development is a complex process influenced by the interaction of biology, cognition, and culture. At birth, babies are capable of making noises in order to gain the attention of their caregivers, such as cooing and crying. The first signs of language, babbling, typically appear at about six months and the language acquisition process that follows occurs in a recognized pattern. Language development studies in infants differentiate between **receptive language** (words that babies understand) and **expressive language** (words babies are capable of producing). Similar to other types of development, language acquisition varies among individuals and the ages presented are only approximate. The typical sequence of language acquisition in children is presented in Table 9.3.

Table 9.3. Language Acquisition

Stage	Description	Example(s)
Babbling 4 to 6 months	The first speech-like but meaningless sounds infants make, including phonemes that are not a part of the child's native language. The early appearance of babbling suggests this behavior is "wired in," or biological and that an infant is capable of learning any language.	In English the sounds are typically short consonant vowel combinations, such as "ba, ba, ba," or "la, la, la."
One-word Stage Holophrasic 10 to 18 months	Stage when infants communicate by using only single words, called *holophrases*, to express themselves.	First words are often those that represent important people in the infant's world, such as "mama" or "dada," or significant objects such as "doggy," "milk," or "ball."
Two-word Stage 18 to 24 months	Stage when the child communicates in two-word phrases called telegraphic speech.	"more milk" "give ball" "mama walk"
Telegraphic Speech 18 to 30 months	Type of speech that begins in the two-word stage and continues until about 30 months as children build utterances containing more words. This speech contains only the words essential to meaning, typically nouns and verbs, and lacks other parts of speech.	Two-year-old Marta says merely, "give doll" or "give doll me," rather than the more complete "Give the doll to me."

(continued)

Table 9.3   (continued)

Stage	Description	Example(s)
Overgeneralization (Overregularization)	Error in language when young children apply rules about grammar to every example before they learn about exceptions.	Julian wants to say that he has two pet mice and overgeneralizes when he says that he has two pet mices instead of mice.
Overextension	Error in language when young children are too broad in their use of a particular word.	Eric refers to all types of moving vehicles as "car." A child that refers to all snacks, including crackers and pretzels, as "cookie."
Underextension	Error in language when young children are too restrictive in terms of how they use a word.	Liza uses the term doll to refer only to her doll and not any other dolls.
Sentences 2+ years	Following the development of telegraphic speech, children quickly begin to create complete sentences and gradually become capable of more sophisticated grammar and sentence construction.	

Cognitive psychologists are interested in how children acquire the complex skills required for language and how nature, nurture, cognition, and culture contribute to this unique human ability. As is the case with other complex human behaviors, the answer is a combination of both nature and nurture, which is best explained by incorporating aspects of several theories that present evidence for each approach.

An early theory that language acquisition was the result of environmental influences was based on the behaviorist approach of B.F. Skinner. According to Skinner, children learn language in the same way they learn everything else, through operant conditioning, imitation, modeling, and association. Children learn the rules of language because they are reinforced with smiles and encouragement when they are correct and punished by being misunderstood or corrected when they are wrong. One major criticism of this approach is that children are likely to be reinforced even when they are incorrect because, although the child says "give cookie me," which is incorrect, they may still be given the cookie. Second, behaviorism does not have an answer for why children overgeneralize by applying grammatical rules more broadly than is appropriate. One example of this linguistic error that children make even though their parents do not make it is adding "-ed" to make words past tense when the rule should not be used, such as saying "holded" instead of "held."

As interest in biological and cognitive psychology grew, psychologists sought a rival explanation for language acquisition which focused more on the influences of biology and genetics. This rival idea is known as the **nativist approach** and contends that language development is the result of a genetically based innate ability. A major proponent of the nativist approach is linguist **Noam Chomsky**, who observed that children learn language much too quickly for it simply to be the result of imitating others or responding to rewards and punishments. Chomsky pointed out that grammar and syntax are acquired even if children are not corrected for the errors in speech they make. He argued that humans, therefore, must come equipped with a **language acquisition device**, or built-in biological readiness to learn the grammatical rules for any language, including syntax, semantics, and pronunciation. Chomsky's language acquisition device is a theoretical idea, but researchers are interested in determining where language development occurs physiologically in the brain. Another important aspect of Chomsky's theory is that language acquisition is the result of a genetic predisposition that he believes is related to the existence of a **universal grammar**, meaning that all human languages have commonalities in terms of their basic underlying structure. As evidence for the biological basis of language, nativists cite the fact that children achieve developmental milestones in linguistics at the same age and in the same order across cultures.

Further support for the biological factors involved in language acquisition comes from evidence regarding critical periods. A **critical period** is a fixed time period very early in life when particular events result in long-lasting effects on behavior. Very young children can easily acquire any language or even more than one language, but as individuals become older, learning a second language becomes increasingly challenging, suggesting a possible critical period when the brain is more receptive to learning language. Similarly, children who are not exposed to normal speech early in their lives have a difficult time learning language later. Ultimately, biological factors also interact with cognitive factors to influence the learning of language.

Language and Thought

Psychologists are interested in how language impacts thought and if thinking is impacted by the particular native language of an individual. Not only does the way we think, such as the grammatical rules we generate, influence the learning of language, the learning of language can also influence the way we think. The most well-known theory regarding how language contributes to thinking was proposed by **Benjamin Whorf** in his theory called **linguistic determinism**. According to linguistic determinism, the language that a person speaks determines how they think. Whorf cited evidence based largely on Native American languages and how they differed in comparison to English and hypothesized that these differences impacted how members of each culture viewed the world. Psychologists disagree with Whorf's hypothesis that language determines thought, but most agree that language does influence thought in what is now thought of as the **linguistic relativity hypothesis**.

Thinking

Thinking, a type of cognition in terms of psychology, involves the conscious processes involved in reasoning, problem solving, and imagining. Although thinking encompasses the interaction of many various brain regions, the area most directly associated with the complex processes of planning, choice, judgment, impulse control, and even humor is the prefrontal cortex. The building blocks for human thinking consist of imagery, concepts, and prototypes. **Mental images,** or complex cognitive representations for objects and ideas that are not immediately present, are a critical part of the thinking process. **Concepts** are mental categories we create for objects or experiences that are similar to one another, allowing us to represent information about large numbers of specific events, objects, and ideas in an efficient way. Concepts allow us to communicate easily, to remember more, and to solve problems. Examples of concepts used to organize what we know range from simple to more complex, including flowers, trees, action movies, democracy, truth, beauty, and fairness. We typically condense the common features of similar objects by creating a **prototype** or best example of a category. Prototypes can vary among individuals and are even impacted by where people live. For example, the best example of a tree for one person might be an oak tree and another an apple tree, but someone living in a tropical region might immediately think of a palm tree. When faced with new experiences, we solve the problems of identifying them and predicting their impact on us by assessing their resemblance to our prototypes. For example, the more closely your psychology teacher matches your prototype for what a kind teacher is like, the more likely you would be to ask them for extra help. Having assigned them to the category of kind teacher, you would be more likely to remember the characteristics they have that represent kindness and understanding and even recall them having characteristics of the prototype that they may not actually have. For example, you may correctly recall their concern over your sick pet, but also "remember" them allowing you to be exempt from a major assignment when they, in fact, did not do that. Thus, concepts help us remember events, but they also color the ways in which we perceive and remember them.

Problem Solving

The area of cognitive psychology related to problem solving considers the various mental processes involved in generating solutions including both insight and problem solving strategies. **Insight** is the "Aha!" experience people have when a solution to a problem suddenly appears or becomes obvious. Because insight is so startling, it can be used to point out how problem solving entails both conscious and unconscious aspects. The attention and conscious exertion an individual directs toward finding a solution may in turn trigger unconscious sources, resulting in the sudden arrival at a correct answer. Creative solutions to problems do not always flash effortlessly into a person's mind. It is also the case, however, that **metacognitive processing,** or the deliberate and conscious process of talking oneself through a problem, contributes to problem solving. Metacognitive processing essentially allows people to expand their awareness of the problem solving process by watching themselves trying out solutions.

One of the most basic problem solving strategies is using the method of **trial and error** in which individuals attack a problem by making random guesses using little reasoning or analysis. Trial and error is most effective if there are only a small amount of possible solutions to try, but for larger problems this method is often unsuccessful or time consuming. For example, Craig cannot remember the password he used when he signed up for a study-help website and is having trouble logging on. Because Craig uses only four different passwords, he uses trial and error until he figures out the password that works. If Craig had a large selection of possible passwords to choose from, this method would not be effective.

Two general categories of problem solving strategies are algorithms and heuristics. An **algorithm** is a strategy that involves using a set of rules that if followed correctly will guarantee a solution. For example, if you were deciding how to get to a party, you could use an algorithm, or standard procedure, by taking out a map and carefully tracing each possible route you could use to drive there. Potential drawbacks for this method are that a specific algorithm does not exist for every problem, and, while algorithms guarantee a solution, their extensive time commitment may be problematic. A **heuristic** is a problem-solving strategy that is likely to produce a solution quickly, but does not guarantee a correct answer. People often use these mental shortcuts or rules-of-thumb as a way to solve problems, especially those involving estimates of likelihood. (See Table 9.4.) While heuristics are faster and more efficient, they are also more prone to error than algorithms.

STUDY TIP

Algorithms take more time to determine the solution, but are the most accurate way to solve a problem. Heuristics take less time to determine the solution, but are more prone to errors.

Table 9.4.   Definitions and Examples of Heuristics

Heuristic	Definition	Example
Representativeness	Judging the likelihood of an event in terms of how well it seems to match a particular prototype, which can result in either a correct or incorrect analysis of the situation.	If you see a man on the street with long hair and tattoos dressed in leather you are more likely to assume that he is a musician than a doctor because his appearance matches your prototype of a rock star. Note: You might be wrong!
Availability	Judging the likelihood that an event will happen in terms of how readily it comes to mind, based on either personal experience or exposure through the media. Events that are more vivid or that have happened more recently tend to be judged as more likely to happen again than those that are less vivid or recent even though this may or may not be true.	Based on how easily an event or solution comes to mind (availability), you might come to the conclusion that judicial trials are relatively common and plea bargains are relatively rare, when the reverse is actually true. News reports of trials tend to be more sensational and, therefore, more memorable than reports of plea bargains, which cause us to expect them to happen more often.

Reasoning

Reasoning is a type of cognition that relates to the processes individuals utilize to reach conclusions based on available information. Two major methods of making conclusions are deductive and inductive reasoning. In **deductive reasoning** individuals start with a premise they have strong reason to believe is accurate and then create conclusions based on that initial premise. Deductive reasoning is used when psychologists create a hypothesis based on an existing and well-established theory. **Inductive reasoning** involves basing a conclusion on what is most likely truth-based on specific examples or determining general principles from analyzing examples. In psychology inductive reasoning is involved when a hypothesis is created based on data obtained through observation. In other words, deductive reasoning goes from established general principle to specific examples and inductive reasoning involves determining general principles based on specific examples. The use of inductive reasoning can lead to a number of potential biases in thinking including **belief bias** or the error in thinking in which individuals are more likely to agree with conclusions that match up with their existing opinions rather than conclusions appearing to be logically valid.

Obstacles to Problem Solving

Psychologists evaluate how various types of bias or flaws in thinking inhibit individuals from effectively solving problems. **Confirmation bias** involves the tendency to selectively attend to information that is consistent with our viewpoint and ignore or minimize information that challenges our beliefs. If the solution to the problem being investigated is very different from what we believe it will be, this bias can prevent us from looking at every possible alternative. Carmelo is in love and notices only the wonderful positive qualities about his girlfriend and ignores any potential negatives, such as the fact that they have nothing in common, illustrating confirmation bias. **Belief perseverance** is the tendency to hold onto an assumption or belief even after it has been disproven. Cody believes that he is able to drive safely while sending text messages. After reading several articles that present extensive evidence that driving while texting is dangerous, Cody still believes that it is safe when he texts while driving because of the error of belief perseverance. Another error in thinking results from **anchoring bias** that leads an individual to place too great an emphasis on an initial estimate when making decisions under conditions in which one is unsure. Although we realize that we need to modify our original answer, we are so tied to the initial estimate (anchor) that we fail to make a large enough adjustment. Even the way in which problems are worded can make finding solutions more difficult. **Framing effect** results when individuals reach a conclusion to a problem based solely on how it is worded. If potential students read that 75 percent of graduates from Psychology College find a job in their field after graduation, they may be more likely to apply to Psychology College than if they heard that 25 percent of graduates could not find jobs after graduation, due to the effects of framing.

Another obstacle to finding solutions is the idea of **mental set** or the tendency for people to cling to old methods of solving problems even when they are no longer working. A problem related to mental set, **functional fixedness** occurs when the set of ideas people have about the purpose or use of objects prevents them from using objects in new ways. If you have ever sat in a room with a can and no can opener, you know the difficulties involved in trying to find another object that can be used in the same way.

Creativity

Psychologists define the term **creativity** as the ability to generate novel and useful products or solutions to problems. No matter how many other people may have thought of the same idea, a solution is novel if it is new to the person who thinks of it. Another way to think of creativity is in terms of the difference between convergent and divergent thinking. Simple arithmetic is solved by **convergent thinking,** which determines one correct answer through applying consistent rules and categorizing events. **Divergent thinking** produces a variety of solutions to any particular problem. Writing, playing chess, creating pottery, or entertaining children all require divergent thinking because they require the generation of many possibilities. Typically divergent thinking is considered to be more closely related to creativity. A commonly used measurement device for creativity is the Minnesota Test of Creative Thinking. This creativity test asks questions like "How many uses can you think of for an old tire?" or "How can you improve a bicycle?" Creativity tests are often scored in terms of number of original ideas that are generated. These tests have been questioned regarding their construct validity. In other words, it is not clear if they are actually measuring the abstract idea of creativity or not.

Take Mini-Test 1
on Chapters 3–9
Go to the REA Study Center
(www.rea.com/studycenter)

Motivation and Emotion

Chapter 10

Human behaviors are driven by both motivation and emotion. The psychology of **motivation** is the study of biological and psychological factors that influence the arousal, direction, and persistence of behavior toward a goal. Human motivations can be categorized in terms of physiological or social motives that will be discussed further in this chapter. **Emotion** is defined by psychologists as a complex state generally characterized by a heightened level of physical arousal, cognitive appraisal of the situation, and a subjective feeling. Motivation and emotion are closely connected concepts that influence each other. Psychologists have presented a variety of theories to explain motivation and emotion and how they are impacted by both genetic and environmental factors.

Motivation Theories

Why do people act the way they do? It is generally agreed that motives energize and provide the purpose behind behavior, but how motivations operate and where they come from are still debatable. There are basic biological motives, including hunger, thirst, sex, and sleep, and learned motives such as need for achievement and affiliation. Additionally, humans experience emotional motives like pleasure, pain, anger, fear, and frustration. Various theories have been presented to explain the complex processes of human motivations and are listed below.

Instinct Theory

The earliest theories of motivation were influenced by the work of Charles Darwin and focused on the identification of human instincts. An **instinct** is an unchanging sequence of behaviors observed in all members of a species in response to specific stimuli without learning. Behaviors produced by instinct are not affected by practice. During the early part of the century, hundreds of instinct theorists published long lists of newly identified instincts that were supposed to determine the reasons for the arousal and direction of behavior. The methods utilized by these early instinct theorists have been highly criticized because they did not involve any attempts to measure, predict, or explain their existence. Merely generating long lists of potential instincts does not actually result in an explanation of human motivation or behavior. The entire concept of listing instincts led to circular reasoning: we love because we have a love instinct, and we know we have a love instinct because we love. Today, evolutionary psychologists accept that innate tendencies interact with experience to produce behavior, and psychologists continue to investigate why particular motivational tendencies were naturally selected to aid in human survival.

Drive-Reduction Theory

According to **drive-reduction theory**, human motivation is influenced by a combination of needs and drives. **Needs** are biological requirements essential for survival, including food, water, oxygen, and sleep. Physiological needs create a **drive**, or internal state of tension, that results when our bodies are deficient in some need, creating a motivation to relieve the tension. Psychologists identify two general categories of drives—primary and secondary drives. **Primary drives** are associated with innate bodily functions. Examples of stimuli having a primary motivational effect are food, water, air, temperature, or an intense stimulus such as a loud noise or electric shock. All **secondary drives** are learned through experience. For humans, these sources of motivation include learned desires such as success, power, affection, money, appearance, and security. Some psychologists include fear, anxiety, and certain verbal cues as learned drives as well.

The **drive-reduction theory** emphasizes that a deficiency in a particular biological need creates a drive, a state of tension, that causes the individual to behave in a manner that reduces that drive and returns the body to homeostasis. Generally, motivation for behavior according to the drive-reduction theory is directed toward maintaining **homeostasis**, a balanced internal state or equilibrium that our bodies attempt to control in order to stay alive. When the equilibrium of a particular biological need is disrupted, an individual is motivated or driven to regain homeostasis. Achieving homeostasis requires the body to continually monitor levels of water, oxygen, and temperature to assure that these levels remain within an optimal range. A major problem with the drive-reduction theory is that while it explains the drive for homeostasis in terms of biological needs, it does not provide an explanation for motives that are not directly linked to survival such as curiosity or adventure.

STUDY TIP

Be able to describe the basic components of drive-reduction theory and how they explain a motivated behavior in a specific example.

After Michael finishes a 5K race, biological *needs* are created because his body temperature is higher than normal and the water content in his blood is low. These biological needs result in a *drive*, or motivation, to drink water and rest, to return his body to *homeostasis*.

Incentive Theory

Incentive theory recognizes that humans are not only pushed into action by internal drives, but that they are also motivated by the pull of an incentive or external stimulus. The incentive theory is complimentary to the drive-reduction theory as seen in the motivation to eat a freshly baked chocolate chip cookie, because it involves both drives and incentives. The push of a drive (hunger) and the pull of an incentive (smell of the cookie) combine to powerfully motivate an individual to eat the cookie. What is interesting to psychologists is why individuals have different responses to the same stimuli. The value of a particular incentive is impacted by biological factors; for example, the incentive of a chocolate chip cookie has a significantly less powerful pull on behavior if the person is not hungry. The effect of a particular incentive also varies among individuals and can change from one situation to another. This is illustrated by the fact that the opportunity to earn good grades or work bonuses does not motivate everyone in the same manner, and each individual may respond differently to the same incentive from day to day or year to year.

Arousal Theory

Biological explanations offered by the drive-reduction theory do not offer a clear explanation for risky, curious, and exploratory behaviors such as skydiving and rock climbing. These motivations may be better explained with the **arousal theory** of motivation. According to the arousal theory, an individual is motivated by the desire to remain at a personally determined *optimal level of arousal*, which is the level of alertness or the amount of excitement preferred by that person. If an individual's level of arousal falls below their personal optimal level, they will be motivated to act in a manner that increases their arousal. For instance, if a class is not very exciting and causes Ross to fall below his optimum level of arousal, he will be motivated to increase his arousal by tapping his foot, drawing pictures on his notebook, or talking in class. Optimum levels of arousal vary from person to person and can be used to explain why some individuals enjoy risky behaviors while others do not.

In general, research findings in both animals and humans suggest that increased arousal levels result in improved performance, as evidenced by increased alertness, interest, and positive emotion. However, after the optimum level is reached, there is an increase in anxiety, and emotional disturbances and performance ultimately declines; therefore, everyone needs to have a personal level of arousal that is moderate for them. The reason that moderate levels of arousal are usually best for performance is that, if arousal levels are too low, individuals may feel bored or unmotivated, but, if arousal levels are much too high, individuals may become fearful, anxious, or tense. The **Yerkes–Dodson law** explains the relationship between the level of arousal and performance; on simple tasks performance is better if arousal levels are somewhat higher, and performance is best on difficult tasks if arousal levels are slightly lower. An extremely high level of arousal can impair performance in situations that are too difficult and require completing complex tasks. In real life, a student who has a high level of anxiety often does not perform well on a difficult exam. If a student has a very low level of arousal, the student may be likely to perform poorly on an easy exam because he or she will make careless mistakes.

STUDY TIP

Be able to interpret the Yerkes–Dodson graph that creates an *inverted U curve;* it is shown in Figure 10.1. Note: The location of the curve changes with the complexity of the task.

The graph presented in Figure 10.1 illustrates the Yerkes–Dodson law of arousal and performance. Although for most tasks individuals will perform the best at moderate levels of arousal, there are differences in optimal levels for very simple or difficult tasks. Performance is best for individuals on very simple tasks if the arousal level is slightly higher than the moderate optimum level. Conversely, on very difficult tasks, performance is best if the arousal level is slightly below the moderate optimal level. This concept is often used by sport psychologists when motivating atheletes for competition against opponents that might be more or less challenging in order to ensure success.

Figure 10.1.   The Yerkes–Dodson Graph

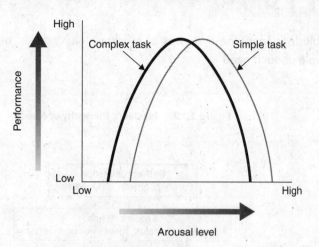

Maslow's Hierarchy of Needs

Abraham Maslow, a humanist, is most widely known for his **hierarchy of needs**. According to Maslow there are a total of five needs in the hierarchy—physiological, safety, belonging and love, esteem, and self-actualization. In this stage model of motivation, the needs at the bottom of the pyramid take precedence over the others. In other words, the primary needs control an organism's actions until those needs are fulfilled. For example, when a lower need such as hunger is fulfilled, the next need in the hierarchy, which is safety, becomes dominant and the individual will begin to focus on fulfilling that need. The highest level on the pyramid of **self-actualization**, or the process of developing to one's fullest potential, is the ultimate motive for all individuals.

Maslow's hierarchy of needs theory is important because of the practical applications associated with basic biological and safety needs being met before individuals can pursue the higher level needs. Individuals living in war-torn areas and concerned for their personal safety and with providing food for themselves and their families are unlikely to be motivated to pursue achievement or self-actualization goals. Maslow's theory is also valuable because it provides a general starting point for discussing human motivation, but there are many significant criticisms of his approach. Evidence supporting Maslow's idea that individuals proceed through the stages in the same order has not been found, and the abstract concept of self-actualization has proven difficult to measure. Furthermore, the hierarchy of needs does not explain why some individuals choose to sacrifice meeting lower level needs in order to pursue others, such as skipping a meal in order to spend time talking with friends, or why individuals choose to risk their own safety for the thrill of skydiving. Each level in the hierarchy of needs is presented in Figure 10.2.

STUDY TIP

Be able to identify the five steps of Maslow's hierarchy of needs in order and provide an example of each need.

Figure 10.2.   Maslow's Hierarchy of Needs

Self-actualization
Personal growth and fulfillment

Esteem Needs
Achievement, status, responsibility, reputation

Belonging and Love Needs
Family, affection, relationships, work group

Safety Needs
Protection, security, order, law, limits, stability

Biological and Physiological Needs
Air, food, drink, shelter, warmth, sleep

STUDY TIP

Be able to compare and contrast the various motivational theories in terms of strengths and weaknesses. See Table 10.1.

Table 10.1.   A Comparison of Motivational Theories

Motivation Theory	Strength	Weakness
Instinct/ Evolutionary	Evolutionary theory may provide an explanation for the adaptive value of behaviors.	Instinct theory is incomplete because it simply names types of behaviors as instincts, but it does not provide an explanation of them as motivations.
Drive-Reduction	Effectively explains motivations to satisfy basic biological needs required for survival.	Does not explain the motivation behind behaviors such as curiosity or risk taking. In addition, fails to account for the importance of external incentives, for example, why, after we are full from eating Thanksgiving dinner, we are still motivated to eat apple pie.

(continued)

Table 10.1.   *(continued)*

Motivation Theory	Strength	Weakness
Incentive	Effectively explains motivations that are not related to maintaining biological homeostasis, such as the drives for achievement, adventure, and affiliation.	Not all behavior can be explained by incentives, for example, altruistic behaviors. An incomplete theory because it fails to account for motivations related to drives to maintain homeostasis.
Arousal	Effectively explains how personal needs for preferred levels of excitement or arousal motivate individuals to engage in various behaviors.	Does not explain some biological motivations as well as drive-reduction theory can.
Maslow's Hierarchy of Needs	Effectively demonstrates how basic biological and safety needs often have to be met before individuals are motivated toward self-actualization.	Evidence supporting the idea that individuals proceed sequentially through the stages in the same way has not been found. Self-actualization has proven difficult to explain and measure objectively. Some individuals are motivated to purposely place higher level needs before lower ones.

Hunger Motivation

A key human motivation studied by psychologists is **hunger**, or the drive that motivates all animals to engage in behaviors aimed at obtaining food and nutrition. The opposite of hunger is **satiety**, or the feeling of being full and not hungry that results in decreasing the likelihood that an individual will eat. On the surface, hunger motivation is merely a basic biological drive necessary for survival, yet there is evidence that hunger is influenced by psychological and cultural factors as well. As a consequence, hunger is often used to illustrate how both nature and nurture interact within one type of human motivation.

STUDY TIP

Remember the term *satiety* by associating it with the word *satisfied*. Satiety involves the general feeling of being full or satisfied that decreases the likelihood that a person will be motivated to eat.

Biological Factors Impacting Hunger

Complex biological factors combine to influence feelings of hunger, including stomach contractions, hormones in the bloodstream, and signals from the brain. Researchers Cannon and Washburn investigated the role of stomach contractions in signaling hunger. Washburn, a graduate student at the time, swallowed a balloon that was then inflated inside his stomach, causing stomach contractions that were recorded and measured. Washburn signaled when he was hungry by pressing a button and a high positive correlation was discovered between feelings of hunger and stomach contractions. Defining hunger in terms of stomach pangs alone is incomplete, because individuals who have had their stomachs removed still report hunger.

Another biological factor influencing hunger is the levels of certain substances in the blood. In an early experiment completed by Davis and others, hungry rats deprived of food were injected with the blood of rats that had been well-fed. When the hungry rats were then given food, they showed no interest in eating. This finding led the researchers to wonder what actually made the rats feel that they were full when they were not. Psychologists are still searching for how the brain and endocrine system specifically control hunger and satiety signals, but some key hormones have been identified as being related to the hunger drive. (See Table 10.2.)

Table 10.2.   Hormones Involved in Hunger and Satiety

Hormone	Area Where Hormone Is Released	Signal
Leptin	Fat cells	Satiety
PYY	Digestive tract	Satiety
Orexin	Hypothalamus	Hunger
Grehlin	Empty stomach	Hunger

Glucose, or blood sugar that provides energy for bodily functions, is broken down by the body from foods that have been eaten recently. As a general rule, people and animals are more likely to eat when glucose levels are low because the brain perceives that they have not had food for a while. However, high levels of glucose in the blood trigger the release of **insulin**, a hormone produced in the pancreas that converts glucose to stored fat and removes it from the blood stream. In addition to insulin, other hormones are involved in sending hunger and satiety signals that effect behavior. Orexin, released by the hypothalamus, and ghrelin, released in response to an empty stomach, both send hunger signals. Leptin, a protein secreted by fat cells, and PYY, a digestive track hormone, send satiety signals to the brain and reduce the motivation to eat.

DIDYOUKNOW?

The direct and indirect cost of obesity in the United States is as much as $147 billion annually. Therefore, a great deal of research is dedicated to finding the causes and solutions to the obesity epidemic. In late 2011, scientists from Harvard University, Harvard Medical School, Massachusetts General Hospital, and Beth Israel Deaconess Medical Center successfully rebuilt diseased brain circuitry in obese mice by transplanting new neurons. Carefully selected embryonic neurons were transplanted into mutant mice that lacked responsive leptin receptors in the hypothalamus, which causes extreme obesity. Studies such as this could also have therapeutic benefits for other diseases, such as Lou Gehrig's disease (ALS) and Parkinson's disease.

STUDY TIP

Orexin is released by the hyp**O**thalamus, and ghrelin (think of your stomach *ghr*rowling) is released by an empty stomach; both send hunger signals to the brain.

The part of the brain that seems to be most important to monitoring hunger-related signals is the **hypothalamus**. Specifically, the **ventromedial hypothalamus** appears to be responsible for stopping hunger; stimulation of this region in animals will depress hunger and destruction of this region results in overeating behavior. On the other hand, the **lateral hypothalamus** is responsible for increasing hunger: stimulation of this region causes a well-fed animal to eat and damage to it will result in a starving animal refusing to eat. See Table 10.3.

STUDY TIP

Eat *late* at night with your *lateral* hypothalamus. The lateral hypothalamus sends hunger signals.

Table 10.3. Hypothalamus Regulation of Hunger and Satiety

Brain Structure	Location	Stimulation	Destruction
Lateral hypothalamus	Both sides of hypothalamus	Desire to eat	Desire to not eat
Ventromedial hypothalamus	Lower middle area of hypothalamus	Desire to not eat	Desire to eat

One hypothesis suggests that the hypothalamus may also be involved in the regulation of weight through the maintenance of homeostasis in terms of set point. **Set point theory** states that individuals have a genetically determined range of weight that is maintained by biological processes without effort. When an individual's weight drops below set point, hunger increases (you will take in calories) and activity level decreases (you will become lethargic, using fewer calories) resulting in an increase in weight. When an individual's weight rises above set point, hunger decreases (you will take in fewer calories) and activity level increases (you will burn more calories), resulting in a drop in weight. According to the set point theory, the brain regulates hunger and satiety drives as well as altering the **basal metabolic rate** or how much energy our body expends at rest to keep weight levels within a certain set range. Some theorists question the existence of a specific set point and look to other factors to explain weight control.

Psychological Factors Impacting Hunger

Non-biological factors can override the brain's regulatory processes and lead to increases in hunger motivation. These environmental factors include conditioning, social and cultural traditions, and external incentives. Learned associations, for example, develop between eating and specific times of day, which is why we become hungry at lunch time even if we have eaten a large breakfast or have had a snack recently. Social and cultural traditions also provide information regarding when to eat, how fast to eat, how much to eat, and what types of foods are appropriate. Finally, external incentives may impact whether or not an individual is likely to be motivated to eat. External incentives can include the smell, appearance, variety, and availability associated with a food. For example, when Jeff lands at a Wisconsin airport and passes the food court on the way to baggage claim, he may be tempted to eat by the wonderful smell of freshly baked cheese curds and a variety of other foods on display even if he is not hungry.

Eating Problems

Obesity is typically defined as a condition in which a person's excess weight results in serious health risks. The World Health Organization measures obesity by a body mass index (BMI) of greater than 30. An individual's BMI is a measurement of the person's body fat in relationship to his or her height and weight and indicates if the individual's weight is at a healthy level. Obesity-related health problems include heart disease, high blood pressure, and diabetes, making this a disease linked to shorter life expectancy. In addition to negative health effects, obesity has negative social and emotional effects due to prejudice and discrimination, as well as higher rates of depression and anxiety. Based on evidence from twin studies, obesity has been found to have a significant genetic component, but the recent dramatic increases in the rates of obesity have been generally attributed to environmental factors. Exposure to a greater variety of inexpensive high-calorie foods, larger portion sizes, and an overall decrease in physical activity levels are significant contributors to what some people consider to be an obesity epidemic.

Eating disorders are illnesses associated with major disturbances in the relationship an individual has with food. Behaviors indicative of an eating disorder include extreme food restriction or the intake of large amounts of calories in short time periods, and stress and worry regarding weight and appearance. Anorexia nervosa and bulimia nervosa, two very serious eating disorders, typically occur more frequently in females and develop during adolescence. While the specific cause of eating disorders is unknown, it appears to stem in part from the desire to achieve a culturally determined ideal of beauty. **Anorexia nervosa** is characterized by the fear of gaining weight, distorted body image, and self-starvation through extreme reduction in the amount of calories taken in. Anorexics are often obsessed with food, but avoid eating it. As a result, they drop far below normal body weight, resulting in severe and permanent damage to their bodies. A diagnosis of anorexia nervosa typically involves individuals who weigh less than 85 percent of their normal weight. **Bulimia nervosa** is an eating disorder marked by repeated episodes of binging and purging in which an individual takes in a large amount of calories in a single sitting (binging) and then eliminates the calories (purging), often through the use of vomiting, laxatives, or diuretics. Bulimics like anorexics are extremely concerned with body image and often consumed with dieting behavior.

Sexual Motivation

Sexual motivation like hunger, thirst, and other biological drives is also impacted by psychological and cultural influences. Physiological aspects impacting the development of primary sex characteristics and sex drive include the presence of specific sex hormones. Sex hormones include androgens such as **testosterone** (the male sex hormones), and estrogens (the female sex hormones). An early researcher of sexual motivation and behavior was **Alfred Kinsey**, who along with his colleagues conducted surveys with thousands of American men and women, asking about their sexual behaviors. Kinsey's controversial research provided statistics and increased public and scientific understanding of sexual behavior. Researchers Masters and Johnson expanded the understanding of sexual motivation by investigating the anatomy and physiology of the human sexual response cycle in laboratory studies. Their research revealed the four stages of the **sexual response cycle** including the excitement, plateau, orgasm, and resolution phases. This research was used to develop methods of treatment for individuals with physical sexual disorders.

Social Motivation

The area of social motivation includes the human drives to belong with others, to form relationships, and to achieve success and excellence. Humans have a strong need to relate to others, and evolutionary psychologists believe that this motivation to create bonds was naturally selected because it allowed for increased chances of survival. **Affiliation motivation** involves the human need to belong and form attachments with others. The drive to develop social bonds leads individuals to seek connections with others by participating in clubs, attending social events, and establishing friendships. Social motivations also include drives to engage with others in order to attain a level of excellence in a particular skill, career, or behavior.

Achievement Motivation

Achievement motivation involves the desire or drive to attain a level of excellence or success by overcoming difficult challenges. Psychologists have found that individuals differ in terms of their levels of achievement motivation. It has also been discovered that there is a high correlation between independence in childhood and high achievement motivation levels during adulthood. Furthermore, individuals who possess high levels of achievement motivation typically select tasks that are challenging, but of moderate difficulty, because those tasks would have a high likelihood of success. Individuals with low levels of achievement motivation tend to avoid or perform less well on challenging tasks due to the fear of failure. David McClelland created a scoring method to measure achievement motivation on the **Thematic Apperception**

Test (TAT) developed by Henry Murray, another leading researcher in motivation. The TAT is a projective test in which participants are asked to create a story to go along with a picture. McClelland then systematically analyzed the stories participants created to search for achievement-related references according to a standardized coding system. The need to achieve appears to be a learned motivation that is typically acquired from parents during childhood or through cultural influences. The impact of culture in achievement motivation can be illustrated in terms of the differences discovered between individualist and collectivist cultures. Achievement motivation in individualist cultures is focused on reaching goals and overcoming difficulties in order to gain individual or personal satisfaction. On the contrary, achievement motivation in collectivist cultures is directed at achieving excellence as a part of a larger group such as a family or community.

STUDY TIP

Individuals taking the Thematic Apperception Test (TAT) will need to **T**ell **A** **T**ale (TAT).

Intrinsic and Extrinsic Motivation

One common way to distinguish among motives is in terms of whether the behaviors they produce are satisfying for their own sake or as a result of consequences. **Intrinsic motivation** involves the desire to perform a behavior out of genuine interest rather than any potential benefit associated with the activity. Performing a behavior in order to obtain a reward or avoid punishment is referred to as **extrinsic motivation**. Reading a book for pleasure involves intrinsic motivation and reading a novel that is assigned in English class in order to pass the class is the result of extrinsic motivation. When individuals are motivated intrinsically as opposed to extrinsically, they tend to achieve more, such as increased productivity at school or work. An interesting finding related to motivation is the **overjustification effect**, or the unusual result that happens if a person is given an extrinsic reward for performance that causes their level of motivation to decrease in the future. This reduction in motivation for performing the task in the future occurs because the original intrinsic motivation is weakened due to the individual explaining their behavior as being the product of the reward rather than interest. When the external reward is taken away, the individual is no longer motivated because the task does not interest them anymore.

Work Motivation

The field of **industrial-organizational psychology** is concerned with psychological issues related to the work environment and investigates how psychological research can be applied to employee motivation or improving the workplace. There are multiple subfields of industrial-organizational psychology, including human factors, personnel, and organizational. **Human factors psychology** is concerned with creating, designing, and producing machines and systems that are functional and easy to use by people. Simply stated, the study of human factors involves psychology plus engineering. In this subfield, psychologists attempt to describe the limitations and capacities of humans in order to effectively design machines that will be used by humans. Effective product design requires knowledge of human sensation, perception, psychomotor behavior, and cognitive processes, as well as an understanding of the properties of the physical world. An example of human factors is utilizing research about perceptual processes to design a complicated dashboard for an airplane that is easy to read and allows pilots to immediately notice potential problems. **Personnel psychology** assists companies with the process of hiring and evaluating worker performance based on data from empirical research. Personnel psychologists may also be involved in administering tests and providing employee training. **Organizational psychology** supports companies and organizations by creating more productive work climates in order to increase employee morale and productivity. Organizational psychologists examine management methods to determine the techniques that are the most effective and how to foster leadership and motivation among the employees. Several management styles that have been researched are outlined in Table 10.4.

Table 10.4. Management Styles

Style	Definition
Task-motivated leadership	Leadership style that emphasizes specific goals (tasks) that groups or teams are required to complete. Communication and feedback are specifically related to goal attainment.
Relationship-motivated leadership	Leadership style that emphasizes developing and maintaining strong supportive bonds among coworkers, minimizing conflict, and offering encouragement. Communication and feedback are designed to develop positive team-centered environments.

(continued)

Table 10.4. *(continued)*

Style	Definition
Theory X management style	Management philosophy based on the assumption that employees are lazy and can only be motivated through extrinsic methods such as rewards and punishments. This management approach results in a self-fulfilling prophecy and employees begin to display the characteristics that management expects of them.
Theory Y management style	Management philosophy based on the assumption that employees are intrinsically motivated to acquire and achieve responsibility. This management approach results in a self-fulfilling prophecy, and employees begin to display the characteristics that management expects of them.

Emotion

An **emotion** involves a complex internal state including physiological, cognitive, and behavioral components that result from a stimulus or event in the environment that is of personal importance. Emotions can create motivations to behave in a particular way; for example, fear may lead individuals to avoid certain situations. Emotions can be goals or motives themselves because people will work harder in order to experience powerful positive emotions such as love or happiness. Finally, emotions also create responses; for example, the emotion of anger may lead to an aggressive reaction. Psychologists measure emotions by using self-report questionnaires or surveys, behavioral observations, and physiological responses.

Emotion as a response is useful because it can be objectively measured through changes in physiological arousal, such as activation of the sympathetic and parasympathetic branches of the autonomic nervous system. During arousal of the sympathetic nervous system (fight or flight), one or more of the following changes result: heart rate or pulse increases, breathing becomes faster, blood pressure rises, pupils dilate, and galvanic skin responses change. A **galvanic skin response** (GSR) is a measure of conductance, or how well skin transmits an extremely weak electrical current. When people sweat, their skin conducts electricity better, and the GSR increases, creating a measurable emotional response. In general the stronger the arousal level, the more intense the emotion. Different emotional states lead to different bodily changes. For example, fear produces higher blood pressure and heart rate changes than anger does. Cross-cultural research suggests that these basic autonomic responses associated with emotions are universal.

Although it has been determined that the physiological reactions associated with each emotion vary, the differences are often so subtle that individuals are unable to ascertain the emotion they are experiencing based solely on the reaction of their body. Ultimately, individuals need to make cognitive appraisals of situational and environmental cues to determine the emotion they are experiencing.

Emotion Theories

Psychologists investigate how the physiological, cognitive, and behavioral aspects that make up emotions combine to create the experience of particular emotions. A variety of theories have been presented to explain how these factors relate to each other. Some approaches suggest that physiological factors create emotions, and others suggest that emotions in fact generate the physical reactions we experience. Additionally, cognition is an important factor in how we explain emotion that is incorporated in many theories.

James–Lange Theory of Emotion

The **James–Lange theory**, named in part for **William James**, asserts that the individual's perception of their physical reactions creates emotions. According to this theory, the emotional experience occurs *after* the bodily change and as a result of it. William James believed that if we find ourselves trembling, then we will feel the emotion of fear, and if we find ourselves crying, that will result in the emotion of sadness. The sequence of events for an emotion include the perception of a situation, the actual bodily reaction to the situation, and the onset of the emotional reaction as a result. The James–Lange theory would explain that an individual experiences fear because the person feels his or her heart pounding. Without the physical arousal the individual would not be afraid. Support for the James–Lange theory is provided by the **facial feedback hypothesis**, which proposes that the activity of the facial muscles that create expressions determines the emotions that we experience. In fact, people asked to hold a pen with their teeth (activating muscles involved in smiling) report finding cartoons to be funnier than people asked to hold a pen with their lips (activating muscles involved in frowning). There are a number of criticisms of the James–Lange theory including the fact that many emotions have very similar corresponding physiological reactions and this approach does not provide an explanation for how the brain recognizes the difference between anger and fear, both of which lead to increased heart rate and breathing. This theory also fails to explain instances when physiological arousal occurs without the experience of emotions in situations like exercise or how emotions sometimes happen before the bodily reaction is detected.

Cannon–Bard Theory of Emotion

According to the **Cannon–Bard theory** of emotion, bodily reactions do not cause emotional responses; rather, the two occur simultaneously. After receiving information from the sensory receptors, the thalamus sends messages to the cerebral cortex where conscious recognition of the emotion happens while also directing the autonomic nervous system to create physiological arousal at the same time. The results of modern research have shown that the thalamus does not play as critical a role in the process as was originally believed, and that other limbic system structures are also involved. Joseph LeDoux's *dual path theory* of fear proposes that information entering the eye travels to the thalamus and then is routed along one of two pathways to separate brain structures. The fast pathway travels along the low road from the thalamus directly to the amygdala. The slow pathway consists of the high road as information travels from the thalamus to the cerebral cortex for interpretation. Due to the fact that information about fear reaches the amygdala faster than the same information reaches the cortex, individuals may experience the emotional reaction of fear before they recognize what has caused the reaction.

Schachter-Singer or Two-Factor Theory of Emotion

The Schachter-Singer or **two-factor theory** involves adding a cognitive aspect to the previous theories. In this theory, emotion is the result of an individual's interpretation (the first factor) of his or her aroused bodily state (the second factor). Emotions seem different from one another because we interpret them or have thoughts about them, and we feel the emotion we believe to be the most appropriate for the situation. The interpretation and cognitive label leads to an emotion, rather than physiological arousal leading to an emotion. Schachter and Singer devised a variety of experiments to examine how individuals explained their emotions. In one classic experiment, participants were told that they would be given an injection of a vitamin, but in reality they were given epinephrine, which creates physiological arousal in the form of increased heart rate and breathing, responses typically associated with strong emotions. Participants were then randomly assigned to wait alone in one of two different rooms. In one condition the participant was joined by a confederate who acted hostile and angry. In the second condition the participant was placed in a room with a confederate who was enthusiastically happy and even tossed paper airplanes around the room. In both cases the participants were asked to report their own emotional state at the end of the experiment. Those who waited with the angry confederate reported feelings of anger, and those who waited with the happy confederate reported feelings of happiness. The results indicated that participants looked to their environment for clues to create a cognitive label for their physiological reaction (increased heart rate due to the epinephrine) in order to determine the emotion that they were experiencing.

Cognition and Emotion

Cognitive theorists continuously debate which comes first—the emotion or thought process. Richard Lazarus's cognitive appraisal theory states cognition must happen before the subjective experience of an emotion. Emotions are the result of a cognitive appraisal of the personal meaning of events and experiences. There are two components of appraisal that include a primary appraisal, which decides if an event will affect an individual personally, and a secondary appraisal that decides how one should deal with the event. Robert Zajonc argues to the contrary: that emotion can occur prior to cognition. In other words, we feel before we think.

STUDY TIP

The term *opponent-process theory* can relate to motivation and emotion or to a theory that explains color vision (see Chapter 6, Sensation and Perception).

Opponent-Process Theory of Emotion

The **opponent-process theory** claims that all emotions are accompanied by an opposite emotional reaction; for example, fear is followed by relief, sadness by happiness. According to Solomon and Corbit, with each experience of the same emotion, the dominant emotion becomes weaker, while the opponent emotion becomes stronger. Solomon and Corbit studied skydivers who were frightened on their first jump, but after repeated jumps became more relieved and finally overjoyed. Opponent-process theory has also been suggested as a factor contributing to drug addiction. For drug users, the first dose of heroin might be very pleasurable, yet with time the opponent negative reaction takes over. To achieve the pleasurable state that was experienced the first time and avoid unpleasant emotion, the addict must take larger and larger doses of the drug.

STUDY TIP

Be able to compare and contrast the major theories of emotions. See Figure 10.3.

Figure 10.3. Different Theories of Emotion

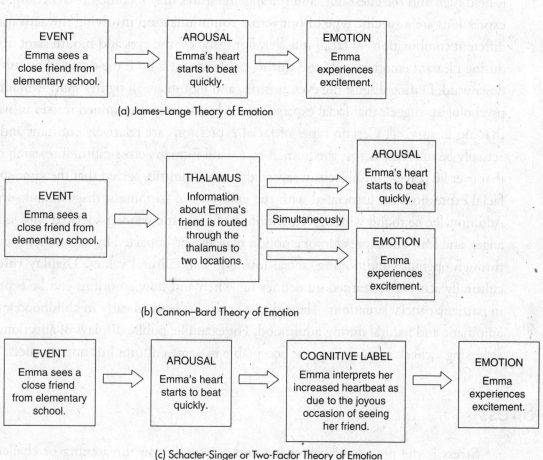

(a) James–Lange Theory of Emotion

(b) Cannon–Bard Theory of Emotion

(c) Schacter-Singer or Two-Factor Theory of Emotion

Types of Emotion and Expression

Psychologists have long debated the existence of basic emotions and emotional expressions across cultures. Research by multiple theorists has sought to identify basic universal emotions. To date a limited number of **primary emotions**, which are universally recognized across cultures, have been identified—fear, anger, joy, sadness, disgust, contempt, and surprise. The additional emotions of shame, shyness, and guilt are accepted as primary emotions by some theorists. Theorists have also sought to identify the types of emotional expression and the cause of differences in expression in relation to the impact of nature and nurture. Emotional expression provides a visible sign of the internal feelings an individual is experiencing. There are several different types of emotional expression, including differences in voice, posture, gestures, and facial expressions. For example, the voice can indicate emotion through laughter, sobbing, screaming, and groans. A low voice or a tremor may indicate deep sorrow. Anger is usually expressed in a sharp, loud, high-pitched voice. As for posture and gestures, in happiness the head is held high and the chest out, and for anger gestures may include fist clenching. Facial expressions are a specific type of nonverbal communication involving the activation of different combinations of facial muscles. For instance, the eyes and mouth slant upward during pleasant emotions, whereas during unpleasantness both the eyes and mouth slant downward. During disgust the eyes, nostrils, and mouth are all tightly shut. Evolutionary psychologists suggest that facial expressions are biologically determined reactions (nature) that aid in survival. Certain types of facial expressions are relatively constant and may actually be universal across the human race. Paul Ekman's cross-cultural research noted that over 90 percent of subjects in several different countries agreed that the same specific facial expressions are associated with the emotions of happiness, disgust, and surprise. Additionally, he found wide agreement on the facial expressions associated with sadness, anger, and fear. The expression of emotion may also be impacted by experience (nurture) through operant conditioning, social learning, and cultural values. **Display rules** are culturally acceptable learned guidelines for when and how emotions can be expressed in particular social situations. These display rules are learned early in childhood and are automatic and natural during adulthood. For example, public displays of affection, such as kissing a cheek as a greeting, are acceptable in some cultures but not in others.

Stress

Stress is the process of perceiving and responding to threatening or challenging events, and can involve a variety of emotional and behavioral responses. Psychologists refer to the stimulus or event in the environment that results in psychological tension and threats to internal homeostasis as the **stressor**. Stressors can be physical, such as injuries, pain, exhaustion, or other types of aversive stimuli. Psychological or environmental stressors may include loneliness, traumatic events, social obligations, or more extreme societal issues such as poverty and discrimination. Other stressors categorized as daily hassles include normal everyday problems that lead to frustration, such as long lines, traffic jams, and interpersonal conflicts.

Stress can be adaptive, such as when it motivates us in constructive ways, or maladaptive when it causes health risks. Hans Selye identified two separate categories of stress—eustress and distress. **Eustress** or positive stress is the result of accepting challenges and pursuing goals. Individuals need some level of eustress in order to be productive, happy, and inspired. Negative stress, or **distress**, involves high levels of tension, resulting in impaired decision making, negative physical consequences, appetite or sleep disturbances, and negative coping mechanisms. Research by health psychologists have discovered that chronic stress results in a depletion of your body's resources and negative effects on the brain and other organs.

Responses to Stress

In response to information received from the senses or the environment, the body reacts to stress with a two-tiered response. First, the sympathetic nervous system activates the release of epinephrine and norepinephrine into the bloodstream. Second, the hypothalamus and pituitary gland send messages that result in the release of glucocorticoid hormones, including cortisol. This two-tiered response leads to the physiological changes associated with the fight or flight reaction. Furthermore, when a person undergoes great emotional stress, the body will go through a three-stage physical response identified by **Hans Selye** and collectively called the **general adaptation syndrome**. The first stage is the **alarm reaction**, consisting of the body's typical sympathetic nervous system response to heightened emotion, such as increased heart rate. If the stressor continues, the individual enters the second stage, called resistance. During **resistance**, increased physiological reactions continue, including the increased presence of stress hormones, as the body attempts to adapt to this high arousal state by using other resources. The excessive amount of epinephrine and other stress hormones increase heart rate and blood pressure. During this stage, diseases such as hypertension (high blood pressure) and heart disease become likely. If the stress continues even longer, the body's resources will become more strained, and the third stage begins, the stage of exhaustion. During the **exhaustion** stage, the body's internal resources for dealing with stress are depleted, and the body cannot tolerate any further stress. Long periods of stress have resulted in accelerated aging, illness, permanent organ damage, and even death.

Individuals may react to stress in one of two broad ways, as Type A or Type B responders. **Type A** individuals are usually in a rush and respond to increased stress by working more, competing harder, or with aggression. Type A's may be impatient and intolerant of slowness. These individuals are more likely to blow their horns and swear during a traffic jam. **Type B**'s, on the other hand, tend to be more relaxed and patient. They allow stress to "roll off their backs" and are generally less driven. Consequently, Type A people are more severely affected by stress than Type B's. Type A's have a higher incidence of heart attacks, ulcers, and other stress-related diseases.

Stressful events are unavoidable, and, because of their potentially dangerous effects, psychologists have promoted a number of techniques for dealing with them. Effective stress management therapy potentially includes exercise, meditation, setting aside time each day for peace and quiet, and deliberately walking, talking, and eating more slowly. Social support also appears to counteract the effects of stressful events. Those who have close relationships with friends or spouses tend to have lower blood pressure, better immune system functioning, and lower levels of stress hormones circulating in their bloodstreams than those who are socially isolated. An important factor related to being able to successfully cope with stress is the ability for an individual to be able to predict and control the amount of stress in his or her life.

Conflict

A **conflict** is a scenario in which an individual is forced to make a choice between two or more incompatible options, which often results in a strong emotional reaction. Psychologists have identified four different types of conflicts; they are explained in Table 10.5.

Table 10.5. Four Types of Motivational Conflict

Conflict	Description	Example
Approach–approach	An individual is forced to make a choice between two equally desirable goals. Both options are appealing, which makes the choice difficult.	Lindsay has to choose between going to a baseball game and hanging out with her friends, and she enjoys both activities.
Avoidance–avoidance	An individual is forced to make a choice between two equally undesirable or threatening options. Neither choice is good, so the individual is essentially choosing the lesser of two evils.	Trisha must choose whether she will clean her room or study for her upcoming exam. She dislikes both activities equally.
Approach–avoidance	An individual is both attracted to and repelled by the *same* goal. Within one particular situation there are both positive and negative parts.	Nathan must choose whether or not to buy a new stereo system. If he gets the new system, his friends will want to ride in his car, but the sound system is very expensive.
Multiple Approach–avoidance	An individual must choose between *two* different options, both of which have positive and negative parts.	Jessica received acceptance letters from two colleges and must choose to go to college in Arizona or Wisconsin. Attending college in Arizona will allow for warm, sunny weather (positive) but family will be far away (negative). Attending college in Wisconsin will involve cold weather (negative), but family will be close by (positive).

Time for a quiz
- Review strategies in Chapter 2
- Take Quiz 4 at the REA Study Center
  (www.rea.com/studycenter)

Developmental Psychology

Developmental psychology focuses on the physical, cognitive, social, and moral development of humans that occurs across the lifespan from conception to death. Typically developmental psychologists examine these various changes at distinct periods in life, in particular, prenatal and newborn, childhood, adolescence, and adulthood. Developmental psychologists are ultimately attempting to answer questions about how we become who we are and how much of whom we are is related to nature and how much is influenced by nurture. In regard to developmental psychology, the term **nature** specifically references influences on development that are genetic or biological. Aspects of developmental change influenced by nature are often related to the process of maturation. **Maturation** includes the biological growth processes that enable changes in behavior and is connected to an individual's genetic blueprint, meaning that it is relatively uninfluenced by experience. The term **nurture** involves the influence of environmental factors on development, such as family, nutrition, culture, interactions with others, education, wealth, etc. Developmental psychologists agree that both nature and nurture contribute to physical, cognitive, social, and moral development in people.

STUDY TIP

Be able to describe how nature and nurture influence physical, cognitive, and social development.

Research Methods

Developmental psychologists seek to understand how individuals develop over time and determine whether differences among age groups are related to changes in cognitive, emotional, or behavioral abilities for example, if older children can remember longer lists of words than younger children. Because age cannot be manipulated (individuals cannot be randomly assigned to a particular age group), developmental research is often correlational. In order to address the specific needs of measuring change over long periods of time, psychologists have distinguished four specific types of developmental research.

In **cross-sectional studies**, psychologists study individuals of different ages who are evaluated at a single point in time. Individuals in several age group categories, for example, five-year-olds, ten-year-olds, twenty-year-olds, thirty-year-olds, and forty-year-olds, are all interviewed or tested regarding a particular behavior or skill such as memory, attachment, commitment in relationships, attitudes toward particular issues, or biological differences including hormone levels. The advantages of this method of study include a short duration that leads to faster results with lower costs. Cross-sectional studies are also used because they have a low participant dropout rate due to a lack of a long-term research commitment. However, caution must be used due to possible cohort effects. A **cohort** consists of a group of people that were all born during a particular period of time and collectively exposed to the same social forces. Members of a cohort may develop similar attitudes, beliefs, and expectations due to shared life experiences that make that particular population different than other cohorts. A **cohort effect** is a chance result that occurs because individuals are influenced by the era or generation that they are part of rather than their age. Cohort effects might be evident if a study were conducted to measure the ability to learn how to play new video games. The results of the research might indicate that individuals in the forty-year-old group had significantly lower video game scores than individuals in the twenty-year-old age group. Does the ability to learn new video games really decline with age, or is it possible that members of the younger cohort have more experience or motivation to play video games that is causing the difference in the scores? Ultimately, cross-sectional studies have the ability to highlight how cohorts differ in terms of their attitudes and behaviors. However, it is difficult to determine how much of the differences are related to aging and how much are related to cohort effects.

Longitudinal studies are research methods that study the same group of individuals over a lengthy period of time to examine changes in the development of behaviors and attitudes related to growth and aging. These studies investigate the important developmental issue of stability versus change across the lifespan for characteristics like personality traits.

Stability versus change refers to the degree to which, as we age, our personalities stay the same (stability) or transform (change), resulting in new traits and behaviors. While longitudinal studies can provide extensive detail, this research method is expensive and time consuming. A major problem with longitudinal studies is that they often have a high rate of participant dropout because participants may move, lose interest in the research, or pass away. In addition, although longitudinal studies are effective at eliminating differences between groups related to cohort effects, they provide data for only one cohort. Thomas Bouchard at the University of Minnesota began the famous longitudinal study of identical twins raised apart in 1979, referred to as the Minnesota Twin Family Study (MTFS), which continues today. The Minnesota Twin Family Study found that monozygotic twins raised apart had remarkable similarities in behavioral traits, including intelligence, personality, interests, fears, and talents, suggesting a genetic cause for these complex human behaviors. Longitudinal data from the Minnesota Twin Family Study is meaningful because the same participants are continually evaluated over time, enabling researchers to study stability of the similar traits observed in twins over time.

> **DID**YOU**KNOW?**
>
> In addition to MTFS, the Minnesota Center for Twin and Family Research (MCTFR) conducts another longitudinal study—the Sibling Interaction and Behavior Study (SIBS). According to the MCTFR, over 9,800 individuals have contributed to these studies. "By studying twins and siblings and their families, we can estimate how genes and environment interact to influence character, strengths, vulnerabilities and values."

Cohort-sequential studies involve studying participants of different ages over time, thus combining the cross-sectional and longitudinal approaches, and allowing the researchers to determine whether aging or social factors influence changes in behavior. This approach is expensive and time consuming, but provides for the greatest amount of data possible in a developmental study.

STUDY TIP

> Be able to discuss the differences, advantages, and disadvantages between a longitudinal and cross-sectional study.

Meta-analysis studies involve combining data from numerous already published studies on the same developmental topic to generate a hypothesis based on a large sample. These studies can indicate if research on the same topic has led to consistent results. The advantages of meta-analyses are that they are relatively inexpensive, and because the data is based on a larger sample size, it is easier to draw conclusions related to the population. A major drawback of this method is that it is difficult to draw a conclusion from numerous studies that were not conducted in the same manner. Furthermore, these studies are subject to potential bias due to the fact that statistically significant results are more likely to end up being published than results that do not support the theory being investigated.

Conception and Gestation

Developmental psychologists study the entire lifespan and are interested in how development is impacted from the moment of conception. **Conception** is the biological process that occurs when fertilization creates a **zygote**, or single-celled organism containing the genetic information contributed by each parent. This cell will divide and multiply, ultimately forming each cell in the body. The zygote then travels along the fallopian tube until it reaches the uterus where implantation occurs. The **prenatal period** consists of the germinal, embryonic, and fetal stages occurring from conception until birth. The term **gestation** involves only the embryonic and fetal stages of development and begins when the zygote attaches to the uterine wall. The embryonic stage lasts from two to eight weeks, and the final and longest stage of gestation, the fetal stage, lasts from nine weeks until birth. At approximately six months, the fetus has developed sufficiently to survive if born prematurely. A fetus that is fewer than six months old will have a more difficult time surviving because the central nervous system and organs may not be completely formed. If very premature infants are provided with exceptional medical care, it is possible for them to survive. The characteristics and developmental changes associated with each of the three stages of prenatal development—germinal (zygotic), embryonic, and fetal—are described in Table 11.1.

Table 11.1. Prenatal Stages of Development

Stage	Time Frame	Characteristics
Germinal (Zygotic)	0 to 2 weeks	• Zygote travels along the fallopian tube to the uterus where it will attach during implantation and form the placenta that provides oxygen and nutrients to the organism.
Embryonic	2 to 8 weeks	• The nervous system, major organs, and body parts, such as the eyes and limbs, begin to form. • Cell division is more specialized, and particular cells are formed to become parts of specific organs. • Period of great vulnerability due to possible teratogens.
Fetal	9 weeks to birth	• Rapid period of organ and body growth during which bodily systems reach maturity in order to ensure survival outside the womb. • Fetus becomes responsive to sound at about 20 to 24 weeks.

Prenatal Risks

During the gestational or prenatal period, environmental factors can have long-lasting or permanent effects on the developing fetus. Various aspects related to the mother, for instance, age, diet and nutrition, drug use, illness, and mental health, have been shown to impact fetal development either positively or negatively. Exceptional prenatal medical care, good nutrition, and emotional support have been shown to result in positive effects for the fetus. Throughout pregnancy the developing organism receives oxygen and nutrition from the mother via the selectively permeable placenta that allows much of what the mother is exposed to, including harmful substances to reach the developing fetus. **Teratogens** are any chemical, virus, or other agent that reaches the fetus and results in harm or a birth defect. Examples of teratogens include radiation, flu virus, prescription medications, and illicit drugs. Many commonly used drugs, such as tobacco, caffeine, nicotine, antibiotics, aspirin, and alcohol, are known teratogens. Of particular risk is the consumption of alcohol during pregnancy. Heavy drinking is known to cause developmental problems and is associated with a condition referred to as **fetal alcohol syndrome (FAS)**. Typical complications of FAS include physical and cognitive abnormalities.

Physical Development

Across the lifespan physical development involves changes in the body, nervous system, senses, and motivational drives related to growth and aging. Changes in people occur due to genetic differences between individuals and automatic biological processes like maturation, as well as environmental and cultural factors. Developmental psychologists investigate how the physical changes in the body impact behavior and mental processes.

Physical and Sensory Development During Infancy

Physically the neonate or newborn child is already very developed and capable of receiving information from their surroundings using all their senses. After birth physical development continues to progress rapidly as both motor skills and sensory abilities improve and expand. In terms of motor development, the neonate is born armed with a set of sophisticated reflexes (newborn superpowers) that allow for survival immediately after leaving the womb. Many of these early **reflexes**, or unlearned involuntary behaviors, are lost relatively quickly after three or four months as the infant develops muscle control, but others last throughout life. Several of these reflexes are clearly essential for survival, yet the purposes for others are unknown. The presence of the major reflexes at birth indicates normal neurological development. Examples of common newborn reflexes are listed in Table 11.2.

STUDY TIP

Be able to identify newborn reflexes and their survival value.

Table 11.2. Newborn Reflexes

Reflex	Description	Duration
Rooting	Newborns open their mouth and turn toward the source if touched on the cheek. Directs the newborn to the mother's breast to allow for feeding.	Gradually weakens during the first six months after birth
Sucking	Newborns suck on an object placed in their mouth. Allows the newborn to be able to feed.	Gradually altered by experience
Swallowing	Newborns swallow when liquid is placed in their mouth. Allows the newborn to be able to feed.	Permanent reflex that is altered by experience
Blinking	Newborns blink their eyes for protection from bright lights and foreign objects.	Permanent
Grasping	Newborns close their fingers around items that touch the palm of their hand. Allows the newborn to cling to the caregiver.	Disappears after approximately four months
Babinski	Newborns stretch their toes outward if the soles of their feet are touched.	Disappears after approximately one year
Moro	When startled, newborns extend their limbs outward and then bring them back in, potentially to grab onto something or brace themselves.	Disappears after approximately seven months

Although it was previously believed that newborns were essentially unaware of their surroundings, current research suggests that they are responsive to changes in their environment immediately after birth. In fact, evidence suggests that sounds are registered during the prenatal period as well. Researchers have been able to demonstrate the sensory capabilities of newborns using a variety of methods, including evaluating facial expressions and other observable behaviors. Newborns are capable of hearing and responding to the voices of their parents, as well as demonstrating startle reactions to loud or unexpected noises. Taste abilities are present at birth, and babies display an inborn preference for sweet and salty tastes and an aversion to bitter tastes. Responsiveness to touch can be observed because many reflexes in newborns focus on touch, for instance, grasping and rooting. Although the sense of vision is limited at birth due to immaturities in both the eye and brain, vision gradually improves throughout the first year of life. A newborn can see as far away as approximately eight inches, recognize color, and track or follow moving objects. Researchers determine what babies prefer to look at and what they notice by what holds their attention the longest. Overall, newborns show the greatest preference for faces, but tend to focus the longest on what they are capable of seeing most clearly—bright colors, movement, and areas of greater contrast. Because infants are unable to verbally report what they are experiencing, stimuli are provided and attention and responses are measured in terms of eye movements and physiological changes. Psychologists conducting research on the capabilities of young infants also monitor habituation during experiments. **Habituation** is a type of conditioning in which organisms demonstrate weaker responses to a stimulus that has been presented repeatedly, indicating that they have become used to or familiar with that particular stimulus. Typically, researchers measure infant responses and attention in terms of the amount of time they spend looking at objects, sucking behavior, or heart rate. If the amount of attention that the infant pays to a stimulus decreases after it is presented repeatedly, habituation has occurred. After habituation has taken place, researchers present infants with a new stimulus along with the familiar one and compare their reactions. Typically, infants pay greater attention to the new stimulus, indicating that they are capable of making distinctions between stimuli, a skill that will help aid learning of complex behaviors in the future.

Physical Development During Childhood

The process of **maturation** involves biologically driven growth processes that enable changes in behavior, connected to each individual's genetic blueprint, and are relatively uninfluenced by experience. In other words, maturation relates to behaviors that are driven mainly by nature and less influenced by nurture. After birth the most important physical milestone is acquiring the ability to walk. The progression of motor skill development that culminates in walking occurs in generally predictable stages, as the result of maturation. Although the exact age for each stage in motor development may not be the same for every infant, the steps in the process follow the same basic pattern. Developmental norms or milestones refer to the average age when children typically achieve particular skills associated with development. In terms of motor development the early norms include learning to lift the head, rolling over, sitting up unassisted, crawling, and ultimately walking. The ability to walk is typically achieved between the ages of ten and fifteen months. Cross-cultural research indicates that, although motor development is related to maturation (nature), the environment (nurture) also influences how soon babies learn to walk or master other motor skills. Considerable amounts of variation among different cultures exist in terms of the age that infants first begin walking, and the variation is generally believed to be due to different parenting methods. Cultures that provide greater opportunities for movement and exploration tend to have infants who achieve developmental milestones for motor movement earlier than cultures that restrict movement.

STUDY TIP

Maturation focuses on the biological growth processes that enable change in behavior. These changes are connected to an individual's genetic blueprint, meaning that they are relatively uninfluenced by experience. This definition of maturation supports the *nature* side of the nature versus nurture controversy regarding developmental influences.

Physical Development During Adolesence

The developmental stage of **adolescence** begins with the onset of puberty and spans the teen years, typically starting at around the age of fourteen for boys and the age of twelve for girls. **Puberty** is defined as the period of development when individuals reach sexual maturity and have the ability to reproduce. The precise beginning of puberty is hard to determine, but many researchers have defined the start of puberty for girls as coinciding with the first menstrual period, called **menarche**. Pinpointing the start of puberty for boys is even more difficult, though some researchers claim that it begins with the first ejaculation. One of the earliest signs of physical changes associated with adolescence is the growth spurt. Increases in height coincide with increases in weight and changes in body proportions. The onset of puberty is marked by the development of primary and secondary sexual characteristics. **Primary sexual characteristics** are traits directly related to reproduction, including the reproductive organs and external genitalia that develop during puberty, allowing individuals to become capable of producing viable sperm or eggs. **Secondary sex characteristics** have no effect on physical reproduction, but they also develop during puberty. Secondary sex characteristics in males include the lowering of the voice and the appearance of facial, chest, and pubic hair. Secondary sex characteristics in females include the enlargement of the breasts and the appearance of armpit and pubic hair. The timing of puberty, like other aspects of physical development, is related to both biological maturation (nature) and environmental influences (nurture). Evidence for the biological influences on the timing of puberty comes from both twin and family studies. Environmental influences on puberty include nutrition and access to health care, and consequently adolescents in wealthier nations reach puberty earlier than those from poorer countries. The timing of puberty for individual adolescents can have important social and emotional effects and differs for the two genders. In general, early maturation is associated with more positive consequences for males than for females.

Physical Development During Adulthood

The developmental period of adulthood encompasses the long period of the lifespan beginning between ages eighteen and twenty-one and can be divided into three stages—early, middle, and late adulthood. Individuals are at the peak of their physical development, such as reaction time, speed, and strength, during early adulthood. Middle adulthood, however, is marked by a gradual physical decline. The senses of hearing, visual acuity, and smell begin to become less sensitive and reaction time decreases. During middle adulthood women will experience **menopause** or the period when a woman no longer has the ability to reproduce and is marked by the end of the menstrual cycle. Men do not have a comparable experience; however, their sperm count does decline with age. Late adulthood involves a more rapid physical decline, which can be seen in lengthened reaction times and reduced motor control. Significant health concerns often emerge in late adulthood, for example, chronic illnesses such as heart disease and cancer, which affect older adults in greater numbers. Late adulthood may also be characterized by dementia and Alzheimer's disease. **Alzheimer's disease** is an irreversible neurological brain disorder involving the deterioration of neurons producing acetylcholine. Symptoms of Alzheimer's disease include increasing deterioration of memory, cognitive, language, and physical abilities. Evidence indicates that the physical and cognitive declines associated with aging can be reduced or slowed by environmental factors. Individuals that remain physically and mentally active and eat a healthy diet are better able to slow the signs of aging.

Life expectancy has increased within the last several decades due to technological and medical advances resulting from research. Considering that individuals are living longer lives, developmental psychologists are becoming important contributors to the interdisciplinary field of **gerontology,** the scientific study of late adulthood and the aging process. A major contributor to the field of gerontology, psychiatrist **Elizabeth Kübler Ross**, studied the psychosocial reactions of individuals who were terminally ill. The series of five stages that characterize the reactions of an individual facing death outlined by Kübler Ross are denial, anger, bargaining, depression, and acceptance. These five stages are regarded as coping methods that an individual utilizes for varying amounts of time. The theory of the five stages of dying continues to receive attention in the popular press, but further research has not provided evidence to support this theory. The work of Elizabeth Kübler Ross is significant because it focused the attention of psychologists and others on researching methods to help individuals and their families cope with life-ending illnesses.

Cognitive Development

In addition to examining physical development, psychologists are also interested in how thinking and intellectual abilities grow, change, and decline across the lifespan. Specifically, developmental psychologists examine differences in learning, problem solving, memory, and comprehension that are affected by the biological processes of maturation and aging, as well as cultural and environmental influences.

Cognitive Developing During Childhood

Cognitive development continues throughout the lifespan and begins as the infant's brain enters a period of rapid growth. While most of the brain cells an individual will ever have are present at birth, the synapses and neural networks grow considerably during this period. In addition, the frontal lobes and association areas are starting to expand so that the processes of language, memory, reasoning, problem solving, and creativity can develop. **Jean Piaget**, a Swiss psychologist and major theorist associated with cognitive development, established an influential theory concerning how thinking develops in children. Piaget believed that the cognitive processes of children were dramatically different from those of adults and that a series of stages led to the acquisition of adult intellectual abilities. During each of the stages there is a distinct change in how children approach problems and what they are capable of achieving. Piaget believed that children advance cognitively through an active exploration of their world, resulting in the development and expansion of schemas. A **schema** is a mental framework that organizes past experiences in order to make faster or more accurate perceptions. According to Piaget, the two processes of assimilation and accommodation are involved in creating and expanding schemas in order to guide cognitive development throughout life. **Assimilation** is the process of trying to fit new information into existing schemas. When we encounter new information or stimuli, we attempt to organize our experience by placing it into an existing category or schema that we already understand. **Accommodation** is the process of changing schemas to incorporate this new information. Sometimes a new experience or event does not fit accurately into any existing schema, and it is necessary to create a new category.

STUDY TIP

Be able to discriminate between assimilation and accommodation. For example, three-year-old Savannah hears a motorcycle for the first time. Savannah may call the loud noise a vacuum when she tries to *assimilate* this new experience into an existing schema. After being told the loud noise is a motorcycle by her mother, Savannah will *accommodate* her schema for loud noises to include both vacuums and motorcycles.

Piaget's Cognitive Development

Jean Piaget described cognitive development in terms of four distinct stages that follow a fixed order from birth to adolescence. Furthermore, he hypothesized that movement from one stage to another is dependent on both biological maturation and exposure to experiences with the environment. The first stage, **sensorimotor**, occurs during infancy and lasts until approximately the age of two. Infants in this stage are preoccupied with experiencing their world by placing objects in their mouth and also by investigating their surroundings through both accidental and purposeful movements. These actions help infants develop cognitively by coordinating information received from the senses and through physical actions to learn about their world and expand their schemas. During the sensorimotor stage at approximately nine months of age, infants develop **object permanence**, or the awareness that items (objects) continue to exist even when they cannot be seen. If a child younger than nine months of age is given a toy that is then covered up with a towel, they will not search for it because they have not yet learned that objects that are out of sight continue to exist. If this same test is repeated later in the sensorimotor stage, the child will remove the towel to look for the missing toy, demonstrating mastery of object permanence.

STUDY TIP

Object permanence appears around nine months, half-way through Piaget's sensorimotor stage of cognitive development.

The second stage of cognitive development, the preoperational stage, begins at approximately age two and lasts until about age seven. During the **preoperational stage** children begin to explore their environment by using symbolic but pre-logical thought and not merely sensory and motor experiences. This stage involves the use of representational thought and symbols, for example, the use of words for classifying and naming objects. Preoperational children make rapid advancements in language and engage in pretend play. Although preoperational children are beginning to use logic and reason, their thought processes are fragmented, rigid, and based wholly on appearance. Additionally, Piaget explained that the thought processes during this period are egocentric. **Egocentrism** involves having difficulty seeing how the world looks from the perspective of others. For instance, egocentrism is displayed when three-year-old Anthony proudly displays his drawing and does not understand why others cannot tell that it is a picture of him and his dog. Anthony thinks that, because he knows what the picture represents, others must also be able to tell what the drawing depicts.

STUDY TIP

Around the age of four, children develop a *theory of mind* and are able to understand the thoughts and intentions of others and predict their behavior. It has been theorized that autism, a developmental disorder marked by impaired social communication, is related to an impaired theory of mind. Autistic children have a difficult time understanding what others are thinking and feeling.

Conservation is the understanding that the mass, volume, weight, and quantity of an object(s) does not change, even though the appearance has been altered in some way. Preoperational children *cannot* conserve. Three-year-old Lily asks for more cookies, but, after her father breaks her cookie into three pieces, she is happy because she now believes she has more. Lily has not mastered the concept of conservation of mass. In another example, Benjamin's brother pours his juice into a tall, narrow glass, and Benjamin now believes he has more juice than when it was in a short, wide glass. Benjamin, who is in the preoperational stage, has not mastered conservation of liquid.

Centration is the error in thinking that contributes to the inability of preoperational children to conserve and involves focusing (centering) on just one feature of a problem, while ignoring other important aspects of the problem. Benjamin was unable to be successful in the conservation of liquid because he focused on only the level of the juice in the glass. Because the level of the juice was higher in the tall, narrow glass, he perceived it as containing more juice. In addition, preoperational children often exhibit **animism,** or the belief that all objects are living and capable of actions and emotions. For example, two-year-old Vince demonstrates animism when he complains to his parents that the slide was bad and made him fall down. Three-year-old Brad demonstrates animism by consoling and petting the bushes after his father has trimmed them because he believes that they are in pain.

Piaget believed children from the ages of approximately seven until eleven were in the **concrete operational stage** characterized by the emergence of logical thought about concrete or tangible ideas. Logical thinking at this stage is confined to tangible objects that are immediately present. Elementary-school-age children are capable of more sophisticated use of symbols than preoperational children—for example, arithmetic and geography. Children in the concrete operational stage have mastered conservation, reversibility, and classification. **Reversibility** is the cognitive ability to perform actions and mentally undo or reverse them. **Classification** is the ability to sort objects by a variety of common attributes. Although a preoperational child would be capable of sorting marbles by size, the concrete operational child would be able to sort them according to numerous categories such as size, color, weight, and value.

STUDY TIP

Children in Piaget's concrete operational stage of cognitive development *can* conserve.

The final stage in Piaget's cognitive development theory, **formal operational**, begins during adolescence, around the age of twelve, when children become capable of formal operations, or the ability to think abstractly, and apply logical rules to envision objects and ideas that they have never seen. This new capability to formulate and test hypotheses goes beyond appearances to deal with the truth or falsity of abstract propositions. Thirteen-year-old George is now able to understand algebra problems that require the ability to think about numbers that cannot be seen and that change from one problem to the next. For example, *x* may equal 7 in one situation and 9 in another. Fourteen-year-old Percy is now capable of discussing theoretical concepts such as truth, freedom, and love. Furthermore, individuals within the formal operational stage are able to evaluate the potential consequences of their actions and recognize or imagine ideal circumstances.

STUDY TIP

Be able to identify significant characteristics in each stage of Piaget's theory of cognitive development and describe how children's thinking (their ability to solve problems) changes in predictable ways as they get older. See Table 11.3.

Table 11.3. Piaget's Four Stages of Cognitive Development

Stage	Significant Characteristics
Sensorimotor (0 to 2 years)	• Learning develops through sensory and motor experiences. • Achievement of object permanence.
Preoperational (2 to 7 years)	• Learning develops through symbolic thought, language, and pretend play. • Lack the ability to conserve. • Thought demonstrates egocentrism, centration, animism, and irreversibility.
Concrete Operational (7 to 11 years)	• Learning develops through the use of logical thought about concrete concepts that are tangible or physically present. • Acquire the skills of conservation, reversibility, and classification.
Formal Operational (12+ years)	• Learning develops through the use of logical reasoning to examine abstract theoretical concepts.

Piaget is considered one of the greatest child psychologists of the twentieth century, and his theories of cognitive development in children have had enormous influence in a variety of fields and education in particular. Cross-cultural studies have supported the idea that the four general stages occur in the same order for all children. However, modern research finds that the transitions between stages are not as distinct as Piaget hypothesized. Improved methods for testing cognitive abilities in very young children have revealed that some children achieve specific cognitive milestones much earlier than he anticipated. Overall Piaget's broad descriptions of how thinking develops in children have withstood the test of scientific scrutiny over time, but the specific onset of various cognitive skills varies across cultures.

Vygotsky's Sociocultural Development

The theory of cognitive development presented by Piaget stated that children develop intellectually as a result of both biological maturation and active interaction with their environment in order to make sense of the world. On the other hand, Russian child psychologist **Lev Vygotsky** presented a **sociocultural theory** of cognitive development that emphasized the combined influences of language, culture, and interactions with others, such as parents, teachers, and older peers. According to Vygotsky, a gap called the **zone of proximal development** existed between what children were capable of learning and doing without assistance, and what they could accomplish with the extra help provided by others. The concept of **scaffolding**, or giving just enough assistance to the learner in order for them to understand, is related to the zone of proximal development because the teacher continually adjusts how much support is needed as learning progresses. Vygotsky believed that children need to be given the opportunity to work with others who have more sophisticated thinking in order to advance cognitively. Importantly, Vygotsky emphasized the role of language, both in terms of communicating with others and self-talk, in the development of cognitive skills. While Piaget emphasized that the self-talk of preoperational children was egocentric and indicative of cognitive immaturity, Vygotsky believed that private speech was critical to helping children organize, guide, and regulate their actions. As children mature, private speech becomes **internalized speech** that individuals rely on to learn about their world.

STUDY TIP

Be able to recognize differences between the two main cognitive developmental theories. See Table 11.4.

Table 11.4. Comparison of Piaget and Vygotsky's Theories of Cognitive Development

Piaget	Vygotsky
Stage theory or discontinuity	Gradual change or continuity.
Cognitive development is influenced by the child being an active explorer that investigates the world.	Cognitive development is influenced by the social world that interacts with the child.
Egocentric speech suggests that the child is self-centered.	Private speech suggests that the child is organizing and guiding their actions.
Development precedes learning.	Learning precedes development.

Cognitive Development During Adolescence

Throughout childhood the brain continues to grow and develop new connections, but during puberty excess or idle connections are selectively pruned. Adolescence is a period of time marked by the development of the frontal lobe. Because the frontal lobe, which is central to planning, judgment, and impulse control does not mature until the mid-twenties, adolescents are more likely to engage in risky behavior.

Developmental psychologist David Elkind examined specific aspects of cognitive development within the social context among adolescents. Young adolescents, according to Elkind, experience what he called **adolescent egocentrism,** or the tendency of teenagers to view the world only from their own perspective. The imaginary audience and personal fable, two specific kinds of social thinking unique to this age group, are both examples of adolescent egocentrism. The tendency of adolescents to believe that other people are watching their every move and talking about them more than is actually happening is called the **imaginary audience**. The concept of an imaginary audience can lead to stress as adolescents attempt to cope with what they imagine others are thinking or saying about them when they are not around. Furthermore, adolescents may develop a sense that they are completely unique and invincible in what is called the **personal fable**. The sense of invincibility associated with the personal fable places adolescents at risk for engaging in dangerous behaviors, such as driving too fast, using drugs or alcohol, or engaging in criminal activities. Due to the personal fable, adolescents may take chances and make dangerous choices because they believe that harmful consequences will not happen to them, only to someone else.

Cognitive Development During Adulthood

Cognitive changes continue during adulthood, but specific differences exist between the abilities of individuals in early, middle, and late adulthood. During early adulthood cognitive abilities, namely vocabulary expansion, planning, reasoning, and memory, are improved and applied to achieving long-term goals. Overall, cognitive abilities and achievement remain high throughout middle adulthood. During late adulthood beginning after approximately age sixty, there may be a slight decline in the speed of processing and capacity of memory storage. Generally, older adults show a more noticeable decrease in problem solving that involves working memory than they do on tasks related to the use of long-term memory. In addition, individuals in late adulthood have a more difficult time on tests requiring the recall of episodic memories for specific events, than those related to the recall of semantic of factual knowledge. It is important to remember that the overall decline in cognitive ability is moderate and does not apply to all individuals. Late adulthood is further associated with changes in specific intellectual abilities in relationship to types of intelligence. **Crystallized intelligence,** or acquired knowledge of vocabulary, verbal skills, cultural knowledge, and factual information, remains the same or increases throughout adulthood. On the other hand, **fluid intelligence**, which involves the rapid processing of information and memory span needed to solve new types of problems, decreases in late adulthood. Environmental factors can help minimize the effects of aging on cognitive abilities. The best evidence for reducing age-related cognitive decline suggests maintaining a regular fitness program and participating in intellectually demanding activities such as reading, working, educational classes, and solving crossword puzzles.

STUDY TIP

Be able to differentiate between crystallized and fluid intelligence and describe how aging impacts these abilities. Crystallized intelligence remains stable or increases with age, while fluid intelligence decreases with age.

Social Development

In addition to examining physical and cognitive development, psychologists are also interested in how social relationships grow, and change across the lifespan. Specifically, developmental psychologists examine the biological factors of temperament and the environmental factors of parenting styles that affect the development of attachments across the lifespan.

Social Development During Childhood

Attachment is the long-lasting emotional bond that develops between the infant and caregiver, which provides the child with a sense of security and comfort. Infants form an attachment with their primary caregiver, usually their mother, by the age of six to ten months. The formation of this attachment takes time, but is clearly visible by the distress caused when the caregiver leaves, in what is known as **separation anxiety**. The close emotional bond for the caregiver is further evidenced by stranger anxiety, which develops as the infant begins to differentiate his or her primary caregiver from others. **Stranger anxiety** is the stress and fear experienced when infants or small children are around individuals who are unfamiliar to them; it typically appears around the age of eight months and lasts until approximately the age of two. A variety of factors influence how attachments develop and are expressed. The type of attachment an infant develops with a caregiver is influenced by both temperament (nature) and parenting styles (nurture).

Temperament

In developmental psychology, the term **temperament** refers to the biologically influenced activity level, behaviors, and emotional responses typically demonstrated by individuals. These differences in temperament are observable in infants from the time of birth.

Alexander Thomas and Stella Chess identified three general types of temperament—easy, difficult, and slow-to-warm-up—based on longitudinal research. *Easy* babies can be described as children that consistently display positive emotions, are able to adjust to changing circumstances, and establish regular patterns for eating and sleeping. Conversely, *difficult* babies demonstrate negative emotions more frequently, have trouble with changes in their environment, and do not have regular eating and sleeping routines. *Slow-to-warm-up* babies are the least active, experience some negative emotions, and adjust to changes slowly. Finally, some infants display a temperament that is a combination of the three main types. Research suggests that temperament has a biological basis and that it is likely to remain consistent over time, but questions remain about when temperament is stable enough to predict adult personality traits. While it may be true that temperament is mainly determined by biology, this does not mean that the environment does not influence temperament, because nature and nurture both contribute to enduring emotional and behavioral patterns.

Imprinting

Konrad Lorenz studied the formation of attachments in newborn baby chicks. Interestingly, Lorenz discovered that baby chicks would form an attachment with him as their primary caregiver if he was the first moving stimulus they saw. **Imprinting** is a phenomenon that occurs in some birds; they are biologically programmed to form an attachment to and follow the first moving object they see. This inborn tendency to form a bond during a critical period is necessary for small vulnerable animals to survive. A **critical period** is a fixed time period very early in life when particular events result in long-lasting effects on behavior. While human infants do not have a critical period for attachment, a strong bond with the caregiver is considered necessary for normal development. Because infants are not capable of physically following their mother through imprinting, they gain their caregivers' attention through other methods, such as crying, making noises, and facial expressions. These behaviors are tools for survival as well because they result in gaining the attention of their caregivers to let them know when they need something or are in danger.

Contact Comfort

During the first year of life, as infants develop an attachment to their caregivers, the factor of contact comfort plays a critical role in bonding. **Contact comfort** is the positive emotions that result when the baby has close physical contact with the caregiver. In a series of famous experiments psychologist **Harry Harlow** raised baby rhesus monkeys in cages with no live mother, only two artificial ones. One artificial mother was made of wire and held a bottle for the monkey to feed from, and the other artificial mother was covered in a soft fuzzy cloth. Overwhelmingly, the baby monkeys preferred the cloth mother to the wire mother, evidenced by the fact that they spent most of their day on the cloth mother. Furthermore, the monkeys would run to the cloth mother and not the wire mother if they were frightened in order to alleviate their anxiety and build their confidence. Monkeys were not forming attachments solely on the basis of a biological need for food, as behaviorists and others at the time believed, because they also craved the softness and warmth of contact comfort when making an attachment. Harlow's research is important because it demonstrated scientifically that attachments between infants and caregivers are impacted by the need for contact comfort as well as nourishment and other basic needs. The research conducted by Harlow is controversial because the animals in the studies suffered negative long-term effects as a result of being raised in isolation; this included aggression and withdrawal. Harlow's monkeys became seriously disturbed and could not successfully interact with other normal monkeys in later life. Similar negative long-term effects have been seen when human infants are deprived of attachment and contact comfort in cases of severe abuse.

Attachment Types

Mary Ainsworth and colleagues used the Strange Situation to investigate different types of attachment. The **Strange-Situation** experiment involves a series of orchestrated scenarios involving a baby, a caregiver, and a stranger designed to assess the type of attachment bond present between the child and caregiver. In the Strange Situation, the first step involves taking the mother and baby into a strange room and allowing the baby to explore. Second, a stranger enters the room and the mom leaves and the baby's reactions are noted. Finally the mother returns and the responses of the baby to his or her mother are observed. Results from the Strange-Situation experiment found four main types of attachment noted in Table 11.5.

Table 11.5. Ainsworth's Four Types of Attachment

Attachment	Mother Is Present	Mother Leaves	Mother Returns
Secure	The child uses the mother as a secure base to explore the environment and interact with strangers.	The child is visibly upset when the mother leaves.	The child seeks contact with the mother when she returns.
Insecure **Anxious-Avoidant**	The child seeks little contact with the mother and is less likely to explore the environment.	The child shows little emotion when the mother leaves.	The child avoids or ignores the mother when she returns.
Insecure **Anxious-Resistant**	The child is unsure of whether to explore when the mother is present.	The child is upset when the mother leaves.	The child seems angry toward the mother when she returns and resists being comforted.
Insecure **Disorganized**	The child is inconsistent about exploring the environment when the mother is present and demonstrates confused or contradictory behaviors.	The child does not show consistent behavior when the mother leaves.	The child does not show consistent behavior when the mother returns and is generally anxious and confused.

Results from the Strange-Situation experiments reveal that infants demonstrate their attachment to their mother by exploring in her presence, usually objecting when she leaves and seeking contact when she returns. The more sensitive and responsive the mother is to the child, the more securely attached the child will become. However, the development of attachment is also influenced by the temperament of the child, the stability of the family environment, and culture. Children who develop secure attachments tend to show greater resilience, self-control, and curiosity when they become preschoolers. Critics argue that the Strange-Situation experiment is flawed because of the correlational nature of the results and the fact that children may behave differently in laboratory experiments than in real life. An equally important criticism is that the experiment may be subject to cultural bias because certain types of insecure attachment are more frequent in particular cultures, due to differences in parenting styles. Overall, regardless of culture, the most prevalent type of attachment style among children is secure.

Parenting Styles

Psychologists and parents alike are interested in discovering the best methods for assisting children in developing into kind, responsible, independent, and self-confident individuals. Developmental psychologist **Diana Baumrind**'s research on parenting styles has been especially influential. The original research described three different types of parenting styles—authoritarian, permissive, and authoritative. Each style differs in terms of discipline, expectations, communication levels, and emotional warmth. Overall, the authoritative parenting style has been found to be the most strongly correlated to positive self-esteem and high levels of self-reliance.

However, parenting is only part of the reason children develop the way they do, because genetics, peer groups, social influence, and experience also contribute to personality. In fact, individuals raised in the same home by the same parents may develop very differently, due to these other factors. The various components of each of the parenting styles are outlined in Table 11.6.

Table 11.6.   Baumrind's Three Parenting Styles

Parenting Style	Parent and Child Relationship
Authoritarian	The parent demands obedience and controls the child's behavior through punishment. There is limited communication between the parent and child. This restrictive parenting style offers the child limited love and warmth.
Permissive	The parent provides few expectations and rules and allows the child to make his or her own decisions. There are high levels of communication as well as warmth and love.
Authoritative	The parent establishes clear limits and provides explanations for consequences. There is open communication between the parent and child, but the parent makes the ultimate decision. This collaborative parenting style offers the child love and warmth.

Social Development During Adolescence

During adolescence, social and emotional development involves expanding the self-concept, building an identity, pursuing autonomy, and developing relationships. Adolescents refine their self-concept, making it more accurate through self-evaluation and the incorporation of the opinions of others. A major aspect of this period is the development of an identity illustrated in James Marcia's work expanding on Erikson's adolescent stage of identity versus role confusion. An individual's **identity** is actually a collection of many separate components that include career, culture, gender, political, religious, personality, and interests that will shape adult behavior. Marcia proposed that adolescents occupy one or more of four statuses (states) at least temporarily as they work to develop various aspects of their identities. Each of the four statuses results from a combination of the adolescent's degree of commitment and on whether or not exploration of an identity is taking place (crisis). Each of the four statuses is described in Table 11.7.

Table 11.7.   Marcia's Four Identity Statuses

Identity Status	Description
Identity Diffusion	The adolescent has *not committed* to an identity and is *not exploring* possible identities.
Identity Foreclosure	The adolescent has *committed* to an identity and is *no longer exploring* possible identities. Often an identity provided by a family member or significant other is blindly accepted.

(continued)

Table 11.7. (*continued*)

Identity Status	Description
Identity Moratorium	The adolescent has *not committed* to an identity but is *actively exploring* possible identities.
Identity Achievement	The adolescent has *committed* to an identity and continues to *explore* to refine their identity. Identity achievement is correlated with the positive benefits of high self-esteem, achievement motivation, and emotional stability.

The developmental period just prior to adulthood also involves significant changes as adolescents seek more autonomy, often resulting in increased family conflicts. Traditionally it was assumed that relationships with parents became more detached during adolescence, but new studies suggest that relationships with parents continue to be important and provide a source of support during the transition into adulthood. Although some parent–adolescent relationships are stormy, most conflict is moderate and serves to assist with the process of preparing for independence. Adolescents from families with a high degree of long-lasting and intense conflict have a greater risk for delinquency, failure to graduate, and moving out before they are prepared to support themselves. As adolescents become less dependent on their parents and more involved with their peers, they explore a variety of possible identities. During this period of identity exploration, adolescents experiment with changes in their appearance and beliefs by trying different styles and investigating possible political, religious, or career paths.

Social Development During Adulthood

The period of adulthood is dominated by concerns regarding marriage, relationships, children, family, and work. Socially, during early adulthood, individuals focus on the development of meaningful relationships, as well as entering into careers. The average age of marriage is steadily climbing because young adults are delaying marriage in order to pursue personal and career goals. Social development in middle adulthood involves working to establish an active role in society through increased involvement in family and career goals in order to establish feelings of accomplishment or generativity. Some middle aged individuals experience a lack of fulfillment that results in stress and upheaval, called a *midlife crisis,* but this is not true for most adults and many people regard this time of life as particularly rewarding. The changes occurring during middle adulthood are now more accurately referred to by developmental psychologists as a *midlife transition*, because although new challenges emerge, the adult finds their career has become more rewarding and, because children have left the home, they have more time to pursue personal interests. As individuals enter the period of late adulthood, a major aspect of social development involves reflecting on their life experiences, which can result in feelings of either fulfillment or disappointment. Retirement is a major social event during this period and results in changes to both self-concept and lifestyle as individuals look for additional ways to find fulfillment as careers come to an end.

Erikson's Psychosocial Development

Erik Erikson, a neo-Freudian, created an influential psychosocial stage theory that explains how individuals develop through social interaction with others across the lifespan. Unlike Freud, Erikson believed that development continued throughout life rather than ending at about age six or seven. Erikson divides his theory of psychosocial development into eight stages, ranging from birth to old age. Each stage involves a **psychosocial crisis,** or turning point, that can result in either a positive or negative outcome. The crisis requires the individual to cope with new demands in the environment and successful development depends on balancing two alternatives, one adaptive and one maladaptive. Despite the fact that no crisis is ever completely resolved, individuals must deal with each one effectively in order to proceed to the next stage in development. If an individual does not resolve a crisis successfully, that individual will become "stuck" in that crisis and may develop a psychopathology related to that stage of development.

STUDY TIP

Be able to recognize which crisis you are experiencing in regards to Erikson's psychosocial development and how the other stages apply to your lifespan. The first four stages are from your past. Identity versus role confusion is your present crisis that occurs during adolescence. The final three stages of psychosocial development are your future. See Table 11.8.

Table 11.8.   Erikson's Eight Stages of Psychosocial Development

Stage (Age)	Crisis	Explanation of Crisis	Resolution of Crisis
Infant Birth to 1 year	**Trust vs. Mistrust**	Developing a sense that the world is supportive and safe	Infants who are nurtured and loved develop a sense of security and basic optimism (trust) about others. Infants whose needs are not met reliably will be suspicious of others (mistrust), timid, and withdrawn.
Toddler 1 to 3 years	**Autonomy vs. Shame and Doubt**	Developing a sense of control and responsibility by caring for oneself	Toddlers provided with opportunities to demonstrate control over their world develop a sense of independence (autonomy) and become self-assured. Parents should encourage autonomy by promoting opportunities for toddlers to explore their surroundings within safe boundaries. Toddlers who fail to have success or are restricted by overprotective parents doubt their abilities, experience feelings of humiliation (shame), and act impulsively.
Preschool 4 to 6 years	**Initiative vs. Guilt**	Developing a sense that one is capable of purposeful behavior	Preschool children who are exposed to a larger social world and engage in planning activities (initiative) and fantasy play feel capable. If the child is supported in his or her attempts to initiate activities, they develop confidence in their ability to make decisions. Preschool children who are criticized or prevented by overprotective parents from attempting to take responsibility develop a sense of anxiousness and fear (guilt).
Elementary School 7 to 12 years	**Industry vs. Inferiority**	Developing critical social and academic skills	School-age children who master the knowledge and social skills required for success develop a sense of themselves as competent (industry), which results in high self-esteem. School-age children who have problems learning or mastering social skills may develop a sense of inadequacy and disappointment (inferiority), which results in low self-esteem.

(continued)

Table 11.8. (*continued*)

Stage (Age)	Crisis	Explanation of Crisis	Resolution of Crisis
Adolescence 13 to 19 years	**Identity vs. Role Confusion**	Achieving a sense of self and making a successful transition to adulthood	Adolescents who are able to determine who they are and their individual strengths and weaknesses develop a strong sense of self (identity). Determining a strong identity provides a solid basis for future development. Adolescents who are unable to develop a personal identity develop a weak sense of self and are confused about how they fit into the world (role confusion).
Young Adulthood 20 to 40 years	**Intimacy vs. Isolation**	Developing relationships based on love and friendship	Young adults who develop strong, healthy relationships that are open and warm (intimacy) resolve this crisis successfully. Young adults who are unable to establish close, loving relationships by opening up to others experience loneliness (isolation).
Middle Adulthood 40 to 60 years	**Generativity vs. Stagnation**	Finding fulfillment and providing guidance for future generations	Middle-aged adults who take an active role in society through their family or career establish feelings of usefulness and accomplishment (generativity). Individuals who successfully resolve this crisis direct their attention toward assisting the next generation. Middle-aged adults who do not develop an investment or connection to the world and are self-absorbed experience frustration and depression (stagnation) because they have not made a difference for future generations.
Late Adulthood 60+ years	**Integrity vs. Despair**	Reflection and evaluation on whether or not life was meaningful and avoiding regrets	Late adult individuals who reflect back on their life experiences and evaluate them favorably believe that life was successful and meaningful (integrity). Late adult individuals who look back at their life experiences and are dissatisfied because of regrets and missed opportunities experience anger or depression (despair) because they believe that their life was meaningless, wasted, or unsuccessful.

Moral Development

How do children decide right from wrong? **Moral development** involves changes in the understanding and interpretation of how the concepts of justice, conscience, and ethics apply to their own behavior and the actions of others. Piaget investigated how children develop moral reasoning by observing and questioning children as they played games with each other. As a result of these observations, he determined that morality, like cognition, develops in a series of stages. According to Piaget, moral reasoning progresses as cognitive abilities become more sophisticated and children learn to understand the point of view of others. Initially young children are very rigid and expect that all rule infractions will be followed by a consequence, but as they develop cognitively, children realize that rules are formed by mutual agreement among individuals and may be altered under specific circumstances, which he called *moral relativity*.

Kohlberg's Moral Development

Lawrence Kohlberg extended the research on moral development started by Piaget by creating a more comprehensive theoretical stage theory. Kohlberg believed that morality is a decision-making process and not a fixed set of behaviors, and investigated how this process develops. Data for Kohlberg's theory was gathered by presenting dilemmas or problems to children, adolescents, and adults and asking participants what the individual in the dilemma should do and why. Kohlberg's famous scenario, known as the Heinz dilemma, was about a man who stole a drug that he was unable to afford in order to save the life of his wife. The question posed to the subject was whether or not Mr. Heinz should have stolen the drug and why. Kohlberg was not interested if participants agreed or disagreed with the behavior of Mr. Heinz, but the reasoning for their judgments. As a result of evaluating the responses of participants to various dilemmas, Kohlberg discovered three levels of moral reasoning, each of which was divided into two stages.

The **preconventional level** typical of young children focuses on external consequences as the source for determining what is moral. Preconventional morality is based on whether particular behaviors result in punishment or reward, and coincides with Piaget's preoperational stage of cognitive development. During stage one (punishment) of the preconventional level, children determine what is moral based on what is punished and might suggest that Mr. Heinz should steal the drug so that he will not get yelled at by his wife or that he should not steal the drug because he would go to jail. In stage two (reward) of the preconventional level, actions that are in the person's best interest or that are likely to result in a reward are considered moral. A child in stage two might suggest that Mr. Heinz should steal the drug in order for him to be happy and save his wife. At the preconventional level, children decide if a particular behavior is moral or not based on its consequences or whether it is punished or rewarded.

The **conventional level** focuses on social rules and develops as individuals reach Piaget's concrete operational stage of cognitive development. Decisions about what is right and wrong are based on approval from others such as parents, teachers, and peers or following the laws and rules set forth by society. Rules at the conventional level are rigid and inflexible. In stage three (social approval) of the conventional level, individuals base moral decisions on what others will approve of or their desire to conform. A typical response to the Heinz dilemma at stage three might be that Mr. Heinz's family will think badly of him if he does not steal the drug to save his wife. In stage four (law and order) individuals base their decisions on strictly following the rules, and so Mr. Heinz should not steal the drug because it is against the law or he should steal the drug because it is his duty to care for his family. Being moral at the conventional level involves gaining approval and conforming to the rules and norms of society.

The third and highest level of morality in Kohlberg's theory is the **postconventional** level. At this level individuals develop and evaluate their own moral standards. They can see beyond the literal interpretation of rules and laws and distinguish between good and bad laws. This level reflects individual principles of conscience and typically begins in adolescence when individuals reach Piaget's formal operational stage of cognitive development. In stage five (social contract) of the postconventional level, individuals reason that although Mr. Heinz broke the law, his behavior was moral because he saved his wife's life and the law should be changed to allow for this type of exception. Universal ethics, which trump the rules of society, are expressed in stage six (universal ethics) and responses to the Heinz dilemma might indicate that the life of any person is worth any potential risks. Being moral at the postconventional level involves living up to individual moral principles and the willingness to violate laws that go against these beliefs.

The development of morality is part of the process of **socialization,** or learning behavior, which is appropriate and inappropriate for a particular culture. In addition, moral development is related to cognitive development. The child cannot develop a moral system until certain intellectual abilities have developed, such as the ability to imagine the results of their actions and their effect on others. Kohlberg believed that many people never get past the early stages of moral development and that very few individuals actually reach the highest stage of moral development. In Kohlberg's own studies, only about 10 percent of twenty-four-year-olds consistently operated at the postconventional level. Much of Kohlberg's theory of moral development has been supported by subsequent research and it has generally been established that individuals do progress through stages that coincide with cognitive advances. Although Kohlberg's stages appear to be universal, based on cross-cultural studies, the highest stages are not as prevalent in all cultures, suggesting a potential bias.

Gilligan's Moral Devleopment

Kohlberg's theory has been criticized for being biased against women, especially by **Carol Gilligan**. Through her research Gilligan determined that women consistently scored lower than men when evaluated based on Kohlberg's theory, but she did not believe that they were really less moral. Gilligan found that the lower scores on Kohlberg's scale resulted from the expected roles of women in society that focused on caring for others and the fact that women place greater value on maintaining relationships. The highest level of morality for women according to Gilligan is based on compassion and concern for others, which she believed contrasted with the male emphasis on individual rights and justice. It is generally believed that men and women both use combinations of compassion and care as well as justice and individual rights when making moral decisions. The most important criticism of moral development theory for both Kohlberg and Gilligan involves the fact that ultimately what individuals say they would do in a moral hypothetical and what they actually do in a real-world situation may not be consistent.

Developmental Stage Theories

Another controversy in developmental theory in addition to nature versus nurture is the debate regarding whether development is continuous or discontinuous. In other words, does development occur gradually or in a series of distinct stages? Continuous development involves gradual changes that result as each new accomplishment builds on previous gains. An example of continuous development would be the physical maturation associated with puberty that involves numerous gradual changes over a period of a few years. Conversely, discontinuous development involves changes occurring in distinct stages marked by significant differences. An example of discontinuous development is demonstrated by the distinct changes proposed by Piaget's theory of cognitive development, such as when a child becomes capable of logical thought and conservation, they progress to the next stage. A comparison of the developmental stage theorists (including Freud, whose psychoanalytic theory is presented in the next section) are outlined in Table 11.9.

Table 11.9. Comparison of Developmental Stage Theorists

Freud	Erikson	Piaget	Kohlberg
Oral	Trust vs. Mistrust	Sensorimotor	Preconventional
Anal	Autonomy vs. Shame and Doubt	Preoperational	Preconventional
Phallic	Initiative vs. Guilt	Preoperational	Preconventional
Latency	Competence vs. Inferiority	Concrete Operational	Conventional
Genital	Identity vs. Role Confusion Intimacy vs. Isolation Generativity vs. Stagnation Integrity vs. Despair	Formal Operational	Post conventional

Freud's Psychosexual Development

Freud's psychoanalytic theory stresses unconscious sexual and aggressive drives, and the importance of early childhood experiences as the driving forces in development. Changes in patterns of behavior and personality according to Freud happen as individuals pass through a series of five psychosexual stages during which the focus of a person's sexual energy or **libido** moves to a different area of the body seeking release. At each stage individuals are confronted with a conflict between their need to find a release for their sexual energy and the demands of society. According to Freud, failure to resolve any of the conflicts associated with the stages results in **fixation** or concerns that remain with the individual, unconsciously resulting in problems during adulthood. Fixations can be the result of either a person's needs being ignored or overindulged during a particular stage. The five stages of psychosexual development identified by Freud as universal and sequential are the oral, anal, phallic, latency, and genital stages. According to Freud, the first three stages were the most critical to development, and an individual's personality was essentially fixed at the end of stage three or around the age of six. During the oral stage, the libido or sexual energy is located in the mouth, and the child derives pleasure from placing things in their mouth. The major task of this stage is breastfeeding and weaning. Oral fixation leads adults to continue to seek gratification by putting things in their mouths and may result in overindulging in activities such as smoking, gum chewing, overeating, or excessive sarcasm. Oral fixation may also result in adults that are excessively clingy or dependent on others. During the anal stage, the source of libido release and main task is toilet training and learning to control bowel movements. Anal fixation can result in adult personalities that are either excessively stingy or rigid, or out of control, impulsive, and rebellious. During the phallic stage, the libido energy is focused on the genitals, and individuals experience either the **Oedipus complex** if they are male or the **Electra complex** if they are female, which both involve developing a sexual attraction to the opposite-sex parent and a desire to eliminate the parent of the same sex who is seen as a rival. This love for the opposite-sex parent causes anxiety in children, because in order to win their affection the child must replace their powerful same-sex parent. For boys, the fear takes the form of **castration anxiety** or a concern that the father will castrate him. Eventually, most boys, according to Freud, decide to identify with their fathers by adopting their values and trying to become just like them in order to reduce their fears. Girls resolve their Electra complex in a similar manner by choosing to identify with their mothers, adopting their values and behaviors. In both boys and girls, the process of **identification** involves resolving the phallic stage conflict by adopting the values, behaviors, and social roles of the same-sex parent. During the latency stage, the sexual or libido energy remains hidden (latent) and no type of fixation occurs. The genital stage is the fifth and final stage, which coincides with the arrival of puberty and lasts through adulthood. During this time sexual impulses reappear and are centered on the genitals but are no longer directed toward the parent. The five stages of Freud's psychosexual development are described in Table 11.10.

Table 11.10. Freud's Five Psychosexual Stages

Stage	Age	Description
Oral	0 to 1 year	Sexual energy is focused on the mouth. The baby is concerned with sucking and biting objects. Fixation can result in an oral personality.
Anal	2 years	Sexual energy is focused on the parts of the body involved with controlling urination and defecation. This is the stage when toilet training takes place. Fixation can result in an anal personality.
Phallic	3 to 5 years	Sexual energy is focused on the genitals and children are attracted to their opposite-sex parent and feel hostility toward the same-sex parent in what is known as the Oedipus or Electra complex.
Latency	6 to 11 years	Sexual desires are dormant and focus is concentrated on developing intellectual and social skills with members of the same sex. Children are interested in identifying with the same-sex parent.
Genital	12+ years	Sexual energy is focused on the genitals and is no longer directed toward the parent. This stage continues for the rest of their lives.

Sex and Gender Development

An individual's **sex** is related to the biological definition of being male or female and is determined by specific anatomical differences. The chromosomes, responsible for determining the sex of each individual, are the **X** and **Y chromosomes**. Only X chromosomes are donated by the mother and the father contributes either an X or a Y chromosome. An individual with an XX combination is female and an individual with an XY combination is male.

An individual's **gender** involves the cultural, psychological, and behavioral characteristics associated with being male or female. Gender is acquired as children develop and are socialized. **Gender identity** involves the internal recognition that an individual is male or female and the assimilation of this belief into their self-concept. For most individuals gender identity is consistent with one's biological sex. Some individuals adopt a gender identity that incorporates both male and female traits in what is known as **androgyny**.

Gender roles or the expected appearance, personality traits, and behaviors connected to being male or female mainly relate to environmental factors such as family and cultural interactions. Characteristic male gender roles include men being independent, strong, and self-assured. Typical female gender roles include the expectation that women will be nurturing, dependent, and emotional. Gender roles help individuals develop a sense of identity and understand others. It is very difficult to tell whether gender roles reflect an inherited tendency or are the result of simple socialization. There are some observable differences in male and female development, but separating the nature from the nurture influences in the study of gender differences is difficult due to many intervening variables. One clear biological fact is that females tend to mature earlier than males, typically at age twelve, as compared to age fourteen for males. However, other differences between the genders are less likely to be related to biological causes. For example, girls who reach puberty early have more anxiety than do boys who mature early. Other characteristics—aggression, for example—are more complicated because, although males demonstrate higher levels of aggression, it is difficult to tell if this is the result of differences in biology, such as the fact that males have more testosterone, or differences in how aggression is reinforced or shaped by family and culture. The problem with attributing these gender differences to genetics is that it is very difficult to separate heritable traits from cultural experience and training, especially in the realm of complex social behaviors, including aggression or performance on standardized tests. **Socialization** or the process of developing the abilities, attitudes, and behaviors required for successful functioning within a particular culture or group includes the acquisition of gender roles, which is called **gender typing**. Socialization to gender roles begins at birth. The first question about any new baby is usually "Is it a boy or a girl?" The introduction of pink or blue blankets begins the process of socialization.

There are two general theories for how gender roles are acquired. The **social learning theory** states that gender roles may be acquired through the observation of models and operant conditioning. Children imitate individuals in their family or culture of the same sex, especially regarding behaviors that are reinforced or punished. Children learn gender appropriate behaviors by observing how boys and girls are treated differently after engaging in the same behavior. For example, if a boy falls and begins to cry and the parent frowns, this punishment will likely lead him to suppress emotions of sadness and pain in the future. If a girl falls and begins to cry and the parent consoles her, she learns that expressing sad emotions leads to reinforcement and acceptance. Children also learn culture-appropriate gender roles though increasing exposure to television, movies, and video games that often present very stereotypical examples of both genders. Other psychologists use the **gender schema theory** which emphasizes a cognitive component to explain how gender roles are learned in childhood. According to this theory, children develop separate mental categories (schema) for each gender and organize information about behavior and activities into these two specific gender categories. Young children who are beginning to develop gender schemas and have limited cognitive skills tend to apply schema rules rigidly. For example, a girl in preschool may decide that pants are for boys and dresses are for girls and refuse to wear pants.

Personality

Personality refers to the pattern of behaviors, thoughts, and characteristics an individual possesses and displays consistently that differentiates one person from another. Personality psychologists attempt to identify personality characteristics similar among people and devise general principles to explain particular motives. Each theorist approaches the development of personality with somewhat different assumptions, strategies, and objectives. Currently, there is no way to empirically test competing theories for their validity and reliability; some theories are constructed in such a way that they defy testing. However, these theories form a strong basis for establishing hypotheses regarding the development of personality and possible explanations for differences in personality. Personality theorists are concerned with the characteristics that all humans share, those that groups of humans share, as well as those that describe specific individuals. Additionally, the study of personality involves how characteristics develop and the relative influences of genetics, biology, cognition, experience, and culture on personality. Finally, personality theory involves how information about characteristics can be utilized to help determine how to improve human relationships and interactions in a variety of settings, including career, love, family, and across cultures.

Psychoanalytic Theory of Personality

The **psychoanalytic** theory of personality, developed by **Sigmund Freud**, explains that an individual's personality is the result of unresolved unconscious conflicts from childhood or unconscious sexual and aggressive instincts. Freud's psychoanalytic theory proposes that the mind, which includes personality, is structured in three levels: unconscious, preconscious, and conscious. These three levels of the mind are often described symbolically as an iceberg because the largest part of the mind, like the largest part of an iceberg, is located below the surface. The **unconscious** is the level of the mind that contains hidden thoughts, wishes, memories, and feelings that an individual cannot bring into conscious awareness. Freud believed that the unconscious was mainly filled with unacceptable sexual or aggressive thoughts and wishes and unresolved conflicts from childhood, which could result in personality difficulties for individuals. The unconscious is hidden deep inside the individual, similar to the part of the iceberg hidden deep below the surface of the water. The **preconscious** is the level of the mind that contains information an individual is aware of but not currently thinking about; it is located between the unconscious and conscious. Similar to the part of the iceberg that is just below the surface of the water, the preconscious is hidden for the moment but capable of becoming quickly visible. For example, an individual may not be thinking of what he or she had for dinner the night before, but if asked, the individual could easily

provide that information from his or her preconscious. Finally, the **conscious** is the part of the mind that is currently active and responsive to events and stimuli in the environment. Individuals are aware of their internal thoughts, making the conscious mind similar to the part of the iceberg visible above the water.

Psychosexual Development

In psychoanalytic theory, an individual's personality is shaped by instincts and needs in the unconscious. According to Freud, there are two biologically based instincts, known as thanatos and eros, that influence personality. **Thanatos**, the Greek word for death, represents the dark side of human nature, including aggressive urges and self-destructive behaviors. **Eros**, the Greek word for love, represents the life instincts or the desire to live, including basic survival needs, self-preservation, and sexual drives. All of the life instincts, especially the sexual drive, and the energy associated with them are simply referred to as the **libido** by Freud. Personality develops as individuals pass through a series of psychosexual stages during which the libido is focused on different areas of the body. The five stages of psychosexual personality development consist of the oral, anal, phallic, latency, and genital stages. During the **oral stage**, occurring from birth to approximately one year, the libido or sexual energy is located in the mouth, and the infant derives pleasure from placing things in his or her mouth. The main tasks and focus of the libido during the **anal stage** is toilet training and learning to control bowel movements, which occurs at approximately two years of age. During the **phallic stage**, occurring from three to five years of age, the libido is focused on the genitals.

Within this psychosexual stage Freud proposed the **Oedipus complex** in which a boy develops a sexual attraction to his mother and a hatred for his father. A girl may also experience sexual attraction to her father in what is sometimes referred to as the **Electra complex**. This love for the opposite-sex parent causes anxiety in children, because in order to win that parent's affection the child must replace his or her powerful same-sex parent. Also, during this time boys and girls are figuring out how they physically differ from one another, and a castration complex develops for both boys and girls. For boys, there is **castration anxiety** or a concern that their fathers will castrate them for desiring their mothers. Girls experience a castration complex when they realize that they do not have the male sex organ and blame their mothers for the fact that they do not have one. The desire to possess a male sex organ is known as **penis envy**; this theory is hardly ever accepted by modern psychology. In both boys and girls, resolution of the phallic stage requires the process of **identification**, which involves adopting the values, behaviors, and social roles of the same-sex parent, resulting in the expansion of their superego or conscience. Freud considered identification to be a defense mechanism or a method that is used by the ego, or problem-solving part of the personality, to reduce anxiety and fear. The process of identification for boys during the phallic stage allows them to reduce their fears of castration. During the **latency stage**, occurring from approximately ages six to eleven, the libido or sexual energy remains hidden, and the individual focuses on academic tasks and social activities with members of the same gender. The **genital stage** is the final stage and lasts through adulthood when sexual impulses reappear and are centered on the genitals but are no longer directed toward the parent.

According to Freud, the first three psychosexual stages are the most critical, and an individual's personality is essentially fixed around the age of five or six. Personality problems in adulthood can be traced to unresolved childhood conflicts that remain with individuals in their unconscious. These conflicts are the result of a failure of the child to completely move from one psychosexual stage to another. **Fixation** is what happens when the needs associated with a particular stage of development are either over- or under-indulged, resulting in an individual getting stuck in that stage. Individuals who are fixated at a particular stage continue to search for gratification by engaging in activities associated with the stage that has the unresolved conflict. Oral fixation leads adults to continue to seek pleasure by putting things in their mouths and may result in overindulging in activities such as smoking, gum chewing, overeating, or excessive sarcasm. Oral fixation may also result in adults being excessively clingy or dependent on others. The control of toilet training can result in fixation at the anal stage, which can lead to specific personality characteristics in adulthood. If parental control of toilet training is too strict, an *anal-retentive personality* can develop, which refers to individuals who are excessively orderly, stingy, or rigid. If toilet training is too lenient, an *anal-expulsive personality* can develop, which refers to individuals who are messy, out of control, impulsive, or rebellious.

Personality Components

Freud divided personality into three components: the id, the ego, and the superego. The **id** is the most primitive aspect of the personality and the only component individuals possess when they are born. The id operates outside of awareness and resides in the unconscious part of the mind. This part of one's personality is ruled by instinctual urges for food, warmth, sex, and aggression and works according to the **pleasure principle**, or the desire for immediate satisfaction and the avoidance of pain. The id does not have any ethical or moral standards and often comes into conflict with reality. The **ego**, or the problem-solving and rational aspect of the personality, develops after about the age of eight months as the id is forced to deal with reality and the child begins to understand what is and is not possible. The ego is located in both the conscious and preconscious areas of the mind and works according to the **reality principle**, which balances the impulses of the id with the constraints of reality and the superego's desire for perfection. The third component of the personality, the **superego**, reminds individuals what ideal behavior consists of and begins developing during childhood. Through the process of identification children expand their superego by adopting the morals of their parents, which typically reflect the values of society. Serving as a conscience and internal critic, the superego determines what is right and wrong and generates a sense of guilt. The superego is located in all three levels of the mind—conscious, preconscious, and unconscious—and is often in conflict with the id because fulfilling many of the id's urges would be socially unacceptable.

According to Freud, the overall personality of an individual is related to the component of the personality that is the most dominant. A personality dominated by the id will be impulsive, selfish, aggressive, and pleasure seeking without regard for consequences. Individuals with a personality dominated by the superego are rigidly moralistic and controlling, and repress desires. A healthy personality involves a strong ego capable of balancing the demands of both the id and the superego.

STUDY TIP

Be able to identify how the individual components of personality would respond to a particular event. For example, during a football game, Walter, a wide receiver, is hit very hard illegally after the play by a member on the other team. How each individual component of personality would respond to Walter's situation is described in Table 12.1.

Table 12.1. **Freud's Components of Personality**

Component	Principle	Application
Id	Pleasure	Walter's id would urge him to shove the other player to the ground or start a fight. The id demands immediate release for aggressive or sexual instincts.
Superego	Morality	Walter's superego would provide the voice in his head saying that he should never resort to violence and always be kind and forgiving. The superego demands perfection.
Ego	Reality	Walter's ego would find a socially acceptable solution to the demands of the id by convincing him to not retaliate against the other player, because it would only result in him being ejected from the game. A possible solution that the ego could use would be to direct his energy into making big plays.

Defense Mechanisms

In order to protect the ego from excessive levels of anxiety, individuals utilize **defense mechanisms** or unconscious methods that reduce anxiety caused from unacceptable thoughts or desires by distorting reality. (See Table 12.2.) These methods allow individuals to convince themselves that nothing is wrong so that they can avoid coming face to face with conflicts or shameful situations. Defense mechanisms may be healthy if used in moderation, but, when they are excessive, they result in stress, due to the large amount of cognitive energy being wasted on maintaining them.

Table 12.2.   Freud's Defense Mechanisms

Defense Mechanism	Definition	Application
Repression	Unconsciously reducing anxiety by blocking a painful incident or event from awareness. Anxiety producing unacceptable wishes and thoughts are pushed into the unconscious.	Dede has forgotten the fact that her dress ripped as she was walking off the stage during her eighth-grade graduation because it was very embarrassing. If her friends mention the event, she does not remember it at all because she has placed it in her unconscious in order to reduce her anxiety.
Denial	Unconsciously reducing anxiety by refusing to accept reality even when presented with large amounts of evidence. Denial involves rejecting external events that pose a threat to the ego.	Drug addicts refuse to accept that they have a problem even after their substance use has led to physical deterioration, the loss of their job, and damaged relationships.
Displacement	Unconsciously reducing anxiety by taking out aggression on someone or something that is less powerful or threatening than the true source of anxiety.	Owen is very angry with his teacher but is afraid to say anything because he would get in trouble. Later that day Owen takes his anger out on his mom by yelling at her because she is a safe target, which allows him to displace his anger.
Sublimation	Unconsciously reducing anxiety by directing aggression toward a more socially acceptable outlet such as exercise, hard work, sports, or hobbies. *Note*: Sublimation is a healthier version of displacement.	Oscar is very angry at his boss, but is afraid to say anything because it might result in him being fired. In order to reduce his feelings of anger and hostility, he puts all of his energy into working in his garden.
Projection	Unconsciously reducing anxiety by attributing one's own fears, feelings, faults, or unacceptable thoughts and behaviors to another person or group.	Angel, who doesn't realize how flirtatious she actually is, complains about other girls in her class being flirtatious.
Rationalization	Unconsciously reducing anxiety by creating logical excuses for unacceptable thoughts and behaviors.	After Kami finds out that she has been rejected by Happy College, she tells everyone that she never wanted to go to that school anyway. This excuse reduces the anxiety and shame she feels because she was not accepted to that college.
Reaction Formation	Unconsciously reducing anxiety by acting or saying the exact opposite of the morally or socially unacceptable beliefs held by an individual.	In order to disguise his dislike for his teacher, Timmy brings him an apple every day and gives him compliments.
Regression	Unconsciously reducing anxiety by reverting to thoughts and behaviors that would be more appropriate during an earlier period of development. Individuals may behave in a childlike manner to get what they want.	Marcie is faced with making a decision that is causing anxiety and begins to use baby talk around her friends and family.

STUDY TIP

Be able to identify and distinguish among the defense mechanisms proposed by Sigmund Freud. Several key comparisons that students often confuse are listed here.

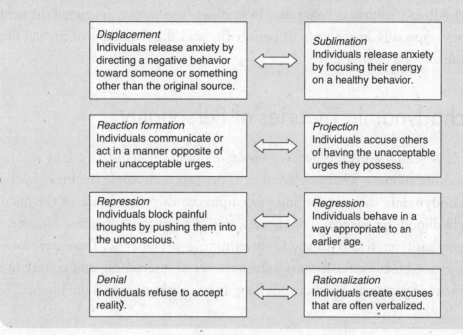

Displacement
Individuals release anxiety by directing a negative behavior toward someone or something other than the original source.

Sublimation
Individuals release anxiety by focusing their energy on a healthy behavior.

Reaction formation
Individuals communicate or act in a manner opposite of their unacceptable urges.

Projection
Individuals accuse others of having the unacceptable urges they possess.

Repression
Individuals block painful thoughts by pushing them into the unconscious.

Regression
Individuals behave in a way appropriate to an earlier age.

Denial
Individuals refuse to accept reality.

Rationalization
Individuals create excuses that are often verbalized.

Criticisms of Freud

Freud's psychoanalytic theory was controversial when it was first introduced and continues to be heavily criticized today for being unscientific, placing too great of an emphasis on childhood, and being sexist. Many of Freud's ideas are difficult to test empirically and are not falsifiable. Freud conducted his research through the use of case studies that consisted mainly of wealthy European women with emotional problems; he then extended those observations to all people across different cultures. The research method of case studies utilized by Freud is limited because it does not allow for causal relationships and the sample is not representative, making it impossible to extend the observations to a larger population. Additionally, Freud explained the adult personalities of these women based on childhood experiences that he did not study directly. Freud's belief that personality is fixed by the age of five or six has also been shown to be incorrect. Current research supports personality development and change during both adolescence and adulthood. Furthermore, psychoanalytic theory focuses too much on the past childhood experiences of an individual and neglects to take current situations into account when explaining behavior. Finally, concepts such as penis envy and the fact that women have an inferior superego to men have resulted in the criticism of the theory as being sexist. Despite the considerable criticisms the psychoanalytic theory has received, Freud's influence is undeniable. His continuing influence is most apparent in the psychodynamic perspective, which also focuses on the unconscious and how early childhood influences behavior. His findings have forever impacted the field of psychology, especially in the areas of personality and the treatment of mental illness through the use of a talking cure.

Psychodynamic Theories of Personality

Several theorists, called *neo-Freudians,* built on Freud's work by making important modifications in what is referred to as the psychodynamic theories of personality. **Psychodynamic** theories continue to emphasize the importance of the unconscious and childhood experiences, but those working from these theories disagree with Freud's emphasis on sexual drives in determining personality. These revisions include an increased focus on conscious influences, social interaction, and culture in the development of personality and how development continues across the lifespan.

STUDY TIP

Be able to differentiate between the psychoanalytic and psychodynamic theories of personality development.

- The *psychoanalytic* theory of personality was proposed by Sigmund Freud and focuses on how unresolved unconscious conflicts and sexual and aggressive drives influence personality.

- The *psychodynamic* theory of personality includes several theories developed by Freud's followers, who also emphasize the importance of childhood and the unconscious. However, psychodynamic theories downplay Freud's emphasis on the importance of aggressive and sexual impulses and focus instead on social and cultural influences in childhood.

Carl Jung, one of the most influential neo-Freudians, found it difficult to accept that sexual motives were the chief force driving human behavior. He discussed forces and content within the unconscious, unlike anything Freud had ever mentioned. Where Freud was concerned with biology, Jung was interested in the spirit. Jung began to explore universal symbols of the human race's experiences, symbols that transcend the individual's immediate concerns. In his theory of personality structure, Jung wrote of both a personal and collective unconscious. The **personal unconscious** of each individual is very similar to what Freud called the unconscious and contains an individual's painful or upsetting memories and information that has been repressed. Jung differed from Freud in his belief that individuals also share a **collective unconscious** or a set of inherited images and experiences common to all humans throughout evolutionary time. The images that comprise the collective unconscious are called **archetypes** and allow individuals to respond universally to particular situations. Archetypes are evident in art and literature; common examples include the wise old man, the mother, the hero, and the quest. Two of the archetypes Jung mentions frequently are the shadow and the persona. The **shadow** represents the repressed, unconscious drives and desires of the personal unconscious, the "dark side" of all humans. The **persona** is an archetype which is described as a front or mask that a person presents to other people; this mask is shown to the outside world when an individual is acting out a role from the collective unconscious. In addition to the collective unconscious and its components, one of the most influential aspects of Jung's personality theory is the identification of several personality types based on general attitudes and perceptions of the world. In particular, Jung suggested that extroversion and introversion represent two important differences among the personalities of individuals. An **extroverted** personality is expressed by individuals who are confident, social, and externally focused. Conversely, an **introverted** personality is expressed by individuals who are internally focused, more self-conscious, less social, and quiet. Jung's extroversion and introversion personality types have greatly influenced many other personality theories.

STUDY TIP

Be able to differentiate between introverted and extroverted personality types.

Alfred Adler was trained in the psychoanalytic perspective, but like Jung, also broke with Freud because he believed that the central core of personality is not related to repressed sexual drives. Adler preferred to think of the person as a whole rather than considering the separate parts of a personality; thus, he focused on how social interactions and conscious thought influenced individual growth. Adler believes that an individual's failures serve to motivate him or her to overcome difficulty which he calls **striving for superiority**. When Adler refers to striving for superiority, he does not mean gaining power over others, but instead finding personal fulfillment and overcoming challenges. Although feelings of inferiority are normal and lead to growth, some individuals may develop an **inferiority complex** if constant criticism and repeated failure happens, causing them to feel helpless and insecure. Individuals with inferiority complexes may become socially isolated and fearful or develop an exaggerated competitive and aggressive nature. Another area of research that Adler pursued was the influence of **birth order** on personality—being the oldest, middle, youngest, or only child. Adler believed that the unique set of challenges presented by these different positions in the family created particular personality traits.

Karen Horney argued against Freud's claim that developmental stages are biologically determined and instead believed that culture played an important role in personality development. Horney is especially well known for her criticisms of Freud's view on female development. Freud believed that girls develop penis envy, or a desire to possess a male sex organ, a concept rarely accepted by modern psychologists. Horney argues that penis envy represents the desire girls have for the social power and status enjoyed by males, as opposed to a desire for the actual organ itself. In addition, she suggests that some men experience **womb envy**, or the unconscious desire to be able to have the ability to give birth. A major component of Horney's psychodynamic personality theory is the idea that healthy personality development depends on the fulfillment of the basic biological need of security that is provided through social interaction. If a child is provided with love and security by his or her parents, the result will be a healthy personality as an adult. If a child does not develop a sense of security as a result of the relationship with his or her parents, they may develop basic anxiety, which leads to difficulties coping with negative events. **Basic anxiety** is defined by Horney as the feelings of helplessness, loneliness, and fear created by the fact that a child is alone in a hostile world. Ultimately, personality development is based largely on the social interaction between the parent and the child.

Erik Erikson, a neo-Freudian, created an influential psychosocial stage theory of personality. Unlike Freud, Erikson believed that development continued throughout the lifespan rather than ending at about age five or six. Erikson divides his theory of psychosocial development into eight stages from birth to old age. Each stage involves a psychosocial crisis or conflict that can result in either a positive or negative outcome (see the development chapter). An effective resolution of a psychosocial crisis for healthy personality development involves finding a balance between the two outcomes. After an individual successfully resolves a particular crisis, the result for personality is the acquisition of a virtue that serves to increase the ability of the ego to handle challenges.

The virtues associated with successful resolution of each of Erikson's eight psychosocial stages are hope, will, purpose, competency, fidelity, love, care, and wisdom.

Humanist Theories of Personality

The **humanist** perspective emphasizes the human capacity for goodness, creativity, and freedom. Humanistic personality theories see humans as spiritual, rational, autonomous beings and emphasize the "whole" person instead of component parts. Although humanists acknowledge that personality is influenced by temperament (nature) and negative factors in the environment (nurture), they focus on the fact that individuals have free will and make choices about how to respond to situations. Both of the major humanist theorists, Carl Rogers and Abraham Maslow, propose that individuals are striving for **self-actualization**, the motive that drives people to reach their greatest potential. Because humanism developed in response to the psychoanalytic and behaviorist perspectives, it is sometimes referred to as the *third-force*.

One of the most influential theorists associated with the humanist perspective was **Carl Rogers**, who believed that self-concept was at the heart of individual personality. **Self-concept** refers to all the unique beliefs and personality characteristics an individual has. For example, a person's self-concept might include the belief that he or she is talented, intelligent, conscientious, and responsible. Rogers believed that a difference sometimes existed between a person's self-concept and reality. This difference determines whether the person will have either incongruence or congruence. **Incongruence** occurs if a person's self-concept is not consistent with reality and leads to feelings of disappointment and failure. For example, if a student believes that he or she is good at a particular subject but consistently does poorly, the student will end up feeling threatened, anxious, and defensive. **Congruence** occurs if the self-concept of an individual is consistent with what the person is generally experiencing, or, in other words, reality. For example, if a person believes that he or she is athletic and coordinated and that person is successful in sports, congruence exists for this aspect of his or her self-concept. Although Rogers acknowledged that nobody experiences complete congruence, he believed that high levels of congruence are related to positive self-esteem and mental health. Individuals, especially children, are blocked or prevented from achieving congruence if *conditions of worth* are imposed on them by parents or others. That is, if parents communicate the message to a child that he or she is valued only when doing what the parents want, the child is forced to deny his or her true self in order to please the parents, which limits the child as he or she works toward self-actualization.

Rogers believed that, in order to develop a healthy personality, children and adults need to be surrounded by others who offer unconditional positive regard and are **accepting** (supportive), **genuine** (honest), and **empathetic** (understanding and compassionate). **Unconditional positive regard** involves the acceptance and appreciation of an individual—faults and all. This unwavering acceptance allows an individual to develop a sense of innate goodness and reach his or her full potential. Unconditional positive regard is one of Rogers' most influential concepts, significantly influencing counseling and treatment methods.

STUDY TIP

According to Rogers, in order to build a positive self-concept, individuals need to **AGE**—**a**cceptance (unconditional positive regard), **g**enuineness, and **e**mpathy—to reach their full potential.

As one might imagine, most of the extensive literature on the topic of **self-esteem** has stemmed in one way or another from Rogers' theories. **Self-esteem** is the amount that one values oneself, for good or for bad. Studies have found that children with high self-esteem are more likely to lead group discussions, make friends, be nonconformist, and be less self-conscious. Clearly, self-esteem plays an important role in personality. However, it is unclear whether having many positive traits gives a person high self-esteem or if having high self-esteem promotes the development of beneficial traits. That is, characteristics can develop as part of a **self-fulfilling prophecy**, in which people who see themselves in some particular way place themselves in situations that bring out that sort of behavior.

Another theorist, **Abraham Maslow**, is famous for his **hierarchy of needs** (see the motivation chapter). His theory of self-actualization holds some interest for personality theorists, because it emphasizes healthy behavior, not just psychological symptoms. According to Maslow, there is a marked difference between the behavior patterns of people motivated by lower needs (aimed toward correcting deficiencies) and the behavior of people driven by self-actualization, or growth-oriented needs. The person who is still motivated to satisfy lower needs is characterized by a tendency to be self-centered and concerned with his or her own needs, to behave mainly on the basis of external cues, to look for gratifications that are short-term and temporary, and view others in terms of how they can satisfy their needs. Growth-oriented people, on the other hand, are likely to be more concerned with the world at large than with themselves, to attain unique, individual goals, and to view people for who they are and not just as useful objects.

Humanist theories are criticized for being based on ideas that are difficult to test scientifically because terms such as *self-actualization* are hard to define operationally and measure accurately. Another criticism is that the humanist idea that individuals are innately good and striving for perfection may be too optimistic because the aggressive and selfish aspects of human nature are not being recognized. Despite the criticisms, humanism has expanded the field of personality psychology to focus more on healthy individuals, which in part has led to the development of the positive psychology movement. **Positive psychology** is the scientific study of human virtues, such as wisdom, altruism, justice, and courage. One major area of research among positive psychologists is the study of happiness, or *subjective well-being,* and factors—including biology, experience, and environment—that contribute to higher or lower levels of joy.

Behaviorist Theories of Personality

Behaviorist theories of personality are based on patterns of observable behavior. Behaviorists assume that behavior is learned and not innate, and they credit personalities with almost infinite flexibility. A child can be conditioned to fear objects or people, such as what happened with poor Little Albert, or to admire and enjoy almost anything. John B. Watson, the founder of behaviorism, is famous for having stated that he could make a child into any sort of person if he had complete control over the child's environment. B.F. Skinner, another behaviorist, did not create a systematic theory of personality development, but he believed that each new experience helps to determine a person's future responses. Skinner and others were proponents of the idea of *determinism* in which all human behavior, including what other theorists called personality, occurred in response to stimuli in the environment. In other words, Skinner explains personality the way he explains all behavior: it is the result of reinforcements and punishments. This idea is heavily criticized by theoretical approaches, such as humanism, that emphasize the importance of free will.

Social Cognitive Theory of Personality

The **social cognitive theory** of personality explains how personal characteristics, social interactions, and cognitive evaluations are involved in developing an individual's personality. One important contribution to this theory is **Albert Bandura's** idea of **reciprocal determinism**: how people think, how people behave, and what their environment is like all interact to influence the consistency of behavior. For instance, if you are interested in tennis (personal/cognitive variable), you will consistently choose to play or watch tennis (behavioral variable), and you will be rewarded by being around people who share your enthusiasm for tennis (environmental variable), further strengthening your interest in tennis.

STUDY TIP

According to reciprocal determinism personal/cognitive, behavioral, and environmental variables continuously interact with one another to influence personality (see Figure 12.1).

Figure 12.1

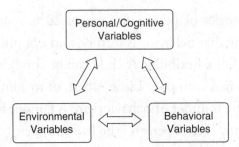

STUDY TIP

Bandura's concept of self-efficacy is very influential and has been included on several free-response questions. Be able to create an original example of self-efficacy. For instance, if Sophie has *high self-efficacy* regarding her math abilities, she will be confident about learning calculus in college. However, if Sophie has *low self-efficacy* regarding her test-taking abilities, she will not be confident about her ability to perform well on her college placement exam and will be anxious.

Among the many personal variables that Bandura studied in terms of personality, the one he focused on the most was the concept of self-efficacy. **Self-efficacy** is the level of confidence an individual has regarding his or her ability to perform particular tasks or skills. In other words, what does an individual believe he or she is capable of accomplishing? Individuals who have high self-efficacy for a particular task believe that success is possible and are more likely to continue to pursue goals when setbacks occur and to accomplish what they set out to do than those with low self-efficacy.

STUDY TIP

Be able to differentiate among the multiple terms referring to the self.

- *Self-efficacy* is the level of confidence an individual has regarding his or her ability to perform particular tasks or skills.
- *Self-esteem* is the amount that one values oneself, for good or for bad.
- *Self-concept* is the unique beliefs and personality characteristics an individual has about himself or herself.
- *Self-fulfilling prophecy* refers to the expectations people have about themselves that lead them to alter their behavior, causing their expectations to come true.
- *Self-serving bias* is the tendency to attribute one's successes to dispositional factors and failures to situational factors.

George Kelly's social cognitive theory explains that personality differences are related to the unique personal constructs that an individual holds. **Personal constructs** are concepts that individuals create to help them predict or explain their experiences. If the personal constructs an individual creates come true, they will be reinforced. However, if the personal constructs provide undesirable results, they will be discarded or revised. For example, if Jeannie meets her boss for the first time and decides that she is intelligent, Jeannie will assign her boss to the construct of "intelligent." If Jeannie's boss continues to behave in ways that Jeannie considers to be smart, she will use that construct to predict the future behavior of her boss. Constructs are highly individual, which means that a man with long hair, tattoos, and a lot of piercings might be placed in a construct for "dangerous" by one person and "interesting" or "cool" by another. Kelly's theory suggests that the way each individual categorizes his or her experiences into different personal constructs represents the individual's personality.

Julian Rotter investigated how differences in personality were related to an individual's perceived control over the environment. **Locus of control** refers to the amount of confidence people have regarding the level of influence (control) they believe they have over events in their lives. People who have an **internal locus of control** believe they are capable of influencing what happens to them though their hard work or effort. Those with an **external locus of control** believe that what happens to them may be largely determined by fate, luck, or the actions of others. Correlational studies show that individuals with an internal locus of control are more successful, less likely to become depressed, more likable, and have higher levels of self-esteem.

Biological Theories of Personality

Biological psychologists investigate how genetic and physiological factors contribute to differences in personality through the use of temperament and twin studies. **Temperament** refers to the biologically influenced activity level, behaviors, and emotional responses typically demonstrated by individuals that is a part of personality. Longitudinal studies that follow infants through early childhood indicate that babies with specific temperaments retain many of these same characteristics as they get older. Researchers have also identified specific patterns of brain activity associated with particular temperaments that are present in babies and remain stable overtime. The heritability of temperament is estimated to be approximately 0.50, indicating that, although there is a biological component to an individual's temperament, environmental factors are also significant.

Further evidence for the genetic basis of personality comes from twin studies. Monozygotic twins who are genetically identical are more alike in regard to personality traits than are fraternal twins, who have only 50 percent of the same genes, indicating the possibility of a genetic component to personality. Traditionally, it has been difficult to measure the effect of heredity without the influence of the environment. Personality traits that identical twins have in common may have been due to genetics or simply because they lived together and shared similar experiences. Therefore, the best evidence for the heritability of personality traits comes from studies of identical twins who have been raised apart and who did not share a similar environment. The Minnesota Twin Family Study concluded that heritability estimates for most personality traits are approximately .40 to .50 for both identical twins raised together, as well as for identical twins raised apart. However, it is important to note that these results also indicate that the environment contributes to personality differences. It appears that heredity may provide a capacity for a wide range of behavior that is also impacted by the environment.

Personality Types

The **type approach** to personality attempts to group individuals according to categories that consist of particular characteristics. One of the earliest personality theories created by ancient Greek physicians was based on types. Hippocrates and Galen classified people into different personality types according to the dominance of one of four bodily fluids, called **humors**. Individuals dominated by the blood humor have a *sanguine* personality and are generally kind, flexible, and optimistic. Passionate, angry, and aggressive personalities are *choleric*, which results from too much yellow bile. *Melancholic* personalities produce too much of the humor black bile and are generally unhappy and depressed. *Phlegmatic* personalities result from too much phlegm and can be apathetic, lazy, or calm. Another not so ancient theory based on personality types was presented by William Sheldon during the twentieth century. Sheldon's theory suggested that differences in personality were related to the overall body type of an individual. According to this theory, individuals who were thin had an *ectomorph body type* that created a personality that was nervous, shy, introverted, and sensitive. The *endomorph body type* characterized as heavyset and round results in a highly social or jolly personality. The *mesomorph body type* was described as physically fit and muscular and leads to a personality that is courageous and assertive. Sheldon's type theory is not supported by psychological research because further analysis indicates a weak or non-correlation between body type and personality. Another more familiar type theory places individuals into one of two personality types in terms of how they respond to stress. **Type A** individuals are usually in a rush and respond to increased stress by working more, competing harder, or with aggression. Type A's may also be impatient and intolerant of slowness. Heart attacks, ulcers, and other stress-related diseases have been associated with type A personalities. **Type B** individuals tend to be more relaxed and patient. They allow stress to "roll off their backs" and are generally less driven.

Hans Eysenck's theory explains that an individual's personality is determined by biologically based levels of influence. Individuals can be categorized according to personality types that fall along two separate dimensions: introversion to extroversion and neuroticism (instability) to emotional stability. A third dimension of psychoticism or levels of hostility was added later by Eysenck, but this level is mostly associated with severe mental illness. For Eysenck, each of these dimensions was characterized by specific biological differences. For example, he believed that individuals high in neuroticism also had greater autonomic nervous system activity.

Trait Theory

Historically, personality has been most commonly described in terms of traits rather than types. **Traits** are patterns of enduring and stable characteristics that influence a person to act in a consistent way and trait theories of personality look for consistencies in behavior. Traits are usually measured using **self-report inventories** that ask people to judge their agreement with statements describing behavior that might be indicative of some particular trait. Agreeing with the statement, "I'm willing to help people who need it," for example, might indicate the trait of "altruism." Trait theory also includes the use of both nomothetic and idiographic studies. **Nomothetic studies** involve the use of large numbers of participants in order to generate basic principles of behavior that can be applied to all individuals. The Big Five personality traits were discovered from nomothetic studies, as well as many other personality theories. **Idiographic studies** involve the selection of research methods that will reveal specific traits that explain how a particular individual is unique. The research for idiographic studies often takes the form of case studies or clinical interviews involving more descriptive analyses of individuals.

Gordon Allport, a major trait theorist, was one of the first psychologists to stress the difference between nomothetic and idiographic studies. He preferred to use the idiographic method by doing case studies to examine individual traits that determine personality. Allport's theories stress that an individual's personality is determined by his or her conscious motivations and intentions. The personality structure consists of a collection of traits, which develop as a result of a person's interaction with the environment. Allport began his research by systematically going through a dictionary and identifying any word that described a human characteristic; the result was a list of 18,000 traits. Next, Allport differentiated between **common traits** that are universal to all people within a culture and **individual traits** that are unique to individuals. These individual traits are referred to as **personal dispositions.** Personal dispositions are divided into three types: cardinal, central, and secondary. **Cardinal dispositions (traits)** influence almost all of a person's behavior and are so significant that these characteristics essentially define the person. Cardinal traits are not present in every individual and are especially rare. **Central dispositions (traits)** represent groups of characteristics that describe how a person behaves most of the time and dependably predict how individuals will act in a given situation. **Secondary dispositions (traits)** influence behavior to a much lesser extent and include individual preferences in terms of food, music, fashion, and hobbies.

STUDY TIP

An essay on a scholarship application may ask a student to select five central traits that distinguish them from other applicants.

Raymond Cattell utilized the statistical method of factor analysis to combine like terms, in this case personality traits, into groups to reduce the total number of possible traits. Cattell divided personality traits into two categories: surface traits and source traits. Surface traits are clusters of highly related behaviors, while source traits are the underlying causes of these behaviors. Source traits are not easily put into categories and may not have common names. Cattell also developed a well-known objective personality test called the 16 PF (Personality Factor) Questionnaire that measures an individual's personality in terms of sixteen important source traits that he identified as being present at some level in all individuals. Psychologists use the 16 PF today to evaluate individuals and to compare their scores with other larger groups, including different age ranges.

Paul Costa and Robert McCrae also attempted to reduce the lengthy list of potential traits for describing individuals into a few fundamental dimensions of personality. Factor analysis, a statistical procedure, was used to pare down the number of traits by clustering together traits that were highly correlated with another. The statistical analysis revealed the Big Five: openness (inquiring, independent, curious), conscientiousness (dependable, self-controlled), extraversion (outgoing, socially adaptive), agreeableness (conforming, likable), and neuroticism (excitability, anxiousness). Each of the Big Five traits actually represents one-half of a dichotomous pair. For example, individuals that are high in openness would be creative, imaginative, and prefer change. However, individuals that are low in openness would be the opposite or conventional, down-to-earth, and prefer routine. The Big Five personality traits are measured in individuals through the use of the *NEO Personality Inventory (NEO-PI-R)*, an objective personality test.

STUDY TIP

To remember the Big Five personality traits, think of the ocean.

- **O**penness
- **C**onscientiousness
- **E**xtraversion
- **A**greeableness
- **N**euroticism

A major criticism of the trait theory is that characterizing individuals solely in terms of their personality traits fails to take into account how people behave differently, depending on the situation. For example, a person reading a description of introverted and extroverted behavior is likely to identify with both traits because, although the individual may be extroverted under most circumstances, he or she may recognize that there are times when they are more reserved and introverted. As a consequence, the predictive power of a self-report inventory is limited because the traits people express tend not to be consistent from situation to situation. Psychologist Walter Mischel was one of the first to call attention to this problem, which resulted in the person-situation controversy. The **person–situation controversy** is the ongoing debate in psychology regarding whether or not traits (person) or the situation are more reliable in terms of predicting behavior. In his research, Mischel found that the behavior of an individual under different circumstances was not consistent with a particular trait that a self-report inventory said they possessed, such as honesty or agreeableness. Some trait theorists countered Mischel's criticism by saying that individual behavior is consistent under most but not all circumstances. In fact, most research shows that traits on average do in fact accurately predict individual behavior in most situations.

Culture and Personality

Although evidence indicates that the Big Five personality traits exist across a wide range of cultures, providing support for a biological influence, there are also differences in personality among cultures. Cross-cultural research discovered differences regarding self-concept when they asked participants to indicate what they considered to be their most important traits. In individualist cultures, such as those found in the United States and Western Europe, individuals described themselves more often with characteristics like "I am outgoing" or "I am athletic," reflecting self-concepts that emphasize independence and self-reliance. Individuals in collectivist cultures, like those found in Eastern Asia, Western Africa, and parts of South America, described themselves more often in relation to others, such as "I am a daughter" or "I am a student." These descriptions align more closely with self-concepts that emphasize the importance of group membership and harmony over individual achievement. Despite differences between individualist and collectivist cultures in terms of self-concept, it is important to remember that there is always individual variation within a group.

Personality Assessment Techniques

As a scientific discipline, personality psychology utilizes a variety of methods to evaluate similarities and differences in the characteristics of individuals. Psychoanalytic and psychodynamic theories, such as those developed by Sigmund Freud and Carl Jung, investigate differences through the use of case studies and projective testing. Humanist personality theorists, Abraham Maslow and Carl Rogers, for example, attempted to measure theoretical ideas such as self-concept and self-actualization based on data obtained in therapy sessions. Biological theories rely more heavily on brain imaging and family studies. The social-cognitive and behavioral theories utilize data from personality tests and generate some of the most effective data. Similarly, trait theory is based on data that is created through factor analysis and personality tests. How can personality actually be measured effectively on a test? Personality psychologists from various approaches have attempted to create psychometric measures that are reliable and valid for assessing personality. The wide range of personality tests in use fall into two large categories, objective and projective, and are outlined in the sections below.

Objective Tests

Objective personality tests, also called **self-report inventories**, are questionnaires that ask individuals to indicate if specific statements about behaviors, symptoms, emotions, or thoughts relate to them personally. The format of these tests is often true/false or multiple choice, and they may be administered to either an individual or large groups. Objective tests are useful because they are easy to score and can be given easily to large groups of individuals. The most frequently used objective personality test is the standardized **Minnesota Multiphasic Personality Inventory (MMPI-2)**. The MMPI-2 is used to measure differences in personality and identify emotional and behavioral problems. The statements on the MMPI-2 are divided into ten scales based on psychiatric categories, including measures for depression, schizophrenia, distrust (paranoia), anxiety, and others. There are a total of 567 statements to which the subject is asked to answer true, false, or cannot say in respect to their own behavior. Examples of statements similar to those on the MMPI-2 are "I do not tire quickly" or "I am sure I am being talked about." In addition to these ten scales, there are validity scales which represent checks on lying, carelessness, and misunderstanding, among other factors. The lie scale consists of statements for which a particular answer is socially desirable, but also extremely unlikely, such as answering true to "I never lie." The test is considered invalid for individuals who score too high on any of these validity scales. The MMPI-2 is frequently used by clinical psychologists and psychiatrists to evaluate the mental health of clients, but it is also used by personnel psychologists in private and government settings. Potential applicants for careers in medicine, law enforcement, or the military have been given this objective test to evaluate mental stability. The *California Personality Inventory (CPI)* is also a well-known objective personality test, but it differs from the MMPI-2 because it is designed to measure a variety of factors, such as personality characteristics, self-control, interpersonal skills, and achievement potential.

Objective personality tests are widely used and have both strengths and weaknesses as assessment measures. The strengths of objective personality tests are that they are relatively easy to administer and generate a great deal of information about particular individuals. Also, in the case of frequently used tests such as the MMPI-2, a large sample which is more representative of the population is created, allowing for standardization and comparison of the score of an individual with the scores of others. The MMPI-2 has been translated for use in cross-cultural studies and has been shown to have high levels of reliability and validity for recognizing mental health issues in a wide range of cultures. Although objective personality tests have greater validity than projective tests, they still have many problems. Individuals from other cultures may have higher overall scores because some items do not apply to them. For example, the statement "Evil spirits sometimes possess me" may not be considered abnormal in some cultures. Additionally, participants may not report accurate information about themselves or, alternatively, interpret the questions differently than how they were intended. Finally, another potential problem with objective personality tests is the **Barnum effect**, the tendency individuals have to agree with descriptions of themselves that are generally positive, but also unclear or ambiguous. Individuals may be likely to believe any personality description of this sort, such as a horoscope, regardless of its validity.

Projective Tests

In a **projective personality test**, the participant is given a vague or ambiguous stimulus and is asked to respond to it, often with a story. Projective testing attempts to measure the symbolic expression of conflicts and impulses and, therefore, is most closely associated with psychoanalytic or psychodynamic methods. Psychologists from these perspectives are attempting to discover deeper insights about the participant's personality and discover unconscious drives that are affecting behavior. Unlike an objective questionnaire, the projective test is unstructured, and participants are presented with open-ended questions. A large variety of projective tests exist, including Draw-A-Person, word-association tests, and sentence-completion tests.

A famous projective test is the **Rorschach Inkblot Test**, in which the participant is presented with a series of cards that have blots of ink on them; the cards are presented one at a time in a specific order. The participants are then asked to describe what they see and are provided with as much time as they wish. After the participant has responded, the examiner asks questions to find out where the item was seen in the blot, what aspects of the blot determined the response (form, color, shading, and movement), and the content of the response (what was seen). The interpretation of these results is supposed to reveal how a subject solves problems, the subject's intellectual level, and emotional stability. However, the validity of these associations has never been satisfactorily proven, and the test is currently of questionable diagnostic value.

The **Thematic Apperception Test (TAT)**, developed by Henry Murray, is another well-known projective test consisting of a series of cards, each of which has a different picture. The participants are instructed to create a story by providing a setting for the action in the picture, indicating what the future outcome will be, and identifying the emotions the characters are experiencing. Whatever the subject chooses to discuss is considered to be important. The TAT is frequently utilized to measure both achievement and affiliation motivations or as a starting point for conversations between clients and psychologists. A great method to help remember that the Thematic Apperception Test requires participants to create a story about an ambiguous drawing is to think of the initials TAT as spelling the phrase "Tell a Tale."

Projective tests continue to be utilized in clinical settings, but they have many significant criticisms. Projective tests are vulnerable to experimenter bias because of preexisting expectations that test examiners may have about how participants ought to respond. Furthermore, despite elaborate and complex scoring systems, interrater reliability is low. A lack of interrater reliability takes place when different psychologists evaluating the same individual's responses do not arrive at the same conclusions, making the findings questionable. Overall, problems exist concerning the reliability and validity of these tests in terms of measuring personality traits and motivations, assessing mental illness, and predicting behavior. The question remains, of course, as to why psychologists would use projective testing if reliability and validity are low. Typically, when projective tests are used, they are methods for gathering additional information about clients or providing an opportunity to stimulate discussion.

Time for a quiz
- Review strategies in Chapter 2
- Take Quiz 5 at the REA Study Center
  (www.rea.com/studycenter)

Testing and Individual Differences

Our society believes that intelligence is very important; in fact, intelligence tests are used to decide what schools people may attend, what jobs they are qualified for, and whether or not they are capable or brilliant. Interestingly, psychologists generally cannot agree on what exactly intelligence is or an effective way that it can be measured. Experimental psychologist E.G. Boring once famously declared, "Intelligence is what intelligence tests measure." If that were the only meaning of intelligence, no one but psychologists would care about it. Broadly defined, **intelligence** involves the capacity to acquire knowledge, reason effectively, and adapt to one's surroundings by utilizing a combination of inherited abilities (nature) and learned experiences (nurture). Intelligence may be described as a collection of separate abilities or as one significant factor. The study of intelligence is closely related to the field of **psychometrics**, or the scientific study of using mathematical or numerical methods to measure psychological variables by creating reliable and valid tests. Psychometrics involves the use of a mathematical concept called **factor analysis**, which utilizes statistics to reduce the number of variables by placing them in clusters of related items. This technique can be used to determine groups of similar variables on a test to determine if an individual's score on a measure of intelligence is related to one type of ability (factor) or many. In regard to intelligence it is important that you are able to describe the main theories, the history of testing, and the elements of good test construction.

Intelligence Theories

As psychologists have researched intelligence, a variety of different theories have been proposed to explain how intelligence can be defined and potentially measured. The theories differ in terms of how they explain the overall concept. Some theories describe intelligence as one type of ability; others describe intelligence as being comprised of several different abilities. Psychologists ultimately disagree as to whether intelligence is a single function or several different abilities. The major theories of intelligence, both historical and contemporary, that are required for the AP Psychology exam are outlined below.

Spearman's Two-Factor Theory of Intelligence

Utilizing factor analysis, **Charles Spearman** created the **two-factor theory** of intelligence that is comprised of both a main **general factor (g-factor)** that represents an individual's overall ability and several other **specific abilities (s-factors)** that are needed for certain types of cognitive tasks. Spearman believed that the g-factor was of greater importance and was the best predictor of intellectual ability. Some modern psychologists still support the idea of a single general factor for intelligence that can be measured on some IQ tests and can be used as a predictor of academic success. However, a downfall of using general intelligence is that the score focuses mainly on cognitive abilities and does not measure other important types of abilities.

Thurstone's Primary Mental Abilities

L.L. Thurstone disagreed with Spearman and believed that intelligence is not dependent on one general factor, but on several primary mental abilities. He considered the idea of a single general intelligence to be too narrow a concept for the wide range of human talents and identified a total of seven different **primary mental abilities**—verbal comprehension (vocabulary), verbal fluency, inductive reasoning, spatial visualization, number computation, memory recall, and perceptual speed. Based on Thurstone's idea of the existence of several specific types of intelligences, J.P. Guilford identified over 100 separate and measurable mental abilities. The advantage of a multifactor theory is the identification of specific mental abilities, which is useful in education because it can help discover areas in which students may need assistance, such as math or reading, in order to be successful.

Gardner's Multiple Intelligences

Another multiple factor theory was proposed by **Howard Gardner;** his theory originally consisted of seven intelligences that exist independently of each other. Currently there are eight **multiple intelligences**—verbal-linguistic, logical-mathematical, spatial, musical, bodily-kinesthetic, interpersonal, intrapersonal, and naturalist with the possibility of more to come. Although these intelligences are independent, they are often used together to solve complicated problems. Gardner gathered evidence by examining the effects on specific intelligences resulting from damage to particular brain areas and testing prodigies and savants. An advantage to Gardner's theory is that it includes other types of intelligence not measured on traditional IQ tests. However, it is difficult to identify how many specialized intelligences exist and to devise an accurate method of measuring them. There is also skepticism regarding how bodily-kinesthetic can be labeled as a mental ability, as opposed to a talent.

STUDY TIP

Be able to distinguish between Howard Gardner's intrapersonal and interpersonal intelligences.

- *Intrapersonal intelligence* refers to an individual's level of self-awareness, including an understanding of one's own emotions, behaviors, and cognitions.
- Interpersonal intelligence refers to an individual's level of understanding the emotions and motivations of others in order to form positive relationships and work effectively with others. To remember *inter*personal, think of an interstate that connects two cities.

Sternberg's Triarchic Theory of Intelligence

Robert Sternberg, another multifactor theorist, identifies three sets of mental abilities—practical, analytical, and creative intelligence. **Practical intelligence** refers to the realistic and useful thinking abilities that enable a person to cope with and thrive in their environment. **Analytical intelligence** is the logical reasoning typically measured on traditional IQ tests. Finally, **creative intelligence** is the inventive problem-solving abilities required to generate new ideas and learn from experience. This theory differentiates between what is commonly referred to as "book smarts" (analytical) and "street smarts" (practical). To remember the three parts of Sternberg's triarchic theory of intelligence, use the acronym PAC (**p**ractical, **a**nalytical, and **c**reative).

Two Types of Intelligence

Raymond Cattell divided general intelligence into two different types—fluid and crystallized intelligence. **Fluid intelligence** involves the rapid processing of information and memory span needed to solve new types of problems and make new associations and analogies with existing knowledge. **Crystallized intelligence** involves knowledge acquired over the lifespan, including vocabulary, verbal skills, cultural knowledge, and factual information. With old age, fluid intelligence tends to decrease, but crystallized intelligence remains steady or even increases with old age.

Emotional Intelligence

Peter Salovey and John Mayer first introduced the idea of emotional intelligence. **Emotional intelligence** is the ability to recognize emotion in others and in oneself and incorporate knowledge about emotion into reasoning and thought processes. Emotionally intelligent individuals are capable of managing their own emotions and are better at expressing empathy. This concept was popularized by Daniel Goleman and is now taught in many schools and companies. Psychologists agree that individuals who possess the attributes associated with emotional intelligence are better prepared for success in personal relationships and the world of work, but many believe that this does not constitute a separate type of intelligence. A major criticism of this theory is that emotional intelligence assessments may in fact do little more than measure personality traits.

STUDY TIP

Be able to compare and contrast historic and contemporary theories of intelligence, including the two-factor (Spearman), primary mental abilities (Thurstone), multiple intelligences (Gardner), and the triarchic theory of intelligence (Sternberg).

History of Intelligence Tests

One of the earliest attempts at determining intelligence was the use of **phrenology**, or the study of how bumps on an individual's head indicated personality traits, skills, and intelligence. Other early efforts searched for a strong correlation between brain size and intelligence, but these efforts were unsuccessful. **Sir Francis Galton,** a cousin of Darwin and pioneer in psychometrics, introduced the idea that intelligence was hereditary because intelligent individuals often had intelligent children. As a nativist, Galton examined differences in inherited intelligence by utilizing statistical methods. He attempted to measure intelligence by testing the basic sensory and motor abilities of individuals; he included reaction time, sensory ability, and memory, but was unable to determine any significant conclusions.

Modern intelligence testing began with the development of the first instrument to measure intellectual ability in France during the early 1900s. **Alfred Binet** and Theodore Simon were hired by the French Ministry of Education to devise a method to determine which students were unable to succeed in regular classrooms, in order to arrange for them to be placed in special schools. Unlike Galton, who measured intelligence in terms of sensory and motor abilities, Binet and Simon created a test that evaluated children in terms of reasoning and comprehension tasks. Binet introduced a new concept, **mental age** or the score on an IQ test that indicates the typical age group an individual's score represents. Mental age provided a framework for comparing individuals, and Binet inferred that children with cognitive disabilities would have scores more typical of a child who was younger. Based on this concept of mental age, Binet created the first intelligence test that was used to evaluate mental abilities.

The concept of **intelligence quotient (IQ)** was created by William Stern to provide a specific score, indicating the level of intelligence in a particular individual, which enabled comparisons to be made between individuals of different ages. Stern's formula for IQ is mental age divided by chronological age multiplied by 100. This type of IQ score is called a *ratio IQ*. If mental and chronological ages are equivalent, the individual is said to have an average IQ, which is 100. Individuals who have a mental age that is greater than their chronological age have above-average IQs. The major flaw in the traditional IQ formula is that it is not effective for creating ratios in older individuals. Modern IQ scores are not determined by using Stern's formula and are instead based on comparing individual performance to a pretested group and establishing norms. The modern IQ formula is called a *deviation IQ* and is obtained by dividing an individual's score on the IQ test by the average test score of individuals their same age in a pretested group and then multiplying that result by 100.

STUDY TIP

Be able to compute a ratio IQ for a simple example: IQ = (mental age/chronological age) × 100. Also, be aware that a modern IQ score is based on comparing an individual's test score to a pretested group (deviation IQ).

Lewis Terman, a psychologist and professor at Stanford University, translated and revised the original intelligence test created by Binet for use in the United States. This test initially used the ratio IQ formula and was renamed the **Stanford-Binet** test. The Stanford-Binet test is known for its high reliability and predictive value. It is very accurate in terms of predicting future academic achievement and may be best thought of as a measure of scholastic aptitude or achievement. The original version of the Stanford-Binet test has been revised multiple times, and the current Stanford-Binet Intelligence Scale is widely used today to assess intelligence and cognitive abilities for individuals ranging from two to eighty-nine years of age. In addition, scores are now based on comparisons to pretested groups resulting in a deviation IQ score.

David Wechsler criticized the Stanford-Binet test because it was too heavily focused on verbal skills. Wechsler designed a set of intelligence tests that were capable of measuring cognitive skills and evaluating individuals with lower verbal abilities for overall intelligence. Currently the Wechsler Intelligence Scales include separate tests for adults (WAIS), children (WISC), and preschoolers (WPPSI). Wechsler's scales include both **verbal and performance subscales** and measure a variety of abilities through the use of eleven subtests. The verbal subscale includes tests on general information, comprehension, arithmetic reasoning, digit span, and vocabulary. The performance subscale includes tests on digit–symbol substitution, picture completion, block design, picture arrangement, and object assembly. Final test results are broken into three subscale scores: verbal, performance, and the total. The separation of subscale scores allows for areas of weakness to be easily identified. The three scores are then converted into deviation IQ scores, with the mean set at 100 and a standard deviation of 15.

Measuring Intelligence

Intelligence is not the same as IQ. Intelligence is a complex concept whose exact meaning psychologists continue to debate. An IQ, or **intelligence quotient**, on the other hand, is a specific score on an intelligence test that may or may not be an accurate measure of the cognitive capabilities of that particular individual. If intelligence is the same as academic achievement, then an IQ is an excellent way to measure intelligence because IQ test scores are usually positively correlated with school grades. Intelligence tests are separated into two general categories in terms of measuring cognitive abilities. **Achievement tests** are intelligence tests created for the purpose of determining the level of knowledge an individual has regarding a particular subject or skill that has resulted from learning or education. For example, after completing the AP Psychology course, students take the Advanced Placement exam in psychology, which is an achievement test, to determine how much material has been learned. **Aptitude tests** are assessments that are designed to predict the success of an individual by evaluating his or her level of skill on a variety of general abilities necessary for success in academic or career environments. Typically aptitude tests measure abilities such as mathematical calculation, language ability, and reasoning. Intelligence tests like the Stanford-Binet or Weschler Scales are aptitude assessments created to determine if an individual has the potential to learn based on the possession of basic skills. Other examples of aptitude tests include the SAT and ACT exams, both of which are utilized to determine if students have the skills required for success in college or, in other words, predict college success. As measures of aptitude SAT and ACT scores are checked against college grades to make sure that those scores correlate with future academic achievement. In reality, college entrance exams measure both aptitude (likelihood of college success) and achievement (accumulated knowledge based on high school course work.) It is important to realize, however, that the line between achievement and aptitude tests is unclear.

Intelligence tests may be given individually or in group settings. **Individual tests** are given to the person by a psychologist trained in the administration of the test in a one-on-one setting. Individual tests are more time-consuming and expensive than group tests, but they provide an opportunity for the test administrator to work closely with the examinee and develop a stronger understanding of their cognitive processes. The Stanford-Binet and Weschler Intelligence Scales are both administered individually. Because of the costs associated with individualized testing, many intelligence tests are now given as **group tests** in which large numbers of examinees take the same test at the same time under standardized conditions. Group tests allow for easier scoring and require little training to administer, but it is difficult to gain detailed information about specific thought processes because there is no relationship between the administrator and test taker. Sometimes intelligence tests are created to measure the speed of processing. In **power tests**, abilities are measured under testing conditions involving little or no time pressure, and in **speed tests** examinees' scores are based in part on how quickly they solve the problems presented.

Test Construction

The accuracy of conclusions based on the results of intelligence tests is directly related to the quality of their design. Psychometricians base test construction on standardization and the utilization of norms. It is important to note that psychometricians are not only interested in creating intelligence tests, but also generating useful measurement devices for other psychological variables, including personality traits. In order to be prepared for the AP Psychology exam, you will need to be able to differentiate between different types of reliability and validity and understand how tests are standardized.

Standardization

One aspect involved in test construction includes creating a standardized test that ensures uniformity of procedures and establishes reliability and validity. During the administration of the assessment, **standardization** would require that the procedures be kept the same. For example, standardized national tests like the AP Psychology exam use the same directions, time frames, and scoring rubrics for all individuals taking the exam. Standardization of procedures eliminates potential confounding variables and ensures, to the extent that it is possible, that no individuals have an advantage over others due to testing conditions. **Standardized tests** are created after they are first provided to a large pretested group to determine norms. **Norms** indicate typical scores for a pretested group that allows for the comparison of an individual test subject with the larger group. For example, the SAT, which is a standardized test, has a mean of 500 and a standard deviation of 100, enabling the comparison of individual scores to the larger group. The results of both the pretested group and the actual test subjects are analyzed for reliability and validity based on the procedures explained later in the chapter.

Once norms have been established they often form normal distributions as in the case of intelligence tests. **Normal distributions (curves)** create bell-shaped curves in which the mean, median, and mode are equivalent and located at the center of the distribution and have a predictable distribution of scores. In a normal distribution, approximately 68 percent of scores fall within one standard deviation of the mean, 95 percent of scores fall within two standard deviations of the mean, and 99 percent of scores fall within three standard deviations of the mean. In a normal distribution, standard deviations are measured in z-scores. Positive z-scores indicate standard deviations above the mean, and negative z-scores represent standard deviations below the mean. Therefore, based on the percentages of a normal distribution, approximately 68 percent of all scores will fall between a z-score of −1 and a z-score of +1. IQ scores form a normal distribution with an average score of 100 and a standard deviation of 15, this means that 68 percent of all scores fall between 85 and 115. The z-scores and their associated percentages are indicated in Figure 13.1.

Figure 13.1. Normal Distribution

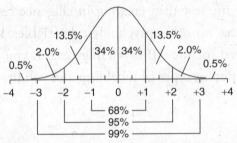

The diagram above illustrates the percentages of scores in a normal distribution that fall within specific z-scores. Percentile rank for any score in a normal distribution can be computed using this diagram, as long as the mean and

standard deviation are provided. The nature of normal distributions makes it simple to determine the percentile rank of any individual test taker, as long as the mean and standard deviation of the distribution of scores have been identified. **Percentile rank** refers to the percentage of scores equal to or below a specific score in a distribution. Different standardized tests will have different means and different standard deviations that can be used to determine percentile rank for scores within that distribution—see Table 13.1. In terms of most intelligence tests, the mean is 100 and the standard deviation is 15. Therefore, if an individual scored 100 on an intelligence assessment, that person would be at the 50th percentile, which means that 50 percent of the tested sample scored at or below the test score of 100. The steps in determining percentile rank are provided in Table 13.1, along with an example for identifying the percentile rank for an IQ score of 115.

Table 13.1.   Determining Percentile Rank

Steps to Determine Percentile Rank	Example for IQ Percentile Rank (Score of 115)
Determine the mean located at the center of the normal distribution.	The mean for IQ is 100.
Identify the test score associated with each z-score based on the standard deviation of the distribution.	Each z-score is equivalent to 15 points for IQ. A score of 115 is located at Z+1.
Percentages of individuals in the ranges of the normal curve can be seen in Figure 13.1 and include: $Z-1 = 34\%$ $Z+1 = 34\%$ $Z-2 = 13.5\%$ $Z+2 = 13.5\%$ $Z-3 = 2\%$ $Z+3 = 2\%$	A total of 34% of the scores in the distribution fall between the mean (100) and Z+1 (115).
Determine the percentile rank of the particular score that needs to be identified by adding the percentages of the scores to the left of the particular score in the normal distribution. Note: the mean score will always be 50% of the distribution.	The mean score in the distribution is 50% of the scores, plus the percentage of Z+1, which is 34% (50 + 34), creating a total of 84% of scores falling at or below an IQ score of 115. Therefore, an IQ score of 115 is at the 84th percentile.

Reliability

An important aspect of constructing intelligence tests or other types of assessments is ensuring reliability. **Reliability** refers to the consistency or repeatability of a particular assessment. There are a variety of methods for checking the reliability of an assessment, and they are explained in Table 13.2.

Table 13.2. Tests for Reliability

Test	Definition	Example
Split-half Reliability	Comparing the scores on one half of the test to the scores on the other half of the test. If a strong positive correlation is found between scores on the two halves of the test, it is said to be split-half reliable. *Note:* Split-half reliability involves giving the test only *one* time.	Alan is given a test designed to measure his current stress level, and, if his stress level is low on both odd- and even-numbered questions, the assessment demonstrates split-half reliability because it is consistent.
Test-retest Reliability	Comparing the scores of the *same* individual who takes the *same* exact test on *two* different occasions. If a strong positive correlation is found between the scores on both occasions, the test is said to be test-retest reliable and indicates the stability of the measurement tool. A major problem with test-retest reliability for achievement or aptitude tests can be practice effects.	Karlee is given a personality test that reveals she is very high in the trait of extraversion. If the personality assessment has test-retest reliability Karlee will have the *same* or a very similar score if she takes the exact *same* test two weeks later.
Alternate-forms Reliability	Comparing the results of two different but equivalent versions of a test given to subjects. If a strong positive correlation is found between the scores on the two different versions of the test, it is said to have alternate-forms reliability, which means that the two versions are equivalent. The use of alternate-forms eliminates practice effects.	The ACT is considered to have alternate-forms reliability if there is a strong positive correlation between the distribution of scores on version A and version B or if individuals who take both versions receive similar scores.
Interrater Reliability	Comparing the scores given by two different examiners of the same individual test subject. If both examiners give the *same* subject the *same* score, the testing instrument is considered to be interrater reliable. Interrater reliability is often important in determining if subjective data collected through observation is consistent, regardless of whom is recording the behavior of the subjects.	Kathee is interviewed by two separate clinical psychologists who both arrive at the same diagnosis based on the criteria listed in the *DSM-IV TR*. Because both examiners using the same testing tool arrived at the same conclusion, the *DSM-IV TR* would be considered interrater-reliable.

Validity

In addition to being consistent and repeatable (reliable), tests used by psychologists to measure intelligence or other variables must be valid. **Validity** refers to the accuracy of the test or measurement instrument being used. It is possible for a test to be reliable, but not valid, which would mean that every time an individual took the assessmenthe or she will receive the same inaccurate results. Various methods exist to assess the validity of a particular assessment tool; they are explained in Table 13.3.

Table 13.3. Common Types of Validity

Type	Definition	Example
Face Validity	The extent to which the material on a test appears on the surface to accurately measure what it intends to measure. Face validity is determined either by a non-expert or an expert who gives only a quick evaluation of the test.	A psychology teacher who is asked to evaluate the accuracy of the art history final exam could provide face validity only because the teacher does not have experience in the field.
Content Validity	The extent to which a test accurately measures the entire breadth of the subject it is intended to measure. For example, an ACT math test that included only geometry questions would lack content validity because it does not include other areas within the domain of math, such as algebra.	Because specific phobias are defined in the *DSM-IV TR* as requiring seven specific criteria, a diagnostic test for specific phobias would need to include questions related to all seven criteria in order to have content validity.
Construct Validity	The extent to which a test accurately measures the abstract theoretical idea (construct) or skill it is intended to measure. Constructs include ideas that are often difficult to define operationally, such as intelligence or personality traits.	If an intelligence test actually measures cognitive abilities and not a different theoretical idea (construct) such as language ability or cultural knowledge, it has construct validity.
Criterion Validity	Scores on a particular test that are positively correlated with scores on another existing and well-established test (criterion) of the same skill, trait, or ability.	Dr. Taber created a depression-screening instrument, and individuals who scored high on her test also scored high on the well-known Beck's Depression Inventory indicating criterion validity.
Predictive Validity	The extent to which a test score forecasts (predicts) future behaviors or results.	If high scores on the Stanford-Binet Intelligence Scale are strongly positively correlated with academic success or high GPA, the Stanford-Binet can be said to have high predictive validity.

Selecting testing instruments for research that are both reliable and valid is a critical part of the research process for psychologists who study intelligence and cognitive abilities. Since achievement tests and aptitude tests have different uses, they are validated in different ways. An achievement test is evaluated for content validity, while aptitude tests are compared to other tests or indicators of the same behavior in order to determine criterion validity. For example, an aptitude test might be designed to predict college performance. Therefore, its scores would be checked against college grades to make sure that those scores correlated with the examinee's future academic achievement.

Extremes of Intelligence

Intelligence test scores create normal distributions, and almost all individuals fall within two standard deviations of the mean (95 percent of the population). Psychologists, however, are interested in studying both extremes, including cognitively disabled individuals on the low end of the distribution and gifted individuals on the high end. Because intelligence tests identify where individuals fall on the cognitive continuum, they can be highly controversial and at times have been misused. IQ test scores, especially on the low end, can lead to negative stereotypes or create self-fulfilling prophecies. It is important to remember that an IQ score is not the only gage of cognitive ability and that IQ tests often do not reveal all types of intelligence.

Cognitive Disability

Individuals with cognitive disabilities are classified as belonging to one of four levels of mental retardation, according to the current diagnostic manual published by the American Psychiatric Association. A new edition of the manual is currently being produced, and when the revised version is released, it is likely that the classification of mental retardation will be changed to cognitive or intellectual disability (due to the stigma associated with the term *retardation*). **Mental retardation** refers to individuals at the lower extreme of intelligence and is generally determined by IQ tests and problems coping with the basic demands of independent living. An IQ score of less than 70 is considered cognitively disabled, but enormous diversity in terms of ability is present among the four levels—mild, moderate, severe, and profound (see Table 13.4). Altogether, the four levels of cognitive disability make up about one percent of the population. Each of the four levels is explained in greater detail in the chart below.

Table 13.4. Classification Levels of Cognitive Disability

Level	IQ	Characteristics
Mild 85% of cognitively disabled individuals	50–70	• Eligible as children and teens for special education in school which is beneficial for social and vocational skills. • Capable of developing academic skills at approximately a sixth-grade level. • Adults in this group can achieve independence and occupational success, although they may need help with social and financial problems.
Moderate 10% of cognitively disabled individuals	35–50	• During childhood, special classes that emphasize self-care instead of academic achievement are beneficial. • Capable of developing academic skills ranging from approximately a second- to fourth-grade level. • Adults in this group are able to succeed at unskilled or routine jobs, often in sheltered workshops, and most are dependent on their families.
Severe 4% of cognitively disabled individuals	20–35	• Individuals at this level are mostly institutionalized and require a controlled environment. • With prolonged training, may develop limited speech and the ability to take care of their basic needs.
Profound 1% of cognitively disabled individuals	Below 20	• Individuals at this level require total supervision and care for their entire lives. • Language ability is extremely limited, and there are severe physical and motor impairments.

The most common cause of cognitive disability is **Down syndrome,** which accounts for 10 to 20 percent of all moderately to severely disabled children. This chromosomal disorder is caused by a genetic abnormality involving an additional chromosome on the twenty-first pair. Children with Down syndrome seldom have an IQ above 50, and many have specific physical abnormalities. Two additional genetic causes of cognitive disability, Phenylketonuria (PKU) and fragile X syndrome, are discussed further in the biological psychology chapter. Cognitive disability can also be attributed to exposure to teratogens, such as in the case of **fetal alcohol syndrome,** which results when the mother drinks alcohol in excess during pregnancy.

Autistic spectrum disorder refers to a range of permanent developmental disorders that are diagnosed in childhood, including autism and Asperger's syndrome. Autism is a developmental disorder that results in difficulties with communication and social interactions. The exact cause of this disease is unknown, but researchers suspect a genetic link. Additionally, some scientists believe that the difficulties autistic children have in terms of empathy and social relations may be due to a deficiency in mirror neurons. **Savant syndrome** is a rare condition marked by an island of brilliance in relation to limited cognitive abilities. A savant is someone who is diagnosed as cognitively disabled or with a developmental disorder such as autism, but the savant also displays an exceptional skill in a limited domain such as music, art, math, or calculating dates. Obsessive fixations on particular topics and memorization of trivia can also be present.

DID YOU KNOW?

As the Academy-Award winning lead actor in the 1988 movie *Rain Man*, Dustin Hoffman met with and researched a number of savants, including the real "Rain Man," Kim Peek. Kim, who passed away in December 2009, had an encyclopedic memory and could recite facts about world and American history, the Bible, sports, geography, the space program, popular culture, current events, and music and literature as well as do calendar calculations (including a person's day of birth, present year's birthday, and the year and date the person would turn 65 years old so he or she could retire) and list the area code, ZIP code, and television stations for any locale. Some other remarkable savants—and well worth an Internet search—include Leslie Lemke, Alonzo Clemons, Daniel Tammet, and Brittany Maier.

Giftedness

On the other side of the spectrum are gifted children. Although **gifted** is commonly defined as children who have an IQ over 130, the term *gifted* is also used to refer to individuals who have special talents, creativity, or leadership ability. In 1926, **Lewis Terman** published his book, *Genetic Studies of Genius,* a longitudinal study of one thousand gifted children possessing IQ scores greater than 140 whom he sometimes referred to as *Terman's Termites.* Contrary to the stereotypical expectations of the period that gifted children would become maladjusted, Terman found that children with high IQs grew up to be well-adjusted adults who achieved significantly higher levels of professional success and reported high levels of happiness and physical health.

Creativity and Intelligence

Creativity and intelligence are not the same thing, but creativity, like intelligence, is a difficult concept to define. Psychologists observed that creativity is influenced by personality and encouraged by a receptive, as opposed to critical, attitude toward new ideas. Modern cognitive psychologists define **creativity** as cognitive processes resulting in original and useful ideas.

Many aspects of creativity cannot be measured on intelligence tests, and creating reliable and valid measures of creativity have proved difficult. Tests of **divergent thinking**, or the ability to generate a variety of solutions to one problem, are a common psychological method of measuring creativity. Questions for **convergent thinking**, or thought processes that are designed to produce just one end result, are not generally used during creative thinking, but are often included on intelligence tests. The question of whether or not a creative person must also be intelligent remains. Once IQ reaches a certain level, correlations between creativity with intelligence test scores are fairly low. An intelligent person would naturally have more information at his or her disposal to use creatively, but the secret of creativity seems to be that there is something unique about how creative individuals think that distinguishes them from others with similar levels of intelligence.

Intelligence Controversies

Does intelligence remain stable throughout the lifespan? As was previously noted, during old age there is a difference between fluid and crystallized intelligence, but psychologists also wonder if intelligence is stable earlier in life. In general, two variables affect IQ stability: the interval of time between the initial test and retest, and the subject's age. The shorter the interval between test and retest, the more stable the IQ will be. Also, the older a person is at the time of the initial IQ test, the more stable that IQ will be. Intelligence changes dramatically during childhood, and the greatest changes occur early. The difference in the intellectual capacity of a three-year-old and a four-year-old is much greater than the difference between a fifteen-year-old and a sixteen-year-old. In general, however, IQ scores are fairly stable measures after the age of approximately seven. The purpose of determining the stability of an individual's IQ is to anticipate problems one might encounter during intellectual development. Then it is often possible to develop intervention programs and change that person's intellectual future.

Another vigorous debate in the field of intelligence is the source of intellectual abilities. Psychologists agree that both genetic and biological factors (nature) and environmental influences (nurture) contribute to differences among individuals regarding intelligence. Evidence for the influence of genetics on intelligence is typically generated by twin, family, and adoption studies which result in heritability measurements. **Heritability** is a mathematical measure that indicates the estimated amount of variation among individuals that is related to genes translated into a percentage. Biological factors that can have a negative effect on individual intelligence include genetic disorders such as Down syndrome, Phenylketonuria (PKU), and fragile X syndrome.

Environmental factors also contribute significantly to differences among individuals in terms of intelligence. Evidence supporting the influence of nurture on IQ comes from poverty studies and research comparing how intelligence is impacted by the addition of an enriched environment. Factors that may influence the development of intelligence include intellectual advantage (such as a house full of books), parental concern with a child's educational achievement or general welfare, environmental change (such as attending summer school), or that the child is developing more quickly than normal. External or environmental factors that are known to have a negative effect on intelligence are problems with exposure to teratogens during pregnancy, physical trauma and illness, drastic changes in the family (such as divorce, loss of parents, adoption or a foster home), and lack of opportunity. The **Flynn effect** is a recently discovered phenomenon that demonstrates that the average IQ has been rising dramatically over successive generations. Most researchers believe that the Flynn effect must be the result of environmental factors because the time period over which the changes have been noticed is much too short for evolution within the gene pool to have occurred.

Group Differences and Bias

Misconceptions about the relationship between heredity and intelligence have caused pain for millions of people. In the United States alone, Americans of Irish, Italian, Jewish, Chinese, and African descent and women have all been accused of being less intelligent than white men. These individuals have been denied jobs, education, and legal rights in part because of these claims. It is true that, in the United States, the IQ scores of certain groups are, on average, lower than other groups. However, the range of IQ for European Americans and other groups is actually the same; every race contains genius. The mean IQ difference has no meaning for specific individuals, only the distribution of scores for the entire population. The problem with comparing different racial or gender groups is that IQ tests have traditionally been developed for only one population: relatively affluent Americans of white European ancestry. IQ tests may be measuring cultural similarity and rules for white affluent Americans as well as intelligence.

Cultural Bias

Psychologists are concerned that intelligence tests might be unfair because individuals who belong to particular ethnic groups score lower on tests because they do not possess enough of an understanding of the dominant culture; thus some questions are unclear. Equally important is the fact that some cultures may have very different interpretations about what intelligence consists of. There seems to be no question that IQ tests, achievement tests, and aptitude tests are culturally biased. The mere fact that a person needs to have good English skills to do well on them is evidence of cultural bias. Standardized intelligence tests that require language skills are the most likely to be culturally biased. For example, the cultural bias of the Wechsler exam is most noticeable on the verbal sections. Although intelligence tests are excellent at evaluating language skills required for success, they do not measure levels of creativity, persistence, or relationship skills that are also necessary for success.

A **culture-fair test** is one that is designed to allow all individuals, regardless of culture, the opportunity to perform equally well. The advantage of developing a culture-fair test to be used across cultures is that it would be possible to measure innate abilities, such as Spearman's general intellectual ability. Psychologists have tried to develop culture-fair tests by first eliminating the problem of different languages and either translating the test or removing language altogether. In addition, psychologists have paid particular attention to speed of performance. In some cultures and rural environments, the tempo of life is slower and there is less emphasis on finishing tests quickly. Thus, culture-fair tests often allow longer time limits and give no credit for fast performance, while traditional tests typically have rigid time restrictions and may be scored according to the total number of items completed. The most important way that culture-fair tests differ is in test content. Many tests are culturally biased because they require the subject to be familiar with objects that are absent in their culture, or that have different uses or values. For example, a person raised with the British game of cricket would assume that a baseball bat is used for hitting balls on the ground and perhaps fail a portion of a test that was developed in the United States. The idea of being able to design an intelligence test that is completely **culture-free** may be out of reach, and perhaps a culture-relevant test is more appropriate. A **culture-relevant test** focuses on skills and knowledge that are specific and important to a particular culture and would be administered only to members of the culture for which it was designed.

Gender Bias

Males and females typically score equally on measures of general intelligence; however, they differ in their scores regarding specific abilities. Males, on average, may score higher on tasks that involve visual-spatial skills, mathematical calculations, and some motor skills. Females, on average, tend to score higher on tasks of verbal ability, reading comprehension, spelling, and speed of processing for recall of semantic information. It must be noted that these average differences apply only to the group, not specific individuals. There is actually a greater average difference within genders than there is between genders. When conducting research regarding group differences, researchers need to be cautioned about the impact of stereotype threat. **Stereotype threat** happens when an individual's belief that negative stereotypes will be used by others to rate his or her performance results in the individual experiencing anxiety that leads to low performance. For example, if a girl is led to believe, either directly or indirectly, that girls are unable to perform well in math and is then given a math test, she may do poorly, due to anxiety caused by this expectation.

Abnormal Behavior

Psychopathology or **abnormal psychology** involves the scientific investigation of the cause (etiology), diagnosis, and treatment of mental illness. This specialty in psychology involves both basic and applied research, as well as clinical practice, and can overlap with a variety of other fields, including cognitive psychology, medicine, biology, and pharmacology. The term psychopathology is also frequently used as a synonym for mental illness or abnormal behavior. Mental illness is extremely difficult to define; therefore, a variety of models to explain this concept have been proposed. The **statistical model** defines abnormality as something that is rare and unusual. This definition is incomplete and inaccurate because, although some mental illnesses, such as dissociative disorders, are extremely rare, others, such as anxiety disorders, are more common. Also, it bears mentioning that if abnormal behavior were defined simply as being rare, then individuals with Olympic medals would be considered abnormal.

Another way to define mental illness is the disturbances in cognition, behavior, or emotions that are deviant, dysfunctional, distressing, and potentially dangerous. Mental illness can be seen as being **deviant** if the resulting thoughts or actions differ from normal behavior that is determined by cultural norms. For example, in some cultures today it would be considered deviant for a woman to be seen in public with her shoulders visible. It is also important to note that cultural norms can change over time. In the United States it would have been considered deviant, until recently, for the father to stay home and raise the children while the mother worked to support the family. A second aspect of mental illness is whether or not particular thoughts or behaviors are **dysfunctional**, also referred to as maladaptive. Thoughts and behaviors are considered dysfunctional if they prevent individuals from caring for themselves, meeting obligations, and being productive. For instance, the behavior of an addict who continues to use drugs even after losing his or her job and going bankrupt would be considered dysfunctional. Also, individuals with extreme social phobias that prevent them from leaving their home when they want to are dysfunctional. A third aspect of mental illness includes thoughts and behaviors that are **distressful** or upsetting to an individual. Although stress and worry are typical emotions that everyone experiences, they become abnormal if they are excessive, constant, and long-lasting. Finally, some definitions of mental illness include the category of **dangerous** thoughts or behaviors. While most individuals with mental illness do not pose a threat to either themselves or others, behaviors that are dangerous may provide a very serious indicator of mental illness. Suicidal behaviors or persistent starvation that can lead to death as seen in anorexia nervosa are considered to be abnormal because these behaviors are dangerous. Psychological disorders, or mental illness, are generally diagnosed based on a pervasive pattern of thoughts or behaviors that are dysfunctional and distressing, making these the most important criteria.

STUDY TIP

While there is no one specific definition for mental illness, many psychologists use the 4 D's—*deviant, dysfunctional, distressful,* and *dangerous*—when discussing abnormal thoughts and behaviors.

The term *insanity* is not the same as mental illness. **Insanity** is a legal definition that indicates if a particular individual can be held responsible for his or her actions in a court of law. The term *insanity* was designed to protect defendants who were not capable at the time of the crime of differentiating between right and wrong and individuals who are not capable of understanding what is happening during their trial (competency), preventing them from participating in their own defense. Despite the fact that insanity is not a psychological or medical term, forensic psychologists and psychiatrists are often asked to evaluate the competency of accused individuals and testify in court as to whether or not an individual fits the criteria for insanity, as defined by the law, when the crime was committed. It is especially difficult for a psychologist to determine the mental state of an individual at the time of the crime after the fact. Legally most individuals with mental illness are not considered insane. Despite public misconceptions, the insanity defense is almost never used (less than one percent of cases), and, when used, it is often unsuccessful. Individuals considered not guilty by reason of insanity by a court are committed to psychiatric hospitals and remain there until it is determined that they no longer pose a threat.

Diagnosis of Psychological Disorders

Psychologists typically make a diagnosis of mental illness through the process of assessment. Assessment refers to the accumulation of data about an individual through the use of clinical interviews, psychometric tests, and the results of medical and neurological exams. Clinical interviews involve a one-on-one interaction between the individual and the psychologist that is designed to gain background information about the person from what the person says, as well as his or her body language. Because medical conditions can impact emotional and behavioral functioning, assessment often includes information about a person's physical health. Psychometric tests include a variety of assessments such as IQ tests, personality questionnaires, and self-report screenings for depression or anxiety. Finally, the psychologist determines whether or not a diagnosis can be made for the individual. A diagnosis is typically made when information gathered during the assessment process is assembled and evaluated according to the criteria of the *Diagnostic and Statistical Manual of Mental Disorders* published by the American Psychiatric Association, although other classification systems also exist.

DSM-IV-TR

The American Psychiatric Association's classification system of mental illnesses, known as the ***Diagnostic and Statistical Manual of Mental Disorders*** (DSM), is the classification system most often used in the United States. The current edition of the manual, ***DSM-IV-TR***, uses five axes of classification (see Table 14.1). Work is currently being done on the *DSM-V* is tentatively scheduled to be released in 2013. The multi-axial format allows psychologists and psychiatrists to make a mental illness diagnosis and also acknowledge medical and environmental factors that contribute to the overall mental health of a particular individual. The diagnostic manual includes the common symptoms, prevalence, specifically required diagnostic criteria, and differential diagnosis (how to distinguish a particular mental illness from others that are similar) for hundreds of specific disorders. The *DSM-IV-TR* does not provide recommendations for treatment or indicate the causes of mental illnesses.

Table 14.1.   The Multi-Axial System for the *DSM-IV-TR*

Axis	Title	Explanation
Axis I	Clinical Disorders	Diagnostic categories that describe all major mental illnesses except personality disorders.
		Major diagnostic categories including mood, anxiety, somatoform, dissociative, and schizophrenia are all listed under Axis I.
Axis II	Personality Disorders and Mental Retardation	Personality disorders and mental retardation (cognitive disability)

(continued)

Table 14.1. *(continued)*

Axis	Title	Explanation
Axis III	General Medical Conditions	Description of medical conditions that are not mental illnesses, but may potentially impact functioning. Examples might include high blood pressure, diabetes, chronic pain, or physical injury.
Axis IV	Psychosocial and Environmental Problems	Description of environmental factors that may potentially impact functioning including social or family problems, economic hardship, work problems, legal difficulties, and housing or healthcare disparities.
Axis V	Global Assessment of Functioning	Description of an individual's ability to function as a whole based on a scale of 1 to 100 and determined by a clinician. Higher scores (closer to 100) indicate superior functioning, and the person is usually successful in many activities and relationships. Extremely low scores are indicative of grossly impaired functioning in which the individual struggles with basic hygiene without assistance and may be in immediate danger of severely injuring him-/herself or others.

Diagnosis of mental illness according to the criteria listed in the *DSM-IV-TR* is effective because it provides a common language to describe patterns of dysfunctional and distressing cognitions, behaviors, and emotions among a variety of mental health and medical professionals enabling better treatment. The most recent version of the DSM has made significant improvements in terms of reliability and validity of diagnosis for most of the mental illnesses listed. The improvements are the result of more precise and observable symptoms and specific instructions designed to differentiate among similar conditions. However, questions have been raised regarding issues of reliability and validity for some categories, especially personality disorders, and problems remain in terms of differentiating among similar disorders, making diagnosis difficult. The *DSM-IV-TR* has also been criticized for being culturally and gender biased. The manual does attempt to address this by including some basic guidelines for understanding how the culture of an individual influences mental health, as well as a glossary of various culture-bound syndromes. One of the most important criticisms is that a diagnosis required by insurance companies creates a label, which may increase problems for individuals. Those with a mental illness diagnosis may suffer from discrimination as a result of the stigma that sometimes can be attached to these labels.

STUDY TIP

It is possible for one individual to receive a diagnosis on all five DSM-IV-TR axes. An example of a diagnosis across each of the five axes is included in Table 14.2.

Table 14.2.   An Example of a Diagnosis Across the Five DSM-IV-TR Axes

Axis	Title	Diagnosis
Axis I	Clinical Disorder	Generalized anxiety disorder
Axis II	Personality Disorder or Mental Retardation	Dependent personality disorder
Axis III	General Medical Conditions	Migraine headaches
Axis IV	Psychosocial and Environmental Problems	Stressful career
Axis V	Global Assessment of Functioning	80 out of 100, indicating no major impairment of function

Labels

Psychologist **David Rosenhan** did a famous study that investigated the power of labels. Rosenhan and others gained admittance to psychiatric hospitals by faking the complaint of hearing voices. All the individuals, referred to as pseudopatients, were admitted to a facility with the diagnosis of schizophrenia or manic depression, based on only this one symptom. After being admitted, the pseudopatients proceeded to act normal and informed the staff that the voices they had been hearing were gone. However, during their stay in the facility, professionals at times interpreted their normal behavior as further symptoms of mental illness. For example, the note-taking of one patient was interpreted as "peculiar note-taking behavior" in the patient's file. In addition, the pseudopatients explained that they felt ignored by hospital staff. On average the patients stayed for three weeks, and, when they were released, they were provided with a diagnosis of schizophrenia in remission. According to the Rosenhan study, the power of labels was apparent, and once labels were attached to a person, the labels were very hard to remove. Diagnostic labels can also be stigmatizing, resulting in discrimination. Despite these concerns, labels do have benefits because they can help individuals to better understand their own behavior and predict future behaviors, as well as allowing for clear communication among mental health professionals. There must be a thorough consideration of all relevant factors before a person's behavior is labeled abnormal.

Models of Abnormal Behavior

Throughout history, three general explanations for the causes of psychological illnesses have been consistently presented. Some theories explain that psychological illness, like physical illness, is the result of a disruption within the body. Many cultures offer supernatural theories for abnormal behavior, including possession by evil spirits, witchcraft, curses, divine punishment, and, in some cases, blessings. Evidence for supernatural explanations for abnormal behavior can be found in ancient Chinese, Egyptian, and Hebrew cultures, as well as in medieval Europe. A final general theory is that mental illnesses have stress, trauma, or psychological causes. The various modern explanations and theories for abnormal behavior are outlined in Table 14.3.

Table 14.3. Models of Abnormal Behavior

Model	Description
Medical (Organic)	Proposes that mental illness originates in the mind and body due to some internal disease or injury (systemic or infectious) or external injury (traumatic). The medical model views mental illness as a disease that requires medical care; it developed as a result of advances in science during the Renaissance and scientific revolution. It replaced the belief that mental illness was caused by demonic possession. The medical model is evident today in the biological approach.
Biological	States that mental illness is related to physical differences in the brain in terms of structure and function, such as problems with specific neurotransmitters and hormones. This perspective also explores how genetic predispositions influence mental illness. Family studies reveal inherited risks for specific mental illnesses and brain imaging research demonstrates differences in brain structure and neurotransmitter function in individuals with mental illnesses.
Psychoanalytic/ Psychodynamic	Explains that mental illness is the result of unresolved unconscious conflicts from childhood and sexual and aggressive urges or instincts. The modern *psychodynamic* perspective also focuses on how social interactions influence mental illness.

(continued)

Table 14.3. *(continued)*

Model	Description
Humanist	Mental illness results from a lack of unconditional positive regard or self-acceptance and failure to genuinely and honestly evaluate one's own behavior. Problems come from the inability to reach one's full potential due to being blocked by society. Humanism as a perspective has been most effective in terms of treatment methods and explaining problems with adjustment, but has been less useful in terms of providing explanations for severe forms of mental illness.
Cognitive	Stresses the influence of thought processes on the development of mental illness. Dysfunctional or maladaptive cognitions are major factors that determine whether an individual will develop a mental illness. An individual's perception regarding the level of control he or she has over events and the attributions that the person makes to explain what happens to him or her influence whether or not psychological disorders will develop or persist.
Behaviorist Social Learning	Emphasizes that abnormal behavior is learned in the same way as most other human behavior through classical conditioning, operant conditioning, and modeling. Although most extreme behaviorists do not refer to any internal states or mental processes, others use a more moderate approach and consider intervening mental and emotional variables.
Biopsychosocial	Because each perspective has strengths and weaknesses, modern psychology combines the biological, psychological, and social perspectives to explain a given situation. The growing influence of the biopsychosocial perspective is evident in the most recent revision of the DSM, which includes greater detail regarding the interaction of biological, psychological, and social influences on human thought and behavior. Additionally, the most recent DSM includes information regarding the influence of culture in terms of the prevalence and observed symptoms associated with various psychological disorders.

Categories of Psychological Disorders

The various diagnostic categories included in the *DSM-IV-TR* identify groups of psychological disorders that share similar diagnostic symptoms. In order to be prepared for the AP Psychology exam, you will need to be able to identify the main diagnostic categories, as well as common psychological disorders. Axis I categories include anxiety, mood, somatoform, dissociative, schizophrenia, cognitive disorders, and others. Axis II categories include personality disorders and cognitive disabilities. It is important to note that the symptoms and diagnostic criteria for each of the specific psychological disorders discussed in the sections below are only summaries.

Anxiety Disorders

Individuals with anxiety disorders experience fear that is extreme, chronic, and interferes with daily functioning. This fear is exaggerated or not in proportion to what is actually being experienced. All anxiety disorders include some form of anxiety as the predominant symptom. Symptoms of anxiety include physical symptoms (e.g., accelerated heart rate and breathing, sweating, dizziness, muscle tension or trembling, nausea), cognitive symptoms (e.g., worry, fear, irritability), and behavioral symptoms (e.g., avoidance, escape, aggression, distraction). According to the DSM-IV-TR, there are five types of anxiety disorders: panic disorder, generalized anxiety disorder, phobic disorders, obsessive-compulsive disorder, and stress disorders.

Panic Disorder

A **panic attack** is the unexpected onset of fear and anxiety. Panic attacks have a minimum of four symptoms, reach a peak level of exaggerated arousal within ten minutes, and then gradually dissipate. The physical symptoms of a panic attack amount to an extreme fight-or-flight reaction, despite the absence of a threat. Cognitive symptoms that accompany a panic attack may involve the thought that the individual is losing control, having a heart attack, or dying. The chief features of **panic disorder** are recurrent unexpected panic attacks followed by at least one month of persistent concern about having another panic attack. Individuals with panic disorder experience ongoing anxiety because they are worried about future panic attacks happening, which can then in turn make more panic attacks likely.

Generalized Anxiety Disorder

Chronic, widespread, and persistent anxiety characterizes a **generalized anxiety disorder (GAD).** Individuals with GAD are uneasy, anxious, and experience excessive amounts of worry, although they cannot identify the source of their anxiety. Because the source of the anxiety cannot be identified, this type of anxiety is sometimes called *free floating.* In order for a diagnosis of GAD, the individual needs to experience symptoms on most days for at least six months. Physical and cognitive symptoms that disrupt functioning include difficulty concentrating, irritability, muscle tension, sleep disturbance, problems making decisions, and restlessness.

Phobic Disorders

Phobias are intense, irrational, and persistent fears of specific objects or situations that pose no actual danger, which lead to avoidance and anxiety that disrupts normal life. The *DSM-IV-TR* divides phobias into separate categories of specific phobias, social phobias, and agoraphobia. Individuals with **specific phobias** have irrational fears of objects and situations, such as heights, closed spaces, snakes, and spiders, which do not pose any actual threat, which prevents them from normal functioning. Individuals with **social phobias** or **social anxiety disorder** fear social situations or performing in public, which prevents them from taking part in normal interactions because of the potential threat of embarrassment. Social phobias, for example, could include the fear of speaking, performing, or eating in public, which leads individuals to decline social invitations and avoid situations in which they believe they might be judged. **Agoraphobia** involves the fear of public places and open spaces due to the worry that one would not be able to escape. Agoraphobics avoid crowded locations such as airports, stores, concerts, or college campuses. In extreme cases, they may be unable to leave their own home. Individuals with agoraphobia may also have panic disorder. Although individuals suffering from phobias realize that the fear is irrational, they remain unable to explain or control it.

Obssessive-Compulsive Disorder

Obsessive-compulsive disorder (OCD) is diagnosed when unreasonable thoughts result in anxiety that the individual can reduce only through the use of specific behaviors or rituals. The high levels of anxiety and the amount of time required to complete the rituals disrupts the person's ability to function in many areas of his or her life, such as school, work, or family. Obsessive-compulsive disorder consists of two main symptoms: obsessions and compulsions. An **obsession** is a persistent, often unreasonable thought which cannot be dismissed and results in high levels of anxiety. Common obsessive thoughts include fear of infection or germs, fear that something terrible will happen to the person or to someone else, or fear that he or she will hurt someone else. A **compulsion** is a persistent act which is continuously repeated in order to reduce the anxiety created by the obsessive thought. Virtually any behavior can be viewed as a compulsion if the individual reports an irresistible urge to perform it and experiences considerable distress if prevented from performing that action. Common compulsions include hand washing, checking doors or light switches, counting, or hoarding. Most individuals with OCD realize that their obsessions are irrational and unlikely to actually happen and that their compulsions are disrupting their lives, but they continue to take part in the rituals because the level of anxiety becomes too great if they do not complete their compulsions.

STUDY TIP

Be able to differentiate between an obsession and a compulsion.
- *Obsessions* are irrational, persistent *thoughts* that result in anxiety.
- *Compulsions* are repetitive *actions* or rituals that individuals with OCD use to reduce anxiety.

Stress Disorders

Stress disorders, characterized as anxiety disorders, are caused by exposure to an extreme traumatic event. The person may have experienced, witnessed, or have been confronted with an event that was life-threatening, involving serious harm to self or others, or was perceived as such. The two main types of stress disorders are **acute stress disorder** and **posttraumatic stress disorder (PTSD)** which share common symptoms, including sleep difficulties, dissociative episodes, numbness, intrusive recollections of the event, flashbacks, exaggerated startle response, problems concentrating, and irritability. Acute stress disorder lasts between two days and four weeks and must happen within four weeks of the triggering event. Posttraumatic stress disorder is distinguished from acute stress disorder because the symptoms last longer than four weeks.

DID YOU KNOW?

According to the U.S. Department of Veterans Affairs, experts believe PTSD occurs:
- In about 11 to 20 percent of veterans of the Iraq and Afghanistan wars (Operations Iraqi and Enduring Freedom).
- In as many as 10 percent of Gulf War (Desert Storm) veterans.
- In about 30 percent of Vietnam veterans.

Causes of Anxiety Disorders

A variety of causes for anxiety disorders have been identified by the various psychological perspectives. The biological perspective emphasizes the genetic and physiological influences on anxiety disorders. Twin and family research studies indicate that genetics play a part in anxiety disorders. Low levels of the neurotransmitter GABA is involved in many anxiety disorders including GAD and anti-anxiety medications, such as *Valium* and *Xanax,* work by increasing the transmission of this inhibitory neurotransmitter. Low levels of serotonin are also correlated with symptoms associated with anxiety disorders. The behavioral approach is often used to explain how phobias are developed through classical conditioning and maintained with operant conditioning. Additionally, individuals who are exposed to high levels of environmental stress have a greater risk for developing an anxiety disorder. Cognitive factors related to anxiety disorders include the influence of irrational thoughts or worry which therapists attempt to replace with more realistic self-talk. Finally, the psychoanalytic approach would explain anxiety disorders as being the result of unresolved unconscious conflicts from childhood.

Mood Disorders

Mood disorders are characterized by disturbances or extremes in emotion and vary in terms of duration and severity. *Episodic* mood disorders involve a particular occasion or episode of severe and persistent mood disturbance that is clearly distinguished from prior functioning. *Chronic* mood disorders imply a long-standing (at least two years) illness with either continuous or intermittent disturbance in mood. Generally, these mood disturbances are more prolonged but not as severe as those associated with episodic disorders. In mood disorders the individual's overall mood tends to fall at one extreme or the other, that is, depressed or manic. Symptoms of **depression** include loss of energy, extreme sadness, sleep or eating disturbances, guilt, and recurrent thoughts of death or suicide. On the other extreme, symptoms of **mania** include hyperactivity, euphoria, decreased need for sleep, talkativeness, inflated self-esteem, and excessive involvement in activities without regard to their painful consequences (e.g., buying sprees, foolish business investments, sexual indiscretions, and reckless driving). Another symptom of mania is the **flight of ideas,** which refers to rapid shifts in conversation from one subject to another, based on superficial associations. The most commonly diagnosed mood disorders are listed in Table 14.4.

Table 14.4.   Mood Disorders

Disorder	Description
Major Depressive Disorder	One or more major depressive episodes lasting for longer than two weeks resulting in a signjficant impairment of physical, emotional, cognitive, and behavioral functioning. Suicidal risk is a significant concern associated with this diagnosis. *Note:* Major depressive disorder is also referred to as unipolar depression.
Dysthymic Disorder	Milder, but more chronic, form of depression that lasts for more than two years. During these two years, symptoms cannot be absent for more than two months at a time. Involves long-lasting but milder depression symptoms that can last for extremely long periods if not treated. Everyday functioning is less impaired than is the case with major depression.
Bipolar Disorder	Involves periods of major depression and mania, resulting in a significant impairment of physical, emotional, cognitive, and behavioral functioning. *Note:* Bipolar disorder was formerly called manic-depression.
Cyclothymic Disorder	Milder but more chronic form of bipolar disorder with depressive and hypomanic symptoms that lasts for more than two years. During these two years symptoms cannot be absent for more than two months at a time.
Seasonal Affective Disorder (SAD)	Referred to in the *DSM-IV-TR* as depression with a seasonal pattern which indicates at least two years of episodes of major depression that occurs only during particular times of the year. Depression is usually during the winter months and is believed to be associated with reduced amounts of sunlight.

Causes of Mood Disorders

A combination of various psychological perspectives can be used to provide a more complete description for the causes or etiology of mood disorders. In terms of the biological perspective, heritability rates obtained through twin, family, and adoption studies indicate that genetic predispositions for mood disorders exist. Disturbances in the levels or receptors for the neurotransmitters serotonin, norepinephrine, and dopamine are associated with mood disorders. Additional biological explanations include problems with the endocrine system, biological rhythms, or differences in brain structure and activity. Cognitive theories of depression focus on the impact of irrational thinking in explaining mood disorders. **Aaron Beck**, a prominent cognitive theorist, proposes that exaggerated negative thoughts and maladaptive beliefs contribute to the development and prolonging of mood disturbances. Beck describes the maladaptive thinking patterns of individuals with depression in terms of what he calls a *negative cognitive triad*. The **cognitive triad** includes the depressed individual's negative interpretations about who he or she is, the experiences the person has, and his or her future. A major theory for explaining the causes of depression from the social-cognitive perspective is the concept of **learned helplessness** proposed by Martin Seligman (see chapter 8) which explains that depression results when individuals believe that they no longer have the ability to determine the course of their own lives, due to repeated failure or negative consequences. If individuals determine that the negative experiences that they are having are the result of internal personal causes which are global (affecting most areas of their lives) and stable (permanent), learned helplessness will develop because they will believe that they do not have any control over their future. The tendency to explain setbacks and failures in terms that are personal or internal, global, and stable is referred to as a **pessimistic explanatory style,** which is associated with a higher risk for depression. Conversely, individuals with an **optimistic explanatory style** who explain negative events in terms that are external, unstable (things will get better), and specific (impacting only part of their life) are more resistant to depression.

STUDY TIP

Be able to identify how a *pessimistic explanatory style* can lead to learned helplessness and depression. For example, if Thor loses his job and uses a pessimistic explanatory style, he will attribute the failure to *internal personal causes,* such as "I am a terrible person," and decide that "I am a failure at everything," (global) and that "I'll never be good at anything" (stable) which will make learned helplessness and depression more likely.

Behavioral theories suggest that high levels of stress and the incidence of traumatic events also appear to be related to the onset of mood disorders. Stressful events including divorce, death, illness, job loss, or military deployment; all potentially increase the chances that an individual will develop a mood disorder because the stressors can be viewed as either punishments or the loss of rewards. However, individuals might interpret the same events differently. The end of a relationship for one person might be stressful, but for another it might result in a reduction in anxiety. According to the behaviorist perspective, the actions of a depressed individual gain for the person reinforcements potentially in the form of compassion, understanding, and attention from others, which would, in turn, lead them to repeat those behaviors.

Somatoform Disorders

Somatoform disorders involve individuals who experience physical problems or symptoms which have only psychological causes. The victim does not have conscious control over the disorder, and he or she is not faking the symptoms. A major potential problem in the diagnosis of somatoform disorders is the fact that, although medical professionals have not been able to identify a physical cause that explains the symptoms the individual is experiencing, that does not mean that one does not potentially exist. Medical conditions that are extremely rare or difficult to diagnose can be missed, resulting in a false diagnosis of a somatoform disorder. The three main types of somatoform disorders are explained in Table 14.5.

Table 14.5.   Somatoform Disorders

Disorder	Description
Hypochondriasis	Individuals who are convinced that they have a very serious medical condition, despite the fact that they remain in good health and medical tests come back negative. These individuals may dramatically misinterpret small physical changes as indicators of serious medical conditions and suffer from chronic fear and worry. Functioning is disrupted because they have trouble meeting obligations due to worry, fear, and continually seeking additional medical advice.
Somatization Disorder	Individuals suffer from a large number of vague long-lasting physical complaints that do not have an identifiable physical cause. The wide range of reported symptoms is often unlikely to exist simultaneously. Unlike hypochondriasis, they do not have a fear of a specific serious illness.
Conversion Disorder	Individuals experience impaired voluntary motor or sensory function, despite the fact that no medical reason can be found to explain the problem. Patients with conversion disorders have reported symptoms such as paralysis, mutism, blindness, seizures, and anesthesia (loss of feeling in a limb), all without any sign of a physiological cause.
	Conversion disorders appear abruptly, usually following trauma or stressful situations, and typically last for several weeks, disappearing when anxiety levels are reduced. Frequently individuals behave inappropriately by showing an indifference to what should be considered a serious loss of function.

Causes of Somatoform Disorders

Many of Sigmund Freud's case studies involved patients with conversion disorders, or what was at that time called *hysteria,* and the psychoanalytic and psychodynamic perspectives attribute these conditions to unresolved unconscious conflicts. Behavioral theories suggest the importance that reinforcements play in somatoform disorders as sufferers receive attention and sympathy from family, friends, and medical workers. The cognitive perspective focuses on how faulty thinking and catastrophic thoughts lead individuals to misinterpret normal bodily functions as problematic symptoms.

STUDY TIP

Glove anesthesia is a conversion symptom in which individuals report a complete loss of feeling below the wrist. Because damage to the nerve that receives sensory information in the hand would also result in a loss of feeling partway up the arm, this type of damage is not anatomically possible.

Dissociative Disorders

In **dissociative disorders,** a portion of the mind "splits off" from the mainstream of consciousness, producing behavior that is incompatible with the rest of the individual's identity. Dissociative disorders are the topic of heated debate in the psychological community. Many researchers do not believe that these conditions exist, but say they are the product of an overactive imagination. The *DSM-IV-TR* lists five categories of dissociative disorders: dissociative amnesia, dissociative fugue, dissociative identity disorder, depersonalization disorder, and dissociative disorder not otherwise specified.

Dissociative Amnesia

Dissociative amnesia occurs when an individual experiences a loss of memory of a traumatic occurrence in their life, such as witnessing violence or death, a physical injury, or abandonment. There is no identifiable medical cause such as a tumor or brain disease for dissociative amnesia, and it often begins suddenly following severe psychological stress. In some forms of dissociative amnesia, the individual forgets personal details about his or her life (episodic memories), yet still retains the knowledge required to function in the world (semantic and procedural memories).

Dissociative Fugue

Dissociative fugue is a type of amnesia with no physical cause; an individual forgets the details of his or her personal identity and suddenly travels away from customary surroundings. Frequently a person with this disorder will move to a new place and start an entirely new life. This new identity will usually be more outgoing and uninhibited than the prior personality, which is typically quiet and very ordinary. Like dissociative amnesia, dissociative fugue is usually produced by psychological stress, and only episodic memory appears to be affected. Marital quarrels, personal rejections, wars, and natural disasters are common examples of stressors that can lead to dissociative fugue. Fugue states are usually brief, lasting for only hours or days, though in rare cases a fugue will continue for months.

STUDY TIP

Think of *dissociative fugue* as consisting of amnesia plus travel.

Dissociative Identity Disorder

Dissociative identity disorder (DID), or the presence of two or more separate and distinct personalities in one person, is the most dramatic type of dissociative disorder. This disorder was formerly referred to as multiple personality disorder. The individual personalities present in this disorder are quite distinctive from one another and may be of different ages and genders. Transition from one personality to another is sudden and frequently associated with psychosocial stress. The primary personality typically remains unaware of the actions or thoughts of the secondary personalities. On the other hand, the secondary personalities are often fully aware of the thoughts and actions of the primary personality of the individual. This diagnosis is considered to be rare overall, although the number of individuals with DID is greater in the United States, where it receives more attention than in other parts of the world.

Causes of Dissociative Disorders

The psychoanalytic and psychodynamic explanations for dissociative disorders both maintain that the symptoms that individuals experience result from the repression of memories and events that are too painful or anxiety-producing to confront directly. Generally, dissociative identity disorder is associated with severe childhood abuse, and an important criterion for diagnosis is the inability to remember extremely painful information. Individuals who experience severe abuse or witness violent events, especially as children, may create additional personalities as a natural response to escape from the trauma. Other dissociative disorders, such as dissociative amnesia and dissociative fugue, happen most frequently as the result of an extreme stressor, but very little is known about their causes. According to behavioral theories, individuals learn that thinking about negative memories causes pain or a punishment, and allowing their minds to wander and ignore upsetting thoughts and memories results in negative reinforcement because anxiety is removed. Other theories contend that dissociative disorders are the result of a form of self-hypnosis in which individuals hypnotize themselves in order to escape from feeling pain or anxiety. Some clinicians doubt that DID even exists and suggest that cases are actually the product of unintentional suggestion on the part of the therapist or the result of a highly suggestible personality. Although differences in brain wave activity and other physiological responses exist between different personalities, critics still contend that this does not provide conclusive evidence of the existence of this condition.

STUDY TIP

Be able to differentiate between *dissociative identity disorder* and *schizophrenia*.

Schizophrenia

Contrary to common understanding, **schizophrenia** does not involve having multiple personalities; it is a group of disorders involving a breakdown of the thinking process, disengagement from reality, and flattened affect (emotion). About 1 percent of the population of the United States will suffer from schizophrenia at some point in their lives, and diagnosis most often occurs during early adulthood. Schizophrenia is characterized by significant disturbances in cognition, emotion, perceptions, behavior, and speech that dramatically impair functioning. Usually a patient diagnosed with schizophrenia will exhibit only some of these disturbances. Many schizophrenics have little or no grasp of reality and may withdraw from contact with the world into their own thoughts and fantasies. Usually a schizophrenic becomes unable to distinguish between their own fictitious constructions of reality and what is really happening. The symptoms of schizophrenia are divided into three separate categories: positive symptoms, negative symptoms, and psychomotor disturbances.

Positive Symptoms

Positive symptoms of schizophrenia are thoughts and behaviors that are unpleasant additions to the functioning of an individual. Positive symptoms are not something pleasant or helpful; they are unwanted distortions or additions to normal thought and behavior. Examples of positive symptoms of schizophrenia include hallucinations, delusions, and disorganized thought. **Hallucinations** are false perceptual experiences in which the individual sees, hears, smells, tastes, or feels something that is not actually present. The most common type of hallucination is auditory and involves the person hearing voices or sounds that are not actually present. Another common positive symptom is the presence of **delusions,** or beliefs contrary to reality that the individual firmly holds, despite contradictory evidence. Delusions can be either simple and short-term or elaborate and long-lasting and schizophrenics often have more than one type. Although delusions are most frequently associated with schizophrenia they can also be present in cases of severe depression or mania. The main types of delusions experienced by schizophrenics are listed in Table 14.6.

Table 14.6.   Delusions

Delusion	Description	Example
Delusions of Persecution	Belief that someone is plotting against the individual or others and the fear of being followed or watched. Individuals who suffer from these types of delusions are overly vigilant, experience extreme levels of agitation, and are extremely mistrustful. Delusions of persecution are especially associated with paranoid schizophrenia.	A schizophrenic who believes that the CIA, foreign governments, aliens, or even their teachers are plotting to steal their mind.

(continued)

Table 14.6. (*continued*)

Delusion	Description	Example
Delusions of Grandeur	Belief that an individual holds special powers or is especially important or influential; this belief may lead the person to demand special treatment. Delusions of grandeur can lead a schizophrenic to believe that he or she is a famous individual, such as a movie star, Jesus, Moses, or Gandhi.	The belief that they have the power to read other people's thoughts or that they are the general of a secret alien army.
Delusions of Control	Belief that an individual's thoughts, behaviors, and emotions are being manipulated by an outside force.	The belief that radar waves being released by the government through street lights or aliens are controlling their actions.
Delusions of Reference	Belief an individual holds in which they interpret objects or the behaviors of others to have important meaning designed only for them.	The belief that song lyrics, newscasts, gestures made by strangers or even objects in the environment are directed toward them specifically.

STUDY TIP

Be able to differentiate between hallucinations and delusions.

- *Hallucinations* are *false perceptual experiences* in which the individual sees, hears, smells, tastes, or feels something that is not actually present.
- *Delusions* are *false beliefs* contrary to reality which are firmly held despite contradictory evidence.

Thought disorders, or the various types of disorganized cognitions present among schizophrenics, are also considered to be positive symptoms. Usually a schizophrenic will speak incoherently, making references to ideas or images which are not connected. Often they will use **neologisms**, or words made up by the speaker. Disordered thought involves numerous loose associations and the individual may have problems sticking to one topic, often drifting off into a series of associations that are peculiar to a specific individual. One such idiosyncratic association is the use of **clang associations** where connections between words are based on how they sound or rhyme instead of on meaning. In a clang association, a patient's speech will be dominated by many words associated only by rhyme, for example, "How are you in your shoe on a pew, doctor dew?" **Word salad** is a type of speech in which the words that are selected have little or no meaning or connection to each other, making it impossible to understand the speaker.

Disturbances of perception and attention (aside from hallucinations) suffered by schizophrenics include changes in the way their bodies feel. Parts of the body may seem too large or too small, or there may be numbness or tickling. Some schizophrenics remark that the world appears flat or colorless. Schizophrenics often have trouble attending to what is happening around them. A schizophrenic, for instance, may be unable to concentrate on television because he or she cannot watch the screen and listen to what is being said at the same time.

Negative Symptoms

Negative symptoms of schizophrenia are behaviors, thoughts, or emotions that are usually a normal part of functioning are absent or dramatically decreased in the individual. Examples of negative symptoms include problems initiating and completing activities or even minor goals (*avolition*), the absence of communication or speech (*alogia*), the inability to experience pleasure (*anhedonia*), social withdrawal, or frequently a flat or inappropriate affect. A **flat affect** is a condition in which virtually no stimulus can produce an emotional response. Individuals who are displaying a flat affect show no emotion on their face or in the tone of their voice in reaction to what is happening around them. However, the inability to express an emotion does not necessarily mean that the individual is not experiencing emotion. Others display *inappropriate affect*, where their emotional responses do not fit the situation, or *ambivalent affect*, where a person or object simultaneously arouses both positive and negative emotions.

Psychomotor Disturbances

Psychomotor disturbances or peculiarities of movement associated with schizophrenia are often obvious and bizarre. A schizophrenic may grimace or adopt strange facial expressions. The overall level of activity may be increased (catatonic excitement), with the patient running around and flailing his or her limbs wildly, or there may be **catatonic immobility**, where unusual postures are adopted and maintained for very long periods of time.

Subtypes of Schizophrenia

Because of the wide variety of symptoms associated with schizophrenia, psychologists have found it helpful to distinguish among **five main types of schizophrenia**, listed in the *DSM-IV-TR*: paranoid, disorganized, catatonic, undifferentiated, and residual. See Table 14.7.

Table 14.7. Schizophrenia Subtypes

Type	Description
Paranoid	Individuals are diagnosed through the presence of numerous and organized delusions, usually of persecution, but sometimes of grandeur or control. Auditory and visual hallucinations may accompany the delusions. Generally, paranoid schizophrenics are more alert and verbal than other schizophrenics and tend to intellectualize.
Disorganized	Individuals display a variety of unusual symptoms including numerous hallucinations and delusions that are plentiful and poorly organized. Prominent features include disorganized speech (word salad, clang associations, and neologisms) and behavior, and flat or inappropriate affect. Disorganized schizophrenia is marked by odd facial and body mannerisms, patterns of silly or absurd behaviors, and impaired personal hygiene. Individuals with this type of schizophrenia have great difficulty managing to support and care for themselves.
Catatonic	Disturbances in motor functions are the most obvious symptoms of the catatonic type of schizophrenia. Individuals typically alternate between immobility and wild excitement, but often one or the other type of motor symptoms predominate. In the excited state the catatonic may shout and talk continuously and incoherently, all the while pacing back and forth. The immobile state is characterized by physical rigidity, mutism, and unresponsiveness.
Undifferentiated	This type applies to schizophrenics who do not exhibit a pattern of symptoms that fits the other subtypes. A patient may have highly organized delusions or motor disorders, but not to the extent that he or she is considered either a paranoid or a catatonic schizophrenic.
Residual	Someone who has had at least one schizophrenic episode, but no longer has significant positive symptoms. They may have some remnants (residual) symptoms such as social withdrawal, unusual beliefs, or peculiar behaviors.

Causes of Schizophrenia

The genetic and biological causes of schizophrenia have been researched extensively. The results of numerous twin studies have revealed that schizophrenia is influenced by genetics by examining rates of concordance. **Concordance** is the percentage of pairs of twins or other family members who have the same trait. Higher levels of concordance among relatives who are more genetically similar than other groups of relatives indicate the likelihood that a particular trait is influenced by genetics. The concordance rate for schizophrenia among monozygotic (identical) twins that share 100 percent of the same genes is approximately 48 percent, while the concordance rate for fraternal twins or siblings is about 17 percent, compared to a member of the general population who is not related to anyone with schizophrenia, which is 1 percent. However, if schizophrenia were solely the result of genetic factors, the concordance rate would be 100 percent. The results indicate that environmental factors play an important role in whether or not someone with a genetic predisposition for schizophrenia will develop the illness.

Biological differences in terms of neurotransmitter activity and physical brain structure have also been identified in individuals with schizophrenia. The **dopamine hypothesis** suggests that schizophrenia is the result of overactive dopamine systems in the brain. Antipsychotic medications alleviate symptoms of schizophrenia by working as dopamine antagonists. The dopamine hypothesis, however, does not provide a complete understanding of the causes of schizophrenia because not all individuals with schizophrenia respond to antipsychotic medications. Unfortunately, some antipsychotic medications block dopamine so effectively that the individual begins to exhibit the trembling and loss of motor control associated with Parkinson's disease, which is linked to insufficient dopamine. More recent research has indicated that, in addition to dopamine, the neurotransmitters serotonin and glutamate may be involved in schizophrenia. Specific abnormalities in brain structure and activity have also been identified, including enlarged ventricles, decreased frontal lobe activity, and differences in blood flow in the brain. A variety of environmental risk factors have been associated with schizophrenia, including prenatal exposure to flu viruses and complications during birth. The sociocultural perspective considers the effect of stressful situations and dysfunctional family systems as key triggers for schizophrenia.

Diathesis-Stress Model

An important theory for explaining the relative influences of both nature and nurture in understanding the causes of psychological disorders that is frequently applied to the study of schizophrenia is the diathesis-stress model. According to the **diathesis-stress model,** psychological disorders are the result of the interaction of both a genetic predisposition and stressful life events. This theory proposes that individuals inherit particular genes that make them vulnerable to particular conditions (diathesis) and that the disease will be expressed as a result of exposure to stressful events. An individual with a genetic vulnerability for depression may develop the psychological disorder of depression after experiencing severe loss or trauma, while another individual who experienced the same events but did not have a genetic predisposition will not develop depression.

Personality Disorders

Personality disorders are characterized by chronic unchanging patterns of perception, behavior, emotion, or thinking that are substantially inconsistent with the expectations of one's culture. In order to result in a diagnosis of a personality disorder, these patterns must be rigid and maladaptive and result in personal distress and difficulty functioning. A diagnosis of a personality disorder requires that patterns of behavior begin in adolescence and continue throughout adulthood. Personality disorders are described in the *DSM-IV-TR* in Axis II and are divided into three groups or clusters. *Cluster A personality disorders* are distinguished by odd or eccentric traits similar to those present in schizophrenia, such as social isolation, mistrust, and the presence of odd perceptions; however, they are much less severe. *Cluster B personality disorders* are marked by dramatic, emotional, or erratic traits that are so exaggerated that individuals have difficulty maintaining normal relationships with others. They may be devious, moody, unstable, or even cold in terms of how they relate with others. *Cluster C personality disorders* all feature anxious or fearful traits and often have symptoms similar to individuals with anxiety- or depression-related psychological disorders. See Table 14.8.

Table 14.8.   Personality Disorders

Cluster A: Odd or Eccentric Personality Disorders	
Disorder	**Description**
Paranoid	Extremely suspicious (paranoid), secretive, scheming, and argumentative, but believe that they are objective and reasonable. Although these individuals are quick to point out faults in others, they are unable to accept responsibility for their mistakes and have a tendency to put the blame on others.
Schizoid	Detached from and not interested in forming social relationships. The individuals have difficulty experiencing pleasure and display a very narrow range of emotional responses in social situations.
Schizotypal	Behavior is marked by social isolation and the presence of odd beliefs and behaviors. This personality disorder is the closest to schizophrenia.

(continued)

Table 14.8. *(continued)*

Cluster B: Dramatic, Emotional, or Erratic Personality Disorders	
Disorder	**Description**
Antisocial	Consistently tramples on or violates the rights of others, is impulsive, ruthless, and lacks a conscience. Behaviors associated with this diagnosis also include selfishness, arrogance, and lying. This is the personality disorder most closely associated with criminal behavior. Individuals must be at least 18 years of age to receive this diagnosis and exhibit similar behavior in childhood. Note: An individual with this diagnosis was formerly referred to as a sociopath.
Borderline	Trouble maintaining relationships due to unstable behaviors, moods, and self-image. Individuals have a tendency toward impulsive behaviors that lead to problems with self-destructive behaviors, including substance abuse, gambling, unsafe sex, reckless driving, and spending sprees. Borderline personality disorder is associated with elevated risk for self-injury and suicide.
Histrionic	Individuals whose behavior is highly emotional and dramatic. Histrionics are often conceited, self-centered, and shallow, yet are constantly searching for approval. They have a tendency to act as if they are "on stage" and that all of the events of their life will be of intense interest to other people. Frequently they dress and act in a provocative or overly sexual manner.
Narcissistic	Characterized by the need for undeserved admiration and praise, and narcissists are preoccupied with fantasies of success, accomplishment, and recognition. Narcissists feel that they are entitled to special treatment and may use others to get what they want. They lack empathy for others and frequently believe others are envious of them.

Cluster C: Anxious or Fearful Personality Disorders	
Disorder	**Description**
Avoidant	Excessively shy and uncomfortable in social situations due to a fear of rejection or being evaluated negatively. Although they want to have relationships, their fears of rejection and failure prevent them from making friends. Individuals with avoidant personality disorder have low self-esteem and are highly self-critical and pessimistic.
Dependent	Characterized by an excessive desire to be taken care of by someone else (dependent). Turn to others for even simple decisions and are fearful of abandonment and independence.
Obsessive compulsive	Perfectionist behaviors and a preoccupation with doing things the correct way. Attempt to exert rigid control in all aspects of their lives, including home, work, and relationships. Even small changes to their routines and patterns result in anxiety and stress.

Individuals who have personality disorders frequently also have a diagnosis of a psychological disorder in Axis I, and it is typically for these conditions that they seek treatment. Individuals with personality disorders also may seek treatment due to interpersonal difficulties or problems with coping. The identification of a personality disorder can be helpful to clinical psychologists because these rigid personality traits may prevent effective treatment of psychological disorders. Diagnosis of personality disorders is difficult, and misdiagnosis is common, raising concerns about the reliability and validity of the category and the criteria. The difficulties clinicians have making a personality disorder diagnosis stem from the fact that the *DSM-IV-TR* criteria for these mental illnesses are less specific than those provided for Axis I disorders. In addition, it is often hard to distinguish among personality disorders that are very similar.

STUDY TIP

Be able to differentiate between paranoid personality disorder and paranoid schizophrenia.

- *Paranoid personality disorder* is an Axis II disorder that refers to an overall disposition that is extremely suspicious (paranoid), secretive, scheming, and argumentative.
- *Paranoid schizophrenia* is an Axis I disorder that involves the presence of numerous and organized delusions, usually of persecution, but sometimes of grandeur or control. Auditory and visual hallucinations often accompany the delusions. Paranoid schizophrenics have lost touch with reality.

Cognitive Disorders

Prior to the publication of the *DSM-IV-TR*, the Axis I disorders of dementia, delirium, and amnesia were all called *organic disorders*. The label *organic* was removed because, although these conditions have biological causes, the label may have conveyed the message that only these conditions were biologically based. The psychological disorders of dementia, delirium, and amnesia all involve impairment to thinking that represents a difference from earlier abilities.

Dementia involves the progressive and typically permanent decline in cognitive functioning, including problems with memory, reasoning, language, and problem solving. The causes of dementia encompass various diseases, including Alzheimer's,

Parkinson's, HIV, as well as severe head trauma. **Delirium** is a condition that involves an impairment of cognition and consciousness, including memory problems and mental confusion. Unlike dementia, delirium is acute and most often lasts for a few hours or days. Delirium can result from infection, fever, disease, head injury, stress, stroke, the effects of drugs, or withdrawal. Typically this psychological disorder is divided into three general categories: (1) delirium due to a general medical condition, (2) substance-induced delirium (drugs or toxins), and (3) delirium due to multiple causes or not otherwise specified. **Amnesia** is described as severe memory impairments that may be caused by medical conditions, drug use, or withdrawal. Medical conditions that can result in amnesia include head trauma, nutritional deficiencies, or infection. Amnesia is specified as either chronic or transient (short-lasting).

Time for a quiz
- Review strategies in Chapter 2
- Take Quiz 6 at the REA Study Center
  (www.rea.com/studycenter)

Treatment of Abnormal Behavior

Each of the various psychological perspectives explains human behavior and mental processes differently, and as a consequence, each has served as the basis for separate methods of treatment. **Treatment** or **psychotherapy** refers to the hundreds of different methods and techniques that have been created to help individuals who are suffering from psychological disorders.

Early Treatment

Historical evidence suggests that, in ancient times, humans sometimes believed that abnormal behavior was caused by evil spirits. The philosophers and physicians of ancient Greece and Rome presented some of the earliest theories, regarding biological causes of mental illness in the form of humor imbalances. During the European Middle Ages, however, mental illness was again believed to be a consequence of demon possession and treated with exorcisms involving prayer, flogging, and starvation. In some cases, it was believed that a person was a witch in league with the devil, and many of these individuals consequently were publicly executed. After the Middle Ages, demonic explanations for abnormal behavior became less prevalent and were replaced once again with the somatic idea that mental illnesses had biological causes as the ideas of the Enlightenment spread. European governments began to create asylums or institutions designed to provide housing and care for those suffering from psychological disorders. Although the asylums were created with the best of intentions, they became essentially prisons with inhumane conditions where many were kept against their will because these illnesses were generally considered to be incurable. During the nineteenth century, efforts began to improve treatment in asylums. In France, **Philippe Pinel** was a vital figure in the movement for humanitarian treatment of the mentally ill inside of asylums because he believed in the possibility of improvement or recovery. According to Pinel, recovery would require changes to the conditions in the asylums. Pinel's efforts resulted in ending the policy of keeping patients in chains, ultimately making it easier for them to be managed and treated. The mentally ill needed to be treated with compassion and dignity, and Pinel achieved some remarkable results. Pinel's ideas, grounded in a psychologically oriented viewpoint, were a major aspect of the nineteenth-century *moral treatment movement* that spread through Europe and America. This movement advocated that the mentally ill should be treated with dignity and respect.

STUDY TIP

Be able to identify how **Dorothea Dix** contributed to the reform movement of moral treatment in the United States.

Efforts to reform the manner in which the mentally ill were treated in the United States were led in part by Dix, who was horrified and shocked by the terrible way that people suffering from mental illness were treated. She fought to establish legal protection for individuals with mental illness and to create state mental hospitals with humane treatment in what was called the *moral treatment movement.*

Modern Treatment

Psychotherapy, also called **therapy** or **talk therapy**, refers to a variety of communication techniques and interventions designed to assist individuals suffering from psychological illnesses to identify and overcome difficulties they are experiencing. Individuals may also seek psychotherapy for assistance with adjustment issues or problems coping with stressful events such as divorce or the loss of a job. Although much of therapy is done with individuals, various psychotherapies have been developed to assist families, couples, or groups of individuals that are all coping with similar mental health issues.

The hundreds of psychological therapies can be divided into general categories: insight, behavioral, cognitive, and biomedical. Psychoanalytic, psychodynamic, humanist, and Gestalt methods of therapy are all considered *insight therapies* because they involve one-on-one communication between the therapist and client and are designed to help the individual understand themselves better (achieve insight) in order to be able to make changes that lead to the reduction of symptoms or increase in positive behaviors. Behavioral therapies utilize methods based on classical, operant, and social learning research to influence behavioral change. Cognitive therapies incorporate techniques for making changes in thought processes in order to reduce negative behaviors and improve mental health. Biomedical therapies involve the use of psychotropic drugs and other medical interventions to treat psychological illnesses by controlling or eliminating symptoms. Research indicates that although no specific therapy category provides the best treatment outcomes, specific psychological illnesses are often treated more effectively with certain methods. Most psychologists and other therapists today take an **eclectic approach** and utilize a variety of methods from several theoretical perspectives to most effectively help their clients. Cognitive behavioral therapy, for instance, may be combined with biomedical treatment in the form of antidepressant medication. These medications may alleviate some but not all of the symptoms of depression, but when they are combined with talk therapy, they provide the best outcome for the patient.

STUDY TIP

Increasingly, psychotherapists are using an *eclectic approach* that involves selecting treatment methods from a wide range of theoretical perspectives based on the individual needs of each client.

There are several important facts about psychotherapy that any patient should know. The first is that about two-thirds of adults who undergo psychotherapy either show marked improvement or recover within two years, regardless of the type of therapy. However, studies also show that the recovery rate of untreated patients is also two-thirds. These results can be misleading, since it is difficult to measure the degree of improvement in psychological cases. In addition, although the overall effectiveness of any particular type of therapy does not appear to be superior to the others, certain therapies seem to work better for specific mental disorders. Panic attacks, for example, may be most effectively treated with cognitive behavioral therapy, and specific phobias with exposure therapy.

Fifty years ago or so, psychotherapy was almost exclusively the domain of psychiatrists. As demand for treatment of psychological problems grew, though, there were not enough psychiatrists to satisfy it. Psychotherapy is now performed primarily by clinical psychologists, clinical social workers, and others with varying levels of education and experience (e.g., counselors, psychiatric nurses, religious leaders). A great deal of therapy also takes place through community mental health programs. These programs typically provide therapy of various sorts on an outpatient basis, as well as offering crisis hotlines and other services that help people cope with difficult situations. The term **psychotherapist** is a broad designation that includes a variety of professionals who have been specifically trained and granted a license to practice by a state board to provide therapy to individuals with psychological illnesses or adjustment problems. Several of the major professions that provide psychotherapy are listed in Table 15.1.

Table 15.1. Types of Psychotherapists

Psychotherapist	Description
Clinical psychologist	Psychologist who works with the diagnosis and treatment of mental illnesses. Clinical psychologists have a doctoral degree such as a PhD or PsyD and complete specialized training and state licensure.
Psychiatrist	Medical doctor (MD) who works with the diagnosis and treatment of psychological illnesses. Psychiatrists are licensed to prescribe psychotropic medications as a part of treatment. In addition to biomedical treatment, many psychiatrists also utilize psychotherapy.
Counseling psychologist	Psychologist who works with people coping with everyday problems including making career decisions, marriage counseling, and social skills training. The required level of education and training for licensure is determined by state law, but many have doctoral degrees including PhD or EdD and often work in university clinics.

(continued)

Table 15.1. **(continued)**

Psychotherapist	Description
Licensed professional counselor	Professionals who provide psychotherapy to individuals, groups, couples or families; typically have a master's degree and have been licensed according to state guidelines.
Social worker	Social workers have typically earned a master's degree in social work (MSW) and provide treatment for psychological illnesses. They assist clients by coordinating access to support for occupational training, housing, and financial assistance. Social workers focus more on how environmental factors such as stress, poverty, and interactions with family impact functioning.
Psychiatric nurse	Nurses with an RN degree who specialize in treating individuals suffering from psychological illnesses. Psychiatric nurses dispense psychotropic medications and provide assistance and support to patients.
Psychoanalyst	Therapist who utilizes Freudian psychoanalysis in the diagnosis and treatment of psychological illnesses; usually, although not always, a medical doctor or psychologist with a PhD or PsyD.

Psychodynamic Therapy

Psychodynamic psychotherapies include a large, diverse group of therapy methods based on the ideas originally proposed by Sigmund Freud which explain that unconscious motives are responsible for psychological illnesses. These therapies emphasize helping the individual to gain greater insight into his or her own actions and to develop a deeper understanding of how forces in the unconscious influence the individual's behavior. Psychodynamic psychotherapies typically utilize interpretation of resistance and transference, along with dream analysis, to help individuals understand how forces and conflicts in the unconscious are the causes of current problems. The emphasis in many psychodynamic therapies is on how more recent social relationships contribute to the difficulties patients are experiencing. Psychodynamic approaches conduct therapy face-to-face with the patient as opposed to the Freudian method of having the patient lie on a couch with the therapist listening but not making eye contact.

Psychoanalysis

Psychoanalysis, often known simply as analysis, refers to the specific methods of psychotherapy created by Sigmund Freud. According to Freud, instead of dealing with inner conflicts, the patient represses conflicts and is made helpless by his or her own defenses. The goal of psychoanalysis involves determining the underlying causes for the patient's maladaptive symptoms. The material of the unconscious mind must be brought into the conscious mind so that it no longer serves as a source of anxiety and confusion for the patient. To explore the unconscious, psychoanalysts typically rely on several different methods. One of the earliest methods Freud used to reach the unconscious was hypnosis, but he eventually abandoned the use of hypnosis in favor of a new method he created known as free association. In the technique of **free association**, the patient is instructed to say anything that comes to mind, no matter how trivial or unimportant it may seem. Because unconscious material is always seeking expression, this technique is thought to encourage the expression of repressed material. The therapist directs the flow of associations to the source of the pathology by providing interpretation or asking questions to keep the flow of free association continuing. During the process of analysis, patients may also be asked to recount the content of their dreams for the analyst. Freud's system for interpreting **dreams** (see Chapter 7) is used in analysis as a tool for "entering" the repressed areas of the patient's unconscious mind. Freud believed that dreams provide the clearest example of unconscious processes at work and published his findings in his famous book, *The Interpretation of Dreams*. According to Freud, dreams provide an outlet for wish fulfillment, and he observed two types of interrelated content present within dreams. The **manifest content** is the information about the dream that the dreamer can remember and report afterward which consists of the storyline of the dream. Beneath the manifest content lurks the **latent content**, the unconscious desires causing the dream. These latent (hidden) desires are usually related to sexual or aggressive drives. Freud thought that these desires were too painful to recognize during waking hours and thus entered dreams.

Interpretation occurs as the psychoanalyst offers insight during the process of dream analysis, projective testing, and free association. **Interpretation** refers to the methods that psychoanalysts use to explain the hidden meanings of a patient's actions, thoughts, emotions, and dreams. The therapist is trained to identify signs of inner conflict, the use of defense mechanisms, and patterns of behavior to help patients understand the unconscious motivations for their actions and problems. Patients may be unable to accept the interpretations presented by the therapist resulting in resistance. **Resistance** includes the various methods that patients use to avoid confronting the painful, repressed memories and conflicts that are the actual cause of their problems. Resistance is mostly done unconsciously and often involves the use of defense mechanisms. Arriving late, canceling appointments, avoiding important concerns, trying to direct the conversation away from upsetting topics, or merely pretending to free associate are all examples of how patients resist or sabotage the process of psychoanalysis. Generally, the patient resists recalling painful or guilty memories, and it is the therapist's role to help the patient overcome this resistance.

Freud believed that patients eventually develop **transference** or the tendency to react to the therapist emotionally in the same way that they did toward their parents or other important figures during childhood. Therefore, if a patient expresses hostility toward the analyst that really represents repressed anger and resentment that the patient has about their parents. Transference can also involve placing feelings of love and affection onto the therapist because the patient was never given the love they needed from a parent. One of the main roles of the therapist is to serve as a transference object and bring the problems into the open where they can be analyzed in a rational manner. The resolution of transference is one of the most important aspects of treatment in classical psychoanalysis. Analysts must be able to maintain a stance of compassionate neutrality and not introduce their own personality or transference onto the patient. Partly for this reason, therapists formally trained as psychoanalysts undergo psychoanalytic treatment themselves before they begin to practice.

Traditional Freudian psychoanalysis is a slow and expensive process that involves the patient attending therapy sessions three or four times per week for many years. The major goals of analysis are to achieve insight or make unconscious conflicts conscious in order to resolve them and to strengthen the ego. The role of the therapist in psychoanalysis is to remain emotionally neutral and to offer interpretations of dreams, free associations, projective tests, resistance, and transference that will hopefully help the patient to achieve insights. Today this approach is rarely utilized and instead has been replaced with psychodynamic approaches that are much shorter in duration.

Modern Psychodynamic Therapy

Because few patients have the time and money for traditional psychoanalysis, several short-term psychodynamic therapies have been developed that are connected to the principles of analysis. Often these therapies are shorter in duration, identify specific goals, and involve the therapist taking an active versus a passive role in the process. Psychodynamic therapies involve face-to-face interactions where patients meet with a therapist once a week typically for only a few months rather than the multiple visits per week over several years associated with traditional analysis. Additionally, psychodynamic therapists are more likely to be actively involved and offer advice and suggestions to clients. One psychodynamic therapy that has been shown to be effective is interpersonal psychotherapy. **Interpersonal psychotherapy (IPT)** involves assisting clients in developing skills to improve their relationships with family members, friends, and coworkers as well as dealing with difficult life changes. The focus of this therapy is on resolving problems resulting from social interactions and conflicts that are occurring in the present in addition to those that happened in the past. IPT is short in duration and typically involves only 12–16 weekly sessions. This method has proven to be effective in the treatment of psychological illnesses including depression, eating disorders, and substance abuse. In addition, IPT helps patients cope with interpersonal stresses such as occupational difficulties and family conflicts.

STUDY TIP

Be able to differentiate between the terms *psychotherapy, psychoanalysis,* and *psychodynamic therapy.*

- *Psychotherapy,* or talk therapy, refers to a variety of communication techniques and interventions designed to assist individuals suffering from psychological illnesses in identifying and overcoming difficulties they are experiencing.

- *Psychoanalysis* is a specific type of psychotherapy developed by Sigmund Freud designed to treat psychological illnesses by discovering the unconscious conflicts and motives responsible for the symptoms individuals are experiencing.

- *Psychodynamic therapy* involves the various modern methods of psychotherapy that are based on the principles of psychoanalysis. Often these therapies are shorter in duration, identify specific goals, and involve the therapist taking a more active versus passive role in the process.

Humanist Therapy

Humanistic therapies based on the work of Abraham Maslow and Carl Rogers emphasize the positive, constructive capacities of individuals instead of mental illness. Individuals are motivated toward self-actualization, and mental illness is the result of distorted self-concepts, a lack of self-awareness, or outside forces blocking growth. Unlike psychoanalytic theory, humanist therapies emphasize current problems and stress that individuals have free will, which enables them to determine their future by assuming responsibility for their own actions and emotions. In these treatment methods, the client is considered to be an important collaborator and not a patient dependent upon an expert doctor providing a cure. The results of successful therapy for the client are openness to experience, absence of defensiveness, accurate self-awareness, unconditional self-regard, and harmonious relations with others.

The most significant humanistic therapy proposed by **Carl Rogers** is **client-centered therapy,** also called **person-centered therapy,** which is based on the idea that all individuals are capable and motivated to grow with guidance provided by a caring therapist. This type of therapy is considered to be **nondirective** because the client is in charge of setting treatment goals and determining the length of the process, while the therapist avoids giving advice. The client is at the center of the process, doing the thinking, talking, and problem solving. In client-centered therapy, the therapist has the responsibility of providing acceptance, genuineness, and empathy to the clients in order to help them realize their full potential. **Unconditional positive regard** involves the acceptance of an individual—faults and all—on the part of the therapist. This unwavering acceptance allows an individual to develop his or her sense of innate goodness and reach one's full potential. **Genuineness** or honesty is required of the therapist in order for a trusting relationship to be developed. Therapists must respond in a warm, sincere, and authentic manner, working collaboratively with an equal—not as an expert or authority figure dispensing advice. This means that if the therapist disapproves of a client's behavior, then he or she must be honest about his or her feelings. Genuineness must be demonstrated in the form of **congruence**, in which the sincerity and honesty of the communications of the therapist are consistently conveyed both verbally and nonverbally (through body language and facial expressions). The client-centered therapist is required to express **empathy** or an accurate understanding and compassion for the feelings of the client. Rogerian therapists demonstrate empathy through the technique of **active listening** in which the therapist rewords what the client says to ensure that what the individual intended to convey is what was actually understood. In addition to paraphrasing the meaning of what the client is saying, therapists should also reflect their understanding of the emotions that are being displayed and ask questions for further clarification. The basic factor distinguishing client-centered therapy from other therapies is that this therapy does not view human nature as self-destructive, defensive, or irrational. Humans possess an innate capacity and motivation towards positive self-fulfillment, termed **self-actualization**. Consistent with this optimistic view is Rogers' belief that all behavior is selected with the self-fulfillment goal in mind, and that although some behavior choices might prove to be self-damaging, the intention is always positive.

Gestalt Therapy

Gestalt therapy, another type of insight therapy, was developed by psychiatrist Fritz Perls. The objective of **Gestalt therapy** is to help clients identify their current feelings, behaviors and needs, and confront their problems directly. Like humanist therapies, Gestalt therapy also focuses on developing self-awareness in patients, helping them to create an accurate self-concept and understanding of their own feelings and behaviors that allows for greater self-acceptance. According to Gestalt therapy, psychological illness and interpersonal problems result if a person has not assumed responsibility for his or her thoughts and emotions. Although the Gestalt therapist creates a positive and supportive therapeutic environment, they may directly confront the patient in an effort to stimulate growth or change, making this treatment method more directive than humanist methods. The ultimate goal of Gestalt therapy is to provide clients with the opportunity to develop greater self-awareness, honesty, and control over their lives.

In order to help individuals grow and develop, Gestalt therapists create opportunities for clients to actively engage with their own thoughts and feelings through a variety of techniques including the empty chair, role playing, and taking part in imaginary conversations. In one well-known Gestalt method, the **empty-chair technique**, the client is asked to imagine that some part of himself or herself or an important person from his or her life (e.g., a parent or spouse) is sitting across from them. The client is then instructed to share his or her feelings and experiences from that relationship that are disturbing to the client. In the final step, the client moves to the empty chair and continues the conversation by assuming the role of the other person. Role-playing methods allow the client the chance to articulate, perhaps for the first time, their goals, fears, and desires.

Behaviorist Therapy

Psychodynamic approaches seek to make unconscious conflicts conscious and humanist approaches help individuals reveal their authentic selves, whereas behaviorist therapies are interested in changing how a person behaves in the present. From a strictly behaviorist perspective, all behavior including dysfunctional behavior is learned and therefore can be unlearned. **Behaviorist therapy**, also called **behavior modification**, uses methods drawn from experimental psychology to attempt to change abnormal behavior. In behaviorist therapy, the overall objective is not to alter the entire personality of an individual, but to alter specific behaviors that are causing problems. After John B. Watson's experiments with Little Albert confirmed that fears could be developed through classical conditioning, other psychologists would develop a variety of methods to use conditioning to reduce fears or eliminate behaviors that result in discomfort or pain for individuals. Psychologist **Mary Cover Jones** used the methods developed by Watson to reduce fear in what is considered to be the first example of what is now known as counterconditioning, a common behavior therapy. Mary Cover Jones worked with a young patient named Little Peter who was afraid of rabbits by pairing a positive stimulus (cookie) with the rabbit each time the rabbit was placed closer to the boy, until Little Peter was no longer fearful of rabbits. In **counterconditioning**, an undesired response to a stimulus is eliminated by creating a new response to that stimulus.

STUDY TIP

Be able to identify an example of how *counterconditioning* can be used to treat fears or phobias.

For example, Sadie, who is afraid of birds, is allowed to eat an ice cream cone while she feeds the birds at the park. The fear (undesired response) produced by the birds (stimulus) is replaced with the positive feelings (new response) associated with eating ice cream. Repeated associations of birds with positive feelings would most likely cure Sadie of her phobia.

The basic idea of counterconditioning has been used to create a variety of other behavioral therapies known as *exposure therapies* including systematic desensitization, flooding, and aversive conditioning. **Systematic desensitization**, developed by **Joseph Wolpe**, involves a step-by-step classical conditioning technique in which an anxiety-producing stimulus is paired with relaxation. The goal of the therapy will be to replace the anxiety response with one of relaxation based on the theory that it is not possible to experience these two opposite responses simultaneously. This method has been shown to be an effective treatment for phobias and other anxiety disorders. There are three basic steps involved in systematic desensitization. First, the client is taught specific methods for relaxation, including breathing techniques and methods to relax all of their muscles. Second, the behavior therapist and the client work together to create an **anxiety hierarchy** or series of scenarios related to their fear, ranging from mild to extremely threatening in incremental steps. Finally, the therapy will consist of the client working sequentially through each of the activities on the hierarchy while simultaneously practicing relaxation methods. If individuals directly experience the steps on the anxiety hierarchy instead of visualizing them, then it is called **in vivo** or real-life systematic desensitization. Advances in technology have now made it possible for patients to work through an anxiety hierarchy for a variety of phobias, including heights and flying through the use of three-dimensional computer programs in **virtual reality therapy**.

STUDY TIP

Be able to identify the three steps involved in *systematic desensitization*.

For example, Luanne has been offered her dream job, but unfortunately she will be required to travel by airplane several times per month and she is terrified of flying. In order to be able to accept the exciting new position, Luanne has decided to work with a behavior therapist that recommends systematic desensitization. The steps in Luanne's treatment are explained in Table 15.2.

Table 15.2. Systematic Desensitization

Step	Technique	Description	Example
Step 1	Relaxation	Client is taught specific methods for relaxation including, breathing techniques, and methods to relax his or her muscles.	Luanne is taught by her therapist the technique of progressive relaxation in which she systematically relaxes all of the muscles in her body. Luanne's therapist explains that she will use this technique as she gradually faces her fear.
Step 2	Anxiety Hierarchy	Client creates a series of scenarios related to his or her fear ranging from mild to extremely threatening in incremental steps.	Luanne and her therapist create an anxiety hierarchy consisting of activities related to flying that increase in anxiety. • Watching a video of a plane takeoff • Driving past the airport and watching planes take off • Visiting the airport and going through the procedures associated with checking baggage • Sitting on a plane and listening to the flight attendant speech but not actually taking off • Taking off on a flight
Step 3	Exposure	Client works step by step through each of the activities on the hierarchy while simultaneously practicing relaxation methods.	Luanne and her therapist slowing work through each of the items on the anxiety hierarchy by doing one each week. As Luanne faces each scenario, she practices her relaxation techniques to reduce her anxiety. The treatment was a success and Luanne happily accepts her dream job!

Another example of an exposure technique used to treat anxiety disorders is **flooding**, which involves having the patient immediately confront the most anxiety-producing situation related to their fear in a manner that is harmless, but does also not allow for the opportunity to escape. Flooding, like systematic desensitization, may involve real (in vivo) or imagined fear-provoking situations.

Aversive conditioning or **aversion therapy**, another variant of counterconditioning, attempts to change or remove a negative behavior by attaching a negative experience or emotion to the stimuli. Aversive conditioning is sometimes used in an attempt to help alcoholics develop feelings of revulsion toward alcohol (see Table 15.3). *Antabuse* is a drug that if combined with alcohol leads to nausea and other negative side effects.

During aversive conditioning, the patient takes *Antabuse* and then drinks alcohol in an attempt to create a new association between alcohol and nausea to replace the old association of alcohol and pleasure. Aversive conditioning has been used with varying levels of success for a wide range of conditions, including alcoholism, self-injury, and gambling.

Table 15.3. Aversive Conditioning

	Stimulus	Response
Before Aversive Conditioning	Alcohol	⇨ Pleasure
	New Stimulus (*Antabuse* drug)	⇨ No Response (No effect if alcohol is not added)
During Aversive Conditioning	New Stimulus (*Antabuse* drug) **+** Alcohol	⇨ Vomiting, unpleasant emotions (result of the combination of alcohol and *Antabuse*)
After Aversive Conditioning	Alcohol	⇨ Nausea, unpleasant emotions

Operant conditioning, also called **behavior modification**, was discussed in the learning chapter and involves using operant conditioning methods based on the theories of **B.F. Skinner**. The techniques are designed to end or change unwanted behaviors and increase the frequency of positive behaviors. The results of behavior modification are quite encouraging, especially among children with behavior problems. A specific example of behavior modification based on operant conditioning involves the creation of a **token economy**. Within institutional settings, patients suffering from very severe impairment of function may receive a positive reinforcement in the form of a plastic token for each desired behavior, which typically includes participating in group therapy, personal hygiene, or caring for their room. Ultimately, patients can redeem accumulated tokens for small luxuries. Token economies have been used in a variety of settings for behavior modification such as inpatient facilities for severely cognitively disabled individuals or psychiatric hospitals. Another operant technique, **biofeedback**, involves the use of a device to reveal physiological responses that are usually difficult to observe such as changes in heart rate, respiration, EEG activity, or similar responses, in order to enable individuals to achieve some degree of control over their responses. Biofeedback is often used in behaviorist therapy as a method for teaching individuals to gain control over their physiological states in order to reduce anxiety and its symptoms.

Some behavioral therapy techniques, such as modeling therapy and social skills training, are based on Albert Bandura's research on observational learning. The technique of **modeling** involves having clients observe and replicate positive behaviors demonstrated by others. Modeling therapy has been successful in the treatment of a variety of psychological disorders, especially phobias. Observational learning has also been applied to **social skills training** or assisting clients in acquiring important interpersonal skills including communication and assertiveness. Social skills training incorporates behavioral exercises such as role playing, rehearsal, and shaping in addition to observing skilled models to help clients develop necessary interpersonal skills.

Cognitive Therapy

According to the cognitive perspective, mental processes including thinking, knowing, feeling, and memory impact behavior. Mental illnesses, therefore, are the result of problematic, faulty, or irrational thought processes. **Cognitive therapy** consists of a variety of methods that attempt to treat psychological illnesses through the direct manipulation of the thinking and reasoning processes of the client. During cognitive therapy, faulty or maladaptive thought patterns are identified and replaced. Cognitive approaches to therapy focus on helping clients replace irrational thought processes and think about themselves and the people they interact with in a more positive and effective way as opposed to behavioral approaches that attempt to change overt external behaviors. Cognitive therapists directly challenge clients to recognize the irrational, negative, and maladaptive thought processes that are impacting their functioning and encourage them to replace these cognitions with alternative thoughts that are more logical and rational. Clients are encouraged to apply these new thought processes in their daily interactions and self-talk. Overall, cognitive therapy is based on three general principles: (1) thoughts impact behavior, (2) thoughts can be recognized, and (3) changes in thoughts can result in changes to behavior. A critical component to cognitive therapy is the process of **cognitive restructuring** or the altering of illogical, self-defeating cognitions that an individual has that are resulting in dysfunctional behavior or distress and replacing them with ones that are realistic, genuine, and adaptive.

Aaron Beck developed an influential cognitive therapy based on his experiences with depressed clients who continually expressed thought processes that were negative and self-defeating. He proposed that exaggerated negative thoughts and maladaptive beliefs contribute to the development and prolonging of mood disturbances. Beck described the maladaptive thinking patterns of individuals with depression in terms of what he called a negative cognitive triad. The **cognitive triad** includes the depressed individual's negative interpretations about who they are, the experiences they have, and their future. Additionally, depressed individuals experience automatic negative thoughts that distort their interpretations of what is happening in excessively negative ways. They have reflexive negative thoughts to normal setbacks such as the belief that hope does not exist and they are worthless. Beck identified several specific types of cognitive distortions that depressed individuals experience including overgeneralization. **Overgeneralization** happens when an individual makes a blanket and all-inclusive judgment about who he or she is and his or her entire life based on only one specific incident. For example, if Tadd is corrected by his boss regarding one specific procedure, he will then assume that he is a horrible employee, his boss hates him, and that he is likely to be fired, which is an overgeneralization. During cognitive therapy, Beck has clients identify negative thoughts and faulty assumptions and replace them with cognitions that are more realistic and positive. Cognitive therapists explain how faulty thought processes contribute to anxiety and depression and supply clients with techniques to monitor their own thinking for cognitive distortions and how to replace them with more realistic thoughts. Additionally, cognitive therapists challenge clients to find specific evidence to disprove their faulty hypotheses. For instance, if a client holds the exaggerated belief that they are never successful at anything that they do, they may be instructed to keep a list of anything that contradicts this statement, no matter how small, to provide logical evidence to disprove their cognitive distortion. Although Beck's cognitive therapy was originally designed to treat individuals with depression, it has also been used successfully in the treatment of anxiety, anger management, and eating disorders.

STUDY TIP

Beck's cognitive triad explains that individuals may react to stressful events and failures with elaborate cycles of negative thoughts that typically consist of three broad areas of overall distorted thinking. Individuals create explanations for *themselves*, their *experiences*, and their *future* that are excessively negative.

Cognitive Behavioral Therapy

Cognitive behavioral therapy (CBT) combines aspects of both cognitive and behavioral approaches in order to identify and alter the maladaptive thoughts and behaviors that are causing significant distress or making it difficult for the client to cope. These methods include cognitive techniques such as cognitive restructuring as well as behavioral methods of learning new, more adaptive responses based on classical and operant conditioning, modeling, and social skills training. CBT is focused on the current situation and not past experiences or conflicts.

One of the most influential cognitive behavioral therapies is rational-emotive behavioral therapy developed by cognitive psychologist **Albert Ellis. Rational-emotive behavioral therapy (REBT)** is a type of CBT that is based on the idea that people sometimes cognitively misinterpret what is happening around them and these errors in thinking lead to emotional turmoil or dysfunctional behaviors. REBT involves the identification and replacement of irrational beliefs and the use of behavioral techniques to create new, more adaptive responses. One example of a belief that may lead to distress is the idea that a person must be thoroughly competent in everything that he or she does in order to be a worthy human being. A person who holds this belief will ultimately view every error or mistake as a catastrophe. A rational-emotive behavioral therapist would help such clients by making them aware of their irrational thinking, and then guide them towards logical beliefs and realistic goals. Ellis believes individuals erroneously attribute the unhappiness they experience to outside events. During therapy, individuals learn that it is not the event itself, but how they *explain* it that causes distress.

Psychological illness is explained by REBT in terms of an *ABC model*. In this model, A represents an activating event that appears to result in a negative emotion. The B in the model refers to the belief that individuals have about the event. The C refers to the emotional and behavioral consequences. Contrary to what most people believe, it is not the activating event (A) that causes the consequence (C), but in fact it is the belief (B) that leads to the consequence for the individual. For example, if a student receives a rejection letter from a college (A), the resulting emotion (C) could be either an optimistic attitude or a depressed state depending upon the belief (B) the student chooses. If the student interprets being rejected by the college as evidence that he or she is a complete failure, the result will be a depressed state. However, if the student chooses to adopt a belief that there are many other universities to apply to, then he or she will likely have an optimistic attitude. According to Ellis, the way to eliminate depression is to dispute the irrational beliefs and replace them with thoughts that are more logical and realistic. REBT involves familiarizing clients with irrational beliefs that individuals typically hold and assisting them in determining the ones they may be using that are leading to their dysfunctional emotional reactions. The therapist may assign homework challenging the client to engage in behaviors that directly oppose the irrational beliefs that they think are true.

DIDYOUKNOW?

The field of art therapy emerged in the 1930s, founded in the United States by educator and psychotherapist Margaret Naumburg. Influenced by Freud, Naumburg founded the Walden School, which used psychoanalysis as the base of its educational philosophies. The art program at the school was developed by her sister, who was highly influenced by Carl Jung. Naumburg wrote several books on art therapy and its applications with psychiatric patients in the 1940s and 1950s. Today, the American Art Therapy Association tells us that art therapy is used for children, adolescents, adults, and older adults to assess and treat anxiety, depression, and other mental and emotional problems; substance abuse and addictions; family and relationship issues; abuse and domestic violence; social and emotional difficulties related to disability and illness; trauma and loss; physical, cognitive, and neurological problems; and psychosocial difficulties related to medical illness.

Forms of Therapy

Most of the treatments described above are used in **individual therapy**, where the therapist concentrates solely on one client at a time. In **group therapy**, a professional treats a number of patients simultaneously (see Table 15.4). Group therapy has gained acceptance not only because of its economic advantages but also because many therapists regard it as uniquely appropriate for treating some psychological problems. From the point of view of many therapists, group therapy is a more efficient use of professional time than one-to-one therapies because it provides a way to treat more clients. Proponents of group therapy feel that groups have many other advantages. First of all, the group member has an opportunity to explore his or her interactions with a group and how they differ from the way he or she would like to behave with other people. The social pressures in a group can aid the therapist. For instance, if a therapist tells a client that their behavior is childish, the message may be rejected; however, if three or four other group members agree with the therapist, the client may find it much more difficult to reject the observation. Also, individuals in group therapy learn to articulate their problems, listen, and give support to others. Group therapy provides an opportunity for clients to gain insights through observation when attention is focused on another participant. In addition, many clients are comforted by the knowledge that others have problems like theirs. The process of group therapy has been utilized in a variety of self-help organizations such as Alcoholics Anonymous.

One specific type of group therapy is **family therapy**. Here, the family is viewed as a patient in itself, and the members of the family are treated together. This approach is based on the theory that the individual is a product of his or her environment and that to produce change within the individual, the environment must be altered. Ultimately, the family is viewed as one interconnected entity and not just a group of unique individuals with the goal of improving troubled relationships within the family. The specific theoretical orientation of the therapist determines the techniques and approaches that are used during therapy sessions. This might involve diverse aims such as uncovering the power structure in the family or improving the communications system. **Couples therapy** or **marriage therapy**, in which the therapist works with both individuals, focuses on improving the relationship by increasing intimacy, repairing damage caused by conflict, and facilitating effective communication.

Table 15.4. Treatment Approaches

Approach	Goal	Role of the Therapist
Psychodynamic	Individual gains insight into the unresolved unconscious conflicts that are the cause of maladaptive behaviors. Achieves insight and reduces guilt and anxiety.	Actively involved, offering advice and suggestions, as well as providing interpretations
Humanist	Individual gains a more accurate self-concept and reaches his or her full potential by achieving insight.	Nondirective, genuine, and empathetic partner that offers unconditional positive regard
Behavior	Individual learns new, more adaptive responses to replace dysfunctional or maladaptive behaviors.	Demonstrates and instructs how to apply new behaviors and provides a supportive environment for practicing new skills

(continued)

Table 15.4. *(continued)*

Approach	Goal	Role of the Therapist
Cognitive	Individual identifies and replaces maladaptive and irrational thoughts that are resulting in distressing emotions or dysfunctional behaviors.	Directly challenges irrational thoughts and provides techniques for replacing them with more accurate beliefs
Family	Family members replace maladaptive patterns and improve communication and relationships.	Utilizes a variety of methods depending on the theoretical perspective of the therapist
Couples	Couples resolve conflicts and improve communication and intimacy.	Utilizes a variety of methods depending on the theoretical perspective of the therapist
Biomedical	Individual eliminates symptoms by altering biological processes through the use of psychotropic medications or other medical procedures.	Doctor and patient relationship

The Effectiveness of Psychotherapies

One way of assessing the effectiveness of psychotherapy is to ask the clients themselves whether they are better off after therapy than before. Although results vary, approximately 75–90 percent of clients say they are satisfied with the therapy they received and are doing better. However, as has been documented in other fields of psychology, people often see what they are motivated to see. As *cognitive dissonance theory* would predict, for example, that people would want to see therapy as worthwhile after having invested time, effort, and money in it (in order to make their attitude about psychotherapy consistent with their behavior). Also, people often begin therapy when they are in the midst of a crisis; if they get better after some period of time, they may attribute the improvement to therapy even if the crisis would have passed without any therapy at all. After "hitting bottom," in other words, there is often nowhere to go but up, even without help from a therapist.

Therapists are also subject to bias in their assessments of the effectiveness of psychotherapy. For instance, therapists are more likely to remember cases that were successful than cases that were not. This is referred to as **confirmation bias** or the tendency to selectively attend to information that is consistent with one's viewpoint and ignore or minimize information that challenges one's beliefs. Optimally, experimental research would be conducted that compares people receiving some sort of therapeutic treatment with similar people who do not receive treatment. One reason this is necessary is that people tend to get better over time, even without treatment. In statistics, this phenomenon is referred to as **regression to the mean**, the tendency for unusual or extreme events to move toward the average. A baseball player who hits an extremely high number of home runs one year will be likely to hit fewer the next year; a city that has unusually high rainfall one summer will tend to have a more typical level of rainfall the next summer. Similarly, people who are motivated to begin therapy may be extremely depressed, and thus likely to become less depressed with the mere passage of time. Looking at the improvement only of people who have been in treatment may make it appear that treatment has been more successful than was actually the case.

The results of studies that involve comparing people who receive treatment to similar people who do not (using self-reports, reports from friends or family, or judgments of therapists who do not know which participants received therapy and which did not) have been combined statistically using a procedure referred to as **meta-analysis**. Meta-analyses of these outcome studies show that, on average, people's psychological condition improves over time, but it improves more with therapy than without. There is also evidence that some therapies are more effective for some disorders than others are. Currently, there is a growing movement among therapists using the eclectic approach to match specific psychological illnesses with treatments that have been demonstrated to be the most effective based on controlled studies. These treatments that are supported by research are called *empirically supported* or *evidence-based treatments*. Cognitive and cognitive behavioral therapies, for example, have been shown to be especially effective for treating depression, anxiety, eating, and personality disorders. Behavioral treatments are known to be effective for anxiety, bedwetting, addictions, and couples therapy. The psychodynamic approach of interpersonal psychotherapy (IPT) has demonstrated effectiveness for depression and bulimia. The use of insight therapy has been most effective in terms of helping individuals with adjustment problems or in the area of couples therapy. Insight therapies are the least effective in terms of treatment of mental illnesses that involve severe disturbances to thought, emotion, and behavior such as schizophrenia. Evidence also suggests that some psychological problems respond best to a combination of therapies, such as in the case of depression, which is often most effectively treated by combining the use of antidepressant medications with an empirically supported method such as cognitive behavioral therapy. Schizophrenia has been treated most successfully with family-based therapies in combination with antipsychotic medications.

In addition to the use of specific treatment methods, other considerations that influence the effectiveness of therapy are the client and therapist relationship, specific qualities and traits of the therapist and client, and the influence of culture. In order for therapy to be successful, a trusting and open relationship must be established between the client and therapist that decreases the chances of individuals dropping out of treatment and increases the chances of success. Although research indicates that women and men achieve the same level of success, men are much less likely to enter into therapy. Additionally, members of ethnic and racial minorities also enter treatment less often and are more likely to discontinue treatment even though research indicates that therapy can be effective. Members of ethnic minorities may avoid or leave therapy due to cultural differences in comfort levels regarding expression and disclosure of emotions. Increasingly psychologists and other individuals who provide psychotherapy are undergoing specific training to assist them in working with individuals from diverse cultural or ethnic backgrounds. Research indicates that education and coaching does improve relationships between clients and therapists and prevents individuals from discontinuing treatment early.

Biological Therapy

Biological therapy or **biomedical therapy** involves the treatment of psychological illnesses through the use of medications and other medical treatments designed to influence behavior by altering bodily functions. Treatments utilized in biological therapy include psychotropic medications, psychosurgery, and electroconvulsive therapy (ECT), all of which are based on the medical model that proposes that these conditions have a physical cause.

Psychopharmacology

The most common type of biomedical treatment involves the use of psychotropic medications and is called **psychopharmacology**. These medications focus on increasing or decreasing the amount of specific neurotransmitters in order to eliminate symptoms or impact thought and behavior. Before the introduction of these medications, patients were typically controlled through physical restraint, barbiturate drugs, prefrontal lobotomies, electroconvulsive shocks, and insulin-shock therapy, all of which had severe side effects or limited effectiveness. The use of psychotropic drugs has greatly reduced the amount of time individuals must remain in psychiatric hospitals and has calmed patients, enabling more effective psychotherapy and improved quality of life. It is important to note that psychotropic medications are not a cure for psychological illnesses, but instead a method for controlling symptoms that return if a patient discontinues taking the drugs. Additionally, psychotropic medications almost always involve side effects and require continual monitoring and possible adjustment by a medical professional. The major categories of medications used in the treatment of psychological illnesses are antipsychotics, antidepressants, anxiolytics (antianxiety), and mood stabilizers.

Antipsychotic Medications

Psychopharmacology began with the introduction of *Thorazine (chlorpromazine)*, in the early 1950s. This synthetic drug was first used to control violent symptoms in schizophrenic or psychotic patients. **Psychosis** refers to a loss of touch with reality and significant impairment in thought (delusions), perception (hallucinations), language, and emotion associated with severe mental illness. **Antipsychotic** drugs are used to control symptoms of psychotic disorders by lowering the patient's motor activity and reducing the occurrence of delusions and hallucinations.

The first generation of antipsychotic drugs introduced in the 1950s, called typical or **conventional antipsychotics**, include *Thorazine (chlorpromazine)* and *Haldol (haloperidol)*. These drugs were effective for alleviating positive symptoms of schizophrenia such as hallucinations and delusions, but had little impact in treating negative symptoms such as social isolation, flat affect, or apathy. Conventional antipsychotic medications are also called **neuroleptics** and result in movement side effects. These early antipsychotic medications work as antagonists by blocking dopamine transmission, although researchers have not been able to identify the specific reason for their effectiveness. The development of these medications allowed individuals with severe mental illnesses to escape from debilitating or incapacitating symptoms, allowing many patients to be able to live independently. Despite the effectiveness of these medications to reduce psychotic symptoms, they also have numerous side effects including Parkinson's disease-like tremors and movement problems, cognitive difficulties, sedation, blurred vision, and weight gain. The most serious potential side effect is **tardive dyskinesia** or the usually permanent involuntary movements often of the face or tongue. Tardive dyskinesia can also lead to uncontrollable twitching and jerking motions of the arms and legs. It is believed that as many as 20% of individuals who take conventional antipsychotics for long periods of time will develop this serious and potentially irreversible condition. The severe side effects of these early antipsychotics led some patients to stop using them altogether.

Since the 1990s, newer antipsychotic medications called **atypical antipsychotics** have been developed that have fewer side effects and are more effective at treating both positive and negative symptoms. Side effects associated with atypical antipsychotics include weight gain, dizziness, and potentially elevated blood sugar levels. The most prescribed atypical antipsychotic medications are *Clozaril (clozapine)* and *Risperdal (risperidone)*. Atypical antipsychotic medications work by blocking dopamine transmission but also certain serotonin receptors. These newer medications do not cause tardive dyskinesia and are now prescribed more frequently than conventional antipsychotics.

Antidepressant Medications

The most commonly used drugs in clinical practice are **antidepressants**, a group of psychotropic medications that are most frequently prescribed to alleviate the symptoms of depression. Three main classes of antidepressants include monoamine oxidase inhibitors, tricyclics, and selective serotonin reuptake inhibitors. **Monoamine oxidase inhibitors (MAOIs)** work to block the enzyme monoamine oxidase, leading to increased levels of the neurotransmitters norepinephrine and serotonin. Although MAOIs are effective in many cases in reducing the symptoms of depression, patients using these medications must adhere to specific dietary restrictions because interactions with certain foods can lead to dangerous increases in blood pressure. Other side effects include headaches, dizziness, blurry vision, sleep disturbances, or tremors. **Tricyclic antidepressants** are a group of antidepressant medications that inhibit reuptake of the neurotransmitters serotonin and norepinephrine. Tricyclics were prescribed more frequently than MAOIs because they have fewer and less serious side effects. These drugs however have also been replaced by SSRIs. **Selective serotonin reuptake inhibitors (SSRIs)** alleviate depression symptoms by reducing the reuptake of the neurotransmitter serotonin and include commonly prescribed drugs such as *Prozac (fluoxetine)*, *Paxil (paroxetine)*, and *Zoloft (sertraline)*.

STUDY TIP

In addition to treating depression, antidepressants have been shown to be effective in treating symptoms associated with other psychological illnesses including anxiety and eating disorders.

Antianxiety Medications

Antianxiety medications, also called **anxiolytics**, are prescribed for a variety of anxiety disorders to help decrease anxiety and tension. Low levels of GABA have been linked to a variety of anxiety disorders and biomedical treatments generally focus on influencing the transmission of this neurotransmitter. Antianxiety medications work as agonists for the inhibitory neurotransmitter GABA and therefore increase its transmission. The two main types of anxiolytics are barbiturates and benzodiazepines. **Barbiturates**, also known as sedatives, were previously widely used for anxiety and sleep disorders but are rarely prescribed today because they are highly addictive. The risk of accidental or intentional suicide due to overdose is high with these medications because at high levels these drugs depress the nervous system, leading to coma, or death. Barbiturate withdrawal can be extremely dangerous due to the possibility of increased heart rate and convulsions. The antianxiety medications most widely prescribed today are **benzodiazepines**, which are used to assist patients as a sleep aid, tension reducer, or muscle relaxant. Benzodiazepines include *Librium (chlordiazepoxide)* and *Valium (diazepam)*. Although these medications are regarded as safer than barbiturates because they are less likely to lead to death by overdose, they also have a risk for dependence and abuse. Benzodiazepine medications can also result in tolerance and withdrawal symptoms such as increased heart rate and irritability. Furthermore, benzodiazepines, if combined with other CNS depressants, can result in intoxication, unconsciousness or possibly death.

Mood Stabilizers

Mood stabilizers are a class of psychotropic medications that are used to balance the extremes of emotion that are experienced by individuals suffering from bipolar disorder. **Lithium,** a naturally occurring, metallic element that is found in the form of a salt, was the first mood stabilizer medication to be shown to effectively treat the mania of bipolar disorder. Because lithium can potentially lead to kidney or thyroid problems, regular blood testing must be conducted to ensure that toxic levels are not reached. Some individuals with bipolar disorder respond best to anticonvulsant mood stabilizers such as *Depakote (valproate)* or *Tegretol (carbamazepine)*. Anticonvulsant mood stabilizers have fewer side effects and are less toxic at higher doses than lithium.

STUDY TIP

Be able to identify the main categories of psychotropic drugs and provide specific examples of medications for each category. See Table 15.5.

Table 15.5. Psychopharmacology

Category	Medication	Examples	Information
Antipsychotic or Neuroleptic	Conventional (typical)	*Thorazine*	Reduces dopamine transmission
		Haldol	Risk of tardive dyskinesia
	Atypical	*Clozapine*	Reduces dopamine and serotonin transmission
		Risperdal	
		Abilify	
Antidepressant	MAOIs	*Nardil*	Blocks enzyme activity resulting in increased levels of norepinephrine and serotonin
		Parnate	
	Tricyclics	*Elavil*	Reduces reuptake of norepinephrine and serotonin
		Tofranil	
		Norpramin	
	SSRIs	*Prozac*	Reduces reuptake of serotonin only
		Celexa	Fewest side effects
		Zoloft	
		Lexapro	
Antianxiety	Barbiturates	*Barbital*	Increases GABA transmission
		Nembutal	Serious side effects
		Seconal	Prescribed rarely
	Benzodiazepines	*Valium*	Increases GABA transmission
		Xanax	Prescribed more frequently
Mood Stabilizer	Mineral Salt	*Lithium*	Levels in the blood must be closely monitored to prevent reaching toxic amounts
	Anticonvulsants	*Depakote*	Fewer side effects and less toxic than lithium

Electroconvulsive Therapy

In the 1930s, it was also believed that schizophrenia and convulsions could not exist at the same time in the body. Therefore, theorists reasoned that it might be therapeutic to induce convulsions in schizophrenic patients. For some years, the drug *Metrazol* was used to induce convulsions in patients, but the drug had the disadvantage of causing extreme fear and unpredictably strong seizures. In the 1940s, psychologists began to use electroconvulsive shock treatment because it caused immediate unconsciousness. Unlike drug-induced shocks, electroconvulsive shock left no time for fear reactions, and doses could be controlled so that extreme convulsions could be avoided. **Electroconvulsive therapy (ECT)** involves the brief passage of an electric current across electrodes placed on the temple of the patient. This creates a brain seizure. Today, before administering the shock, the patient is given a muscle relaxant and placed under anesthesia in order to reduce the severity of the convulsions during the seizure and render them unconscious for the entire procedure. The usual treatment consists of 6 to 12 sessions spread over several weeks. The aftereffects of the treatments can include temporary loss of memory, disorientation, and confusion. These effects usually disappear within a month or two after the treatments, but are one of the reasons patients and therapists do not choose this type of therapy. While ECT has been found to be in an ineffective treatment for schizophrenia, it is one of the most effective and speediest treatments available for severe depression. This method relieves symptoms faster than antidepressant drugs, which generally require at least two weeks before their effects can be seen. Currently, no scientific explanation for why ECT is effective has been provided and the results are often temporary. Although ECT continues to be a controversial treatment, it has been demonstrated to be effective for specific conditions. Critics argue that ECT poses a threat of significant cognitive damage, including problems with language and amnesia, but for severely depressed individuals who have not found relief from any other treatment, ECT may be the best possible alternative.

Psychosurgery

Many different and sometimes bizarre medical treatments have been developed for mental illness. Evidence of trephination, believed to be the oldest form of brain surgery, has been found on prehistoric skulls in various parts of the world. *Trephination* involves drilling a hole directly through the skull to expose the brain. Although it is still unknown exactly what this method of treatment was used for, it has been hypothesized that this surgery may have been used to treat medical conditions or mental illness by allowing for evil spirits or demons to be released. **Psychosurgery**, the most drastic form of biomedical therapy is the purposeful surgical removal or destruction of particular areas in the brain. This controversial method was pioneered in the 1930s with the use of the prefrontal lobotomy originally developed by Portuguese neurologist Egas Moniz. **Prefrontal lobotomies** involve various surgical procedures, including the removal of certain areas of the prefrontal cortex of the brain or the severing of connections between the prefrontal cortex and the rest of the brain. The theory underlying this approach was that severing the nerve connections with the thalamus, then believed to be the controlling center for the emotions, would relieve severe emotional disturbance. In many cases, this procedure controlled violent and psychotic behaviors and made patients manageable in an era before the advent of antipsychotic medications. Prefrontal lobotomies were routinely used for a variety of conditions and often performed with inexact methods. One particular method involved inserting an ice pick beneath the eyeball and moving it swiftly back and forth to cut the connections from the prefrontal cortex. Although behavioral improvements were achieved, many patients suffered severe side effects or irreversible brain damage. Many patients experienced severe losses of cognitive function, had extreme changes in personality, and some remained in permanent vegetative states. Furthermore, many individuals died as a result of the surgery. Beginning in the 1950s, the development of antipsychotic medications led to the elimination of prefrontal lobotomies. Modern psychosurgery involves the use of sophisticated brain imaging and precise procedures, although this method is only used in the most extreme cases because of the effectiveness of psychotropic medications.

Community and Preventative Approaches

During the 1950s, the first antipsychotic medications were introduced into American hospitals for the mentally ill, providing relief from the severe symptoms of serious disorders such as schizophrenia to many patients. The improvement that these medications provided became a major factor in a change in government policy regarding state-run hospitals and the creation of community mental health centers. **Deinstitutionalization** involved closing government-run hospitals and providing care to individuals with mental illness through outpatient facilities, or group homes in the community. Although many patients were able to thrive outside of institutions, large numbers were left without sufficient support, and many of these individuals became homeless after they stopped taking their medications. The **community mental health movement** was designed to offer care for individuals formerly treated in mental hospitals by providing therapy and support through outpatient facilities that would be used by individuals with mental illness living either with family members or in group homes. Community mental health services are provided by a variety of mental health specialists, including social workers, psychologists, and psychiatrists who work in a variety of facilities (e.g. halfway houses, nursing homes, group homes, and outpatient clinics). This movement was based on the premise that recovery would be enhanced if individuals could live within and be part of local communities instead of being isolated within hospitals. Within the community setting, it would be easier to focus efforts on prevention as well as treatment and social skills training. Decreases in funding of these facilities have led to problems with availability of care for many individuals. The field of **community psychology**, which is extensively involved in the community mental health movement, involves basic and applied research related to discovering methods to prevent or reduce the prevalence of psychological illnesses by understanding how social interactions in neighborhoods, families, and the larger culture impact functioning.

Social Psychology

Social psychology focuses on the individual in relation to society and emphasizes how we think about, shape, and connect with one another. Although social psychologists draw on the areas of sociology and cultural anthropology, their primary interest is still the psychological level of thought and action. Social psychologists work to explain social thought and behavior through the use of the scientific method and have produced a large body of knowledge about the underlying psychological processes involved in social interactions. Humans are social animals, and behavior is dramatically impacted by interactions with others.

Social Cognition

Social cognition involves how people gather, use, and react to information about the behavior of others. This process occurs, for example, when meeting someone for the first time and forming an initial impression. First impressions form rapidly, are resistant to change, and are especially strong if they are negative. Impressions formed about others can become self-fulfilling prophecies because our own expectations can influence how others behave. A **self-fulfilling prophecy** happens when our beliefs about another person or ourselves lead us to act in a way that brings about the behaviors we expect and confirms our original impression.

In a classic study on the self-fulfilling prophecy called "Pygmalion in the Classroom," researchers Rosenthal and Jacobsen, in order to investigate how the expectations of teachers effected student achievement, told teachers that a group of students were on the verge of a dramatic increase in intellectual growth or "academic blooming." The students were actually randomly selected and did not have any special potential. At the end of the year, the students whom teachers believed were on the verge of a dramatic increase in intelligence, in fact, demonstrated significantly higher increases in their scores compared to the other students. How did this happen? Additional research has shown that teachers treat students with positive academic labels differently by providing them with more feedback and increased opportunities to work with more challenging material, as well as by giving them more chances to respond in class. This additional attention and positive treatment leads the students to work harder and think of themselves as talented and capable, thus making these beliefs a reality. Self-fulfilling prophecies can also pertain to a person's own behavior. This occurs when predictions an individual has about his or her own abilities lead the person to act in a way that results in confirming those expectations. If Robert believes that he is not good at writing, he may give up when given a difficult assignment, confirming his beliefs. However, if he believes he excels at writing and is given a difficult assignment, he will be more likely to work hard and confirm his opinion of himself as a talented writer.

STUDY TIP

Be able to apply the concept of the self-fulfilling prophecy to a specific example.

Earl believes his girlfriend Fiona is going to break up with him. Because of this belief, he frequently checks her text messages and questions her about conversations with other boys. As a result of this behavior, Fiona decides that Earl is too clingy and breaks up with him. Earl's belief about Fiona led him to behave in a way that made his expectation become reality, which is a self-fulfilling prophecy.

Social Comparison

Individuals develop **self-concepts** or **self-schemas** consisting of the beliefs they have about themselves. Self-schemas include the various ways people describe themselves; for example, an individual's self-concept might include a belief that he or she is creative, intelligent, persistent, and stubborn. The term **self-esteem,** however, refers to a value judgment a person makes about how worthy a person he or she is based on comparisons with how he or she was in the past, as well as how the person measures up to others. When we compare our current abilities and traits with how we performed in the past, this is a **temporal comparison** and can result in either an increase or decrease in self-esteem. If we make a temporal comparison between our gymnastic skills now and what we were capable of two years ago, and determine that we have improved, the result will most likely be an increase in self-esteem. However, if our skill level has decreased over time, the temporal comparison may result in a decrease in self-esteem.

Another way to evaluate self-esteem is to make comparisons between others and ourselves; these are called **social comparisons**. Typically we compare ourselves to individuals we perceive to be similar to us or to people who are members of groups to which we belong; these groups are called **reference groups**. The members of a reference group share a common aspect of social identity such as gender, interests, ethnicity, or occupation. **Relative deprivation** occurs when we compare ourselves with our reference group and find that, regardless of how much wealth, status, and appreciation we are receiving, it is less than what others who are similar to us have. For example, a recent college graduate making $60,000 may feel he is not getting what he deserves if others in his reference group are making over $100,000.

Another way we enhance our self-esteem is though the **false consensus effect**, which involves overestimating how much others share our opinions or behave in the same way as we do. Students who believe that a test was really difficult will be more likely to overestimate how many other students share their opinion. When we fail at something or behave badly, we may preserve our self-esteem by saying that most other people would have done the same thing. For example, when people feel bad about speeding, the false consensus effect allows them to justify their actions by convincing themselves that everyone else also drives over the speed limit.

Attitudes and Cognitive Dissonance

An **attitude** is a person's belief about another person, object, or situation. Each attitude consists of a cognition (belief), affect (feeling), and behavior (action). An attitude about attending college may include the understanding that it is essential for future employment (cognition or belief), that it is an exciting opportunity (affect or feeling), and that excellent grades are necessary for admission (behavior or action). Social psychologists investigate how attitudes influence our behavior and how our behaviors influence our attitudes.

Although it would seem that an individual's behavior would be consistent with his or her beliefs, this is not always the case. **Cognitive dissonance** occurs when we experience an unpleasant state because we are holding two conflicting beliefs *or* have an inconsistency between our behavior and beliefs. This tension motivates us to reduce our cognitive dissonance by either changing our behavior or altering our beliefs. For example, John thinks smoking can kill and does not want to harm himself (belief) but continues to smoke (behavior), and this inconsistency causes him discomfort. In order to reduce dissonance, John will be motivated to change his behavior and quit smoking, *or* he will alter his belief to explain his behavior in a way that allows him to feel comfortable again. Because it is usually easier to alter our beliefs than to change our behaviors, John will most likely rationalize that death due to smoking occurs only to people that smoke much more than he does so, and he will continue to smoke.

Cognitive dissonance was demonstrated by psychologist **Leon Festinger** in a famous experiment in which participants were asked to complete a dull task (turning knobs on a board). After completing the task, participants were asked to tell the next participant (a confederate) that the experience was fun. Half of the participants were paid $1 to lie to the next participant, and half were paid $20 to lie. In the final part of the experiment, participants were asked to rate how much they enjoyed the original task. Those who were paid $20 had received sufficient justification for lying to the next participant and reported that they found the task to be boring. The individuals in the experimental group who were paid only $1 did not have sufficient justification for lying and experienced cognitive dissonance. The participants resolved this inconsistency between their belief (the task was dull) and their behavior (telling another participant it was fun) by altering their belief and telling the researcher that the experiment was actually enjoyable. It is important to mention that if a person's beliefs and behaviors do not match, cognitive dissonance does not always occur. If Alfonso hates doing homework (belief) but chooses to do his assignments because there is an incentive (college admission, high grades, etc.), there is no dissonance because he has sufficient justification for acting in a manner that is not aligned with his beliefs. This is why the participants in Festinger's study who were paid $20 did not feel any dissonance.

The phenomenon of **justification of effort** is related to cognitive dissonance and states that if something involves a higher cost in terms of money, pain, or effort, we will value it more. Justification of effort explains why individuals who have to suffer through a difficult initiation process end up valuing membership in the group more than they would if joining required little effort. The hazing rituals used for fraternities and sororities require potential members to suffer in order to gain entrance into the group. Justification of effort explains why individuals who endure hazing value their membership in the organization more.

STUDY TIP

Cognitive dissonance is a key concept that has appeared frequently on both the multiple-choice and free-response sections of the AP exam.

- Tension created when holding two conflicting beliefs or if our beliefs and actions do not match.
- Attitude change results because we are motivated to reduce the tension.

Hint: Cognitive dissonance occurs only within the individual and *not* between two individuals.

Attribution Theory and Biases

Why do people do what they do? Social psychologists study the various types of attributions or explanations people generate for their own behavior and the behaviors of others. Fritz Heider's attribution theory states that the attributions we generate are either dispositional or situational. **Dispositional (internal) attributions** explain behavior in terms of factors inside the person (personality, intelligence, maturity, etc.), whereas **situational (external) attributions** explain behavior in terms of factors outside the person (luck, social etiquette, etc.). The attributions we make about ourselves and others influence our behavior. For instance, if a salesperson complements Amanda's hairstyle and she attributes it to the person's ability to appreciate her style and fashion sense (dispositional), she might respond warmly to the person; if Amanda attributes the compliment to pressure from the salesperson's boss to make a sale (situational), she might walk away. Making attributions can result in various types of errors. The main types of bias in attribution are explained in Table 16.1.

STUDY TIP

Be able to apply attribution theory to specific examples.

Table 16.1. Common Attribution Biases

Attribution Bias	Definition	Study Tip	Example
Fundamental Attribution Error (FAE) *More common in Individualistic Cultures	Tendency to use a dispositional (internal) explanation without considering the situational (external) factors that might be influencing the behavior of someone else.	FAE occurs only when explaining someone else's behavior—it is about *"them."*	Brent is having dinner with his girlfriend, and their waiter is inattentive. He most likely will attribute the waiter's behavior (*"them"*) as being rude (dispositional). Brent is making the FAE because he failed to take into account the potential external (situational) factors involved, such as the fact that his waiter is new and the restaurant is short-staffed.

(continued)

Table **16.1.**   *(continued)*

Attribution Bias	Definition	Study Tip	Example
Actor–Observer Bias	Tendency to explain the behavior of others with dispositional attributions (FAE), but attribute our own behavior as the actor to situational factors. This is due to the greater awareness we have about how our own behavior can vary from one situation to another.	Actor–observer bias involves two individuals in comparison—*"you"* (the person making the attribution) and *"them"* to whom you assigned an attribution.	When Samantha watches her classmate stumble while giving a speech, she believes it is because her classmate (*"them"*) is a bad public speaker (dispositional), but when Samantha stumbles during her speech, she explains that it was because she (*"you"*) was distracted by noise in the hallway (situational).
Self-Serving Bias *More common in Individualistic Cultures	Tendency to attribute our successes to dispositional factors and our failures to situational factors. This is due to the desire to see oneself in a positive way. We serve ourselves by making ourselves look good, taking credit for our successes and avoiding responsibility for our failures.	Self-serving bias involves only your own behavior (*"you"*) and involves choosing attributions that make *"you"* look good.	Jordan believes he aced the chemistry test because he is smart (dispositional), but that he failed the calculus test because his teacher did a poor job explaining the content (situational). In this example, Jordan has explained only his own behavior (*"you"*).
Self-Effacing Bias *More common in Collectivist Cultures	Tendency to attribute our failures to dispositional factors and our successes to situational factors. This results in modesty by taking responsibility for one's failures and crediting the contributions of others for one's successes.	Self-effacing bias involves only your own behavior (*"you"*) and involves choosing attributions that make the group look good and *"you"* seem modest.	When Mari's team loses the soccer game, she takes the responsibility for not being prepared (dispositional), and when her team wins, she attributes it to the effort of her teammates (situational). In this example, Mari has explained only her own behavior (*"you"*).
False Consensus Effect	Tendency for an individual to overestimate how many others act and think the way that they do.	False consensus effect involves *"your"* perceptions about how others think and behave.	Ethan did well on his psychology midterm, leading him to exhibit the false consensus effect by assuming everyone else was successful on the exam as well.

The prevalence of a particular attribution error can be impacted by culture. The self-serving bias and fundamental attribution error occur more frequently in **individualistic cultures,** such as those found in the United States and Western Europe, due to their emphasis on the values of independence and self-reliance. The self-effacing bias is more frequently identified in **collectivist cultures** such as those in Eastern Asia, Western

Africa, and parts of South America; these cultures emphasize group membership and harmony above individual achievement.

Individuals often preserve their self-esteem by using **self-handicapping** strategies to create a convenient situational explanation for potential failures before they happen. Alina realizes she needs to pass her calculus exam, but she is afraid that she will fail, so she chooses to stay up all night watching a marathon of old movies to create an excuse in case she fails. On the day of the test, Alina tells all of her friends that she had no time to study, so that if she is not successful, they will attribute her failure to being tired (situational) instead of saying she is not smart (dispositional). Alina has sabotaged her chances of being successful on the exam in order to preserve her self-esteem.

As humans we feel the need to see our world as fair, in what is known as the just-world phenomenon, and that individuals get what they deserve. The belief in a just world may lead individuals to **blame the victim** or to hold victims responsible for their own misfortunes. Blaming the victim can lead people to believe that someone who was robbed at gunpoint deserved it because the person should have been more careful about walking home alone in a high crime area.

Social Influence

Behavior is contagious! We have all experienced how a collective yawn can spread through a room. **Social influence** is the study of how other individuals' thoughts and actions shape our own beliefs, feelings, and behaviors. Social influence is spread through **norms**, or conditioned social rules, that provide information on how to behave. These rules may be implicit or explicit and learned from parents, peers, teachers, or cultural role models. Failure to adhere to these social rules can result in exclusion from the group. Norms are not universal; for example, the personal space norm, or the acceptable distance required between individuals varies by culture.

Social Roles and the Stanford Prison Study

In addition to norms, social roles have a significant impact on our thoughts and actions. **Social roles** are the expected patterns of behavior required by specific situations or social positions. For example, there are certain behaviors associated with particular social roles, such as mother, employer, student, and teacher. In 1971 **Phillip Zimbardo** conducted the famous **Stanford Prison Experiment**, investigating the power of social roles and the impact of the situation on behavior. Twenty-four male college students were selected to participate in a study located in a mock prison, constructed in a basement of Stanford University. The participants were randomly assigned to the social role of either "prisoner" or "guard" and provided with a wardrobe symbolizing their new status. Although the experiment was designed to last for fourteen days, it had to be canceled after only six days due to the suffering of the participants. The guards and prisoners had started to actually become their social roles, with the guards becoming increasingly aggressive in their psychological torment of the prisoners and prisoners developing signs of extreme psychological stress, such as symptoms of depression. The power of the situation led both the guards and the prisoners to alter their own thoughts and behaviors to align with the social roles that they were assigned.

> **DID**YOU**KNOW?**
>
> In 2004, comparisons were made between the Stanford Prison Experiment and the abuses and human rights violations that came out of the Abu Ghraib prison in Iraq. Phillip Zimbardo compared Abu Ghraib's leader, Brig. Gen. Janis Karpinski, to his own role in the Stanford Prison Experiment. Both operations ended when someone inside—another researcher at Stanford and a soldier in Baghdad—brought to light the events taking place.

Compliance and Persuasion

Persuasion refers to a type of social influence that involves various methods designed to change the behavior of others by convincing them to alter their beliefs or behaviors. **Compliance** is a change in behavior that results from a direct request. Social and organizational psychologists study the necessary motivations required to convince people to buy products or alter their opinions. Salespeople, politicians, and others use a variety of methods designed to gain compliance and persuade individuals to change their opinions. The **foot-in-the-door** technique involves having someone comply with a small request first in order to increase the likelihood that they will agree to a second larger request later. Students utilize this technique in the classroom to convince the teacher to give them help with multiple answers by first asking for assistance on only one question. The **door-in-the-face** technique works in the opposite direction because the individual begins by making a large request that most likely will be turned down. After this large initial request is denied, the person makes a more reasonable request that is now much more likely to be granted. In the classroom students may use the door-in-the-face technique to persuade their teacher to move the date of the test. The students would begin by first asking the teacher to have the date of the test moved to the following week, knowing that they will most likely be denied. The teacher is now likely to agree to their more reasonable request to postpone the test for one additional day. The door-in-the face method is an effective way of persuading someone by first make a request for something that is so extreme that it will be rejected and then asking for what one wanted in the first place. The **low-ball** technique is a compliance method that involves convincing someone to commit to an agreement and then increasing the effort or cost required to fulfill the commitment. The low-ball technique is a two-step process: First, obtain a commitment and, second, increase the effort or cost to fulfill that commitment by revealing hidden or additional costs. A car salesperson might have the customer test drive the car and then convince the customer to commit to purchasing the car by offering an extremely good deal. After the individual has agreed to the deal, the salesperson using the low-ball technique would change the terms and increase the price. Many individuals will accept the new price because they are already emotionally committed to the new car. The effectiveness of a persuasive message is also influenced by the source (who says it), the nature of the communication (how it is said), and the audience. All of these persuasion factors can be applied to print and broadcast media, as well as face-to-face interactions. The **elaboration likelihood model** of persuasion offers two general methods that individuals use to process the claims being presented to them in a persuasive message. The two approaches of the elaboration likelihood model are the *central* and *peripheral* routes to persuasion and they are discussed in Table 16.2.

STUDY TIP

Be able to discriminate between the two methods of persuasion that make up the elaboration likelihood model.

Table 16.2.   Elaboration Likelihood Model

Concept	Definition	Example
Central Route of Persuasion	Focuses on the factual content of the message and uses evidence and logical arguments as the basis for attitude change. Individuals are persuaded based on the strength of the argument presented.	An advertisement for a car that uses the central route of persuasion will include data such as the safety rating or highway/city miles per gallon.
Peripheral Route of Persuasion	Focuses on positive or negative associations and emotional appeals. Individuals are persuaded by surface or external factors and not the strength of the argument presented.	An advertisement for a car that uses the peripheral route of persuasion would involve an emotional appeal such as a celebrity endorsement.

Conformity

Changing one's behavior or beliefs to fit in with others due to real or imagined social pressures is known as **conformity**. In a famous experiment on conformity, **Solomon Asch** assigned participants to work on a panel with seven other participants who were really confederates. **Confederates** are individuals who are part of the research team that pose as subjects and whose behavior in the experiment is determined in advance. Asch asked the participants to choose which of three comparison lines on a card was the same length as a standard line on a separate card. The subject was asked to give an answer to the line question after all of the confederates first gave the same wrong answer aloud. Under these conditions 70 percent of the subjects conformed to the group's wrong answer at least once, but when the subject was given the task alone, that person gave the correct answer 99 percent of the time. Since there were no explicit rewards or punishments, the reason for conformity could be that in the face of such "overwhelming" opposition the subjects agreed with the confederates to gain group acceptance (or avoid group rejection). The results of the Asch study showed that individuals would, under certain conditions, conform to an obviously wrong group norm. Asch and his colleagues repeated this study many times, varying the conditions in attempts to determine what variables play a causal role in decreasing or increasing conformity. The Asch studies revealed that group size and unanimity were the best predictors of conformity. Further research discovered additional factors that increased the likelihood of conformity, including attraction to the group, having no strong preexisting opinion, and being presented with a situation in which the correct answer is unclear or ambiguous.

Obedience

Obedience involves changing one's behavior in response to a demand from an authority figure. **Stanley Milgram** conducted one of the most famous experiments in psychology and discovered that the average American would, under the direction of a legitimate authority figure, give what they believed were severe shocks to other people in an experimental setting. In Milgram's experiment, two men were told that they would be taking part in an experiment on the effects of punishment on learning. One man was predetermined to be the learner (a confederate), and the participant was assigned to be the teacher (the participant). The learner was taken into an adjoining room and strapped into a chair. The teacher was placed in front of a shock generator and told to administer shocks from 15 to 450 volts to the learner when they provided an incorrect answer. However, there were no actual shocks being given to the learner (confederate). The first mistake resulted in a mild shock, and each subsequent wrong answer resulted in a progressively stronger shock. Despite cries from the learner (confederate) of "Let me out of here, I've got a heart condition!", the teacher (participant), with encouragement from the authority figure, would continue administering shocks, although more and more reluctantly. Out of the forty males who took part in the initial experiment, 65 percent went all the way to the maximum shock level of 450 volts. This alarming finding has been replicated many times. It demonstrates that ordinary people will obey orders given by a legitimate authority figure even to the point of committing cruel and harmful actions. The main factors that increased the likelihood of obedience in Milgram's studies were the prestige of the institution, proximity of the authority figure, the behavior of others, and the depersonalization of the victim. Later experiments by Milgram revealed that the most significant factor in reducing obedience to authority was the presence of other teachers who chose not to continue.

DIDYOUKNOW?

The American Psychological Association (APA) put Stanley Milgram's membership application "on hold" because of the questions raised about the ethics of his research—a year before his first journal article on obedience research. After an investigation, the APA finally admitted him.

STUDY TIP

Be able to discriminate among the various types of social influence. The AP exam requirements specifically reference four psychologists and their corresponding experiments on social influence. See Table 16.3.

Table 16.3. **Key Social Influence Studies**

Concepts	Definition	Researcher	Results
Cognitive Dissonance	Altering one's behavior or beliefs to reduce the discomfort caused when there is conflict.	Festinger's $1 or $20 Study	After lying about the task, participants in the $1 experimental condition revised their belief to say that the task was interesting to reduce their cognitive dissonance.
Social Roles	Altering one's behavior to fit the expectations of a social role.	Zimbardo's Prison Study	The study was terminated after six days due to the negative consequences of participants assuming their social role.
Conformity	Altering one's behavior or beliefs to fit in with a group.	Asch's Line Study	Approximately 70% of the subjects conformed to the group's wrong answer at least once.

(continued)

Table 16.3.   *(continued)*

Concepts	Definition	Researcher	Results
Obedience	Altering one's behavior in response to a demand from an authority figure.	Milgram's Shock Study	In response to a demand from an authority figure, 65% of the subjects obeyed and administered what they believed was the maximum shock level to the learner.
Compliance	Altering one's behavior in response to a request, *not* a command, by an authority figure.		
Persuasion	Attempting to alter the attitudes, opinions, and behaviors of others through the use of arguments and techniques designed to exert influence.		

Group Dynamics

The behavior of individuals can be powerfully influenced by the presence of others, and people often behave differently when they are in a group. Depending on a variety of factors, the existence of an audience can lead to either increased or decreased individual performance. In **social facilitation** the presence of others, such as an audience or coworkers, increases individual performance on easy or well-rehearsed tasks. However, if the task is unfamiliar or difficult, the presence of an audience leads to decreased individual performance in what is known as **social interference**. These opposite effects explain why an experienced actor has a better performance in front of a large audience, while a new actor may experience stage fright in front of a crowd.

Membership in a group can also lead to increased or decreased individual performance or changes in behavior. **Social loafing** occurs when a person contributes less when working with others in a group than when performing the same task alone, due to the lessoning of personal accountability. While social loafing is more common in individualistic cultures, **social striving** or an increased effort when working as part of a group is more common in collectivist cultures. If a group is large enough, such as the size of an audience at a sporting event, social influence can lead people to behave in ways that is very different from what they would normally do. **Deindividuation** is a state of lessened personal responsibility and self-restraint due to feelings of anonymity created by being part of a crowd. Deindividuation can lead individuals to participate in **prosocial** or **antisocial behaviors** that they would not otherwise do.

Group decision-making processes can be either improved or hindered by the strength of our prior personal beliefs or the desire for harmony. **Group polarization** occurs when groups of like-minded individuals interact, resulting in an amplification of their existing attitudes and a tendency to make more extreme decisions. For example, if a group of conservative voters gather together to discuss politics, their overall opinion will become more conservative. Groups in general also have a tendency to make more risky decisions than the members would individually in what is known as **risky shift**. Groups working together often make better decisions, but, under certain conditions, group influences can lead to bad decision-making processes such as groupthink. **Groupthink** is a the tendency for a cohesive decision-making group to ignore or dismiss reasonable alternatives because of the desire for a unanimous decision. The likelihood of groupthink increases when contradictory evidence is ignored, disagreement is discouraged, and there is pressure for a quick decision. To effectively prevent groupthink, groups should include members who genuinely challenge the group's beliefs or an individual should be assigned the role of *devil's advocate*. The *devil's advocate* assumes the unpopular role of voicing any possible concerns that other group members might be reluctant to mention. A summary of group dynamics is presented in Figure 16.1.

Figure 16.1.   Group Dynamics Summary

Social Facilitation	Presence of an audience increases arousal.	Social Inhibition
Performance increases on easy or well-learned tasks in the presence of others.		Performance decreases on difficult or unfamiliar tasks in the presence of others.

Social Loafing	Personal accountability within a group	Social Striving
Individuals contribute less effort as members of a group. *More common in Individualistic Cultures		Individuals contribute more effort as members of a group. *More common in Collectivist Cultures

Group Polarization	Factors that influence group decision making	Groupthink
Participation in a group amplifies existing attitudes, which leads to more extreme decisions (risky shift).		Individuals feel pressure for unanimous decisions, which prevents group discussion of possible alternatives.

Prosocial Behavior	Deindividuation	Antisocial Behavior
Kurt is normally reserved, but, during the homecoming pep rally, he chants the school song because he feels anonymous in a large crowd.	Loss of identity or self-restraint because of membership in a group	Citizens who normally respect the law may take part in destructive behavior, such as looting or rioting, when feeling anonymous in a large crowd.

STUDY TIP

Be able to describe the impact of the presence of others or membership in a group on individual behavior.

Conflict and Aggression
Prejudice, Discrimination, and Stereotypes

In addition to forming a self-concept or self-schema, humans also add organization to their world by creating social schemas by grouping similar types of people or events into categories. Individuals we view as similar to ourselves are considered members of our **in-group**, and those perceived as different are categorized as **out-groups**. There is a natural tendency for people to notice negative characteristics in members of out-groups, and not in members of their in-group; this is known as **in-group bias**. People are also more capable of distinguishing differences among members of their in-groups than among members of out-groups, in what is known as **out-group homogeneity**, often leading to stereotyping and discrimination. It is easy for individuals to acknowledge that only some of the football fans at their school are disrespectful (in-group bias), yet still hold the belief that most of the fans of their cross-town rival are disrespectful (out-group homogeneity). In-group bias can be a method individuals use to elevate their self-esteem by associating themselves with successful groups and putting down members of out-groups. **Prejudice** is usually a negative attitude directed toward a particular group and its members. It is translated into behavior through **discrimination**, or any action that results from prejudiced points of view. **Stereotypes** make up the cognitive component of prejudice and are schemas for entire groups that assume that all or most of the members share the same negative traits. **Ethnocentrism** is a specific type of prejudice that involves favoring one's own cultural or ethnic group and holding negative stereotypes about other cultures. A specific type of discrimination known as the **scapegoat theory** occurs when an innocent out-group is blamed by an individual or community for a negative experience. According to scapegoat theory, during times of economic or social hardship when people are angry and frustrated, they may blame out-groups for their problems.

STUDY TIP

The AP exam requirements specifically reference students being able to articulate the processes that contribute to treatment of different groups (i.e., in-group/out-group dynamics, ethnocentrism, and prejudice).

- *Culture:* enduring ideas, attitudes, and traditions shared and transmitted by a large group. Cultural group identifications can include ethnicity, religion, language, customs, etc.
- *Ethnocentrism:* specific type of prejudice in which an individual favors his or her own culture or ethnic group's values, attitudes, and actions over other cultural groups.

All people are ethnocentric to some degree. For example, when traveling people might view their own culture's food as superior to the food in the country they are visiting. When ethnocentrism is extreme, it can lead to discrimination, conflict, or war.

Decreasing Prejudice

One method of decreasing prejudice is to provide opportunities for groups in conflict to spend time together in order to reduce stereotypes. This increased interaction, known as **contact theory**, allows members of groups in conflict to recognize what they have in common and provides an opportunity for them to work together and build relationships. Contact theory is most effective if the opposing individuals or groups are required to collaborate on a **superordinate goal**, or obstacle that requires cooperation to ensure success. These concepts were illustrated in Sherif's Robber's Cave experiment that involved boys who attended a summer camp and were divided into two opposing teams. The researchers created in-group bias and prejudice and then utilized contact theory and superordinate goals to create harmony between the two groups.

Social Dilemmas

Individuals in groups may work collectively toward a common goal, known as **cooperation**, but, if they are working to reach a goal while simultaneously preventing others from doing the same, they are in a state of **competition**. Competition may lead to open clash between individuals or groups known as **conflict**.

Social dilemmas (traps) are situations in which individuals must choose whether to cooperate or compete with others. In social dilemmas, choosing to compete will provide one individual with an advantage, but, if all parties compete, it will result in harmful consequences for everyone. A social trap based on the scenario when two people are immediately separated after being arrested for a serious crime is known as the **prisoner's dilemma**. Prisoners have the choice to cooperate with their partner or to compete by confessing. In this situation there are good reasons to compete and good reasons to cooperate, but the best result would be for both partners to cooperate (see Figure 16.2).

Figure 16.2. The Prisoner's Dilemma

	Prisoner A	
	Remain Silent (Cooperate)	Confess (Compete)
Prisoner B — Remain Silent (Cooperate)	Both prisoners are released.	Prisoner A is released and Prisoner B receives the maximum sentence.
Prisoner B — Confess (Compete)	Prisoner A receives the maximum sentence and Prisoner B is released.	Both prisoners receive a moderate sentence.

Social dilemmas may also involve conflict between the short-term interests of one person and the long-term interest of the group regarding a shared resource. In the **commons dilemma (tragedy of the commons)**, individuals need to determine how much to *take* from a shared supply. If a group of sheep ranchers all share the same pasture area, a commons dilemma emerges because, although it is in the best interest of each individual rancher to allow their sheep to graze frequently, the pasture would not be sustainable if all of the ranchers did this. In a **public goods dilemma**, individuals must decide how much to *contribute* to a shared resource. It is in the best short-term interest of each individual citizen to not pay taxes, but if everyone chose to behave this way, government services would shut down.

Aggression

Psychology defines **aggression** as any action, verbal or physical, meant to hurt others. According to social psychologists, there needs to be a distinction between two main types of aggression. In **instrumental aggression** the goal is not to harm the victim, but to achieve a goal or protect oneself. Aggression intended to cause damage to a victim is called **hostile aggression**, and it is usually the result of anger or frustration. In professional boxing instrumental aggression is involved, because violence against an opponent is a method used to win the match or title. When a street fight breaks out, it is the result of hostile aggression because the goal is solely to inflict harm.

STUDY TIP

Both Sigmund Freud and Konrad Lorenz believed aggression was an instinct that needed to be released when it built up. Freud's theory regarding aggression is known as the **catharsis hypothesis**. This theory states that expressing aggression is needed to release inner tension. Research does not support this theory and has actually shown the opposite to be true. Venting anger increases aggressive behavior.

Aggression is clearly influenced by both biological and psychological factors. Brain structures involved in aggression include the emotional limbic system and the frontal lobes that allow individuals to evaluate the potential consequences of their actions and restrain their aggressive impulses. Increased levels of the hormone testosterone are also associated with aggressiveness.

STUDY TIP

Think of the emotional limbic system as the gas pedal for aggression and the thinking and planning functions of the frontal lobes as the brakes that restrain aggressive responses. Damage to the frontal lobes will lead to increased aggression because it is like driving without brakes.

Many social psychologists believe that aggression, like other behaviors, is learned through conditioning or observation. **Albert Bandura's** work on modeling was designed to explain how aggressive tendencies in children are learned through imitation. Aggression may also be conditioned through reinforcements and punishments. The **frustration–aggression hypothesis** states that frustration or stress resulting from being blocked from reaching a goal produces aggression. For example, if a person is late to school and stuck in traffic, this will result in frustration and stress, increasing the likelihood of aggressive driving. There are various negative environmental factors that can increase the likelihood of aggression. **Aversive conditions** include crowding, pain, foul odors, high temperatures, etc. Within a school setting, overcrowding may lead to increased aggression, measured by an increase in the number of student fights.

Altruism

Altruism and the bystander effect are two opposite responses to situations where another person needs help. In **altruism**, a person will risk his or her own health or well-being to help another. If a large group of people witness an event where someone desperately needs assistance, each person is less likely to intervene than if there were fewer onlookers. This phenomenon is called the **bystander effect** in which the presence of more witnesses decreases helping. The bystander effect results from the belief of each individual in a crowd that they do not need to help because somebody else will take action. This phenomenon is known as **diffusion of responsibility**. Research into the bystander effect was first inspired by the brutal murder of Kitty Genovese. Media coverage of this event highlighted the fact that, although there were many witnesses to the crime, none of them called the police. This example can be explained by diffusion of responsibility because the presence of others decreased each person's obligation to respond or call the police.

Various factors contribute to the likelihood that altruism will occur, including the **social exchange theory**, which states that individuals balance the costs and rewards of helping and are more likely to assist others if the potential for reward is high and potential costs are low. **Reciprocity norms** lead people to help others with the expectation that they would receive help if they needed it or because they had been helped in the past and are now returning the favor. The variable of **time pressure** has a huge impact on helping behavior, because individuals who are in a hurry are significantly less likely to offer assistance.

Attraction

Although what is considered attractive varies by culture and time period, social psychologists have identified factors that influence whether people will like each other or not. One of the strongest predictors of attraction is **proximity**, because people are more likely to be attracted to those who live near them and with whom they have repeated contact. Research indicates that repeated contact with a new stimulus leads to increased liking in what is called the **mere exposure effect**. For example, David did not think that his new coworker Alice was attractive when he first met her, but, after seeing her at work every weekend for several months, he changed his mind and asked her out on a date.

Another factor related to attraction is similarity in both attitudes and physical attractiveness. Individuals are more likely to be attracted to people with whom they share common interests, beliefs, and values. Online dating services collect information from members and suggest matches based on similar beliefs and interests. The theory that individuals pair up in relationships with those who are similar to themselves in terms of their level of physical attractiveness is known as the **matching hypothesis.** It is important to remember that the matching hypothesis applies only to similarity in terms of physical attractiveness.

Robert Sternberg proposed the **triangular theory of love** that includes several different types of love resulting from various combinations of three main components: passion (physical attraction), intimacy (closeness), and commitment (a decision to remain together). **Companionate love** consists of intimacy and commitment, and **passionate** or romantic love consists of intimacy and passion. The ultimate form of love, according to Sternberg, is **consummate love**, which includes all three aspects—passion, intimacy, and commitment—and for that reason is rare. To remember the three parts of Sternberg's triangular theory of love, use the acronym PIC (**p**assion, **i**ntimacy, and **c**ommitment).

STUDY TIP

Be able to apply psychological concepts to a variety of behaviors both within and across chapters. One example within the social chapter is the norm of reciprocity, which can influence a variety of behaviors.

- Reciprocity in Persuasion—Individuals are more likely to comply with a request from someone who has already done them a favor.
- Reciprocity in Altruism—Individuals are more likely to help someone who has helped them in the past.
- Reciprocity in Attraction—Individuals are more likely to be attracted to someone who is attracted to them.

Time for a quiz
- Review strategies in Chapter 2
- Take Quiz 7 at the REA Study Center
(www.rea.com/studycenter)

Take Mini-Test 2
on Chapters 10–16
Go to the REA Study Center
(www.rea.com/studycenter)

Practice Exam

Also available at the REA Study Center (*www.rea.com/studycenter*)

This practice exam is available at the REA Study Center. Although AP exams are administered in paper-and-pencil format, we recommend that you take the online version of the practice exam for the benefits of:

- Instant scoring
- Enforced time conditions
- Detailed score report of your strengths and weaknesses

Practice Exam
Section I

(Answer sheets appear in the back of the book.)

TIME: 1 hour and 10 minutes
100 questions

Directions: Each of the questions or incomplete statements below is followed by five suggested answers or completions. Select the best choice for each question and then fill in the corresponding oval on the answer sheet.

1. The double-blind procedure refers to a method of experimentation in which

   (A) participants in both the experimental and control groups do not know the purpose of the study.

   (B) members of both the experimental and control groups are exposed to the independent variable.

   (C) two different control groups are created.

   (D) neither the participants nor the experimenter know which participants are in the experimental group.

   (E) two different experimental groups are created.

2. Twelve-year-old Nina was told by her parents that she should not slam her bedroom door, but she did not change her behavior. One day when Nina came home from school, she found that her parents had taken the door from her room and put it in the attic. After a month had passed, Nina's parents replaced her door. Nina no longer slams her bedroom door. Nina's change in behavior is the result of receiving a

   (A) negative reinforcement.

   (B) negative punishment.

   (C) positive reinforcement.

   (D) positive punishment.

   (E) fixed-ratio schedule.

3. According to Kohlberg's theory of moral development, a person who follows the law purely because it is the law is functioning at which of the following levels?

   (A) Preconventional

   (B) Conventional

   (C) Postconventional

   (D) Preoperational

   (E) Concrete

4. People who have had a finger amputated often report that their adjacent fingers become more sensitive, particularly if the amputation happens relatively early in life. This change is likely due to which feature of the brain?

   (A) Localization of function

   (B) Lateralization of function

   (C) Long-term potentiation

   (D) Plasticity

   (E) Maturation

5. Which of the following is a method of statistical analysis used by personality psychologists to identify clusters of traits that tend to co-exist in people?

   (A) ANOVA

   (B) Factor analysis

   (C) Regression to the mean

   (D) Standard deviation

   (E) Meta-analysis

6. The first psychology laboratory was founded by

   (A) William James

   (B) Wilhelm Wundt

   (C) Sigmund Freud

   (D) Edward Titchener

   (E) Ivan Pavlov

7. Psychologists conducting research on the effects of morphine on the body discovered that even though morphine is an artificial chemical, the human body seems to have neural receptor sites that are "built" to receive morphine. This happens because the drug morphine closely mimics the chemical structure of which of the following naturally occurring hormones?

   (A) GABA

   (B) Norepinephrine

   (C) Serotonin

   (D) Glutamate

   (E) Endorphins

8. Edward has a fear of heights and is terrified to ride the roller coasters at the amusement park even though he really wants to fit in with his friends and take part in the excitement. Edward's friend Beatrice explains that his fear of heights is genetic and that this apprehension was naturally selected because it helped human ancestors to survive. Matt disagrees and believes that Edward acquired his fear of heights by observing others in his family who are afraid of heights as well. Beatrice is explaining Edward's fear from the _____ perspective, while Matt is using the _____ perspective.

(A) cognitive; behaviorist

(B) behaviorist; cognitive

(C) biological; behaviorist

(D) evolutionary; biological

(E) evolutionary; behaviorist

9. What region of the brain is located in the hindbrain and is most responsible for regulating breathing, blood circulation, reflexes, and other involuntary vital functions?

(A) Thalamus

(B) Reticular formation

(C) Amygdala

(D) Medulla

(E) Hypothalamus

10. Luke stopped hitting his brother after seeing a boy on a TV show hit someone and get punished for it. What type of learning on Luke's part does this illustrate?

(A) Latent learning

(B) Partial reinforcement

(C) Chaining

(D) Generalization

(E) Observational learning

11. The proportion of total variation in a population that is due to genetic variation is referred to as

(A) genotype.

(B) phenotype.

(C) heritability.

(D) the Flynn effect.

(E) natural selection.

12. Wayne is a patient at a mental health facility. During his admission interview, he described how he had been kicked out of his previous home due to disruptive behavior, and how he is now homeless. Under which axis of the *DSM-IV-TR* would this type of information be noted?

(A) Axis I

(B) Axis II

(C) Axis III

(D) Axis IV

(E) Axis V

13. The bias toward thinking of objects only in terms of their normal uses, instead of some novel use for which they might be needed, is called

    (A) divergent thinking.

    (B) breaking set.

    (C) functional fixedness.

    (D) confirmation bias.

    (E) belief bias.

14. Dr. Ruiz has published the findings of his research regarding Howard Gardner's multiple intelligences theory in a scientific journal. After comparing the test scores of all of the participants, the results indicate that participants who scored high in mathematical intelligence also scored fairly high in musical intelligence. Which research method did Dr. Ruiz use?

    (A) Case study

    (B) Experiment

    (C) Naturalistic observation

    (D) Correlational

    (E) Double blind

15. In an experiment to determine if looking at three-dimensional optical illusions results in individuals leaning back and forth more than looking at two-dimensional optical illusions, participants were asked to view both types of images for four minutes each while standing. The researchers then carefully measured how often the participants shifted their weight while viewing each type of image. The number of times participants shifted their weight represents a(n)

    (A) operational definition of the independent variable.

    (B) operational definition of the dependent variable.

    (C) confounding variable.

    (D) set of demand characteristics.

    (E) positively skewed distribution.

16. In which of the following Piagetian stages of cognitive development does a child gain the ability to mentally represent abstract concepts?

    (A) Concrete operational

    (B) Sensorimotor

    (C) Formal operational

    (D) Conventional

    (E) Preconventional

17. Which sleep stage is most closely associated with the appearance of sleep spindles and K-complexes?

    (A) REM

    (B) Stage one

    (C) Stage two

    (D) Stage three

    (E) Stage four

18. Individuals who act in aggressive and manipulative ways for their own benefit, with little concern for their wrongdoings toward others, are displaying signs of which personality disorder?

    (A) Antisocial

    (B) Paranoid

    (C) Histrionic

    (D) Narcissistic

    (E) Obsessive-compulsive

19. When you look at the lights on a theater marquee, they may appear to be "moving" in a circle around the marquee. In reality, they are merely blinking in coordinated order to create the illusion of apparent motion, also known as

    (A) the phi phenomenon

    (B) perceptual constancy

    (C) a perceptual set

    (D) the stroboscopic effect

    (E) motion parallax

20. Which theory of emotion states that after encountering a stimulus, the person first has a physiological response which is subsequently interpreted as an emotion by the brain?

    (A) Yerkes-Dodson

    (B) Opponent-process

    (C) Cannon-Bard

    (D) James-Lange

    (E) Schachter-Singer or two-factor

21. The closing of government-run hospitals in favor of providing care to individuals with mental illness through outpatient facilities, or group homes, was called the

    (A) moral treatment movement.

    (B) deinstitutionalization movement.

    (C) community mental health movement.

    (D) statistical model.

    (E) diathesis-stress model.

22. Dysthymia is a mild form of what psychological disorder?

    (A) Bipolar disorder

    (B) Posttraumatic stress disorder

    (C) Schizophrenia

    (D) Major depressive disorder

    (E) Hypochondriasis

23. When looking at a flock of birds in flight, we often see the "flying V" rather than perceiving each bird as an individual object. This organization of our perceptions into larger, more meaningful units is the focus of which of the following schools of psychology?

    (A) Gestalt psychology

    (B) Behaviorist psychology

    (C) Functionalist psychology

    (D) Evolutionary psychology

    (E) Cognitive psychology

24. John is an extremely organized person. His desk is completely clean and orderly, as is his bedroom. He is regularly on time for appointments and he is careful to follow through on all of his obligations. Based on this information, which of the following personality traits would he score high on?

    (A) Openness

    (B) Conscientiousness

    (C) Extraversion

    (D) Agreeableness

    (E) Neuroticism

25. Addie is trick-or-treating during Halloween and finds a large bowl of candy on the porch at one of the houses and must decide how much candy to take. If all of the trick-or-treaters only take one piece of candy, there will be enough for every kid. However, the opportunity exists for individuals to take as much candy as they want. Addie's situation is best described as

    (A) altruism.

    (B) the prisoner's dilemma.

    (C) groupthink.

    (D) the public goods dilemma.

    (E) the commons dilemma.

26. Which of the following is true of short-term memory (STM)?

    (A) STM has limitless storage.

    (B) Rehearsal does not aid keeping information in STM.

    (C) STM is highly susceptible to interference.

    (D) Information always travels from STM to long-term memory.

    (E) The use of chunking decreases STM capacity.

27. Becky is strongly in favor of requiring students at public high schools to wear uniforms. During a class debate on the topic, she is assigned to generate arguments against creating a uniform policy. In order to reduce cognitive dissonance,

    (A) Becky's classmates will now be more in favor of requiring uniforms.

    (B) Becky's classmates will now be less in favor of requiring uniforms.

    (C) Becky's opinion on requiring uniforms will not change.

    (D) Becky will now be less in favor of requiring uniforms.

    (E) Becky will now be more in favor of requiring uniforms.

28. Which of the following Pearson correlation coefficients represents the highest degree of association between variables X and Y?

    (A) $r = -.70$

    (B) $r = +.60$

    (C) $r = +.50$

    (D) $r = +.10$

    (E) $r = +7.0$

29. According to Carl Jung, where are archetypes common to all individuals found?

    (A) Preconscious

    (B) Superego

    (C) Personal unconscious

    (D) Collective unconscious

    (E) Hidden observer

30. Which theory for pitch perception suggests that the pitch we perceive is the result of sound waves activating cilia in different locations along the basilar membrane?

    (A) Place theory

    (B) Frequency theory

    (C) Volley theory

    (D) Sensory adaptation

    (E) Set point theory

31. The word "dogs" contains _____ phonemes and _____ morphemes.

    (A) 1; 2   (D) 4; 2

    (B) 3; 4   (E) 2; 4

    (C) 4; 1

32. In a well-designed controlled experiment, the researcher manipulates the textbook students use in order to measure the effects of a new and improved book on test scores for a Philosophy class. It turns out that the average test score among participants in the experimental group was 90 and the average score for participants in the control group was 78. If the 12-point difference between the two groups is "statistically significant," what would that mean?

    (A) There is a high probability that the dependent variable caused the independent variable.

    (B) The research conclusions are accurate.

    (C) A difference as big as 12 points, or more, would be unlikely to happen by chance.

    (D) That a 12-point difference is important.

    (E) The populations those samples came from must differ from each other, as well.

33. The distribution of a group of SAT scores has a mean of 550 and a standard deviation of 50 and forms a normal distribution. What percent of the SAT scores fall between 500 and 600?

    (A) 50%   (D) 34%

    (B) 68%   (E) 98%

    (C) 14%

34. Each person who completes an 8-item personality test is given a total score for his or her ratings of item numbers 1, 3 5, and 7, as well as a total score for his or her ratings of item numbers 2, 4, 6, and 8. Thus, each person ends up with two scores; one the total for odd-numbered items and one the total for even-numbered items. The correlation across these individuals' odd-number total and even-number total is then computed. This procedure would be used to assess

    (A) alternate-forms reliability.

    (B) face validity.

    (C) test-retest reliability.

    (D) split-half reliability.

    (E) criterion-related validity.

35. Stacy has a lunchbox that is twice as heavy as Jennifer's. Stacy's lunchbox would have to have 4 more cupcakes in it before it would feel noticeably heavier, whereas Jennifer's would have to have only 2 more cupcakes in it in order to feel heavier. Which of the following concepts best explains this situation?

    (A) Sensory adaptation

    (B) Weber's law

    (C) Young-Helmholtz theory

    (D) Opponent-process theory

    (E) Feature detection theory

36. Which of the following would result if the parasympathetic nervous system was activated?

    (A) Decreased salivation

    (B) Producing perspiration

    (C) Inhibiting digestion

    (D) Slowing heart rate

    (E) Pupil dilation

37. Most cases of classical conditioning require repeated pairings of the associated stimuli before the animal has fully made the connection and learned the association. One notable exception is a _____, which can be formed after even a single pairing.

    (A) negative reinforcement

    (B) taste aversion

    (C) negative punishment

    (D) shaping

    (E) simultaneous conditioning

38. An assessment that measures what a person has already learned in prior training is a (an)

    (A) aptitude test.

    (B) objective test.

    (C) projective test.

    (D) self-report inventory.

    (E) achievement test.

39. Archie is a star athlete at his school and hopes to be drafted to play professional sports after he graduates. One day a teammate offers to sell Archie performance-enhancing drugs that allegedly cannot be detected in drug tests. On the one hand Archie believes that taking the drugs will give him a competitive advantage, but on the other hand the drugs are illegal and dangerous to his long-term health. In what type of situation has Archie found himself?

    (A) Approach-approach conflict

    (B) Approach-avoidance conflict

    (C) Avoidance-avoidance conflict

    (D) Multiple approach-avoidance conflict

    (E) Social trap

40. Young infants enjoy playing peek-a-boo in part because they lack _____, the awareness that something exists even when they cannot see it. They acquire this ability during the _____ stage according to Piaget's cognitive development theory.

    (A) conservation; concrete operational

    (B) egocentrism; preoperational

    (C) assimilation; preoperational

    (D) object permanence; preoperational

    (E) object permanence; sensorimotor

41. Which type of cell allows an individual to distinguish different wavelengths of light?

    (A) Ganglion cells

    (B) Cones

    (C) Bipolar cells

    (D) Rods

    (E) Gustation receptor cells

42. A(n) _____ is an unwanted repetitive behavior that a person cannot help but engage in because it reduces anxiety. Repeated hand washing is one of the most common examples.

    (A) compulsion

    (B) panic attack

    (C) obsession

    (D) phobia

    (E) agoraphobia

43. Which of the following was a finding of Stanley Milgram's experiment when participants were asked to shock a learner (confederate) in increasing amounts in what they believed was a study on the effects of punishment on learning?

    (A) 65% of participants obeyed the authority figure and administered shocks to the maximum 450 volt level.

    (B) 30% of participants obeyed the authority figure and administered shocks to the maximum 450 volt level.

    (C) 30% of participants conformed by going along with others in the group and administering shocks up to the 450 volt level.

    (D) 65% of participants conformed by going along with others in the group and administering shocks up to the 450 volt level.

    (E) 75% of participants refused to participate in the experiment after the learner first indicated pain.

44. After having three cups of strong coffee, Jake finds that he is angrier than usual after being insulted by a co-worker, but happier than he otherwise would be when he finds out he got a modest raise. Which theory of emotion explains this?

    (A) Schachter-Singer or two-factor theory

    (B) Instinct theory

    (C) Opponent-process theory

    (D) Cannon-Bard

    (E) James-Lange

45. An assessment created to make it possible for any individual, regardless of their ethnic, national, or religious background, to perform equally well is considered to be a

    (A) culture-relevant test.

    (B) culture-fair test.

    (C) power test.

    (D) speed test.

    (E) crystallized intelligence test.

46. Whorf's linguistic determinism hypothesis states that

    (A) culture determines the language that we speak.

    (B) language and thought are independent and do not influence each other.

    (C) bilingual people have more flexible and outgoing personalities.

    (D) certain principles and the ability to learn language are "hard-wired" into the human brain.

    (E) language determines the thoughts that a person has.

47. Alice has been living in Seattle for the past six weeks while working at a fast-food restaurant. She has various documents in her purse, though, that say her real name is Lucy; she lives in Chicago with her husband and three kids, and has a job as a tax attorney. Alice remembers nothing about Lucy and her life. Which psychological disorder does Alice most likely have?

    (A) Disorganized schizophrenia

    (B) Bipolar disorder

    (C) Conversion disorder

    (D) Dissociative amnesia

    (E) Dissociative fugue

48. Extinction of a conditioned response occurs when the

    (A) CS is presented without the UCS several times.

    (B) CS is introduced and remains present before the UCS is introduced.

    (C) CS is introduced and then stopped before the UCS is introduced so that the presentation of the two stimuli is separated by an interval of time.

    (D) CS and the UCS are both presented at the same time.

    (E) UCS is presented before the NS.

49. Which brain structure plays the most important role in forming implicit memories?

    (A) Corpus callosum

    (B) Cerebellum

    (C) Hippocampus

    (D) Suprachiasmatic nucleus

    (E) Pons

50. Transduction for the vestibular sense occurs in the _____ and is our sense of _____.

    (A) hair cells on the basilar membrane; balance

    (B) semicircular canals; balance

    (C) semicircular canals; location of body parts

    (D) muscles and joints; location of body parts

    (E) muscles and joints; balance

51. The type of validity which measures the extent to which a test measures an abstract theoretical idea that it is designed to measure is

    (A) content validity.

    (B) face validity.

    (C) predictive validity.

    (D) criterion validity.

    (E) construct validity.

52. A type of therapy that is useful in eliminating bad habits is _____, during which a negative response becomes associated with the habit.

    (A) aversive conditioning

    (B) systematic desensitization

    (C) cognitive behavioral therapy

    (D) psychoanalysis

    (E) cognitive therapy

53. The theory that states that dreams are merely the result of the brain attempting to interpret the stimulation it is receiving during sleep is called

    (A) paradoxical sleep.

    (B) the hypnagogic state.

    (C) the activation-synthesis model.

    (D) microsleep.

    (E) the information-processing theory.

54. A(n) _____ is a method of brain imaging that creates a color-coded image that indicates brain activity by tracking where small amounts of radioactive glucose are consumed in the brain.

    (A) MRI

    (B) fMRI

    (C) CT scan

    (D) PET scan

    (E) EEG

55. Terrance has been depressed for a very long time and finally decides to seek treatment. His depression has started to cause problems in his marriage and he is having difficulty fulfilling his responsibilities at home and work. His therapist recommends weekly sessions for cognitive behavioral therapy and in addition writes a prescription for Prozac. Which type of professional is most likely providing Terrance's treatment?

    (A) Psychiatrist

    (B) Counseling Psychologist

    (C) Clinical Psychologist

    (D) Social worker

    (E) Psychiatric nurse

56. Abby has an overwhelming fear of snakes. She begins to shake and feel nervous whenever she is around a snake. Her therapist begins to treat her by asking her to simply think of a snake while she practices new relaxation techniques. On Abby's next visit, he places a snake in a cage on the other side of the office and she again practices relaxing. On her next visit, Abby has to reach into the cage and touch the snake while relaxing. This process of gradually eliminating phobias is known as

(A) client-centered therapy.

(B) cognitive restructuring.

(C) a token economy.

(D) flooding.

(E) systematic desensitization.

57. The theory that whether or not an individual notices a stimulus depends on the stimulus itself, the background stimulation, and characteristics of the detector is known as

(A) social cognitive theory.

(B) theory of mind.

(C) absolute threshold.

(D) signal detection theory.

(E) the Premack principle.

58. Individuals with a(n) _____ personality disorder are extremely shy and anxious in social situations due to a fear of rejection or being evaluated negatively. Although they want to have relationships, their fears of rejection and failure prevent them from being able to form friendships.

(A) avoidant

(B) schizoid

(C) antisocial

(D) borderline

(E) dependent

59. The _____ are two small, almond-shaped structures in the limbic system, which is the seat of many emotions, most notably fear and anger.

(A) occipital lobes

(B) amygdala

(C) hippocampus

(D) reticular activating system

(E) pons

60. Veronica had a stroke and suffered damage to her hippocampus. After the stroke, she was no longer able to form new memories. However, she could still remember everything that happened in her life before the stroke. What type of amnesia is Veronica experiencing?

(A) Dissociative

(B) Retroactive

(C) Proactive

(D) Anterograde

(E) Retrograde

61. All of the following are monocular cues for depth EXCEPT

    (A) interposition.

    (B) relative size.

    (C) retinal disparity.

    (D) linear perspective.

    (E) texture gradient.

62. Edward Tolman conducted research on how cognition impacts learning in animals and studied how an organism may acquire a new behavior without reinforcement or awareness. This new behavior is not demonstrated unless a need or reinforcement is presented. Tolman referred to this type of learning as

    (A) latent learning.

    (B) a cognitive map.

    (C) centration.

    (D) the law of effect.

    (E) insight learning.

63. Long-term potentiation refers to

    (A) the strengthening of neural connections that are the basis of learning.

    (B) the speed of spontaneous recovery of classically conditioned behaviors.

    (C) the maturation of the peripheral nervous system.

    (D) the growth of new neurons in the brain.

    (E) the ability of feature detector cells in the brain to fire simultaneously to rapidly form interpretations.

64. Individuals with a diagnosis of mental retardation who are the most cognitively disabled are at the _____ level.

    (A) profound

    (B) pervasive

    (C) serious

    (D) severe

    (E) moderate

65. Jane, who is depressed, recently succeeded in getting a job she really wanted. A therapist that was working from a strictly cognitive approach would want Jane to attribute her success to

    (A) her own talent and ability.

    (B) the modeling therapy that she participated in to prepare her for a job interview.

    (C) cognitive restructuring and social skills training.

    (D) achieving insight about unconscious conflicts that were holding her back.

    (E) luck.

66. Participants in experiments have an equal chance of being placed within either the experimental or control condition. This ensures that the average behavior of subjects in the control group will not differ from the average behavior of subjects in the experimental group. What procedure does this statement represent?

    (A) Random sample

    (B) Stratified sample

    (C) Random selection

    (D) Representative sample

    (E) Random assignment

67. The reinforcement schedule that produces the highest and most steady rate of performance is a

    (A) fixed-interval schedule.

    (B) variable-interval schedule.

    (C) fixed-ratio schedule.

    (D) variable-ratio schedule.

    (E) frequency histogram.

68. Antidepressants such as Prozac, Zoloft, and Paxil work by blocking the reuptake of which neurotransmitter?

    (A) Dopamine

    (B) Glutamate

    (C) Acetylcholine

    (D) GABA

    (E) Serotonin

69. Rebecca began noticing some problems sensing touch on her right arm after she hit her head in a car accident. Which area of the cerebral cortex would Rebecca most likely be worried about?

    (A) Left parietal lobe

    (B) Right parietal lobe

    (C) Left temporal lobe

    (D) Right temporal lobe

    (E) Frontal lobes

70. Group polarization refers to

    (A) the tendency for a cohesive decision-making group to ignore or dismiss reasonable alternatives because of the desire for a unanimous decision.

    (B) the tendency of groups of like-minded individuals that interact to make more extreme decisions after an issue is discussed.

    (C) the tendency for individuals to make more extreme (risky) decisions after having a group discussion than they would have made individually.

    (D) a state of lessened personal responsibility and self-restraint due to feelings of anonymity created by being part of a crowd.

    (E) a situation in which individuals must choose whether to cooperate or compete with others.

71. If deception is involved, researchers are legally required to fully explain the true purposes of the study to participants and answer questions that they might have at the end of the experiment. This process is known as

    (A) random assignment.

    (B) random selection.

    (C) priming.

    (D) debriefing.

    (E) informed consent.

72. The second level in Maslow's hierarchy of needs is

    (A) esteem and self-esteem.

    (B) love and belonging.

    (C) safety.

    (D) self-actualization.

    (E) physiological needs.

73. Three-year-old Jimmy, who sees lots of cows on the family farm, saw a rhinoceros at the zoo and thought it, too, was a cow. Which of the cognitive processes described by Piaget does this illustrate?

    (A) Assimilation

    (B) Accommodation

    (C) Conservation

    (D) Egocentrism

    (E) Object permanence

74. Zoey and Zach have been dating for two years and it is almost time to start making plans for prom. Zach has told Zoey that he does not want to go to prom this year and she is very disappointed and angry. Zoey is afraid to tell Zach how she really feels because she is afraid he might break up with her. That night at dinner Zoey is extremely rude to her mom and dad. Which defense mechanism is Zoey most likely using?

    (A) Projection

    (B) Regression

    (C) Displacement

    (D) Reaction formation

    (E) Sublimation

75. All of the following are factors that increase the likelihood of conformity EXCEPT:

    (A) The opinion of the majority is unanimous.

    (B) The group consists of the individual's friends

    (C) The individual does not have a strong pre-existing opinion.

    (D) There are others present who are not conforming.

    (E) The size of the group is large.

76. If a neuron receives more excitatory neurotransmitters than inhibitory and reaches a specific minimum level, the neuron will have reached

    (A) the refractory period.

    (B) threshold.

    (C) repolarization.

    (D) resting potential.

    (E) polarization.

77. Benjamin is trying to decide how likely it is that he will enjoy a new class being offered at his college on positive psychology and decides to compare the characteristics of the class such as the teacher, or other students taking the course with other courses he has liked. Benjamin is ultimately asking himself how similar one event (the positive psychology course) is to a class of events. (other classes he has liked) that are familiar to him. This is an example of the use of the technique of a(n) _____ for problem solving.

    (A) representative heuristic

    (B) anchoring

    (C) availability heuristic

    (D) belief perseverance

    (E) overconfidence

78. All of the following statements describe a feature of classical conditioning EXCEPT

(A) unconditioned and conditioned stimuli are presented to the organism.

(B) the response will always be involuntary.

(C) unconditioned and conditioned responses are the same or similar.

(D) voluntary responses by the organism result from prior reinforcements or punishments.

(E) an initially neutral stimulus becomes a conditioned stimulus.

79. _____ are false beliefs held by schizophrenics ("I am the queen of Oklahoma"), while _____ are perceptions of things that do not exist ("I hear voices in my head").

(A) Neologisms; delusions

(B) Delusions; catatonia

(C) Delusions; hallucinations

(D) Hallucinations; delusions

(E) Neologisms; clang associations

80. Over the past six months, Renee has had unpredictable episodes during which she experiences a fear that something bad is about to happen. Her heart begins to race, she feels dizzy, and she has trouble catching her breath. Between episodes Renee worries a great deal about future incidents. Which anxiety disorder does Renee most likely suffer from?

(A) Specific phobia

(B) Generalized anxiety disorder

(C) Social anxiety disorder

(D) Panic disorder

(E) Obsessive-compulsive disorder

81. Mr. Tagala is a highly motivated volunteer soccer coach who works many hours a week creating innovative plays and drills for his players and providing additional one-on-one help to many kids. After coaching for five years, he learns that coaches whose teams win more than 80% of their games will receive a large bonus. Mr. Tagala receives the bonus the first year and is very excited. Unfortunately, the next year his players do not win enough games for him to earn a bonus and he finds he is less interested in working long hours to help kids or spend time on creating new plays. Which psychological concept best explains why Mr. Tagala's intrinsic motivation level has been diminished?

(A) Overjustification effect

(B) Priming

(C) Self-fulfilling prophecy

(D) Self-reference effect

(E) Display rules

82. Freud believed that sometimes a person in therapy will redirect their positive or negative feelings about life events or other people in their life onto the therapist. He referred to this process as

(A) identification.

(B) resistance.

(C) transference.

(D) rationalization.

(E) repression.

83. Electroconvulsive shock therapy (ECT) has been demonstrated to be most effective in the treatment of which of the following?

    (A) Major depressive disorder

    (B) Schizophrenia

    (C) Hypochondriasis

    (D) Obsessive-compulsive disorder

    (E) Posttraumatic stress disorder

84. Which of the following statements best summarizes the research on intelligence in old age?

    (A) In old age, both crystallized and fluid intelligence increase.

    (B) In old age, both crystallized and fluid intelligence decrease.

    (C) In old age, crystallized intelligence increases while fluid intelligence decreases.

    (D) In old age, crystallized intelligence decreases while fluid intelligence increases.

    (E) In old age, neither crystallized nor fluid intelligence change.

85. Which of the following is an example of the compliance technique of low-ball?

    (A) Estella receives an email from a political organization asking her to sign a petition in support of a presidential candidate. After she signs the petition, the website asks her to make a financial donation to the campaign.

    (B) Maggie was excited to hear that a major department store was giving away free samples of a new perfume. After she received her free sample she ended up purchasing $50 in skin care products from the same store.

    (C) Tristan has decided to buy a very expensive new pair of basketball shoes after seeing a commercial starring his favorite athlete.

    (D) Students in a study were first asked to volunteer at a homeless shelter for 20 hours a week for the entire school year. After they turned down the offer, the students were asked if they would be willing to work one day a month, and many agreed.

    (E) Sue was contacted by the president of the parent organization and asked if she would be willing to help set up the bake sale. Sue agreed, but after she committed, the president informed her that she would need to be a school at 5:00 a.m. If Sue had been told about the early start time when she was first asked to volunteer, she most likely would have said no to the parent organization.

86. In order to study the effects of unpredictable noise on learning, a researcher has one group of college students study a list of words while jackhammer sounds are played sporadically over headphones and another group study the same list while listening to a steady rhythm of jackhammer sounds. After each group has time to study they are both given an identical test on the words. In this experiment, the independent variable would be _____ and the dependent variable would be _____.

(A) the college students; the presence or absence of unpredictable noise

(B) the number of questions answered correctly; the college students

(C) the college students; the number of questions answered correctly

(D) the number of questions answered correctly; the presence or absence of unpredictable noise

(E) the presence or absence of unpredictable noise; the number of questions answered correctly

87. Karen believes that her brother does not clean the house because he is lazy, but she explains that she does not clean the house because she has too much homework. This example best illustrates the

(A) fundamental attribution error.

(B) in-group bias.

(C) actor-observer bias.

(D) self-serving bias.

(E) bystander effect.

88. The unpleasant physical symptoms that result if the addict stops taking the drug associated with substance dependence are known as

(A) psychological dependence.

(B) polydrug abuse.

(C) detoxification.

(D) tolerance.

(E) withdrawal.

89. Which of the following psychologists created a stage model of psychosocial development that suggested a major conflict to be dealt with at each stage of life?

(A) Carol Gilligan

(B) Erik Erikson

(C) Sigmund Freud

(D) Jean Piaget

(E) Lawrence Kohlberg

90. Echoic memory and iconic memory are specific examples of what type of memory?

(A) Sensory memory

(B) Short-term memory

(C) Long-term memory

(D) Episodic memory

(E) Procedural memory

91. Mimi is entering a shoe-tying contest. Mimi's task is to tie as many shoelaces as possible within one minute. Assuming that Mimi has tied many shoes in her life and that this is an easy task for her, what would *social facilitation theory* say about Mimi's performance?

    (A) Mimi will perform at the same level regardless of whether or not an audience is present.

    (B) Mimi will perform better with no one watching than if there is an audience.

    (C) Mimi will perform better in front of an audience than if no one is watching.

    (D) Mimi will perform worse in front of an audience than if no one is watching.

    (E) Mimi will perform worse as a member of a shoe-tying team.

92. Information about how cold Marisa's hands are travels to her central nervous system along _____ neurons, while commands from her brain to rub her hands together for warmth travel along _____ neurons.

    (A) interneurons; afferent

    (B) glial; afferent

    (C) glial; efferent

    (D) efferent; afferent

    (E) afferent; efferent

93. Freud argued that the personality is made up of distinct components that work with and/or against each other. The _____ is the component that operates on the pleasure principle, seeking to act on sexual and aggressive urges, and the _____ operates on the reality principle.

    (A) id; superego

    (B) id; ego

    (C) ego; id

    (D) superego; ego

    (E) ego; superego

94. Which of the following represents the correct order for the three stages of Hans Selye's general adaptation syndrome?

    (A) Alarm, resistance, exhaustion

    (B) Alarm, resistance, adaptation

    (C) Alarm, adaptation, exhaustion

    (D) Resistance, adaptation, recovery

    (E) Resistance, exhaustion, recovery

95. Which of the following is a weakness of correlational research?

    (A) Correlational research only examines one variable at a time.

    (B) Correlational research does not imply causation.

    (C) Correlational research is the most expensive and time-consuming to run.

    (D) Correlational research focuses exclusively on one person or group.

    (E) Correlational research only involves basic and not applied research.

96. A Spanish teacher gives pop quizzes because he wants to reinforce the behavior of studying. The behavior of studying is being reinforced according to a

    (A) fixed-ratio schedule.

    (B) variable-ratio schedule.

    (C) fixed-interval schedule.

    (D) variable-interval schedule.

    (E) continuous reinforcement.

97. The _____ initiates hunger and motivates the animal to eat, while the _____ initiates feelings of satiation.

    (A) medulla oblongata; reticular activating system

    (B) reticular activating system; medulla oblongata

    (C) hippocampus; thalamus

    (D) ventromedial hypothalamus; lateral hypothalamus

    (E) lateral hypothalamus; ventromedial hypothalamus

98. The biologically influenced activity level, behaviors, and emotional responses typically demonstrated by individuals that are a part of personality is called

    (A) attachment.

    (B) temperament.

    (C) maturation.

    (D) identity.

    (E) androgyny.

99. Depression has been correlated with low levels of the neurotransmitter _____, and anxiety disorders are often associated with lower levels of the neurotransmitter _____.

    (A) serotonin; GABA

    (B) dopamine; GABA

    (C) GABA; dopamine

    (D) acetylcholine; serotonin

    (E) GABA; serotonin

100. Which of the following is more likely to occur in a collectivist culture?

    (A) Self-serving bias

    (B) Social loafing

    (C) Fundamental attribution error

    (D) Self-effacing bias

    (E) Greater emphasis on the qualities of independence and self-reliance

Section II
Free-Response Questions

TIME: 50 minutes

2 Free-Response Questions

Directions: After reading the question presented define each of the following terms and describe how they specifically apply to the scenario presented. Although the directions on the AP Psychology exam may indicate that definitions alone will not score, it is to your advantage to include a brief definition of each term to support your application. Remember to always use synonyms for all aspects of the terms in both the definition and application. The AP exam will allow you exactly 50 minutes to answer both free-response questions. It is not necessary to write an introduction or a conclusion.

Question 1

Dr. Wyatt, a sports psychologist is conducting research regarding ways to help young baseball players improve their batting averages. Dr. Wyatt's hypothesis is that if high school baseball players practice batting for one hour per week by playing an interactive video baseball game that their batting averages will improve. Ultimately, Dr. Wyatt's study involves 1600 high school baseball players that all have the same amount of traditional baseball practice each week. Half of the athletes are given one hour of video batting practice every week in addition to their traditional practice schedule.

Explain how each of the following research terms applies to the study presented.

- Random sample
- Confounding variable
- Informed consent

Explain how each of the following terms might affect the players during the study.

- Self-fulfilling prophecy
- External locus of control

Question 2

Manuel went on a senior trip after graduation to Italy along with many of his classmates where they had the opportunity to visit various cities, historical sites, and cultural events. Some of the highlights of the trip were visiting ancient Roman ruins, touring art museums, sampling the local cuisine, and attending a professional soccer match.

Explain how each of the following terms might relate to the senior trip.

- Schema
- Schachter-Singer theory of emotion
- Gate control theory
- Retroactive interference
- Ethnocentrism

Answer Key

Section I

1. (D)	21. (B)	41. (B)	61. (C)
2. (B)	22. (D)	42. (A)	62. (A)
3. (B)	23. (A)	43. (A)	63. (A)
4. (D)	24. (B)	44. (A)	64. (A)
5. (B)	25. (E)	45. (B)	65. (A)
6. (B)	26. (C)	46. (E)	66. (E)
7. (E)	27. (D)	47. (E)	67. (D)
8. (E)	28. (A)	48. (A)	68. (E)
9. (D)	29. (D)	49. (B)	69. (A)
10. (E)	30. (A)	50. (B)	70. (B)
11. (C)	31. (D)	51. (E)	71. (D)
12. (D)	32. (C)	52. (A)	72. (C)
13. (C)	33. (B)	53. (C)	73. (A)
14. (D)	34. (D)	54. (D)	74. (C)
15. (B)	35. (B)	55. (A)	75. (D)
16. (C)	36. (D)	56. (E)	76. (B)
17. (C)	37. (B)	57. (D)	77. (A)
18. (A)	38. (E)	58. (A)	78. (D)
19. (A)	39. (B)	59. (B)	79. (C)
20. (D)	40. (E)	60. (D)	80. (D)

Answer Key

81. (A)	86. (E)	91. (C)	96. (D)
82. (C)	87. (C)	92. (E)	97. (E)
83. (A)	88. (E)	93. (B)	98. (B)
84. (C)	89. (B)	94. (A)	99. (A)
85. (E)	90. (A)	95. (B)	100. (D)

Detailed Explanations of Answers

Section I

1. (D)

In the double-blind procedure both the experimenter and the participants are unaware of who has received the treatment (IV). Studies that utilize the double-blind procedure eliminate both experimenter and participant bias. The double-blind technique is often used in drug research. Option (A) is incorrect because this is an example of a single-blind procedure. Option (B) is incorrect because it does not meet the definition of an experiment due to both groups receiving the exact same conditions. Options (C) and (E) are both incorrect because the creation of multiple groups for research does not necessarily indicate a double-blind design.

2. (B)

Nina received a negative punishment, which is an operant conditioning technique designed to decrease the occurrence of a behavior (door slamming) by removing a desirable stimulus (the door). A negative reinforcement (A) is an operant conditioning technique designed to increase the occurrence of a behavior by removing something undesirable. A positive reinforcement (C) is an operant conditioning technique designed to increase the occurrence of a behavior by adding something desirable. A positive punishment (D) is an operant conditioning technique designed to decrease the occurrence of a behavior by adding an undesirable stimulus. Any time an individual is given a reinforcement, the intended result is a repeat of the behavior. Any time an individual receives a punishment, the intended result is the extinction or disappearance of the behavior. A fixed-ratio schedule (E) is a reinforcement schedule in operant conditioning in which the reinforcement is given after a set number of correct behaviors have occurred. An example of a fixed-ratio schedule of reinforcement is receiving a free car wash after purchasing five car washes from the same store.

3. (B)

According to Kohlberg's theory, individuals in the second level of moral development—the conventional level—follow rules simply because they are the rules. In the conventional level, decisions about morality are based on social approval and law and order. In the preconventional level (A) of moral development, Kohlberg suggests that morality is based on self-interest. In other words, these individuals make moral decisions based on what is best for them in their own life. At the preconventional stage, decisions about morality are based on avoiding punishment or gaining reward. In the postconventional level (C), morality is based on an internalized understanding of what justice means. At this third and final level, decisions about morality are based on social contracts and universal ethics. The preoperational stage (D) is the second stage of Piaget's cognitive development theory and is characterized by the presence of symbolic but pre-logical thought. This stage also involves pretend play, egocentrism, centration, animism, and irreversibility. The concrete operational stage (E) is the third stage of Piaget's cognitive development theory. This stage of cognitive development is characterized by the emergence of logical thought about concrete or tangible ideas. Remember, although both Kohlberg and Piaget are stage theorists, they focus on different types of development. Kohlberg developed a stage theory for moral development and Piaget developed a stage theory for cognitive development. Both Kohlberg and Piaget are extremely influential and very likely to appear on the AP Psychology exam.

4. **(D)**

Plasticity refers to the brain's ability to modify itself and adapt as a result of experiences. Rather than simply letting a certain region go unused, the brain will assign other duties to that region. For instance, the visual cortex is often reassigned to hearing or touch duties among the blind. Localization of function (A) refers to the idea that specific areas in the brain control specific types of behaviors or processes. Lateralization of function (B), also known as hemispheric specialization, refers to the fact that specific functions are controlled by each half of the cerebral cortex. Long-term potentiation (C) is a biological theory for memory that states that repeated stimulation of neural networks strengthens connections between neurons, resulting in the formation of new dendrites that lead to learning and memory. Maturation (E) involves biologically driven growth processes that enable changes in behavior, which are connected to an individual's genetic blueprint and are relatively uninfluenced by experience.

5. **(B)**

Factor analysis takes a large number of variables and groups them together based on which ones are correlated. In personality psychology, there are thousands of potential traits that a person could have. Factor analysis allows researchers to combine similar traits into larger categories. So the traits of "liveliness" and "sociability" might be grouped together under the broader heading of "extraversion." An ANOVA (A) is an inferential statistic used to generate a probability value (p) for an experiment in order to determine if the results of the research were most likely caused by chance. Regression to the mean (C) is a phenomenon in statistics in which unusual or extreme events move toward the average. The standard deviation (D) is a measure of variability that indicates the average differences between the scores and their mean. A meta-analysis (E) is a research method that involves combining data from numerous already published studies on the same developmental topic to generate a hypothesis based on a large sample.

6. **(B)**

Wilhelm Wundt opened the first formal psychology laboratory in 1879 at Leipzig University in Germany. In his laboratory, Wundt studied consciousness by dividing the mind into component elements creating a perspective that would later be known as structuralism. William James (A) was an American psychologist who was influential in the school of thought of functionalism, which emphasized that psychology should focus on the evolved purposes (functions) of behavior and consciousness. Sigmund Freud (C) was the influential founder of the school of thought of psychoanalysis, but did not conduct laboratory research. Edward Titchener (D) was a student of Wundt's who brought his ideas to the United States and started the first theoretical perspective in psychology, called structuralism, which was based on Wundt's work. Titchener would open his own laboratory in the United States at Cornell University. Ivan Pavlov (E), a Russian physiologist, was a pioneer in the study of learning whose research began the investigation into classical conditioning.

7. **(E)**

The term *endorphin* is short for "endogenous morphine," which are the naturally occurring painkillers produced in the body. Endorphins are released in response to pain and strenuous exercise, resulting in the so-called "runner's high." Morphine is an effective painkiller because it is an agonist for endorphins, which means morphine fits into the same receptor sites as endorphins. GABA (A) is the major inhibitory neurotransmitter and is not impacted by morphine. Norepinephrine (B) and serotonin (C) are related to mood and sleep. Low levels of both of these neurotransmitters are associated with depression. Glutamate (D) is the major excitatory neurotransmitter and is associated with memory and learning.

8. **(E)**

Beatrice is taking the evolutionary approach by explaining that the fear of heights was naturally selected because it allowed the human species to survive, while Matt gives an example of learning through observation or modeling, which is associated with the behaviorist approach. Option (A) is incorrect because cognitive psychology would explain fears as being the result of thought processes. Option (B) is incorrect because Beatrice's example is not behavioral, which would explain the fear of heights in terms of learned responses acquired through reinforcements and punishments. Option (C) is incorrect because the biological approach explains that behavior is influenced by the inheritance of specific genes from one's biological parents and not the result of gradual changes over extremely long time periods that lead to species-level survival, the evolutionary explanation that Beatrice is using. Option (D) is incorrect because although Beatrice does give an evolutionary approach, the biological explanation is incorrect. Matt explains that Edward learned to fear heights by observing members of his family demonstrating fear, and not inheriting a genetic predisposition.

9. (D)

The medulla, or medulla oblongata, is located in the hindbrain below the pons and is responsible for survival functions (e.g., heartbeat, breathing, and blood pressure), and reflexes (e.g., sneezing, coughing, vomiting, and swallowing). The thalamus (A) is located in the forebrain and functions mainly as a major relay station for the brain. Information from sensory receptors (except smell) arrives at the thalamus first and is then relayed to the appropriate areas in the cortex. The reticular formation (B) or reticular activating system is a network of nerves running through the brainstem that is responsible for arousal to stimuli, sleep, and attentiveness. The amygdala (C) consists of two small almond-shaped structures in the limbic system involved in emotions (especially fear and aggression). The hypothalamus (E), located under the thalamus, is a collection of nuclei concerned with homeostatic regulations. Electrical stimulation of certain cells in the hypothalamus produces sensations of hunger, thirst, pain, pleasure, or sexual drives. The hypothalamus is involved in many important emotional and physiological motivators of behavior.

10. (E)

Observational learning, also called social learning or vicarious learning, is associated with the research of Albert Bandura and happens when people mentally represent the contingency between a behavior and its consequence, even without doing the behavior or experiencing the consequence themselves. Luke learned that hitting would produce a punishment by seeing that someone else received a punishment for that same behavior. Latent learning (A) is a type of learning that involves an organism mastering a new behavior without effort, awareness, or reinforcement; this behavior is not demonstrated unless a need or reinforcement is presented. Partial reinforcement (B) is the operant conditioning technique of reinforcing the desired behavior only some of the time. Chaining (C) is an operant conditioning method for teaching a complex series of behaviors whereby each response cues the next response. Generalization (D) refers to a phenomenon that can occur during either classical or operant conditioning. In classical conditioning, generalization is when an organism learns to respond (CR) to stimuli that are similar to the conditioned stimulus (CS). In operant conditioning, generalization is when an organism learns to voluntarily respond to stimuli that are similar to the original stimulus.

11. **(C)**

Heritability is defined as a mathematical measure indicating the proportion of the total variation in a population that is due to genetic variation. Since heritability is dependent on a ratio of genetic to environmental variation, its value is affected by both factors. A measure of heritability is only an estimate and applies to the population and not individuals. The concept of heritability is expressed as a numerical value ranging from 0 to 1.0 and can be translated into a percentage. Genotype (A) is the genetic makeup for the traits an individual possesses. Phenotype (B) refers to the traits that are expressed and therefore observable. The Flynn effect (D) is a recently discovered phenomenon that demonstrates that the average IQ has been rising dramatically over successive generations. Natural selection (E) is Darwin's theory that traits and behaviors exist in humans because these attributes allowed our ancestors to adapt, survive, and reproduce.

12. **(D)**

Axis IV of the DSM-IV is used to note any social or environmental problems that the patient is experiencing that may be impacting functioning. Such problems can include issues at home, work, or school. The axes of the DSM-IV provide a framework for a standardized initial interview between a clinician and a client. Axis I (A) includes clinical disorders with categories describing all of the major mental illnesses. Axis II (B) includes personality disorders and mental retardation. Axis III (C) allows the clinician to provide a description of medical conditions other than mental illness that may be influencing functioning. Axis V (E) is for the Global Assessment of Functioning, which the clinician uses to rate the overall functioning of the client on a scale of 1–100.

13. **(C)**

Functional fixedness is an obstacle in problem solving that involves a tendency or mental set in which one considers only the common uses of objects, rather than the possibilities for novel or unusual functions. Divergent thinking (A) is a cognitive process that results in a number of possible answers to a particular problem. This type of cognition is a major element in creativity which is not related to functional fixedness. The term *breaking set* (B) refers to creativity or finding new and innovative solutions to problems. Confirmation bias (C) is a cognitive error that involves the tendency to look for information that agrees with, rather than opposes, one's beliefs. The term *belief bias* (E) is a cognitive error in which individuals are more likely to agree with conclusions that match up with their existing opinions rather than conclusions appearing to be logically valid.

14. **(D)**

Correlational research was used in the example because Dr. Ruiz determined a relationship between scores on two different portions of the test. Correlational studies cannot determine cause and effect, but they can show the direction of the relationship, which in this case is a positive correlation between math intelligence and musical intelligence. A case study (A) would involve an in-depth investigation of an individual or group that includes detailed information from a variety of methods including observation, interviews, surveys, and testing. Dr. Ruiz does not conduct an experiment (B) because there is no evidence that participants were randomly assigned to either a control or experimental group. Naturalistic observation (C) is a method for carefully and systematically watching human behavior as it occurs in the real world. A double-blind (E) is incorrect because it refers to a method used in controlled experiments in which both the researcher and the participants are unaware of who has received the treatment (IV). Double-blind procedures are useful because they eliminate both experimenter and participant bias; however, this example does not involve an experiment.

15. (B)

The number of times participants shifted their weight is the dependent variable and is operationally defined because it offers a precise explanation allowing the experiment to be replicated. The independent variable (A) in this experiment is exposure to optical illusions, which, if operationally defined, would have to identify the specific images used. A confounding variable (C) would be any difference present other than the independent variable between the experimental or control group participants that might have an effect on the dependent variable. Demand characteristics (D) are any potential hints or indications about what is being studied that might be discovered by participants and result in distorted findings. If the participants realized what was being studied, they might consciously or unconsciously shift their weight more or less frequently. A positively skewed distribution (E) refers to a distribution in which most of the scores are low and the tail is pointing toward the right.

16. (C)

The formal operational stage is the fourth and final stage of Piaget's model of cognitive development. During this stage (beginning around the age of 11 or 12), Piaget believed that children begin developing the ability to reason and think about abstract concepts. Formal operations is the logic of science, and individuals at this stage can apply logical rules to things they cannot see, allowing them to understand why experiments are set up the way they are. Concrete operational (A) is Piaget's third stage, which is characterized by the development of logical rules. However, during this stage individuals can only apply these rules to things that they can see or easily imagine, not to things that are abstract. They can solve most conservation problems because they can see or imagine changes in the objects involved, but they would still have trouble with something like algebra. This is because algebra involves thinking about numbers that they cannot see and that change from one problem to the next. The sensorimotor (B) stage, according to Piaget's cognitive development theory, is the first stage that occurs from birth to two years of age. Learning during this stage develops through sensory and motor experiences. The conventional level (D) refers to the second level of Kohlberg's theory of moral development in which moral behavior involves upholding laws and rules just because they are laws and rules. The preconventional level (E) refers to the first level of Kohlberg's theory of moral development in which individuals determine that moral behavior involves doing what will result in tangible rewards and not doing anything that will result in punishment.

17. (C)

Stage two sleep of NREM involves an overall brain wave pattern that is slower and more regular. This stage is marked by the brief appearance of sleep spindles or short high-frequency bursts of electrical activity and K-complexes, extremely short bursts of high amplitude (height) brain waves. REM sleep (A) is characterized by the low amplitude (height) and high frequency sawtooth-like waves that look very much like the beta waves predominant when an individual is awake. REM is named for the rapid eye movements (REM) happening under closed eyelids that often occur during this stage. Stage one sleep (B) represents the very short transition period between wakefulness and sleep in which alpha waves are replaced by even slower theta waves. Stages three and four sleep (D) and (E) are known as *deep sleep* and are dominated by delta waves that have the lowest frequency and high amplitude (height). During the third and fourth stages, heart rate, breathing, and brain waves slow down considerably and it is difficult to wake a person. Stage four is the stage when sleepwalking and night terrors happen.

18. (A)

An antisocial personality disorder manifests as a lack of conscience or remorse for a person's wrongdoings. People with this disorder are known to lie, cheat, and steal for their own benefit, and they do not regret doing those things, even if they are harming friends or family. A paranoid personality disorder (B) refers to an overall disposition that is extremely suspicious (paranoid), secretive, scheming, and argumentative. A histrionic personality disorder (C) refers to an overall disposition that is highly emotional and dramatic. Histrionics are often conceited, self-centered, and shallow, yet constantly search for approval. A narcissistic personality disorder (D) refers to an overall disposition that is dominated by a grandiose sense of self-importance, fantasies of unlimited success, a need for excessive admiration, and a willingness to exploit others to achieve personal goals. Narcissists feel that they are entitled to special treatment, and may use others in order to get what they want. An obsessive compulsive personality disorder (E) refers to an overall disposition that is dominated by perfectionist behaviors and a preoccupation with doing things the correct way.

Individuals with obsessive compulsive personality disorder attempt to exert rigid control in all aspects of their lives including home, work, and relationships. Obsessive-compulsive personality disorder, however, is not the same as obsessive-compulsive disorder, which is an Axis I anxiety disorder.

19. **(A)**

The phi phenomenon is an illusion of movement created when a group of stationary lights placed in a row turn on and off in rapid sequence. The result is the perception by the brain of a single light moving across space. Perceptual constancy (B) is the ability to hold onto a stable perception of an object, allowing us to be able to recognize familiar objects despite changes in color due to illumination, distance, or angle. A perceptual set (C) refers to the predisposition individuals have to interpret an event or stimulus in a particular way based on their beliefs, emotions, or previous experiences. The stroboscopic effect (D) is easily confused with the phi phenomenon, but refers to the illusion of movement created when a series of images that change slightly are presented in rapid sequence. The apparent motion created by a picture flip book is an example of the stroboscopic effect. The motion parallax (E) is a monocular cue for depth perception in which an object appears closer to the viewer if it is moving in the opposite direction as the observer and appears to be moving faster.

20. **(D)**

The James-Lange theory suggests that an emotion begins with the way our physical body feels. According to this view, if we see something scary like a bear in the woods, our body reacts with the usual fight-or-flight response (e.g., pounding heart, short breath). The emotion is then your brain's awareness of this physiological state. The Yerkes-Dodson law (A) explains that an optimal level of arousal helps performances. When arousal is too low, our minds wander and we become bored. When arousal is too high, we become too anxious and "freeze up." People are thus motivated to seek a moderate level of stimulation that is neither too easy nor too hard. Additionally, Yerkes-Dodson explains that on simple tasks performance is better if arousal levels are somewhat higher and performance is best on difficult tasks if arousal levels are slightly lower. Option (B), opponent-process, is a theory of emotion that claims that all emotions are accompanied by an opposite emotional reaction; for example, fear is followed by relief, sadness by happiness.

The Cannon-Bard theory of emotion (C) states that bodily reactions do not cause emotional response; rather, the two occur simultaneously. The Schachter-Singer or two-factor theory of emotion (E) states that emotion is the result of an individual's interpretation (the first factor) of their aroused bodily state (the second factor).

21. (B)

Deinstitutionalization involved closing government-run hospitals and providing care to individuals with mental illness in the community. Although many patients were able to thrive outside of institutions, large numbers were left without sufficient support. The moral treatment movement (A) was a 19th-century movement that spread through Europe and America proposing that the mentally ill should be treated with dignity and respect. The moral treatment movement in the United States was heavily influenced by the work of Dorothea Dix. The community mental health movement (C) was designed to offer care for individuals formerly treated in mental hospitals after deinstitutionalization by providing therapy and support through outpatient facilities. This movement was based on the premise that recovery would be enhanced if individuals could live and be part of local communities instead of being isolated within hospitals. Decreases in funding of these facilities have led to problems with availability of care for many individuals. The statistical model (D) is an incomplete and inaccurate theory for defining abnormal behavior as something that is rare or unusual. Although some mental illnesses are very rare, many are common. The diathesis-stress model (E) is an influential theory for the cause of mental illnesses including schizophrenia. The diathesis-stress model states that mental illness develops when there is a genetic predisposition (diathesis) present and environmental factors (stressors) that trigger the disorder.

22. (D)

Dysthymia is an Axis I mood disorder and individuals experience similar symptoms to those with major depression, but do not experience enough of those symptoms to warrant a full diagnosis. Individuals with dysthymia have a milder but more chronic form of depression that lasts for more than two years. Bipolar disorder (A) is an Axis I mood disorder that involves periods of major depressive disorder and mania resulting in a significant impairment of physical, emotional, cognitive, and behavioral functioning. Posttraumatic stress disorder (B), or PTSD, is an Axis I anxiety disorder characterized by intense feelings of anxiety, horror, and helplessness after experiencing a traumatic event such as a violent crime, natural disaster, or military combat. Schizophrenia (C) is a group of Axis I psychological disorders that involves major disturbances in perception, language, thought, emotion, and balance. Delusional beliefs, hallucinations, and disorganized speech and thought are three key characteristic symptoms. Hypochondriasis (E) is an Axis I somatoform disorder in which an individual is convinced that they have a very serious medical condition despite the fact that they remain in good health and medical tests come back negative. These individuals may dramatically misinterpret small physical changes as indicators of serious medical conditions and suffer from chronic fear and worry. Functioning is disrupted because they have trouble meeting obligations due to worry, fear, and continually seeking additional medical advice.

23. (A)

Gestalt psychology functions on the premise that the whole is greater than the sum of its parts. In other words, Gestalt theorists believe that our minds try to organize individual pieces of information into bigger chunks that have meaning, known as perceptual units. As such, we perceive the entire flock of birds as one thing (the "flying V") rather than as a series of individual, independent birds. Behaviorist psychology (B) stresses that the science of psychology should only involve the study of behaviors that could be both observed and measured, and focused on how organisms learn. Functionalist psychology (C) studied the evolved purposes (functions) of consciousness. Evolutionary psychology (D) would be interested in why the flying V pattern was naturally selected because it aided in survival. Cognitive psychology (E) would focus on how organisms think, solve problems, and utilize memory.

24. (B)

Conscientiousness is a Big Five trait that describes people that tend to be organized, careful, and responsible. People high in this trait place great importance on fulfilling their obligations and maintaining order and discipline in their lives. All of the other traits listed are also part of the Big Five personality model proposed by researchers Costa and McCrae. Openness (A) describes individuals who are inquiring, independent, and curious. Extraversion (C) describes individuals who are outgoing and socially adaptive. Agreeableness (D) describes individuals who are conforming and likable. Neuroticism (E) describes individuals who are excitable and anxious. Individuals may be either high or low in each of these traits. The Big Five personality traits are often measured in individuals through the use of the NEO Personality Inventory (NEO-PI-R), an objective personality test.

25. (E)

Addie is involved in a commons dilemma in which an individual needs to determine how much to take from a shared supply. She has a conflict because she must choose between her short-term interest, taking as much candy as she wants, and taking only one piece to leave enough for everyone. The commons dilemma is also called the tragedy of the commons. Altruism (A) refers to a selfless concern for others or actions taken by an individual to help others that involve a risk or personal cost without any incentives or personal benefits. Although the prisoner's dilemma (B) is also a type of social trap, it involves two individuals and this does not relate to Addie's situation. Option (C), groupthink, was not present because Addie was not involved in making a decision with a group. The public goods dilemma (D), like the commons dilemma, is a resource dilemma, but it involves making a decision about how much to give to a shared resource.

26. (C)

STM is highly susceptible to interference. For instance, when a person begins dialing a telephone number but is interrupted, the number may be forgotten or dialed incorrectly. Interference can disrupt STM because there is no rehearsal time after a response. In addition, interfering information may also enter STM and cause it to reach its capacity for stored items. In either case, displacement of old, unrehearsed items will occur. Option (A) is not correct, because according to research by George Miller, STM can only hold seven items plus or minus two, with seven being the magic number. Option (B) is not correct because the process of rehearsal is important in order to allow items in short-term memory to be retained and facilitates the transfer of material from short-term to long-term memory. Option (D) is incorrect because not all of the information in short-term memory reaches long-term memory because information may be lost due to interference, lack of attention, or failure to rehearse. Option (E) is incorrect because chunking or grouping related items into meaningful units can increase the amount of material that can be held in short-term memory.

27. (D)

Becky's behavior (generating arguments against uniforms) is inconsistent with her preexisting attitude (a favorable view about uniforms). According to cognitive dissonance theory, this inconsistency produces discomfort, motivating Becky to reduce the tension by changing her attitude to one that is more consistent with her behavior. Options (A) and (B) are incorrect because cognitive dissonance theory does not apply to situations involving the behaviors of others. Becky's beliefs (C) do not change in this example, indicating that cognitive dissonance has not decreased. In example (E) Becky's thoughts and behaviors continue to be in conflict; therefore, cognitive dissonance is not being reduced.

28. (A)

The strongest Pearson correlation coefficient is $^-.70$ because it is the closest to a perfect correlation of $^+1.0$ or $^-1.0$. The positive or negative sign in front of the number refers to the direction of the correlation. Correlational coefficients represented as numbers close to zero (B, C, and D) are weaker correlations. The correlation of $+7.0$ (E) is an impossible answer because it is outside of the range of $^-1$ to $^+1$ for Pearson correlation coefficients.

29. (D)

The collective unconscious according to Jung is the set of inherited images and experiences (archetypes) common to all humans throughout evolutionary time. Archetypes are the images that comprise the collective unconscious and allow individuals to respond universally to particular situations. The preconscious (A), according to

Freud and Jung (a neo-Freudian), is the level of the mind that contains information an individual is aware of but not currently thinking about and is located between the unconscious and conscious. The superego (B) is the part of the personality that reminds individuals what ideal behavior consists of and begins developing during childhood. The superego operates on a morality principle, seeking to enforce ethical conduct. The personal unconscious (C), according to Jung, is the unconscious unique to each individual that contains painful or upsetting memories and information that has been repressed. The hidden observer (E) refers to the part of consciousness that is monitoring from the background during hypnosis, according to Ernest Hilgard's theory of hypnosis. Hilgard explains hypnosis as a state of dissociation or divided consciousness in which awareness is split.

30. (A)

Place theory states that we perceive a range of pitches because sound waves activate hair cells in different locations (places) along the basilar membrane. Remember that place theory explains the perception of high-pitched sounds well. Frequency theory (B) states that we perceive a range of pitches because the basilar membrane vibrates at the same rate (frequency) as the sound wave. The frequency theory best explains low-pitched sounds. Volley theory (C) states that for sound waves above 1,000 hertz, multiple neurons must fire one after the other in rapid succession in order for pitch to be perceived. The combination of the place, frequency, and volley theories provides the most complete explanation for the wide range of pitch that humans are capable of detecting. Sensory adaptation (D) is not related to pitch perception and refers to the decline in sensitivity individuals experience as a result of exposure to a constant and unchanging stimulus. Set point theory (E) proposes that individuals have a genetically determined range of weight that is maintained by biological processes without effort.

31. (D)

A phoneme is the smallest unit of sound in a language. The word "dogs" has four distinct sound units (d, o, g, and s) and therefore four phonemes. A morpheme is the smallest unit of sound that carries meaning in a language. There are two units that convey meaning within the word ("dog" and "-s"), and therefore the word "dogs" has two morphemes.

32. (C)

If a 12-point difference in the dependent variable between the control and experimental groups is statistically significant, that indicates that the results were *not* likely to have happened by chance. Statistical significance indicates a high probability that the independent variable caused the change in the dependent variable, allowing the researcher to reject the null hypothesis. Option (A) is incorrect, because statistical significance means the opposite—that there is a strong likelihood that the independent variable caused the dependent variable. Options (B) and (D) are both incorrect because statistical significance does not guarantee that the conclusions are accurate or important, only that they most likely are not the result of chance. Option (E) is incorrect because if the experiment was well designed, then differences between the groups would be eliminated by random selection of the sample and random assignment of participants to either control or experimental groups.

33. **(B)**

In a normal distribution, the mean, median, and mode are equivalent and located at the center of the distribution and have a predictable distribution of scores. Approximately 68% of scores fall within one standard deviation of the mean, 95% of scores fall within two standard deviations of the mean, and 99% of scores fall within three standard deviations of the mean. In this example, the mean is 550 and the standard deviation is 50 therefore 68% of scores will fall within one standard deviation from the mean or between a z-score of $^-1$ and a z-score of $^+1$. The value of z^-1 will be the mean minus one standard deviation or a score of 500. The value of z^+1 will be the mean plus one standard deviation or a score of 600. Therefore, 68% of the scores will be between 500 and 600.

34. **(D)**

Split-half reliability is done by comparing the scores on one half of the test to the scores on the other half of the test to determine if a test is reliable (repeatable). If a strong positive correlation is found between scores on the two halves of the test, it is said to be split-half reliable. Alternate-forms reliability (A) is a method used for determining if a test is reliable (repeatable) by comparing two different but equivalent versions of a test to determine if they produce consistent results. High positive correlations between two comparable versions indicate alternate-forms reliability. Face validity (B) is the extent to which the material on a test appears on the surface to accurately measure what it intends to measure. Face validity is determined either by a non-expert or an expert who only gives a quick evaluation of the test. Test-retest reliability (C) is a method used for determining if a test is reliable (repeatable) by giving the same test on two occasions and finding a strong positive correlation between the scores for the two administrations. Test-retest reliability is determined by giving the same test twice, not splitting one test in half like the example presented. Criterion-related validity (E) is a way to measure accuracy by determining if scores on a particular test are positively correlated with scores on another existing and well-established test (criterion) of the same skill, trait, or ability.

35. **(B)**

Weber's law states that the difference threshold remains in a constant proportion to the size of the original stimulus. The term *sensory adaptation* (A) refers to the decline in sensitivity that is the result of continual exposure to a stimulus. The Young-Helmholtz theory (C) or the trichromatic theory of color vision states that there are three types of color photoreceptors (cones) in the retina of each eye that are either most sensitive to red, green, or blue wavelengths. According to this theory, all of the colors of the visible spectrum can be perceived by combining these three reflected wavelengths. The opponent-process theory (D) is another theory for color vision that states that there are three pairs of opponent neurons that work together. One half of the opponent pair is inhibited by the other half of that pair which is activated. The complementary pairs are red-green, blue-yellow, and white-black. Opponent-process is also a theory of emotion that claims that each emotion is accompanied by an opposite emotional reaction; for example, fear is followed by relief, sadness by happiness. Feature detection theory (E) refers to the manner in which complicated stimuli are perceived by the brain when separate feature detector cells analyze the individual components that make up the stimuli such as straight lines, edges, curves, angles, or direction.

36. **(D)**

A lowered heart rate would be caused by the parasympathetic nervous system as it acts to increase the body's stored energy. The parasympathetic nervous system is associated with a period of rest and digest in which all of the body systems slow down except for digestion. Decreased salivation (A) and the inhibition of digestion (C) are both sympathetic nervous system reactions. Although the sympathetic nervous system arouses the body, the function of digestion is reduced. Perspiration (B) increases when the sympathetic nervous system is activated. Pupil dilation (E) or the enlarging of the pupils is a sympathetic nervous system reaction whereas pupil constriction is associated with the activation of the parasympathetic nervous system. The sympathetic nervous system prepares the body for fight or flight and stops digestion. The parasympathetic nervous system allows the body to rest and digest.

37. **(B)**

If a particular type of food you eat makes you sick one night, you will be unlikely to want to eat that particular food again in the future. That is because you have developed a taste aversion, which is an example of classical conditioning that only requires one pairing. Taste aversions were studied by psychologist John Garcia, who found that this example of learning, unlike other classically conditioned behaviors, is unusual because it typically only requires one pairing for learning to occur. A negative reinforcement (A) is a term that is used in operant conditioning to refer to a consequence that involves removing an undesirable stimulus after the behavior to increase the likelihood of the behavior happening again in the future. A negative punishment (C) is an operant conditioning technique that involves removing a desirable stimulus after the behavior to decrease the likelihood of the behavior occurring in the future. Shaping (D) is an operant conditioning technique of achieving a desired behavior by gradually reinforcing successively closer approximations of a behavior until the entire correct behavior is displayed. Simultaneous conditioning (E) refers to a classical conditioning procedure for acquisition in which the conditioned stimulus and the unconditioned stimulus are presented to the organism at the same time.

38. (E)

An achievement test is an assessment device created for the purpose of determining the level of knowledge an individual has regarding a particular subject or skill that has resulted from learning.

Achievement tests are often administered after training in order to evaluate what the individual has gained through training. An aptitude test (A) is an assessment device that is designed to predict the success of an individual by evaluating their level of skill on a variety of general abilities necessary for success in academic or career environments. A projective test (C) is a personality assessment in which the participant is given an ambiguous stimulus and asked to respond to it. Examples of projective personality tests include the Rorschach Inkblot Test and the Thematic Apperception Test. A self-report inventory (D) is a questionnaire that asks people to judge their agreement with statements describing behavior that might be indicative of some particular trait used in personality psychology.

39. (B)

Archie is involved in an approach-avoidance conflict because he must make a decision about a situation in which he is both attracted to and repelled by the same goal. Within one particular situation there are both good and bad aspects. An approach-approach conflict (A) is a situation where an individual is forced to make a choice between two equally desirable goals. Both options are appealing, which makes the choice difficult. If Archie were offered a position on two professional sports teams and he liked both of them, that would be an approach-approach conflict. An avoidance-avoidance conflict (C) is a situation where an individual is forced to make a choice between two equally undesirable or threatening options. Neither choice is good so the individual is essentially choosing the lesser of two evils. A multiple approach-avoidance conflict (D) is a situation where an individual must choose between two different options, both of which have positive and negative parts. A social trap (E), also known as a social dilemma, is a situation in which individuals must choose whether to cooperate or compete with others. By the way, in case you are wondering, Archie made the right decision and did not take the drugs.

40. (E)

Jean Piaget argued that for very young children, the world consisted entirely of the things they can sense immediately around them. From this perspective, until object permanence develops, children are not able to conceive that something may exist even when it is not in sight. It is important to note that object permanence develops toward the end of the sensorimotor stage of cognitive development and not during the preoperational stage. Conservation (A) is Piaget's term for the cognitive ability to determine that certain quantitative attributes of objects remain unchanged unless something is added to or taken away from them. The ability to conserve is acquired, according to Piaget, during the concrete operational stage. Egocentrism (B), according to Piaget, is the difficulty in seeing how the world looks from the perspective of others, which is typical of the preoperational stage of cognitive development, but is not what is described in the question.

Assimilation (C) is the process of trying to fit new information into an existing schema, which, according to Piaget, is an important method, along with accommodation, for learning in all of the stages. Option (D) is incorrect because although the example describes object permanence, this cognitive ability is acquired in the sensorimotor stage.

41. (B)

The wavelength of a light wave determines the color or hue that is perceived and the photoreceptors responsible for color are cones. Light energy strikes rods and cones: rods enable black and-white vision; cones enable color. A trick to remember all the functions of cones is to think of words that start with the letter **C**. Cones are associated with *color* vision and *clarity* and are mainly located in the *center* of the retina (fovea). After light energy is received by the rods and cones, transduction occurs and the message is then transferred to bipolar cells (C) and finally to ganglion cells (A) whose axons converge to make the optic nerve that carries the message to the brain. Gustation receptor cells (E) are involved in the sense of taste.

42. (A)

A compulsion is an unwanted repetitive behavior individuals with obsessive-compulsive disorder feel they must engage in to reduce anxiety. A panic attack (B) is an unexpected onset of fear and anxiety. Panic attacks have a minimum of four symptoms and reach a peak level of exaggerated arousal within ten minutes and then gradually dissipate. The physical symptoms of a panic attack amount to an extreme fight-or-flight reaction despite the absence of a threat. Cognitive symptoms that accompany a panic attack may involve the thought that the individual is losing control, having a heart attack, or dying. An obsession (C) is the unwanted and anxiety-producing thought that people who suffer from obsessive-compulsive disorder (OCD) experience. A phobia (D) is an Axis I anxiety disorder characterized by an intense, irrational, and persistent fear of a specific object or situation that poses no actual danger, which leads to avoidance and anxiety that disrupts normal life. The DSM-IV-TR divides phobias into separate categories of specific phobias, social phobias, and agoraphobia. Agoraphobia (E) involves the fear of public places and open spaces due to the worry that one would not be able to escape. Agoraphobics avoid crowded locations such as airports, stores, concerts, or college campuses, and in extreme cases may be unable to leave their own home.

43. (A)

In spite of the screams of the confederate and complaints about a heart condition, 65% of the participants reluctantly obeyed orders from the experimenter who was perceived to be a legitimate authority figure and continued with the experiment through the maximum shock level. Option (B) is incorrect because the amount of participants that obeyed the experimenter was 65%. Options (C) and (D) are both incorrect because Milgram's research was about obedience to authority and not conformity. Remember, Milgram studied obedience to authority with the shock experiment and Asch studied conformity in the line experiment. Option (E) is incorrect because most participants did not stop when the learner expressed pain.

44. (A)

In this example, the emotion being experienced varied as a function of how the arousal was interpreted. This is explained by the two-factor theory. The Schachter-Singer or two-factor theory explains that physical arousal and cognitive labeling of that arousal produce the subjective experience of emotion. Instinct theory (B) is an early theory of motivation influenced by the work of Charles Darwin that focused on the identification of human instincts. An instinct is an unchanging sequence of behaviors observed in all members of a species in response to specific stimuli without learning. Merely generating lists of instincts, however, does not actually explain human motivation or behavior and this theory is no longer used. The opponent-process theory of emotion (C) states all emotions are accompanied by an opposite emotional reaction; for example, fear is followed by relief, sadness by happiness. The Cannon-Bard (D) and James-Lange (E) theories consider emotions to be linked to specific patterns of arousal and do not include a cognitive component.

45. **(B)**

A culture-fair test is an assessment that is designed to allow all individuals, regardless of culture, the opportunity to perform equally well. A culture-relevant test (B) is an assessment that focuses on skills and knowledge that are specific and important to a particular culture and would only be administered to members of the culture for which it was designed. A power test (C) is an assessment that measure abilities under testing conditions involving little or no time pressure. A speed test (D) is an assessment that determines an examinee's score based in part on how quickly they solve the problems presented. Crystallized intelligence (E) involves the knowledge individuals acquire over the life span including vocabulary, verbal skills, cultural knowledge, and factual information.

46. **(E)**

Benjamin Lee Whorf was a linguist who believed that our thoughts are shaped and constrained by the language we speak. He believed that people are not capable of thinking about anything that their language cannot express. Psychologists today disagree with Whorf's hypothesis that language determines thought, but most agree that it does influence thought. Option (D) refers to the language acquisition devise theory proposed by Noam Chomsky.

47. **(E)**

Dissociative disorders involve the fragmentation of personality. In Alice's case, she has an "old" self, of which she apparently has no memory, but also a "new" self, around which her current life revolves and her condition also includes fugue or travel. Disorganized schizophrenia (A) is a type of schizophrenia characterized by a collection of unusual symptoms including numerous hallucinations and delusions that are poorly organized. Prominent features include disorganized speech and behavior, and flat or inappropriate affect. Bipolar disorder (B) is an Axis I mood disorder that involves periods of major depressive disorder and mania resulting in a significant impairment of physical, emotional, cognitive, and behavioral functioning. Conversion disorder (C) is an Axis I somatoform disorder in which individuals experience impaired voluntary motor or sensory function despite the fact that no medical reason can be found to explain the problem. Dissociative amnesia (D) is similar to the condition described except that it does not include the fugue or travel aspect of the mental illness affecting Alice.

48. **(A)**

Extinction occurs when the conditioned stimulus (CS) is repeatedly presented without the unconditioned stimulus (UCS). The strength of the response elicited by the CS, and its ability to elicit the CR, gradually decreases if the CS continues to be presented alone. Option (B) involves the process of acquisition and is an example of delayed conditioning, which is a type of forward conditioning. Option (C) involves the process of acquisition and is an example of trace conditioning, which is a type of forward conditioning. Option (D) involves the process of acquisition and is an example of simultaneous conditioning. Option (E) involves the process of acquisition and is an example of backward conditioning, which is not considered to be an effective method of conditioning.

49. **(B)**

The cerebellum is the brain structure that is most closely associated with the encoding of implicit memories. The corpus callosum (A) is a large group of nerve fibers connecting the two cerebral hemispheres that relays information between the two halves of the brain. Explicit memories are encoded primarily by the (C) hippocampus. Because different memory stores are dependent on different brain structures, it is possible for one to be impaired by brain damage while the other remains intact. The suprachiasmatic nucleus (D) is a small region within the hypothalamus involved in the regulation of the sleep cycle by controlling the release of melatonin by the pineal gland. The pons (E) is the section of the hindbrain located above the medulla on the brainstem in charge of sleep, arousal, dreams, and facial expressions.

50. **(B)**

Transduction for the vestibular sense, occurs in the semicircular canals and is responsible for balance. Transduction is the process by which sensory receptors convert the incoming physical energy of stimuli, such as light waves, into neural impulses that the brain can understand. The semicircular canals contain fluid and their inner walls are lined with tiny hair cells. When a person is not upright, these hair cells sense the fluid moving and send neural signals to the brain about the body's position, which provides our sense of balance. (D) and (E) are incorrect because the muscles and joints are the location for the specialized receptor cells for kinesthesis or the sense that provides information about the location of body parts in relation to one another. Transduction for kinesthesis occurs in specialized cells called proprioceptors that are located in the joints and muscles of the body.

51. **(E)**

Construct validity means that a particular test accurately measures the abstract idea (construct) or skill it was created to measure. Constructs include ideas that are often difficult to define operationally such as intelligence or personality traits. If an intelligence test actually measures cognitive abilities and not a different theoretical idea (construct) such as language ability or cultural knowledge it is construct valid. Content validity (A) is the extent to which a test accurately measures the entire breadth of the subject it is intended to measure.

Face validity (B) is the extent to which the material on a test appears on the surface to accurately measure what it intends to measure. Face validity is determined either by a non-expert or an expert who only gives a quick evaluation of the test. Only an expert or an individual familiar with the material can determine content validity. Predictive validity (C) is the extent to which test scores forecast (predict) future behaviors or results. Criterion validity (D) is a way to measure accuracy by determining if scores on a particular test are positively correlated with scores on another existing and well established test (criterion) of the same skill, trait, or ability.

52. (A)

Aversive conditioning is a type of behavior therapy intended to make a person have an unpleasant reaction when they engage in a certain behavior. For instance, there are medications that make people feel nauseous when they drink alcohol. As such, the sick feeling becomes associated with alcohol, and people may be less likely to drink in the future. Systematic desensitization (B) is a type of behavior therapy developed by Wolpe to help people overcome fears and anxiety. The process of systematic desensitization involves the use of step-by-step classical conditioning in which an anxiety-producing stimulus is paired with relaxation. Individuals construct an anxiety hierarchy that they work through by starting at the least anxiety-producing activity and use relaxation techniques. Cognitive behavioral therapy (C) is a type of therapy that combines aspects of both cognitive and behavioral approaches in order to identify and alter the maladaptive thoughts and behaviors that are causing significant distress or making it difficult for the client to cope. Psychoanalysis (D) is a specific type of psychotherapy developed by Sigmund Freud designed to treat psychological illnesses by discovering the unconscious conflicts and motives responsible for the symptoms individuals are experiencing. Cognitive therapy (E) is a type of psychotherapy that uses a variety of methods that attempt to treat psychological illnesses through the direct manipulation of the thinking and reasoning processes of the client.

53. (C)

According to the activation-synthesis model, signals from the brainstem, especially the pons, are reaching areas of the forebrain in charge of vision, hearing, and memory to create meaning from these limited messages resulting in what we experience as dreams. Paradoxical sleep (A) is a reference to the fact that REM sleep represents a contradiction. The paradox is that although the body is asleep it is demonstrating brain wave activity and bodily changes that are commonly associated with arousal. Furthermore, despite the internal state of the individual being very active, the individual cannot physically move. A hypnagogic state (B) is associated with stage one of NREM sleep and is the brief period just before sleep that may include dreamlike experiences, hallucinations, or sudden movements called hypnic jerks. Microsleep (D) refers to the short naps, lasting only a few seconds, that sleep-deprived individuals fall into. Individuals are often unaware of these lapses in consciousness which can occur while working, listening in class, or in a dangerous situation such as when someone is behind the wheel of a car. Information-processing theory (E) is a cognitive approach to the explanation of dreams that states that dreams occur because the mind needs to sort out the events of the day and place them into memory.

54. (D)

Positron emission tomography (PET) scans track the amount of glucose being consumed by different brain regions. Because glucose is a major source of energy for the brain, greater consumption in one area is assumed to indicate greater activity by that brain region. Magnetic resonance imaging, MRI, and computerized axial tomography, or CT scan, (A) and (C) create images of brain structure only and not function. Options (B) and (E) also both provide information about brain functioning, but neither involves the tracking of radioactive glucose.

55. (A)

Terrance is seeing a psychiatrist because that is the only type of therapist that can typically prescribe medications. Prozac is a type of antidepressant called a selective serotonin reuptake inhibitor (SSRI) that alleviates depression symptoms by reducing reuptake of the neurotransmitter serotonin. Counseling psychologists (B) are practitioners who work with people coping with everyday problems including making career decisions, marriage counseling, and social skills training. The required level of education and training for licensure for a counseling psychologist is determined by state law, but many have doctoral degrees including PhD, PsyD, or EdD. Clinical psychologists (C) are practitioners who work with the diagnosis, causes, and treatment of mental disorders that typically have a doctoral degree such as a PhD or PsyD and complete specialized training and state licensure. Social workers (D) are professionals who have a master's degree in social work (MSW) who provide treatment for psychological illnesses. They assist clients by coordinating access to support for occupational training, housing, and financial assistance. Psychiatric nurses (E) are professionals with an RN degree who specialize in treating individuals suffering from psychological illnesses. Psychiatric nurses may dispense psychotropic medications and provide assistance and support to patients, but they rarely have the ability to write a prescription.

56. (E)

Systematic desensitization is the process of gradually exposing a person to a feared stimulus with simultaneous relaxation. The idea is that the person can become comfortable with that stimulus a little bit at a time, without having to immediately confront it directly. This therapy is used most often to treat phobias. Client-centered therapy (A) is a type of humanist psychotherapy developed by Carl Rogers. Cognitive restructuring (B) is a method used in cognitive therapy that involves altering the illogical, self-defeating cognitions that an individual has that are resulting in dysfunctional behavior or distress and replacing them with ones that are realistic, genuine, and adaptive. Flooding (D) is a type of implosion behavioral therapy which involves having the patient immediately confront the most anxiety-producing situation related to their fear in a manner that is harmless, but also does not allow for the opportunity to escape.

57. (D)

Signal detection theory is used by psychologists to evaluate how accurately individuals notice faint stimuli under a variety of conditions. Whether or not an individual notices a faint stimulus depends on the stimulus itself and characteristics of the individual including their level of attention, motivation, and experience.

Social cognitive theory (A) is a theory of personality that explains how personal characteristics, social interactions, and cognitive evaluations are all involved in developing an individual's personality. Theory of the mind (B) refers to the cognitive ability that children acquire around the age of four in which they are able to understand the thoughts and intentions of others and predict their behavior. Absolute threshold (C) refers to the minimum intensity at which a stimulus can be detected at least 50 percent of the time. For example, the absolute threshold for human vision is illustrated by the fact that humans can detect a candle flame from 30 miles away on a clear, dark night under optimal conditions. Signal detection theory is a more detailed method for identifying specific cognitive and environmental factors that affect which stimuli are noticed. The Premack principle (E) is a learning theory that explains that it is possible to use a behavior which is preferred by an individual to increase the likelihood that a behavior that is not as preferred will occur.

58. (A)

Individuals with an avoidant personality disorder are socially insecure and unable to form social relationships and show similarities to social phobias. A schizoid personality disorder (B) is marked by a cold demeanor and a lack of interest in forming relationships. An antisocial personality disorder (C) is marked by impulsivity, ruthlessness, and a lack of a conscience. A borderline personality disorder (D) is marked by instability in a variety of domains. Therapists often find borderline difficult to treat because the person's thoughts and behaviors are so variable and unpredictable. People with borderline will act very clingy and needy on some days, and angry and dismissive on others, without provocation. A dependent personality disorder (E) is characterized by an excessive desire be taken care of by someone else that causes them to be clingy (dependent). Individuals with a dependent personality disorder turn to others for even simple decisions and are fearful of abandonment and independence.

59. **(B)**

The limbic system is a collection of brain structures in the middle of the brain that largely control motivations and emotions. One particular structure in the limbic system is the amygdala, which drives fear and anger responses. Some types of damage to the amygdala in animal subjects can lead to an apparent inability to experience these emotions. The occipital lobes (A) are the portions of the cerebral cortex located at the back of the cortex responsible for visual processing. The hippocampus (C) is a limbic system structure surrounding the thalamus responsible for explicit memory formation and learning. Remember—a hippocampus is like a college campus where you make a lot of memories and you learn a lot of things! The reticular activating system (D) is the network of nerves running vertically through the brainstem and extending to the thalamus responsible for arousal to stimuli, sleep, attentiveness, and the filtering of incoming stimuli. Damage to the RAS can result in coma or death. The pons (E) is the section of the hindbrain located above the medulla on the brainstem in charge of sleep, arousal, dreams, and facial expressions.

60. **(D)**

Anterograde amnesia is an inability to form new memories after the event that caused the amnesia. Dissociative amnesia (A) is characterized by a partial or total inability to recall past experiences and information that does not have a biological cause. Dissociative amnesia is usually associated with a traumatic experience. The term *retroactive* (B) refers to retroactive interference, which is a memory problem that occurs when new information interferes with the recall of old information. The term *proactive* (C) refers to proactive interference, which is a memory problem that occurs when previously learned information interferes with the ability to recall a new memory. Retrograde amnesia (E) is an inability to recall memories that were formed prior to the event that caused the amnesia. Be able to recognize the difference between anterograde and retrograde amnesia as well as proactive and retroactive interference.

61. **(C)**

Retinal disparity also known as binocular disparity is one of two binocular depth or distance aids that require the use of both eyes. The other binocular cue is convergence. All of the other answers are monocular cues or aids for determining depth or distance that require only one eye. Interposition (A) is a monocular cue for depth in which an object appears closer to the viewer if it partially blocks the view of another object. Relative size (B) is a monocular cue for depth that states that objects that are larger compared to others in the visual field are closer. Linear perspective (D) is a monocular cue for depth that states that objects appear closer to the viewer if they are located farther away from the point where two parallel lines appear to converge (meet). Texture gradient (E) is a monocular cue for depth in which objects that have detailed, distinct textures are perceived to be closer and objects that have a less detailed, indistinct texture are perceived to be farther away.

62. (A)

Latent learning was discovered by Tolman through his research with rats. The term *cognitive map* (B) is also a term associated with the research of Tolman and refers to the mental picture of one's environment created by an organism. Centration (C), according to Piaget, is an error in thinking that contributes to the inability of preoperational children to conserve and involves focusing (centering) on just one feature of a problem, while ignoring other important aspects. The law of effect (D) studied by Thorndike states that a voluntary behavior followed by a positive outcome would be repeated, and a voluntary behavior followed by failure would not be repeated. Thorndike's law of effect would significantly influence the work of key behaviorist B.F. Skinner on operant conditioning. Insight learning (E) involves a sudden flash of inspiration rather than a strategy and was researched by Kohler. Kohler investigated how chimpanzees solved problems, by placing a banana outside the cage beyond the reach of the animal. The chimpanzee was given several short, hollow sticks which would have to be pushed together in order to reach the banana. The chimpanzees first attempted to get the banana with one stick, but eventually, realized the sticks could be connected to form a longer stick, thus perceiving a completely new relationship between the sticks which Kohler considered to be an insight.

63. (A)

When we learn something, we create neural connections in the brain to represent that information. When we revisit that information (for example, when we study), the firing thresholds for those connections are lowered and additional receptor sites for neurotransmitters are created. As a result, it becomes easier for these connections to be accessed and are the neural path is "strengthened." This process is known as long-term potentiation. Option (D) is known as neurogenesis or the development of new neurons that occurs in even in adults. Option (E) is known as parallel processing in which a combination of many neurons fire in multiple brain regions at once, rather than individually in order for the brain to be faster and more efficient.

64. (A)

The most severe level of cognitive disability is profound mental retardation and individuals with this diagnosis require complete supervision and care for their entire lives and have limited language and movement ability. A diagnosis of severe mental retardation (D) involves individuals that mostly live in institutions and may develop limited speech and learn to take care of their own basic needs with prolonged training. The terms *pervasive* (B) and *serious* (C) are not categories listed in the *DSM-IV-TR*. Individuals with a diagnosis of moderate (E) mental retardation can develop academic skills at approximately the 2nd to 4th grade level and can be successful as adults in unskilled or routine jobs. Most individuals with a cognitive disability fall into the category of mild mental retardation and are capable of academic skills at approximately the 6th grade level. These individuals can achieve independence and occupational success as adults, although they may need help with social and financial problems.

65. (A)

Depressed people tend to attribute their own failures to internal, stable characteristics ("I am not good at anything"), while attributing their successes to external factors (e.g., an easy test). By changing the way that Jane explains her failures and successes, her depression could be lessened or eliminated. Cognitive therapies incorporate techniques for making changes in thought processes in order to reduce negative behaviors and improve mental health. Modeling therapy (B) is a behavioral approach. Option (C) references cognitive behavioral therapy (CBT) because it combines aspects of both the cognitive approach (cognitive restructuring) and the behavioral approach (social skills training). Option (D) refers to psychoanalytic or psychodynamic approaches that assist individuals in achieving insight into the unresolved unconscious conflicts that are the cause of maladaptive behaviors. Option (E) would not be considered a rational statement or belief by a cognitive therapist.

66. (E)

Random assignment ensures that each participant has an equal chance of being assigned to either the control or experimental group. Assignment refers to placing subjects into experimental conditions (control or experimental group) after they have already been selected for the experiment. The process of random assignment is required in order to determine cause and effect and eliminate confounding variables. All other options (A, B, C, D) are samples. Sampling is the process of selecting subjects from the population to be involved in the experiment.

67. (D)

Variable-ratio schedules produce consistently high rates of performance even after prolonged discontinuance of the reinforcement. In fact, once an operant learning response has been established with a variable-ratio reinforcement schedule, it is difficult to extinguish. This schedule produces the highest rate of performance and a steady response rate with few pauses because the subject does not know how many behaviors are required before reinforcement will occur again. The fixed-interval schedule (A) is a reinforcement schedule in operant conditioning in which the reinforcement is given for the first correct response after a set period of time has occurred. This schedule has a lower yield in terms of performance. However, just before reinforcement time, activity increases. A variable-interval (B) is a reinforcement schedule in operant conditioning in which the reinforcement is given for the first correct response after a changing period of time has occurred. A fixed-ratio schedule (C) is a reinforcement schedule in operant conditioning in which the reinforcement is given after a set number of correct behaviors have occurred. This schedule also creates high response rates but includes short pauses after each time reinforcement is presented, creating a less steady rate of response. The faster a subject responds, the more reinforcements they will receive. A frequency histogram (E) refers to a specialized type of bar graph that displays data from a frequency distribution.

68. (E)

Prozac, Zoloft, and Paxil are all selective serotonin reuptake inhibitors (SSRIs). SSRIs work by preventing reuptake of excess serotonin in the neural synapse. Because depression has been associated with low levels of serotonin, SSRIs can be effective antidepressants because they leave more of this critical neurotransmitter in the system.

69. (A)

The left parietal lobe contains the portion of the somatosensory cortex that is responsible for sensations of touch for the right side of the body. The right parietal (B) is incorrect because it receives sensation for the left side of the body, which is not a problem for Rebecca. The temporal lobes (C) and (D) contain the primary auditory cortex responsible for hearing, as well as areas responsible for olfaction and the recognition of faces. The frontal lobes (E) contain the primary motor cortex, which controls voluntary movement as well as regions responsible for higher-level thinking, reasoning, planning, judgment, and impulse control.

70. (B)

Group polarization is a tendency for people with similar opinions to shift their opinions in a more extreme direction after discussion. Option (A) describes groupthink, which is a desire for group harmony that produces agreement from members when making a decision. Option (C) describes the risky shift, which is sometimes confused with group polarization. Risky shift, unlike group polarization describes how an individual's decisions become riskier after discussion rather than how the group comes to a more extreme conclusion. Option (D) refers to deindividuation or the phenomenon in which a person experiences a lessened sense of personal identity and responsibility. It is a state likely to be experienced by a person in a large group or crowd situation. Option (E) refers to a social dilemma, also called a social trap.

71. (D)

All researchers are required by law to debrief participants at the end of every research session. The debriefing is intended to explain the true reasons for the research, as well as to ensure that the person feels comfortable with his or her participation before leaving. Random assignment (A) is a process used in experiments in which each participant has an equal chance of being assigned to either the experimental or control group and is required in order to determine cause and effect relationships. Random selection (B) is a process creating a random sample by selecting participants in a manner that allows for every member of the population to have an equal chance of being chosen for participation in the study. Priming (C) is the process of being exposed to a stimulus which then makes the individual unconsciously more likely to be able to recall that same stimulus. Informed consent (E) occurs prior to the start of the research and involves telling the participants about the purpose, time commitment, and procedures of the experiment as well as informing them of their rights and any potential use of deception.

72. (C)

The second level of Maslow's hierarchy of needs consists of the need for safety and security. Maslow's hierarchy of needs has five levels. The five levels in order starting from the bottom of the pyramid include: physiological needs, safety and security, love and belonging, esteem and self-esteem, and self-actualization. As one type of need is satisfied, the next level in the hierarchy becomes the dominant motivating factor. Remember that the highest level on Maslow's pyramid is self-actualization or the desire to achieve one's greatest potential. According to Maslow, few people achieve the highest stage in the motivation hierarchy.

73. (A)

Assimilation according to Piaget, is the process of trying to fit new information into an existing schema. Jimmy interpreted what he saw in terms of his current framework for understanding animals. Accommodation (B) is the process of adjusting old schemas to incorporate new information. Had Jimmy changed his understanding of animals (cows and rhinos are different), he would have been accommodating. Conservation (C) is Piaget's term for the cognitive ability to understand that the mass, volume, weight, and quantity of an object(s) does not change even though the appearance has been altered in some way. The ability to conserve develops during the concrete operational stage of cognitive development. Egocentrism (D) is the difficulty in seeing how the world looks from the perspective of others typical of the preoperational stage of cognitive development. Egocentrism is present during the stage of cognitive development that Jimmy is in currently, the preoperational stage, but is not evident in the example. Object permanence, (E) according to Piaget, is the awareness that items (objects) continue to exist even when they cannot be seen. The understanding of object permanence appears around 9 months, halfway through Piaget's sensorimotor stage of cognitive development. Jimmy has already developed an understanding of the concept of object permanence, but that concept is not what is described in the example.

74. **(C)**

Zoey is using the defense mechanism of displacement that involves unconsciously reducing anxiety by taking out aggression on someone or something that is less powerful or threatening than the true source of anxiety. Zoey is really angry at her boyfriend Zach, but instead takes her aggression out on her parents because she knows they will still love her, making them a safer target. Projection (A) is a defense mechanism that involves reducing anxiety by attributing one's own fears, feelings, faults, or unacceptable thoughts and behaviors to another person or group. Regression (B) is a defense mechanism that involves unconsciously reducing anxiety by reverting to thoughts and behaviors that would be more appropriate during an earlier period of development. Reaction formation (D) is a defense mechanism that involves unconsciously reducing anxiety by acting or saying the exact opposite of the morally or socially unacceptable beliefs held by an individual. Sublimation (E) is a defense mechanism that involves unconsciously reducing anxiety by directing aggression toward a more socially acceptable outlet such as exercise, hard work, sports, or hobbies.

Sublimation is viewed as a healthier version of displacement. If Zoey was using the defense mechanism of sublimation she would have found a way to vent her anger and frustration without hurting her family.

75. **(D)**

The presence of others who do not follow the crowd is one of the strongest predictors of resistance to conformity. Options (A), unanimity, and (E), large group sizes, are incorrect because they are the two factors that *most predicted* conformity. Individuals are more likely to conform to a group of their friends (B) because of the strong desire to be liked and accepted by social groups. The lack of a strong prior opinion about a topic (C) *increases conformity*.

76. **(B)**

Threshold refers to the fact that the total amount of EPSPs that an individual neuron receives from other neurons must be greater than the total amount of IPSPs it receives in order for the neuron to fire as well as reaching a minimum level. The firing of the action potential works on the all-or-none principle, either firing at 100% strength or not at all. The refractory period (A) is the stage when repolarization is occurring and the neuron cannot fire because it is resetting itself to its original resting potential state. Repolarization (C) is the stage when the sodium-potassium pump is returning the ions to their original positions either inside or outside of the axon, reestablishing the resting potential. The resting potential (D) is the state when the neuron is waiting for a message, in which the fluid-filled interior of the axon has a negative charge (-70 millivolts) and the fluid exterior has a positive charge.

77. **(A)**

The representative heuristic is being used by Benjamin because he is judging the likelihood of an event (liking the new class) based on how well it matches a typical example or prototype (previous academic experiences that were positive). A representative heuristic is a shortcut that involves judging the likelihood of an event which can result in either a correct or incorrect analysis of the situation. For example, if Jake is 24 years old, 6 feet 8 inches tall and weighs 300 pounds, we may be more likely to guess that he is an NFL lineman instead of a stockbroker based on a representative heuristic. The anchoring bias (B) is a cognitive error that leads an individual to place too great of an emphasis on an initial estimate when making decisions under conditions in which they are unsure. The availability heuristic (C) refers to the tendency to think that easily recalled events happen more frequently than they actually do. However, there are lots of reasons that an event might come to mind easily. Perhaps that event has been in the news, or maybe a similar thing happened to you a long time ago. If these instances leap easily to mind, you are likely to overestimate their frequency. Belief perseverance (D) is a cognitive error in which individuals have a tendency to hold onto an assumption or belief even after it has been disproven. Overconfidence bias (E) is a cognitive error in which individuals have a tendency to overestimate how correct their predictions and beliefs about ideas actually are.

78. **(D)**

Classical conditioning never involves voluntary responses. Voluntary actions are associated with operant conditioning. A helpful hint to be certain that your answer is correct is to check that both the unconditioned and conditioned responses are involuntary; that is, they are either reflexes, automatic bodily reactions like sweating or salivating, or emotions such as fear. Additionally, both the unconditioned and conditioned responses will be the same or similar. During classical conditioning, the neutral stimulus will become the conditioned stimulus. For example, in Pavlov's experiment the neutral stimulus (bell) became the conditioned stimulus (bell) that resulted in salivation after it was paired with the unconditioned stimulus (meat powder).

79. **(C)**

Delusions and hallucinations are two of the hallmark symptoms of schizophrenia. Delusions are false beliefs, and often take the forms of persecution, grandeur, control, or reference. Hallucinations are experiences of things that the senses are not actually detecting. These are typically auditory, though some schizophrenics do have hallucinations involving the other senses. Neologisms (A) are words that are made up by the speaker and are an aspect of the disorganized thought associated with schizophrenia. Catatonia (B) refers to a variety of psychomotor difficulties including immobility, lack of responsiveness, excitability, or the assuming of unusual physical postures characteristic of catatonic schizophrenia. Clang associations (E) are a type of disorganized speech associated with schizophrenia that involves the speaker making connections between words based on how they sound or rhyme instead of their meaning.

80. **(D)**

   Panic disorder is an Axis I anxiety disorder characterized by recurrent unexpected panic attacks followed by at least one month of persistent concern about having another panic attack. Individuals with panic disorder experience ongoing anxiety because they are worried about future panic attacks happening, which can then in turn make more panic attacks likely. People experiencing a panic attack often confuse it for other threatening medical conditions like heart attacks or strokes. A specific phobia (A) is an Axis I anxiety disorder in which the individual has irrational fears of objects and situations such as heights, closed spaces, snakes, and spiders that do not pose any actual threat which prevents them from normal functioning. Generalized anxiety disorder (B) is an Axis I anxiety disorder characterized by chronic, widespread, and persistent anxiety. Because the source of the anxiety cannot be identified, this is sometimes called free-floating. Social anxiety disorder (C) is an Axis I anxiety disorder also called a social phobia in which the fear an individual has regarding social situations prevents him or her from taking part in normal interactions because of the potential threat of embarrassment. Obsessive-compulsive disorder (E) is an Axis I anxiety disorder characterized by persistent, repetitive, and unwanted thoughts (obsessions) and behaviors (compulsions). In obsessive-compulsive disorder the individual performs the behaviors or rituals (compulsions) in order to reduce the anxiety caused by the obsessive thoughts. All of the options in this question are Axis I anxiety disorders, which include posttraumatic stress disorder.

81. **(A)**

   The overjustification effect is the reason that Mr. Tagala's level of intrinsic motivation has decreased. The overjustification effect is the unusual result that happens if a person is given an extrinsic reward for performance that causes their level of intrinsic motivation for the same task to decrease in the future. Priming (B) is an aid for memory retrieval that happens if an individual is exposed to a stimulus previously. This prior exposure or priming will make it more likely that they will recall that same or a similar stimulus later. Self-fulfilling prophecy (C) refers to a phenomenon that occurs when the expectations people have about themselves lead them to alter their behavior which in turn causes their expectations to come true. If Mr. Tagala believed he was a great coach, which led him to work harder and resulted in him having success, that would be an example of a self-fulfilling prophecy. The self-reference effect (D) is the tendency for an individual to have improved recall for information that personally relates to their life. Display rules (E) are the culturally acceptable learned guidelines for when and how emotions can be expressed in particular social situations.

82. (C)

Transference is the shifting of attitudes about external events, individuals and objects toward the therapist directly. Freud believed that patients would sometimes develop extremely strong positive or negative feelings about their therapists, but that these feelings were initially felt about something or someone else. For example, negative emotions about one's parents could result in those same negative emotions being felt toward the therapist. Identification (A), according to Freud, occurs when an individual adopts the values, behaviors, and social roles of the same-sex parent and consequently resolves their phallic stage conflict. Resistance (B) is a method in psychodynamic and psychoanalytic therapy that includes the interpretation of the various ways patients avoid confronting the painful, repressed memories and conflicts that are the actual cause of their problems. Rationalization (D) is a defense mechanism that involves unconsciously reducing anxiety by creating logical excuses for unacceptable thoughts and behaviors. Rationalization is about making excuses and is usually verbal. Repression (E) is a defense mechanism that involves unconsciously reducing anxiety by blocking a painful incident or event from awareness. Anxiety-producing unacceptable wishes and thoughts are pushed into the unconscious

83. (A)

Electroconvulsive therapy (ECT) is a form of biomedical therapy that involves the brief passage of an electric current across electrodes placed on the temple of the patient that creates a brain seizure. This method has been effective in the treatment of severe depression that does not respond to medication. ECT has not been shown to be an effective treatment for the other mental illnesses listed.

84. (C)

Crystallized intelligence, the knowledge and skills that we gather over our lifetimes, tends to increase with experience (and thus with age). However, fluid intelligence decreases. Fluid intelligence is the ability to quickly and easily use reason and to solve problems.

85. (E)

The bake sale organizer is using a low-ball approach by first getting Sue to make a commitment and then revealing hidden costs. After Sue agrees, the terms of the deal are changed. Low-ball differs from foot-in-the-door because the original agreement is never honored; it is only a method to receive the intended larger request. The political organization (A) is attempting to persuade Estella through the foot-in-the-door method by first having her comply with a small request (signing a petition) before asking her for the larger request (a donation). Option (B) is an example of how the norm of reciprocity influences persuasion. After receiving a free gift, Maggie reciprocated by purchasing products. In option (C) Tristan has been influenced by the elaboration likelihood model's peripheral route to persuasion because the commercial succeeded in creating a positive association between the basketball shoes and a famous celebrity. The door-in-the-face technique (D) is being used to increase the chances of compliance by the students by first asking for a very large request (20 hours a week), which is likely to be turned down, and then asking for a smaller favor (one day per month) that is then more likely to be granted.

86. (E)

Experiments test cause-and-effect relationships by manipulating an independent variable (the presumed cause—in this case, the presence or absence of unpredictable noise) and measuring the effect on the dependent variable which in this example is the number of questions answered correctly. The college students are the participants in the research.

87. (C)

Karen has committed the actor-observer bias because she has explained her brother's behavior in terms of a personality trait (dispositional), but attributed her own behavior to the fact that she has a lot of homework (situational). The actor-observer bias always involves a comparison. Fundamental attribution error (A) refers to the tendency to explain the behavior of someone else in terms of dispositional factors only and unlike the example, does not involve a comparison. This situation in this example is not the FAE because Karen also explains her own behavior. In-group bias (B) occurs when individuals have a preference for groups to which they themselves belong. Karen is not identifying specific groups that she prefers. Self-serving bias (D) was not present for Karen because she is explaining her brother's behavior as well as her own. Self-serving bias is the tendency to attribute one's successes to dispositional factors and one's failures to situational factors. This is due to the desire to see oneself in a positive way and is more common in individualistic cultures. The bystander effect (E) is a phenomenon relating to helping behavior in which each individual is less likely to help when others are present than if they were alone.

88. (E)

Withdrawal symptoms vary depending on the drug and often include cold sweats, vomiting, convulsions, hallucinations, depressed mood, and anxiety and is associated with physical dependence.

Psychological dependence (A) is characterized by intense cravings created by the reinforcing properties of the drug. Polydrug abuse (B) refers to the fact that many individuals that abuse or become dependent on drugs use more than one substance. Combining too many drugs with similar effects—for example, mixing depressants such as alcohol with benzodiazepines—can severely impair the central nervous system, resulting in overdoses that can lead to coma or death. Detoxification (C) is the medically supervised process of assisting an individual through withdrawal. Detoxification also includes therapy and medications to assist individuals. Tolerance (D) is a condition in which an individual will need to take greater amounts or stronger versions of a drug in order to achieve the same psychotropic effect that they experienced previously. Tolerance, like withdrawal, is associated with substance dependence or addiction.

89. **(B)**

Erik Erikson's model of psychosocial development divided the lifespan into eight distinct stages. During each of these stages, Erikson believed that people face a developmental conflict to be resolved—called a psychosocial crisis—which can have either a positive or a negative outcome. If the conflict is resolved in a healthy, proactive way, the individual experiences personal growth and development. If not, the person will become "stuck" in that crisis and may develop a psychopathology related to that stage of development. Carol Gilligan (A) created a theory of moral development that stressed compassion and concern for others as the highest level of moral development for women, which contrasted with Kohlberg's theory, which placed an emphasis on the moral value of individual rights and justice. Sigmund Freud (C) created a stage theory of personality that was based on five psychosexual stages. Jean Piaget (D) created a stage theory for cognitive development. Lawrence Kohlberg (E) created a stage theory for moral development.

90. **(A)**

Sensory memory is the first stage of memory in the information-processing model of memory developed by Atkinson and Shiffrin also called the sensory register. Sensory memory is a very short-lived recording of sensory information lasting for a few seconds or less. Sensory memory includes both echoic (very brief auditory memories) and iconic (very brief visual memories) that allow the brain to process the information before it fades from memory. Short-term memory (B) is the second stage of memory in the information-processing model that has a capacity for approximately seven plus or minus two pieces of information and lasts for 10–30 seconds. Long-term memory (C) is the third stage in the information-processing model of memory and is considered to be a generally permanent storage capable of containing a limitless amount of information. Episodic memory (D) is a type of explicit or declarative memory that consists of personal experiences and events tied to particular times and places. Procedural memory (E) is the most well-known category of implicit memory, which consists of the long-term memory for the skills, habits, and cognitive rules involved in particular tasks. Procedural memories can be thought of as "how to" memories such as the memory of how to ride a bike or snowboard.

91. (C)

Social facilitation theory says that we perform better in front of others, if and only if we are performing a task that is well-practiced. If you are doing something simple that you have done a million times in your life, the presence of an audience should cause you to perform the task more quickly and at a higher level. However, if the task is not familiar, the presence of an audience can make us choke under pressure. Choice (D) is incorrect because social facilitation would have Mimi perform better on an easy task, not worse. Choice (E) is an example of social loafing, or the phenomenon in which individuals contribute less when working with others in a group than when performing the same task alone due to the lessoning of personal accountability.

92. (E)

Information from the sensory receptors in Marisa's hands travels to the central nervous system on afferent or sensory neurons and voluntary muscle commands travel on efferent or motor neurons. Glial cells (B) and (C) are the cells that provide nourishment, protection, and produce myelin. Interneurons (A) are located in the brain and spinal cord and facilitate communication between afferent and efferent neurons.

93. (B)

Freud believed that the personality has three parts: the id, the ego, and the superego. The id pursues basic physical urges related to sex, survival, and reproduction. The id is not concerned with social norms or standards, but instead is driven by instinct. In Freud's personality theory the id operates according to the pleasure principle, seeking only immediate satisfaction and the avoidance of pain. The ego operates on the reality principle by balancing the impulses of the id with the constraints of reality and the superego's desire for perfection. The superego is the portion of the personality that serves as an individual's conscience, which operates on a morality principle, seeking to enforce ethical conduct.

94. (A)

According to Selye, the reaction to chronic stress occurs in three stages: alarm, resistance, and exhaustion. The syndrome can ultimately lead to bodily damage during the final stage of exhaustion. At this point, prolonged stress and physical arousal has exhausted the body's resources. This is caused in part by a depletion of the adrenal hormones. When this occurs, disorders such as rheumatism and arthritis can develop. Ultimately, death may result from prolonged exhaustion.

95. **(B)**

Correlations simply tell you whether variables A and B are related, as well as the strength and direction of the correlation. They do *not* tell you anything about causation. If A and B are correlated, it is possible that A causes B, that B causes A, or that there is a third variable that influences both A and B. Only experimental research tells you about causation between variables. Option (A) is incorrect because correlational studies do indicate how variables relate to each other. Option (C) is incorrect because correlational research is often inexpensive and faster than experimental designs or other methods. Option (D) is a criticism typically associated with the case study method. Option (E) is incorrect because correlational research can involve either basic or applied research.

96. **(D)**

The use of pop quizzes involves reinforcing studying on a variable-interval schedule because the students do not know when the reinforcement (a good quiz score) will occur as a result of their studying behavior. A variable-interval schedule involves providing reinforcement for the first correct response after a changing period of time has occurred. The students do not know when the next test will occur and will most likely keep studying at a consistent rate. Fixed-ratio (A) is a reinforcement schedule in which the reinforcement is given after a set number of correct behaviors have occurred. Variable-ratio (B) is a reinforcement schedule in which the reinforcement is given after a changing number of correct behaviors have occurred. Fixed-interval (C) is a reinforcement schedule in which the reinforcement is given for the first correct response after a set period of time has occurred. If the Spanish teacher gave students a vocabulary quiz every Thursday, that would be a fixed-interval schedule and most likely the students would not start studying until Wednesday night.

Continuous reinforcement (E) is the operant conditioning technique of reinforcing the desired response every time it is presented as opposed to providing reinforcement according to one of the previous four schedules. Continuous reinforcement produces a fast rate of learning, but if reinforcement ends, the behavior becomes extinct quickly.

97. **(E)**

The hypothalamus regulates a number of physiological motivations, especially hunger. If the lateral hypothalamus is stimulated, the animal begins to eat, whereas it will stop if the ventromedial portion is stimulated. Conversely, lesioning the lateral hypothalamus will cause the animal to stop eating, while destroying the ventromedial section will lead the animal to overeat. The term *satiety* refers to the feeling of being full and not hungry that results in decreasing the likelihood that an individual will be motivated to eat.

The choices in option (A) and (B) are incorrect because the medulla oblongata is the brain area responsible for survival functions such as heartbeat and breathing, and the reticular activating system is the brain area in charge of arousal to stimuli, sleep, attentiveness, and the filtering of incoming stimuli. Option (C) is incorrect because the hippocampus is a limbic system structure related to forming new explicit memories and learning, and the thalamus is the sensory relay station.

98. **(B)**

Temperament in developmental psychology refers to the biologically influenced activity level, behaviors, and emotional responses typically demonstrated by individuals. These differences in temperament are observable in infants from the time of birth. Three general types of temperament have been identified including easy, difficult, and slow-to-warm-up. Attachment (A) refers to the long-lasting emotional bond that develops between the infant and caregiver that provides the child with a sense of security and comfort. Ainsworth's research on attachment style based on the Strange Situation revealed four types of attachment including secure, anxious-avoidant, anxious-resistant, and disorganized. Maturation (C) refers to the biological growth processes that enable changes in behavior connected to an individual's genetic blueprint. Maturation refers to changes that are driven mainly by nature and less influenced by nurture. Identity (D) is the collection of many separate components including career, culture, gender, political, religious, personality, and interests that shape adult behavior. Androgyny (E) is the development of a gender identity that incorporates both male and female traits.

99. **(A)**

Depressed people tend to have low levels of the neurotransmitter serotonin (and also norepinephrine). Many antidepressants target these serotonin deficits by blocking the reuptake process, leaving more serotonin in the system. Lower levels of the inhibitory neurotransmitter GABA have been associated with anxiety disorders. High levels of dopamine (B) and (C) have been associated with schizophrenia. Acetylcholine (D) is a neurotransmitter involved in memory and movement. Low levels of acetylcholine are associated with Alzheimer's disease.

100. **(D)**

The self-effacing bias is more common in collectivist cultures that value teamwork and group harmony. The self-serving bias (A) is more common in individualist cultures that value personal success. Social loafing (B) is more common in individualist cultures. In collectivist cultures social striving or putting forth a greater effort in a group situation would be more common. The fundamental attribution error (C) is more common in individualist cultures. Option (E) is incorrect because the values of independence and self-reliance are more closely associated with individualist cultures. Collectivist cultures would instead emphasize the values of teamwork, group unity, and harmony.

Rubrics and Sample Essays

Section II

Question 1 Rubric

This is a ten-point free-response question. Two points are assigned for each of the five terms.

General Requirements

1. Answers must be written in complete sentences. Bulleted answers will not score.

2. Correct spelling and grammar are not required as long as the meaning of the response is clear.

3. No points will be scored for introductions or conclusions.

4. The presence of incorrect information does not result in the removal of points, unless the information directly contradicts another part of the response that is correct.

5. Questions must be either answered in order or the specific part of the question being addressed must be identified.

6. All answers must reference the scenario presented.

Point 1: Random sample definition

- A random sample allows everyone in the population to have an equal chance to participate in the study.

- Do not score references to random assignment.

Point 2: Random sample application

- Identification of a method for random selection (random sample) of baseball players. The response must reference selection from a population not assignment to groups. **OR**

- Allows for the results that are obtained from the sample (1600 high school baseball players) to be applied to the population (all high school baseball players). Poor sample selection creates problems in generalizing the results to the population referred to as sampling bias.

- Do not score references to random assignment. An argument stating merely that random sampling must occur for a good experiment will also not score.

Point 3: Confounding variable definition

- A confounding variable is any difference present other than the independent variable between the experimental and control group that might have an effect on the dependent variable.

- Do not score definitions of independent or dependent variables. Also, do not score references to illusory correlations or correlational studies.

Point 4: Confounding variable application

- Cite one example of a confounding variable: culture, gender, motivation, disinterest, familiarity with videogames, or involvement in other sports that might interfere with Dr. Wyatt's results. **OR**

- Dr. Wyatt should eliminate or control possible confounding variables because they would prevent him from being able to draw cause and effect conclusions. **OR**

- Dr. Wyatt can control for confounding variables by using methods such as obtaining a random sample, using random assignment, and standardizing procedures.

- Do not score references to anything that influences both groups in the same manner. Also, examples of independent or dependent variables and references to illusory correlations or correlational studies will not score.

Point 5: Informed consent definition

- Informed consent is an ethical requirement that involves participants knowing that they are involved in research and giving their permission to participate voluntarily.

- Do not score references to other ethical requirements such as debriefing.

Point 6: Informed consent application

- The baseball players' parents give permission for their child to participate in the study. **AND**

- The baseball players or parents are told about the purpose, time commitment, and/or procedures of the experiment. **OR**

- The baseball players or parents are told that they can withdraw from the experiment at any time (*voluntary participation- no coercion*). **OR**

- The baseball players or parents are told about the potential benefits and risks associated with the research. **OR**

- The baseball players or parents are told if they will be paid for participation.

- Do not score permission from the IRB or other ethical requirements such as debriefing.

Point 7: Self-fulfilling prophecy definition

- A self-fulfilling prophecy is an expectation people have about themselves that leads them to alter their behavior causing their expectation to come true.

Point 8: Self-fulfilling prophecy application

- The belief of the baseball player about his or her ability leads to altered behavior, causing the expectation to come true. The player believes he is a good athlete, so he practices more and becomes a good player. The player believes he is a poor athlete, so he does not practice, and becomes a poor player.

- Do not score a self-fulfilling prophecy on behalf of the coach, parents, or other individuals. Also, do not score references to self-esteem alone.

Point 9: External locus of control definition

- External locus of control is a person's belief that what happens to them is largely determined by fate, luck, or the actions of others.

Point 10: External locus of control application

- The baseball player believes that any improvement in his or her batting is the result of fate, luck, or the actions of others. **OR**

- The baseball player's self-esteem can be negatively impacted by an external locus of control.

- Do not score references to the baseball player having control over him- or herself. Also, do not score references to the level of motivation alone. Do not score references to external control for Dr. Wyatt or others.

Sample Free Response for Question 1

A random sample is a subset of the population selected to participate in the experiment that is chosen in such a way that every member of the population has an equal chance of being drawn to participate in the study. In order for Dr. Wyatt to have a random sample he will need to ensure that he has a group of high school baseball players for the study that is selected in a manner that allows every member of the population (all high school baseball players) to have an equal chance of ending up in the study. He could do this by using a computer to generate random numbers for the participants. Random selection is a critical step in the research process because it increases the likelihood that Dr. Wyatt's results can be applied to the larger population.

Confounding variables are any conditions present other than the independent variable that create a difference between the experimental and control group that might have an effect on the dependent variable. Examples of confounding variables in Dr. Wyatt's study might include: culture, gender, motivation, disinterest, familiarity with videogames, or involvement in other sports. Dr. Wyatt will need to prevent confounding variables or aspects of the experiment that vary between the groups, other than the independent variable he is studying so that he can determine cause and effect. For example, Dr. Wyatt can use random assignment to groups to prevent confounding of variables such as the amount of video game experience.

Informed consent is an ethical requirement which ensures that researchers obtain permission from participants that is voluntary and based on the fact that they are told in advance about what the research will involve. Dr. Wyatt will need to obtain informed consent or agreement to participate from all of the players in the study or from the parents of all of the players in the study. Dr. Wyatt's participants must agree in advance to participate after they are told about their rights. The players' rights might include being told of the purpose, time commitment, study procedures, potential use of deception or voluntary nature of the study.

A self-fulfilling prophecy occurs when the expectations people have about themselves lead them to alter their behavior causing their expectations to come true. The player believes they are a good athlete, so they practice more and become a good player. The expectations the players have about themselves lead them to alter their behavior causing their expectations to come true which is a self-fulfilling prophecy.

Locus of control refers to the influence an individual believes they have over a situation. An external locus of control is the belief that what happens to an individual is largely determined by fate, luck, or the actions of others. The locus of control for the players or their beliefs about how much influence that they have over their lives might influence their levels of self-esteem. A baseball player with an external locus of control that believes that their batting can only be improved by luck is more likely to evaluate themselves negatively, which may impact their success with the training.

Question 2 Rubric

This is a ten point free-response. Two points are assigned for each of the five terms.

General Requirements

1. Answers must be written in complete sentences. Bulleted answers will not score.

2. Correct spelling and grammar are not required as long as the meaning of the response is clear.

3. No points will be scored for introductions or conclusions.

4. The presence of incorrect information does not result in the removal of points, unless the information directly contradicts another part of the response that is correct.

5. Questions must be either answered in order or the specific part of the question being addressed must be identified.

6. All answers must reference the scenario presented.

Point 1: Schema definition

- A schema is a mental framework that organizes past experiences in order to make faster or more accurate perceptions.

- Do not score if the response does not contain both components of the definition (framework and organization).

Point 2: Schema application

- A schema for a highlight of the trip. Students need only to cite one example.

- For example, a schema regarding the ancient Roman ruins, art museum, local cuisine, OR a professional soccer match.

- Note—response must apply to an event or an individual that is involved with the trip.

Point 3: Schachter-Singer theory of emotion definition

- An emotion theory that involves a physiological response that is linked to a cognitive appraisal or cognitive label.

- Do not score if only one of the two factors is provided. Also, do not score references to any other emotion theory.

Point 4: Schachter-Singer theory of emotion application

- Students must refer to an example of emotion that results from physiological arousal and a cognitive label while on the trip to Italy.

- For example, Manuel's heart rate increases when he sees the ancient ruins and labels it as excitement about seeing history come alive. He could be excited by new experiences on the trip and interpret his arousal as a positive emotion.

- Do not score a response such as "The soccer match was in overtime and Manuel became nervous, and labeled the game as exciting." This is incorrect because Manuel needs to appraise his own emotion and not an external event such as the game.

- Note—response must apply to an emotion experienced by Manuel or another individual on the trip, not an event.

Point 5: Gate control theory definition

- Gate control theory explains that pain signals travel to the brain via the spinal cord and pass through a series of "invisible gates or doors" that can be opened or closed to reduce pain.

Point 6: Gate control theory application

- While on the trip, Manuel or another individual needs to demonstrate how pain can be reduced as a result of the gate control theory. Information traveling up the spinal cord can close the gate or door and prevent the passage of pain messages. This occurs when you rub the area around an injury and the rubbing sensations temporarily block the door and prevent or reduce the transmission of pain signals. OR

- The brain sends signals down the spinal cord, closing the gate and preventing additional pain messages from traveling to the brain. Factors such as distraction, emotion, and visual input all impact how much or how little pain is perceived.

- Note—response must apply to Manuel or another individual on the trip.

Point 7: Retroactive interference definition

- Two memory tasks must be in conflict with one another. AND
- Retroactive interference is a memory problem that occurs when recently learned information prevents the recall old information.

- Do not score references to proactive interference or a type of amnesia such as retrograde amnesia.

Point 8: Retroactive interference application

- Information about a new experience is preventing the recall of previously learned information while on the trip.

- For example, "The new language interferes with the old language students studied before going on the trip." "Newly learned Italian rules or customs interfere with students' customs."

- Note—response must apply to Manuel or another individual on the trip.

Point 9: Ethnocentrism definition

- Ethnocentrism is a specific type of prejudice in which an individual favors his or her own culture or ethnic group's values, customs, attitudes, and actions over other cultural groups.

- Do not score references to attitude or ignorance alone. In addition, do not score a prejudice just between two individuals or a prejudicial attitude about something other than a cultural or ethnic group.

Point 10: Ethnocentrism application

- An example of a negative prejudicial attitude towards a culture while on the trip.

- For example, "Italy's culture is worse" or "Manuel's culture is better."

- Note—response must apply to the culture of Manuel or another individual on the trip OR Italy's culture.

Sample Free-Response for Question 2

A schema is a mental framework that allows individuals to organize past experiences in order to make faster or more accurate perceptions. Manuel is given a taste of gelato, a frozen Italian dessert, and he immediately assimilates it into the mental framework or category that he already has for ice cream.

Schachter-Singer theory or the two-factor theory of emotion states physical arousal and cognitive labeling of that arousal combine to produce the subjective experience of emotion. When Manuel is watching the soccer game his heart is pounding and his breathing is faster. Based on this physiological arousal and the acknowledgement that he is watching a close game he experiences the emotion of excitement.

The gate control theory is an explanation for how pain can be reduced. In this theory, pain signals travel to the brain via the spinal cord and pass through a series of "invisible gates or doors" that can be opened or closed to reduce pain. When Manuel trips because of the uneven surface of the cobblestone street and hits his knee, he rubs the area around the injury. The sensations from rubbing his knee partially block pain signals allowing him to feel less pain.

Retroactive interference is a memory problem that occurs when recently learned information is in conflict with older information and prevents recall of that old information. Because Manuel practiced his Italian so much during the trip he finds that it is difficult to remember Spanish words for class when he returns home. The new Italian words are blocking his recall of previously learned Spanish vocabulary. While spending time in Italy, Manuel calls his parents on the phone and finds it difficult to remember the English word for goodbye because he has been using the newly learned Italian word for goodbye.

Ethnocentrism is a specific type of negative prejudice in which an individual favors their own culture or ethnic group's values, attitudes, and actions over other cultural groups. While visiting Italy Manuel is hesitant to try new foods because he has a negative prejudicial attitude about Italian food and believes American food is the best.

Answer Sheet

Section I

1. Ⓐ Ⓑ Ⓒ Ⓓ
2. Ⓐ Ⓑ Ⓒ Ⓓ
3. Ⓐ Ⓑ Ⓒ Ⓓ
4. Ⓐ Ⓑ Ⓒ Ⓓ
5. Ⓐ Ⓑ Ⓒ Ⓓ
6. Ⓐ Ⓑ Ⓒ Ⓓ
7. Ⓐ Ⓑ Ⓒ Ⓓ
8. Ⓐ Ⓑ Ⓒ Ⓓ
9. Ⓐ Ⓑ Ⓒ Ⓓ
10. Ⓐ Ⓑ Ⓒ Ⓓ
11. Ⓐ Ⓑ Ⓒ Ⓓ
12. Ⓐ Ⓑ Ⓒ Ⓓ
13. Ⓐ Ⓑ Ⓒ Ⓓ
14. Ⓐ Ⓑ Ⓒ Ⓓ
15. Ⓐ Ⓑ Ⓒ Ⓓ
16. Ⓐ Ⓑ Ⓒ Ⓓ
17. Ⓐ Ⓑ Ⓒ Ⓓ
18. Ⓐ Ⓑ Ⓒ Ⓓ
19. Ⓐ Ⓑ Ⓒ Ⓓ
20. Ⓐ Ⓑ Ⓒ Ⓓ
21. Ⓐ Ⓑ Ⓒ Ⓓ
22. Ⓐ Ⓑ Ⓒ Ⓓ
23. Ⓐ Ⓑ Ⓒ Ⓓ
24. Ⓐ Ⓑ Ⓒ Ⓓ
25. Ⓐ Ⓑ Ⓒ Ⓓ
26. Ⓐ Ⓑ Ⓒ Ⓓ
27. Ⓐ Ⓑ Ⓒ Ⓓ
28. Ⓐ Ⓑ Ⓒ Ⓓ
29. Ⓐ Ⓑ Ⓒ Ⓓ
30. Ⓐ Ⓑ Ⓒ Ⓓ
31. Ⓐ Ⓑ Ⓒ Ⓓ
32. Ⓐ Ⓑ Ⓒ Ⓓ
33. Ⓐ Ⓑ Ⓒ Ⓓ
34. Ⓐ Ⓑ Ⓒ Ⓓ

35. Ⓐ Ⓑ Ⓒ Ⓓ
36. Ⓐ Ⓑ Ⓒ Ⓓ
37. Ⓐ Ⓑ Ⓒ Ⓓ
38. Ⓐ Ⓑ Ⓒ Ⓓ
39. Ⓐ Ⓑ Ⓒ Ⓓ
40. Ⓐ Ⓑ Ⓒ Ⓓ
41. Ⓐ Ⓑ Ⓒ Ⓓ
42. Ⓐ Ⓑ Ⓒ Ⓓ
43. Ⓐ Ⓑ Ⓒ Ⓓ
44. Ⓐ Ⓑ Ⓒ Ⓓ
45. Ⓐ Ⓑ Ⓒ Ⓓ
46. Ⓐ Ⓑ Ⓒ Ⓓ
47. Ⓐ Ⓑ Ⓒ Ⓓ
48. Ⓐ Ⓑ Ⓒ Ⓓ
49. Ⓐ Ⓑ Ⓒ Ⓓ
50. Ⓐ Ⓑ Ⓒ Ⓓ
51. Ⓐ Ⓑ Ⓒ Ⓓ
52. Ⓐ Ⓑ Ⓒ Ⓓ
53. Ⓐ Ⓑ Ⓒ Ⓓ
54. Ⓐ Ⓑ Ⓒ Ⓓ
55. Ⓐ Ⓑ Ⓒ Ⓓ
56. Ⓐ Ⓑ Ⓒ Ⓓ
57. Ⓐ Ⓑ Ⓒ Ⓓ
58. Ⓐ Ⓑ Ⓒ Ⓓ
59. Ⓐ Ⓑ Ⓒ Ⓓ
60. Ⓐ Ⓑ Ⓒ Ⓓ
61. Ⓐ Ⓑ Ⓒ Ⓓ
62. Ⓐ Ⓑ Ⓒ Ⓓ
63. Ⓐ Ⓑ Ⓒ Ⓓ
64. Ⓐ Ⓑ Ⓒ Ⓓ
65. Ⓐ Ⓑ Ⓒ Ⓓ
66. Ⓐ Ⓑ Ⓒ Ⓓ
67. Ⓐ Ⓑ Ⓒ Ⓓ
68. Ⓐ Ⓑ Ⓒ Ⓓ

69. Ⓐ Ⓑ Ⓒ Ⓓ
70. Ⓐ Ⓑ Ⓒ Ⓓ
71. Ⓐ Ⓑ Ⓒ Ⓓ
72. Ⓐ Ⓑ Ⓒ Ⓓ
73. Ⓐ Ⓑ Ⓒ Ⓓ
74. Ⓐ Ⓑ Ⓒ Ⓓ
75. Ⓐ Ⓑ Ⓒ Ⓓ
76. Ⓐ Ⓑ Ⓒ Ⓓ
77. Ⓐ Ⓑ Ⓒ Ⓓ
78. Ⓐ Ⓑ Ⓒ Ⓓ
79. Ⓐ Ⓑ Ⓒ Ⓓ
80. Ⓐ Ⓑ Ⓒ Ⓓ
81. Ⓐ Ⓑ Ⓒ Ⓓ
82. Ⓐ Ⓑ Ⓒ Ⓓ
83. Ⓐ Ⓑ Ⓒ Ⓓ
84. Ⓐ Ⓑ Ⓒ Ⓓ
85. Ⓐ Ⓑ Ⓒ Ⓓ
86. Ⓐ Ⓑ Ⓒ Ⓓ
87. Ⓐ Ⓑ Ⓒ Ⓓ
88. Ⓐ Ⓑ Ⓒ Ⓓ
89. Ⓐ Ⓑ Ⓒ Ⓓ
90. Ⓐ Ⓑ Ⓒ Ⓓ
91. Ⓐ Ⓑ Ⓒ Ⓓ
92. Ⓐ Ⓑ Ⓒ Ⓓ
93. Ⓐ Ⓑ Ⓒ Ⓓ
94. Ⓐ Ⓑ Ⓒ Ⓓ
95. Ⓐ Ⓑ Ⓒ Ⓓ
96. Ⓐ Ⓑ Ⓒ Ⓓ
97. Ⓐ Ⓑ Ⓒ Ⓓ
98. Ⓐ Ⓑ Ⓒ Ⓓ
99. Ⓐ Ⓑ Ⓒ Ⓓ
100. Ⓐ Ⓑ Ⓒ Ⓓ

Glossary: Major Figures in Psychology

Adler, Alfred Neo-Freudian who focused on how social interactions and conscious thought influenced individual growth. He is known for his work on the inferiority complex, striving for superiority, and birth order. See Chapter 12.

Ainsworth, Mary Investigated different types of attachment through the use of the Strange Situation. Infants could be classified as having a secure or insecure attachment. See Chapter 11.

Allport, Gordon Trait theorist who described all traits as falling into three categories: cardinal, central, and secondary. See Chapter 12.

Asch, Solomon Known for his contributions to social psychology, in particular his famous line study that investigated the concept of conformity. See Chapter 16.

Bandura, Albert Known for his work on learning and personality theory. He conducted research on social learning, modeling, and observational learning of aggressive behavior with the famous Bobo doll experiment. See Chapter 8. He is also known for the social cognitive theory of personality, which explains how personal characteristics, social interactions, and cognitive evaluations are involved in developing an individual's personality. Important contributions from Bandura's research include reciprocal determinism and self-efficacy. See Chapter 12.

Baumrind, Diana Known for her research on parenting styles. Her original research described three different types of parenting styles: authoritarian, permissive, and authoritative. See Chapter 11.

Beck, Aaron Psychiatrist who developed an influential cognitive therapy based on the use of cognitive restructuring to replace irrational beliefs and negative thought processes that were causing maladaptive behaviors. Beck's research was especially influential in the treatment of depression. Important contributions from Beck's research include cognitive restructuring, the cognitive triad, and effective cognitive therapy for depression. See Chapter 15.

Binet, Alfred French psychologist who created the first intelligence test used to evaluate mental abilities. Binet introduced a new concept: mental age, or the score on an IQ test that indicates the typical age group an individual's score represents. Mental age provided a framework for comparing individuals, and Binet inferred that children with cognitive disabilities would have scores more typical of a child who was younger. See Chapter 13.

Broca, Paul French physician who discovered that a specific type of aphasia was the result of damage to a particular area of the brain. The area of the brain he discovered that was responsible for language production is now called Broca's area and damage to this area is referred to as Broca's aphasia. See Chapter 5.

Calkins, Mary Whiton Student of William James who developed an important technique for studying memory. Despite being denied the PhD she earned from Harvard because of her gender, Mary Whiton Calkins became the first female president of the American Psychological Association. See Chapter 3.

Chomsky, Noam Linguist known for his nativist (nature) approach to the acquisition of language. Chomsky stresses that humans have a biological predisposition to develop language. His theories are in direct conflict with those offered by B.F. Skinner, who believed that language is learned (nurture). Important contributions from Chomsky's research include the language acquisition device (LAD) and universal grammar. See Chapter 9.

Costa, Paul and McCrae, Robert Known for their work on the Big Five personality model, which includes openness, conscientiousness, extraversion, agreeableness, and neuroticism. See Chapter 12.

Darwin, Charles British naturalist known for his theory of evolution and natural selection. He believed that traits and behaviors exist in humans because these attributes allowed our ancestors to adapt, survive, and reproduce. Darwin's theories have heavily influenced the perspective of evolutionary psychology. See Chapter 5.

Dix, Dorothea American reformer who fought to establish legal protection for individuals with mental illness and create state mental hospitals with humane treatment in what was called the moral treatment movement. See Chapter 15.

Ebbinghaus, Hermann German psychologist most notable for his work on forgetting. Ebbinghaus studied how much individuals forgot over time and what types of techniques could be utilized to reduce forgetting. Important terms associated with Ebbinghaus include *nonsense syllables* and the *forgetting curve*. See Chapter 9.

Ellis, Albert American psychologist known for the development of rational-emotive behavioral therapy (REBT), a type of cognitive behavioral therapy that involves the identification and replacement of irrational beliefs and the use of behavioral techniques to create new, more adaptive responses. Important contributions from Ellis's research include REBT and the ABC model for explaining how irrational beliefs lead to psychological problems. See Chapter 15.

Erikson, Erik Neo-Freudian who created an influential psychosocial stage theory of personality that explains how individuals develop through social interaction with others across the lifespan. Unlike Freud, Erikson believed that development continued throughout life rather than ending at about age five or six. Erikson divides his theory of psychosocial development into eight stages ranging from birth to old age. See Chapters 11 and 12.

Fechner, Gustav German physician and philosopher who trained in both medicine and mathematics and made an enormous contribution to the specialty of psychology known as psychophysics. Psychophysics studies how physical stimuli (sensations) translate to psychological experiences (perceptions). Fechner created scientific methods to study sensation and perception that are still in use today. See Chapter 6.

Festinger, Leon Known for his contributions to social psychology including research on conformity and cognitive dissonance. Cognitive dissonance is the state of psychological tension, anxiety, and discomfort that occurs when an individual's attitude and behavior are inconsistent, which motivates a change in attitude or behavior to reduce the discomfort. See Chapter 16.

Freud, Sigmund Founder of the psychoanalytic school of thought who emphasized the role of unconscious conflicts and early childhood experiences in determining behavior and personality. He was the first major psychologist to consider dreams meaningful and published his findings in his famous book *The Interpretation of Dreams*. See Chapters 3, 7, 12, and 15.

Galton, Francis Cousin of Darwin and pioneer in psychometrics who introduced the idea that intelligence was hereditary because intelligent individuals often had intelligent children. As a nativist, Galton examined differences in inherited intelligence by utilizing statistical methods. Galton developed the statistical measurement of correlation. See Chapter 13.

Garcia, John Psychologist known for his research regarding conditioned taste aversions, which involve an organism learning to avoid a particular food item or liquid after it becomes associated with nausea. Taste aversions were first discovered when Garcia and colleagues noticed that rats that had received radiation treatment in their cage were avoiding their water bottles. A taste aversion is sometimes referred to as the Garcia effect. Research conducted by Garcia provides evidence for the influence of evolution on learning because organisms are predisposed to make certain associations such as taste aversions rapidly because they aid in survival, a phenomenon called biological preparedness. See Chapter 8.

Gardner, Howard Known for his multiple intelligence theory consisting of specific intelligences that exist independently of each other. Currently there are eight multiple intelligences including verbal-linguistic, logical-mathematical, spatial, musical, bodily-kinesthetic, interpersonal, intrapersonal, and naturalist, with the possibility of more to come. See Chapter 13.

Gazzaniga, Michael Researcher whose work with split-brain patients was a continuation of the work of Nobel Prize-winning psychologist Roger Sperry. Gazzaniga's work illustrates differences in hemispheric lateralization, especially with regard to language and communication between the left and the right hemispheres. See Chapter 5.

Gilligan, Carol Known for developing a theory for how moral development differed between males and females. She created her theory in response to Kohlberg's theory, which she believed was biased against women. The highest level of morality for women, according to Gilligan, is based on compassion and concern for others, which she believed contrasted with the male emphasis on individual rights and justice. See Chapter 11.

Hall, G. Stanley Influential in the rapid growth of psychology in the United States. Hall opened the first psychology lab in the United States and started the first American psychology journal. Additionally, he helped found the American Psychological Association (APA) and served as its first president. See Chapter 3.

Harlow, Harry Known for his work with baby rhesus monkeys that were raised in cages with no live mother, only two artificial ones. Harlow's research is important because it demonstrated scientifically that attachments between infants and caregivers are impacted by the need for contact comfort as well as nourishment and other basic needs. See Chapter 11.

Hilgard, Ernest Known for research on learning, hypnosis, and pain. He theorized that hypnosis is a state of dissociation or divided consciousness in which awareness splits into two distinct states that happen concurrently. According to Hilgard, one of the two states of consciousness reacts to the suggestions of the hypnotist while the other, from the background, monitors behavior and processes information not available to the part of the mind responding to the hypnotist. See Chapter 7.

Hubel, David and Wiesel, Torsten Known for the discovery of feature detectors in the brain for which they received the Nobel Prize. Hubel and Wiesel investigated how specific neurons in the brains of cats reacted when black and white geometric drawings were presented to the visual fields of the animals. The results showed that individual neurons were specialized to respond to only certain features or aspects of an image. See Chapter 6.

James, William American psychologist who played a key role in the development of the perspective of functionalism and the growth of American psychology. James published the first textbook of psychology, *The Principles of Psychology*. James was one of the first psychologists to examine the nature of consciousness and spoke of a stream of consciousness in which consciousness was a continuous and constantly changing flow of feelings, sensations, and thoughts. The James–Lange theory of emotion, named in part for William James, asserts that the individual's perception of his or her physical reactions creates emotions. According to this theory, the emotional experience occurs after the bodily change and as a result of it. See Chapters 3, 7, and 10.

Jones, Mary Cover Utilized the methods developed by Watson to reduce fear in a young patient named Little Peter who was afraid of rabbits by pairing a positive stimulus (cookie) with the rabbit each time the rabbit was placed closer to the boy, until Little Peter was no longer fearful of rabbits. This was considered to be the first example of what is now known as counterconditioning, a common behavior therapy. See Chapter 8.

Jung, Carl One of the most influential neo-Freudians who found it difficult to accept that sexual motives were the chief force driving human behavior. Jung was interested in the spirit and is known for his work regarding the personal unconscious, collective unconscious, archetypes, and introversion–extroversion. See Chapter 12.

Kinsey, Alfred Known for his research regarding human sexuality. He and his colleagues conducted surveys with thousands of American men and women asking about their sexual behaviors. Kinsey's controversial research provided statistics and increased the public and scientific understanding of sexual behavior. See Chapter 10.

Kohlberg, Lawrence Extended the research on moral development started by Piaget by creating a more comprehensive theoretical stage theory. Kohlberg believed that morality is a decision-making process and not a fixed set of behaviors and investigated that how this process develops with the use of moral dilemmas. His theory of moral development consists of three levels of morality: preconventional, conventional, and postconventional. See Chapter 11.

Kohler, Wolfgang Gestalt psychologist who investigated insight learning by presenting chimps with a problem of attaining a banana that was just outside of their reach and supplying the animals with various objects to use as potential tools. In one example, sticks were provided in the cage as possible tools for the chimps to use in order to reach the banana. At first, the chimps would try to reach the banana with their hands, sit for a while, and then suddenly connect the sticks together to reach their prize. See Chapter 8.

Locke, John British philosopher who agreed with Aristotle that ideas were not innate; presented the idea of the mind as a blank slate or tabula rasa at birth. See Chapter 3.

Loftus, Elizabeth Cognitive psychologist who demonstrated that memory is not as accurate as we believe it is and that eyewitness testimony is unreliable because false memories or confabulations can be created easily through suggestion. She conducted classic research on the misinformation effect with the famous car crash experiment that showed that the way a question is worded can alter a person's memory. See Chapter 9.

Lorenz, Konrad Studied the formation of attachments in newborn baby chicks. Interestingly, Lorenz discovered that baby chicks would form an attachment with him as their primary caregiver if he was the first moving stimulus they saw. Through his research, Lorenz made important contributions to the field of ethology or the scientific study of a particular behavior among a variety of animals including humans. Lorenz studied both imprinting and aggression. See Chapter 11.

Marcia, James Known for research on adolescent identity. His theory proposed adolescents occupy one or more of four statuses (states) at least temporarily as they work to develop various aspects of their identities. Each of the four statuses results from a combination of the adolescent's degree of commitment and whether or not exploration of an identity is taking place (crisis). See Chapter 11.

Maslow, Abraham Humanist psychologist known for emphasizing healthy behavior. His hierarchy of needs theory of motivation arranges in order of importance a total of five needs including physiological, safety, belonging and love, esteem, and self-actualization. In this stage model of motivation, the needs at the bottom of the pyramid take precedence over the others. See Chapter 10.

McCrae, Robert and Costa, Paul Known for their work on the Big Five personality model that includes the traits of openness, conscientiousness, extraversion, agreeableness, and neuroticism. See Chapter 12.

Milgram, Stanley Known for his contributions to social psychology and his famous, but controversial shock experiment. He discovered that the average American would, under the direction of a legitimate authority figure, give what they believed were severe shocks to other people in an experimental setting. The suffering of participants in Milgram's shock experiment influenced ethical guidelines for research. See Chapter 16.

Miller, George A. Known for discovering that the capacity for short-term memory was seven plus or minus two pieces of information. Miller referred to seven as the magic number for short-term memory. See Chapter 9.

Pavlov, Ivan Russian physiologist who was awarded the Nobel Prize in medicine and physiology for his investigation of the key components of classical conditioning with dogs. See Chapter 8.

Piaget, Jean Swiss psychologist and major theorist associated with cognitive development who established an influential theory about how thinking develops in children. Piaget believed that the cognitive processes of children were dramatically different than those of adults and that a series of stages have led to the acquisition of adult intellectual abilities. Piaget's cognitive development theory has four stages including sensorimotor, preoperational, concrete operational, and formal operational. See Chapter 11.

Pinel, Philippe Vital figure in the movement for humanitarian treatment of the mentally ill inside of asylums because he believed in the possibility of improvement or recovery by treating the mentally ill with dignity and respect. See Chapter 15.

Rescorla, Robert Developed the contingency model of learning and added a cognitive component to classical conditioning based on prediction and expectations. Stimuli that are more consistently paired are more predictable and therefore generate stronger responses. According to Rescorla, cognitive expectations guide learning. See Chapter 8.

Rogers, Carl Humanist who developed client-centered therapy, also called person-centered therapy, based on the idea that all individuals are capable and motivated to grow with guidance provided by a caring therapist. He believed that self-concept was at the heart of individual personality. Important contributions from Rogers' work include client-centered therapy, congruence, active listening, and unconditional positive regard. See Chapters 12 and 15.

Rosenhan, David Known for a famous study that investigated the power and danger of labels. Rosenhan and others gained admittance to psychiatric hospitals by faking the complaint of hearing voices. The pseudopatients were admitted to a facility with the diagnosis of schizophrenia or manic depression based on only this one symptom. After being admitted, they proceeded to act normal and informed the staff that the voices they had been hearing were gone. On average, the patients stayed for three weeks and upon release they were provided with a diagnosis of schizophrenia in remission. See Chapter 14.

Ross, Elizabeth Kübler Proposed the concept of the five stages of grief, including denial, anger, bargaining, depression, and acceptance. She was instrumental in bringing the hospice movement to the United States. See Chapter 11.

Rotter, Jullian Investigated how differences in personality were related to an individual's perceived control over the environment, which he called the locus of control. See Chapter 12.

Seligman, Martin Cognitive psychologist who investigated learned helplessness in animals and theorized about how this concept contributes to depression. See Chapters 8 and 14.

Selye, Hans Known for his research regarding chronic stress. He discovered that when a person undergoes great emotional stress the body will go through a three-stage physical response collectively called the general adaptation syndrome. The three stages include alarm reaction, resistance, and exhaustion. See Chapter 10.

Skinner, B.F. American behaviorist and influential researcher in the area of operant conditioning, which involves how organisms learn voluntary responses. Skinner stressed that reinforcements and punishments influenced future behavior and that free will was an illusion. He created the operant chamber (Skinner box) for studying operant learning concepts in animals. See Chapter 8.

Spearman, Charles Created the two-factor theory of intelligence that comprised both a general factor (g-factor) that represents an individual's overall ability and several other specific abilities (s-factors) that are needed for certain types of cognitive tasks. Spearman believed that the g-factor was of greater importance and was the best predictor of intellectual ability. See Chapter 13.

Sperry, Roger Nobel Prize-winning neuroscientist whose work with split-brain patients illustrated differences in hemispheric lateralization, especially with regard to language. See Chapter 5.

Sternberg, Robert Known for his triarchic theory of intelligence that identifies three sets of mental abilities including practical, analytical, and creative intelligence. Sternberg also created the triangular theory of love, which includes several types of love resulting from various combinations of three main components: passion, intimacy, and commitment. A tip to remember Sternberg's two theories is the acronym PIC PAC. PIC refers to the love theory (passion, intimacy, and commitment) and PAC refers to the intelligence theory (practical, analytical, and creative). See Chapters 13 and 16.

Terman, Lewis Stanford University psychologist who translated and revised the original intelligence test created by Binet for use in the United States. The intelligence test is now known as the Stanford-Binet Intelligence Scale. He also conducted a well-known longitudinal study of gifted children possessing IQ scores greater than 140 that he sometimes referred to as Terman's Termites. See Chapter 13.

Thorndike, Edward Known for his research regarding animal learning. He developed instrumental learning by observing the law of effect in cats as they learned how to escape from puzzle boxes. See Chapter 8.

Titchener, Edward Created the first theoretical perspective in psychology, structuralism, based on Wundt's work. He studied consciousness through the use of the technique of introspection. Titchener brought psychology to the United States by starting his own psychology research lab at Cornell University. See Chapter 3.

Tolman, Edward Cognitive psychologist who was one of the first to investigate the role of cognitive processes in operant conditioning, challenging the viewpoint of strict behaviorists like B.F. Skinner. He conducted research on how cognition impacted learning in animals and developed the concepts of latent learning and cognitive maps. Tolman explored the thinking process that occurred between the stimulus–response patterns in animals by recording how long it took rats to master a maze under three different conditions over seventeen days worth of trials. See Chapter 8.

Vygotsky, Lev Russian psychologist who proposed the sociocultural theory of cognitive development. His theory emphasized the combined influences of language, culture, and interactions with others on a child's cognitive development. Important contributions from Vygotsky's research include the concepts of internalized speech and the zone of proximal development. See Chapter 11.

Washburn, Margaret Floy First woman to formally earn a PhD in psychology under Edward Titchener. She did significant research on animal behavior and greatly influenced the emerging perspective of behaviorism. See Chapter 3.

Watson, John B. American psychologist and the father of behaviorism. Watson rejected introspection, believing instead that psychology should only study observable, measurable behaviors that were the product of stimuli (events in one's environment). Watson's research focused on how classical conditioning worked in humans, especially the development of classically conditioned fears with his famous study involving Little Albert. See Chapter 8.

Weber, Ernst Psychophysicist whose work helped to create Weber's law, a formula for determining the just noticeable difference. Weber's law states that the minimum amount of change needed to create a just noticeable difference is a constant percentage of the original stimulus. Weber discovered that larger stimuli require greater increases in intensity for a difference to be noticed. See Chapter 6.

Wechsler, David Criticized the Stanford-Binet scale because it was too heavily focused on verbal skills. Wechsler designed a set of intelligence tests that were capable of measuring cognitive skills and evaluating individuals with lower verbal abilities for overall intelligence. See Chapter 13.

Wernicke, Carl German physician who discovered the region typically in the left temporal lobe responsible for language comprehension. See Chapter 5.

Wiesel, Torsten and Hubel, David Known for the discovery of feature detectors in the brain for which they received the Nobel Prize. Hubel and Wiesel investigated how specific neurons in the brains of cats reacted when black and white geometric drawings were presented to the visual fields of the animals. The results showed that individual neurons were specialized to respond to only certain features or aspects of an image. See Chapter 6.

Wolpe, Joseph Known for developing the behavioral treatment of systematic desensitization, which involves a step-by-step classical conditioning in which an anxiety-producing stimulus is paired with relaxation. The goal of the therapy is to replace the anxiety response with one of relaxation based on the theory that it is not possible to experience these two opposite responses simultaneously. See Chapter 15.

Wundt, Wilhelm German scientist known by some as the father of psychology. He established the first laboratory solely devoted to the scientific study of psychology in Leipzig, Germany. To analyze mental elements, Wundt used an experimental method called introspection that involved having subjects report the contents of their own mind as objectively as possible. This work led to the psychological perspective known as structuralism formally introduced by Edward Titchener. See Chapter 3.

Zimbardo, Phillip Known for his famous and controversial Stanford Prison Study, Zimbardo investigated the power of social roles and the impact of the situation on behavior. Twenty-four male college students were selected to participate in a study located in a mock prison, constructed in the basement of Stanford University. See Chapter 16.

Glossary: Psychology Terms

Absolute threshold The minimum intensity at which a stimulus can be detected at least 50 percent of the time.

Accommodation (1) according to Piaget, the process of adjusting old schemas to incorporate new information; (2) the process in which the lens in the eye changes shape either by flattening or by curving to focus an image on the retina.

Acetylcholine (ACh) A neurotransmitter involved in memory and movement. Low levels of acetylcholine are associated with Alzheimer's disease.

Achievement motivation The drive to succeed, especially in competition with others. Individuals who have a strong need for achievement most often seek out tasks that are moderately difficult.

Achievement test An assessment device created for the purpose of determining the level of knowledge an individual has regarding a particular subject or skill that has resulted from learning.

Acquisition The initial process of learning in either classical or operant conditioning.

Action potential The nerve impulse; a brief electrical charge that travels down the axon, section by section, to the terminal buttons where neurotransmitters are released into the synapse.

Activation–synthesis model The theory that states that dreams are merely the result of the forebrain attempting to interpret the stimulation it is receiving during sleep from areas in the lower brain. Also called activation-synthesis hypothesis.

Actor–observer bias The tendency to explain the behavior of others with dispositional attributions (FAE), but attribute one's own behavior as the actor to situational factors. This is due to the greater awareness one has about how his or her own behavior can vary from one situation to another. Also called actor-observer effect.

Additive color mixing The addition of light waves to produce color. When all the additive primary colors of light (red, green, and blue) are mixed together, the resulting color is white or the reflection of all colors of light.

Adolescent egocentrism The tendency teenagers have to view the world only from their own perspective, which includes both the imaginary audience and the personal fable.

Adrenal glands The endocrine glands located above the kidneys that are controlled by the sympathetic nervous system's fight-or-flight response, which increases heart rate, blood pressure, and glucose levels to respond to a threat. The adrenal glands control the release of the hormones cortisol, epinephrine (adrenaline), and norepinephrine (noradrenaline).

Adrenaline A substance produced by the adrenal glands, which is related to increases in general arousal. Also called epinephrine.

Afferent neurons The nerve cells that transfer information from the sense organs to the central nervous system for analysis. Also called sensory neurons.

Affiliation motivation The human need to belong and form attachments with others.

Afterimages A misperception that lingers after the visual stimulus is removed. A positive afterimage is viewed in the same color as the original stimulus. A negative afterimage is viewed in the opposite color than the original stimulus and is used as evidence for the opponent-process theory of color vision.

Aggression Any action, verbal or physical, meant to hurt others.

Agonist A drug that works by either blocking reuptake or mimicking the natural neurotransmitters by fitting into receptor sites on the postsynaptic neuron.

Agoraphobia Axis I anxiety disorder that involves the fear of public places and open spaces due to the worry that one would not be able to escape.

Algorithm A logical, step-by-step procedure that, if followed correctly, will guarantee a solution.

All or none principle The law that the axon of a neuron will fire either with full strength (100 percent) or not at all to a stimulus, regardless of its intensity, provided the stimulus is at least at the threshold value.

Alternate-forms reliability A method used for determining if a test is reliable (repeatable) by comparing two equivalent versions of a test to determine if they produce consistent results. High positive correlations between two comparable versions indicate alternate-forms reliability.

Altruism A selfless concern for others or an action taken by an individual to help others that involves risk or personal cost without providing any incentives or personal benefits.

Alzheimer's disease An irreversible neurological brain disorder involving the deterioration of neurons producing acetylcholine.

Amygdala Two almond-shaped structures in the limbic system linked to the regulation of emotional responses, especially fear and aggression.

Anal stage The second stage in Freud's psychosexual development theory in which the libido is focused on controlling bowel movements; occurs at approximately two years of age.

Anchoring bias A cognitive error that leads an individual to place too great of an emphasis on an initial estimate when making decisions under conditions in which one is unsure.

Androgens A class of hormones including male sex hormones such as testosterone, produced mainly by the testes and to a small extent by ovaries and the adrenal cortex.

Androgyny The development of a gender identity that incorporates both male and female traits.

Animism The belief that all objects are living and capable of actions and emotions typical of Piaget's preoperational stage of cognitive development.

Anorexia nervosa An eating disorder characterized by the fear of gaining weight, distorted body image, and self-starvation. A diagnosis of anorexia typically involves individuals that weigh less than 85 percent of their normal weight.

Antagonist A drug that works by occupying the receptor sites on the postsynaptic neuron and blocking the transmission of neurotransmitters.

Anterograde amnesia The inability to retain memories for events after the injury or disease that resulted in amnesia.

Antianxiety medications A category of psychotropic drugs prescribed for a variety of anxiety disorders to help decrease anxiety and tension. The common categories include barbiturates and benzodiazepines. Also called anxiolytics.

Antidepressant medications A category of psychotropic drugs prescribed for a variety of mood and other psychological disorders. The common categories include MAOIs, tricyclics, and SSRIs.

Antipsychotic medications A category of psychotropic drugs prescribed to control symptoms of psychotic disorders by lowering the patient's motor activity and reducing the occurrence of delusions and hallucinations. The common categories include conventional (typical) and atypical.

Antisocial personality disorder Axis II personality disorder characterized by individuals that violate the rights of others, are impulsive, and lack a conscious. This is the personality disorder most closely associated with criminal behavior. Individuals must be at least eighteen years of age to receive this diagnosis and exhibit similar behavior in childhood. Individuals with this diagnosis were formerly called sociopaths.

Anxiolytic medications See *antianxiety medications.*

Aphasia A neurological condition in which brain damage from disease or injury to the portions of the brain responsible for language produce difficulties in communication.

Applied research The psychological research that utilizes descriptive, correlational, and experimental designs to positively influence behavior and solve real-world problems.

Approach–approach conflict A situation where an individual is forced to make a choice between two equally desirable goals. Both options are appealing, which makes the choice difficult.

Approach–avoidance conflict A situation where an individual is both attracted to and repelled by the *same* goal. Within one particular situation, there are both good and bad aspects.

Aptitude test An assessment device that is designed to predict the success of an individual by evaluating their level of skill on a variety of general abilities necessary for success in academic or career environments.

Archetypes According to Jung, the images that comprise the collective unconscious and allow individuals to respond universally to particular situations.

Assimilation According to Piaget, the process of trying to fit new information into an existing schema.

Association areas The portions of the cerebral cortex that are not devoted to motor or sensory functions and are instead responsible for higher level thinking processes including language and reasoning.

Atkinson–Shiffrin model of memory An influential information processing model that explains memory as a sequential process that moves through three distinct stages: sensory memory, short-term memory, and long-term memory.

Attachment The long-lasting emotional bond that develops between the infant and the caregiver that provides the child with a sense of security and comfort.

Attention-deficit/hyperactive disorder (ADHD) A developmental disorder typically diagnosed in childhood that is characterized by difficulty in focusing on tasks or the tendency to be overly active and impulsive, leading to difficulties in functioning within school, work, or social situations.

Attitude A person's belief about another person, object, or situation. Each attitude consists of a cognition (belief), affect (feeling), and behavior (action).

Attribution An explanation created by an individual for his or her own behavior or the behavior of others.

Atypical antipsychotic medications The newer antipsychotic medications that have fewer side effects and are more effective at treating both positive and negative symptoms than conventional antipsychotics.

Audition A synonym for the sense of hearing.

Authoritarian parenting According to Baumrind, the parenting style in which the parent demands obedience and controls the child's behavior through punishment. There is limited communication between the parent and the child and the parent offers the child limited love and warmth.

Authoritative parenting According to Baumrind, the parenting style in which the parent establishes clear limits and provides explanations for consequences. There is open communication between the parent and the child, but the parent makes the ultimate decision. This collaborative parenting style offers the child love and warmth.

Autistic spectrum disorder A range of developmental disorders that are diagnosed in childhood, including Autism and Asperger's syndrome, that often involve impaired social communication.

Autonomic nervous system (ANS) The branch of the peripheral nervous system that consists of the nerves that control automatic bodily functions by integrating the central nervous system with the organs and glands. It is divided into the sympathetic and parasympathetic systems.

Availability heuristic A shortcut for judging the likelihood that an event will happen in terms of how readily it comes to mind based on either personal experience or exposure through the media.

Aversive conditioning A variant of counterconditioning that attempts to change or remove a negative behavior by attaching a negative experience or emotion to the stimuli. Also called aversion therapy.

Aversive condition A situation—such as crowding, pain, foul odors, and high temperatures—that makes aggression more likely.

Aversive stimulus A factor that is negative or unpleasant and often results in avoidance or escape behaviors.

Avoidance conditioning A type of learning where an organism determines how to prevent an aversive stimulus from being introduced in the first place.

Avoidance–avoidance conflict A situation where an individual is forced to make a choice between two equally undesirable or threatening options. Neither choice is good so the individual is essentially choosing the lesser of two evils.

Avoidant personality disorder Axis II personality disorder characterized by individuals who are excessively shy and uncomfortable in social situations due to a fear of rejection or being evaluated negatively.

Axon The long tube-like extension attached to the cell body that sends the electrical message (action potential) away from the cell body of the neuron.

Babinski reflex An automatic response shown by newborns when the soles of their feet are touched that involves stretching their toes outward. This reflex disappears within approximately one year.

Backward conditioning A classical conditioning acquisition procedure in which the unconditioned stimulus is presented before the neutral stimulus. This method is not considered effective for conditioning.

Barnum effect The tendency individuals have to agree with descriptions they are given of themselves that are generally positive, but also unclear or ambiguous.

Basic anxiety According to Horney, the feelings of helplessness, loneliness, and fear created by the fact that a child is alone in a hostile world.

Basic research The psychological research that investigates answers to scientific questions and expands the overall information base of psychology.

Basilar membrane The membrane that runs down the center of the cochlea located in the inner ear. The sound waves cause the cilia (hair cells) located on the organ of Corti supported by the basilar membrane to bend initiating the process of transduction.

Behavior therapy Use of techniques designed to change unwanted behaviors and increase the frequency of positive behaviors. Classical, operant, and observational learning may be utilized. Also called behavior modification.

Behavioral genetics The scientific discipline that attempts to integrate the influences of heredity, environment, and evolution in terms of their effect on human behavior.

Behavioral perspective A psychological perspective that focuses on how human behavior is shaped by environmental influences and learning.

Behaviorism A perspective in psychology founded by John B. Watson, which studied observable, measurable stimuli and responses only, without reference to consciousness or cognition.

Belief bias An error in thinking in which individuals are more likely to agree with conclusions that match with their existing opinions rather than conclusions appearing to be logically valid.

Belief perseverance The tendency to hold onto an assumption or belief even after it has been disproven.

Benzodiazepines A category of antianxiety medications that are prescribed to assist patients as a sleep aid, tension reducer, or muscle relaxant. Examples include *Librium (chlordiazepoxide)* and *Valium (diazepam).*

Big Five personality model The common personality traits identified by Costa and McCrae that include openness, conscientiousness, extraversion, agreeableness, and neuroticism.

Binocular cues The specific cues or aids for determining distance that require two eyes. Examples include retinal (binocular) disparity and convergence.

Biofeedback A method that involves the use of a device to reveal physiological responses that are usually difficult to observe such as changes in heart rate, respiration, EEG activity, or similar responses in order to enable individuals to achieve some degree of control over their responses. Biofeedback is often used in behavior therapy as a method for teaching individuals to gain control over their physiological states in order to reduce anxiety and its symptoms.

Biological constraints The theory that biology sets limits regarding what an animal is capable of learning. The rate and strength of conditioning is dependent upon if the conditioned stimulus can create a natural association for the organism.

Biological perspective A psychological perspective that focuses on explaining human behaviors, emotions, and mental processes as having physiological or genetic causes. Biological psychology covers a wide range of study including genetics, the brain, the nervous system, and the endocrine system.

Biological preparedness A biological predisposition of organisms to learn certain behaviors easier because they have a tendency to pair particular stimuli together over others.

Biological rhythms The physiological and behavioral changes that occur in predictable patterns controlled by an internal clock. Examples include circadian rhythms and annual rhythms.

Biological therapy The treatment of psychological illnesses through the use of medications and other medical treatments designed to influence behavior by altering bodily functions. Examples include psychotropic medications, psychosurgery, and electroconvulsive therapy (ECT). Also called biomedical therapy.

Bipolar disorder Axis I mood disorder that involves periods of major depressive disorder and mania resulting in a significant impairment of physical, emotional, cognitive, and behavioral functioning. Formerly called manic depression.

Blind spot The gap within the field of vision that exists within each eye, which is caused by the optic disk or the place on the retina where the optic nerve leaves the eye.

Blood–brain barrier A network of tightly packed cells in the walls of capillaries that prevents many harmful substances, including poisons, from entering the brain and other parts of the central nervous system.

Borderline personality disorder Axis II personality disorder characterized by trouble maintaining relationships, unstable moods, impulsiveness, self-destructive behaviors, self-injury, and suicide.

Bottom-up processing The assembling of the basic elements of a stimulus in the brain to form a complete perception. For example, the visual system in the brain uses bottom-up processing by creating perceptions based on input from sensory receptors and feature detectors.

Broca's aphasia A neurological condition caused by damage to Broca's area in the left frontal lobe resulting in problems with speech production including pronunciation, speaking, writing, and coordinating the facial muscle movements required for speech. A type of expressive aphasia.

Bulimia nervosa An eating disorder marked by repeated episodes of binging and purging in which an individual takes in a large amount of calories in a single sitting (binging) and then eliminates the calories (purging), often through the use of vomiting, laxatives, or diuretics.

Bystander effect The tendency for individuals to be less likely to assist in an emergency situation when other people are present.

Cannon–Bard theory A theory of emotion that holds that bodily reactions do not cause emotional response; rather, the two occur simultaneously.

Cardinal dispositions According to Allport, the personality characteristics that influence almost all of a person's behavior and are so significant that these characteristics essentially define the person. Cardinal dispositions are not present in every individual and are especially rare. Also called cardinal traits.

Case study A descriptive research method that involves an in-depth examination of individuals or groups.

Catatonia A variety of psychomotor difficulties including immobility, lack of responsiveness, excitability, or the assuming of unusual physical postures. Catatonia is the main symptom associated with a diagnosis of catatonic schizophrenia.

Catatonic schizophrenia Axis I psychological disorder and subtype of schizophrenia characterized by severe disturbances in motor functions. Individuals typically alternate between immobility and wild excitement, but often one or the other type of motor symptoms predominate.

Catharsis hypothesis The psychoanalytic theory that states that individuals need to express aggression in order to release inner tension. Research does not support this theory and has actually shown the opposite to be true.

Central dispositions (traits) According to Allport, the personality characteristics that describe how a person behaves most of the time and dependably predict how individuals will act in a given situation.

Central nervous system (CNS) The nervous system consisting of all the neural cells and nerves making up the brain and spinal cord.

Central route of persuasion The basis for attitude change that focuses on the factual content of the message and the use of evidence and logical arguments. Individuals are persuaded based on the strength of the argument presented.

Central tendency The various statistical procedures that describe the typical or central score within a data set. There are three main ways to measure central tendency: mean, median, and mode.

Centration According to Piaget, an error in thinking that contributes to the inability of preoperational children to conserve and involves focusing (centering) on just one feature of a problem while ignoring other important aspects.

Cerebellum The hindbrain structure responsible for balance, coordination, fine motor movements, and procedural memory. Cerebellum literally means "little brain" and looks like a miniature brain attached to the brainstem.

Cerebral cortex A thin surface layer on the cerebral hemispheres that regulates most complex behavior, including sensations, motor control, and higher mental processes such as decision making. It is made up of gray-tinted cells and thus is sometimes called gray matter.

Cerebral hemispheres The nearly symmetrical left and right halves of the cerebral cortex. The left hemisphere often specializes in verbal and analytical functions. The right hemisphere typically focuses on nonverbal abilities such as art and music and visual recognition tasks.

Cerebrospinal fluid (CSF) The fluid that surrounds the brain and spinal cord and circulates through the ventricles or cavities found in the brain. CSF protects the central nervous system by providing additional cushion and removing toxins.

Cerebrum The largest and most highly developed area of the brain. It includes all of the brain except for the brainstem and cerebellum.

Chaining An operant conditioning method for teaching a complex series of behaviors where each response cues the next response.

Change blindness The failure to perceive a difference (change) in a particular stimulus that has occurred after there has been a disruption in the field of vision.

Chunking The grouping of related items into meaningful units that can increase the amount of material that can be held in short-term memory.

Circadian rhythm A specific type of biological rhythm in which a predictable pattern occurs over a twenty-four hour period. Circadian rhythms control the fluctuations of hormones, blood pressure, temperature, and wakefulness.

Classical conditioning A type of learning based on the pioneering work of Ivan Pavlov that involves pairing a previously neutral stimulus (NS) with an unconditioned stimulus (UCS) to generate a conditioned response (CR). Classical conditioning is based on involuntary responses that include reflexes. Also called Pavlovian or respondent conditioning.

Classification The ability of a child in Piaget's concrete operational stage to sort objects by a variety of common attributes.

Client-centered therapy Carl Rogers' humanist therapy emphasizing the client's natural tendency to become healthy and productive. Key techniques include empathy, unconditional positive regard, and active listening.

Clinical psychologist A psychologist that works with the diagnosis and treatment of mental illnesses. Clinical psychologists have a doctoral degree such as a PhD or PsyD and complete specialized training and state licensure.

Closure A Gestalt principle of filling in missing portions of incomplete figures or other stimuli to form a completed whole or group.

Cocaine A very powerful stimulant that produces a euphoric "high" lasting approximately ten to thirty minutes followed by a crash characterized by cravings and withdrawal.

Cochlea The coiled, snail-shaped structure in the inner ear containing cilia or hair cell receptors for transduction in audition (hearing).

Cochlear implant An electronic device that converts sound waves into electrical signals and works by taking over the function of the hair cells directly stimulating the auditory nerve. Cochlear implants are used for individuals with severe sensorineural hearing loss.

Cocktail party effect The ability to focus attention on one voice while ignoring all other noises. However, information that is of special interest (such as your name) will most likely be noticed.

Cognition The various mental processes studied in psychology that can be translated simply to mean thinking.

Cognitive behavioral therapy (CBT) Psychotherapy that combines aspects of both the cognitive and behavioral approaches in order to identify and alter the maladaptive thoughts and behaviors that are causing significant distress or making it difficult for the client to cope.

Cognitive disability A designation for exceptional individuals whose IQ scores are below 70. Cognitive disability is referred to as mental retardation in the *DSM-IV-TR*.

Cognitive dissonance Leon Festinger's theory about the state of psychological tension, anxiety, and discomfort that occurs when an individual's attitude and behavior are inconsistent, which motivates a change in attitude or behavior to reduce the discomfort.

Cognitive map A mental picture of one's environment. Research on cognitive maps and learning was done by Edward Tolman.

Cognitive perspective A psychological perspective that focuses on the processes of thinking and memory, as well as attention, imagery, creativity, problem solving, perception, and language.

Cognitive restructuring A cognitive therapy technique that involves the altering of illogical, self-defeating cognitions that result in dysfunctional behavior or distress and replaces them with ones that are realistic, genuine, and adaptive.

Cognitive therapy A variety of methods that attempt to treat psychological illnesses through the direct manipulation of the thinking and reasoning processes of the client.

Cognitive triad According to Beck, the depressed individual's negative interpretations about who they are (self), the experiences they have (world), and their future.

Cohort effect A chance result that can affect cross-sectional studies because individuals are influenced by the era or generation that they are part of rather than their age.

Cohort-sequential studies A research method that involves studying participants of different ages over time, thus combining the cross-sectional and longitudinal approaches, and allowing the researchers to determine whether aging or social factors influence changes in behavior.

Collective unconscious According to Jung, the set of inherited images and experiences (archetypes) common to all humans throughout evolutionary time.

Collectivist cultures Cultures that emphasize group membership and harmony above individual achievement. Examples include cultures from Eastern Asia, Western Africa, and parts of South America.

Color constancy The tendency to perceive objects as being the same hue (color) despite the fact that the amount of reflection may change.

Commons dilemma A type of resource dilemma in which individuals need to determine how much to *take* from a shared supply. Also called the tragedy of the commons.

Community psychology A specialty in psychology that involves the basic and applied research related to how social interactions in neighborhoods, families, and the larger culture impact functioning.

Compliance A change in behavior that results from a direct request.

Compulsion A persistent act that is continuously repeated in order to reduce the anxiety created by an obsessive thought.

Computerized axial tomography (CT) A brain imaging method that creates advanced and specific X-rays of the brain's structure.

Concepts The mental categories individuals create for objects or experiences that are similar to one another, allowing for large amounts of information to be represented in an efficient way.

Concordance The percentage of pairs of twins or other family members that have the same trait or disorder.

Concrete operational stage According to Piaget's cognitive development theory, the third stage characterized by the emergence of logical thought about concrete or tangible ideas. This stage occurs between the ages of seven and eleven.

Conditioned response (CR) In classical conditioning, a learned reaction caused by a conditioned stimulus that is the same or similar to the unconditioned response.

Conditioned stimulus (CS) In classical conditioning, something in the environment that was originally a neutral stimulus. When systematically paired with the unconditioned stimulus, the neutral stimulus becomes a conditioned stimulus as it gains the power to cause a response.

Conduction deafness Hearing loss that is the result of problems with funneling and amplifying sounds waves to the inner ear. Damage to the eardrum or the bones of the middle ear that prevent the transmission of sound waves are typical causes of this type of hearing loss.

Cones The cone-shaped photoreceptor cells located in the retina, particularly the fovea, which are responsible for color and high-acuity vision. People who are color-blind typically have deficiencies in their cones.

Confabulation A false memory generated when a person's actual memory becomes distorted because they unconsciously add or remove information received from other sources.

Confederates Individuals who are part of the research team that pose as participants in an experiment and whose behavior is determined in advance.

Confirmation bias The tendency to selectively attend to information that is consistent with one's viewpoint and ignore or minimize information that challenges one's beliefs.

Conflict A situation that occurs when a person is forced to choose between two or more opposing options, goals, or desires. Conflict can be classified as approach–approach, avoidance–avoidance, or approach–avoidance.

Conformity The tendency to change one's behavior or beliefs to fit in with others due to real or imagined social pressures.

Confounding variable Any difference present other than the independent variable between the experimental and the control groups that might have an effect on the dependent variable.

Congruence (Rogers) (1) consistency (congruence) between a person's self-concept and reality that leads to a healthy self-concept; (2) the sincere and honest communications of the therapist, meaning that what is experienced inside and what is expressed outwardly are consistent (congruent).

Connectedness A Gestalt principle in which objects, events, or individuals that are linked together by another element are perceived as a group.

Connectionist model The theory that suggests that encoding of memories happens through the building of connections and that retrieval occurs through the spreading of activation within this large network. Also called the parallel distributed processing model.

Conscious The part of the mind that is currently active and responsive to events and stimuli in the environment and is currently aware of internal thoughts.

Conservation Piaget's term implying that certain quantitative attributes of objects remain unchanged unless something is added to or taken away from them. Characteristics of objects, such as mass, weight, number, area, and volume, are capable of being conserved in the concrete operational stage.

Construct validity The extent to which a test accurately measures the abstract theoretical idea (construct) or skill it is intended to measure. Constructs include ideas that are often difficult to define operationally such as intelligence or personality traits.

Contact comfort The positive emotions that result when the baby has close physical contact with the caregiver.

Contact theory A method of decreasing prejudice by providing opportunities for groups in conflict to spend time together, in order to reduce stereotypes. Also called the contact hypothesis.

Content validity The extent to which a test accurately measures the entire breadth of the subject it is intended to measure.

Context-dependent memory The retrieval process is aided if the individual is in a similar environment to the one where the material was originally encoded. Also called context-specific learning.

Contiguity model The theory states that when events are placed together close in time or space learning occurs.

Contingency (Rescorla) (1) in classical conditioning, one stimulus reliably predicts the arrival of the second stimulus in order for the organism to learn; (2) in operant conditioning, a voluntary behavior reliably predicts a consequence in order for the organism to learn.

Continuity A Gestalt principle in which objects, events, or individuals that create a smooth ongoing shape or pattern are perceived as a group.

Continuous reinforcement schedule The operant conditioning technique of reinforcing the desired response every time it is presented.

Control group A group of participants in an experiment, which is similar to the experimental group, except that it does not receive the treatment of the independent variable. Thus, the control group can be used as a comparison with the experimental group to determine whether subjects were affected by the experimental procedure. Also called the control condition.

Conventional level According to Kohlberg, the second level of moral development in which decisions about morality are based on social approval and law and order.

Convergence A binocular aid or cue that provides information about depth perception based on the amount of muscle strain associated with the inward turning of the eyeballs. A greater amount of muscle strain indicates the object is closer.

Convergent thinking The cognitive process that results in one correct answer to a particular problem; not associated with creativity.

Conversion disorder Axis I somatoform disorder in which individuals experience impaired voluntary motor or sensory function despite the fact that no medical reason can be found to explain the problem.

Cornea The outer transparent coating that protects the eye's interior and focuses incoming light.

Corpus callosum The large group of nerve fibers connecting the two cerebral hemispheres, which relays information between the two halves of the brain.

Correlation coefficient A statistical measure of the strength of the relationship between variables. The most common example is the Pearson correlation coefficient represented by the letter r and ranging from $^+1.00$ to $^-1.00$ that indicates the strength and direction of the relationship between two variables. A positive correlation indicates that the two variables move or vary in the same direction. A negative correlation indicates that the two variables move or vary in opposite directions. A zero correlation or noncorrelation indicates that there is no relationship between the two variables.

Correlational research The researcher observes or measures two or more naturally occurring variables to find the relationship between them. In correlational research, the researcher does not directly manipulate the variables and cause and effect relationships cannot be determined.

Counseling psychologist A psychologist that works with people coping with everyday problems including making career decisions, marriage counseling, and social skills training. The required level of education and training for licensure is determined by state law, but many have doctoral degrees including PhD, PsyD, or EdD and may work in university clinics.

Counterconditioning An undesired response to a stimulus is eliminated by creating a new response to that stimulus. It is used in therapy to replace unacceptable responses with acceptable ones.

Couples therapy A type of psychotherapy that works with both individuals in a couple and focuses on improving the relationship by increasing intimacy, repairing damage caused by conflict, and facilitating effective communication. Also called marriage therapy for married couples.

Creativity The ability to generate novel and useful products or solutions to problems.

Criterion validity The scores on a particular test are positively correlated with the scores on another existing and well-established test (criterion) of the same skill, trait, or ability.

Critical period A fixed time period very early in life when particular events result in long-lasting effects on behavior.

Cross-sectional study A research method that studies individuals of different ages who are evaluated at a single point in time.

Crystallized intelligence The acquired knowledge of vocabulary, verbal skills, cultural knowledge, and factual information that remains the same or increases throughout adulthood.

Culture The enduring ideas, attitudes, and traditions shared and transmitted by a large group. Cultural group identifications can include ethnicity, religion, language, and customs.

Culture-fair test An assessment that is designed to allow all individuals regardless of culture the opportunity to perform equally well.

Culture-relevant test An assessment that focuses on skills and knowledge that are specific and important to a particular culture and would only be administered to members of the culture it was designed for.

Cyclothymic disorder Axis I mood disorder that is a milder but more chronic form of bipolar disorder with depressive and hypomanic symptoms, which lasts for more than two years.

Dark adaptation The chemical changes in the rods and cones, and pupil expansion that allow for an increase in sensitivity to light during dark conditions.

Debrief The ethical requirement that psychologists fully explain the details of the research and inform participants if any deception was involved immediately after the research ends.

Decay theory The theory of forgetting that states that memories disappear with time if they are not retrieved.

Declarative memory See *explicit memory.*

Deductive reasoning The cognitive process in which individuals start with a premise they have strong reason to believe is accurate and then create conclusions based on that initial premise.

Deep processing According to Craik and Lockhart, the thinking and memory processes that involve concentrating on the meaningful aspects of a concept and not simply on its surface characteristics. The result of deep processing is more durable memories that are easier to retrieve.

Defense mechanisms According to Freud, the various unconscious methods individuals use to reduce the anxiety caused by unacceptable thoughts or desires through the process of distorting reality. Examples include repression, rationalization, reaction formation, projection, and regression.

Deindividuation A state of lessened personal responsibility and self-restraint due to feelings of anonymity created by being part of a crowd.

Deinstitutionalization The closing of government-run hospitals in favor of providing care to individuals with mental illness through outpatient facilities or group homes in the community.

Delayed conditioning A type of forward conditioning in which the conditioned stimulus is introduced and remains present before the unconditioned stimulus is introduced. This method is considered an effective technique for conditioning.

Delusion A belief or thought that a person maintains as true despite irrefutable evidence that it is false (e.g. believing that one is being persecuted); this is a characteristic of psychotic reactions.

Demand characteristics Any potential hints or indications about what is being studied that might be discovered by participants and result in distorted findings.

Dendrites The branches extending from the cell body of a neuron that receives messages from other neurons in the form of neurotransmitters.

Denial A defense mechanism that involves unconsciously reducing anxiety by refusing to accept reality even when presented with large amounts of evidence.

Dependent personality disorder Axis II personality disorder characterized by an excessive desire to be taken care of by someone else that causes them to be clingy (dependent).

Dependent variable (DV) The observation and measurement of the behavior or mental process of participants in an experiment.

Depolarization The process that occurs during the action potential when the interior of the axon changes to a less negative or slightly positive charge.

Depressant A category of psychotropic drugs that lead to muscle relaxation, sleep, and inhibition of the cognitive centers in the brain.

Depth perception The awareness of a world that is three-dimensional and an understanding of the distance between an individual and other objects.

Descriptive statistics A group of statistical measurements that are used to illustrate data including tables, graphs, charts, correlations, measures of central tendency, and variance.

Developmental psychology A specialty of psychology that focuses on the physical, cognitive, social, and moral development of humans that occurs across the lifespan from conception to death.

***Diagnostic and Statistical Manual of Mental Disorders* (DSM)** The classification system for mental disorders developed by the American Psychiatric Association. The current edition is the *DSM-IV-TR*, which indicates it is the text revision (TR) of the fourth major revision (IV).

Diathesis-stress model A theory for what causes schizophrenia and other mental illnesses. The diathesis-stress model states that mental illness develops when there is a genetic predisposition (diathesis) present and environmental factors (stress) that trigger the disorder.

Difference threshold The smallest difference in intensity between stimuli that can be detected by an individual. Also called the differential threshold or the just noticeable difference.

Diffusion of responsibility The belief of each individual in a crowd that they do not need to help because somebody else will take action; results in the bystander effect.

Discrimination (1) a phenomenon in classical conditioning in which an organism learns to respond (CR) to *only* the conditioned stimulus (CS); (2) a phenomenon in operant conditioning in which an organism learns to voluntarily respond to only the stimulus that was reinforced; and (3) any action that results from prejudiced points of view.

Disorganized schizophrenia Axis I psychological disorder and subtype of schizophrenia characterized by a collection of unusual symptoms including numerous hallucinations and delusions that are poorly organized. Prominent features include disorganized speech and behavior and flat or inappropriate affect.

Displacement A defense mechanism that involves unconsciously reducing anxiety by taking out aggression on someone or something that is less powerful or threatening than the true source of anxiety.

Display rules The culturally acceptable learned guidelines for when and how emotions can be expressed in particular social situations.

Dispositional attribution An explanation for behavior based on factors inside the person (e.g., personality, intelligence, and maturity). Also called an internal attribution.

Dissociation The splitting of consciousness into two or more simultaneous streams of mental activity. Also called divided consciousness.

Dissociative amnesia Axis I dissociative disorder characterized by a partial or total inability to recall experiences and information.

Dissociative disorders A category of Axis I disorders that involve a portion of the mind "splitting off" from the mainstream of consciousness, producing behavior that is incompatible with the rest of the individual's awareness, memory, or identity.

Dissociative fugue Axis I dissociative disorder characterized by a sudden and unexpected travel away from home as well as amnesia. The individual often assumes a completely new identity and has no memory of their former life.

Dissociative identity disorder (DID) Axis I dissociative disorder characterized by the presence of two or more distinct personality systems in the same individual. Formerly called multiple personality disorder.

Divergent thinking The cognitive process that results in a number of possible answers to a particular problem. This type of cognition is a major element in creativity.

Dizygotic twins Twins that share 50 percent of the same genes because they developed from two separate fertilized eggs and are no more genetically similar to each other than siblings. Also called fraternal twins.

Door-in-the-face technique A persuasion method in which the individual begins by making a large request that most likely will be turned down. After this large initial request is denied, the person makes a more reasonable request that is now more likely to be granted.

Dopamine A neurotransmitter involved in pleasure, reward, voluntary movement, learning, and attention. Certain dopamine pathways are involved in drug addiction. Parkinson's disease is marked in part by low levels of dopamine and schizophrenia is associated with elevated levels of dopamine.

Double blind A procedure in which both the experimenter and the participants are unaware of who has received the independent variable (treatment). Double-blind studies eliminate both experimenter and participant bias.

Down syndrome A condition in which an individual is born with an additional chromosome present on the twenty-first pair resulting in cognitive disability and distinctive facial features.

Drive-reduction theory The theory that emphasizes that a deficiency in a particular biological need creates a drive, or state of tension, that causes the individual to behave in a manner the reduces the drive and returns the body to homeostasis.

Dualism The theory that the body and the mind are separate.

Dysthymic disorder Axis I mood disorder that is a milder but more chronic form of depression that lasts for more than two years. Everyday functioning is less impaired than is the case with major depression.

Echoic memory The storage of a brief auditory stimulation for a few seconds. Also called auditory sensory memory.

Eclectic approach The approach to psychotherapy that involves the use of a variety of methods from several theoretical perspectives to most effectively help clients.

Educational psychologist A psychologist who studies theoretical issues related to how people learn and develops effective teaching practices.

Efferent neurons The nerve cells that transfer information from the brain and spinal cord to the muscles, organs, and glands of the body that are responsible for both voluntary movements, such as walking, and involuntary movements, such as breathing and digestion. Also called motor neurons.

Ego According to Freud, the problem solving and rational aspect of the personality. It operates on a reality principle, seeking to mediate between the demands of the id and the superego.

Egocentrism According to Piaget, the difficulty in seeing how the world looks from the perspective of others typical of the preoperational stage of cognitive development.

Eidetic imagery The ability to retain a visual mental image with great clarity for a fairly long period. Sometimes called "photographic memory."

Elaboration likelihood model The theory of persuasion that includes two general methods for creating attitude change: the peripheral and central routes to persuasion.

Elaborative rehearsal A method of rehearsal that utilizes connections to previously learned material, leading to better retention rates.

Electroconvulsive therapy (ECT) A form of biomedical therapy that involves the brief passage of an electric current across electrodes placed on the temple of the patient that creates a brain seizure. This method has been effective in the treatment of severe depression that does not respond to medication.

Electroencephalogram (EEG) The brain imaging device that measures electrical activity of the neurons below the electrodes placed on the scalp. The EEG is often used to show brain wave patterns of electrical activity during sleep stages and seizures.

Embryonic stage The second stage in prenatal development that lasts from approximately week two until week eight during which the nervous system, major organs, and body parts such as the eyes and limbs begin to form.

Emotion A complex internal state including physiological, cognitive, and behavioral components that result from a stimulus or event in the environment that is of personal importance.

Emotional intelligence The ability to recognize emotion in others and oneself and incorporate knowledge about emotion into reasoning and thought processes.

Empiricism According to Locke, the view that knowledge should be gained through careful observation and from experimental evidence.

Encoding The process of combining, organizing, and placing information into memory.

Endocrine system The body system consisting of ductless glands, which secrete hormones into the bloodstream in order to control and coordinate bodily functions including growth, metabolism, reproduction, and stress responses.

Endorphins The chemical substances associated with the inhibition of pain and the regulation of pleasure.

Engrams The hypothetical memory trace in the brain.

Episodic memory A type of explicit or declarative memory that consists of personal experiences and events tied to particular times and places.

Eros The Greek word for love which Freud used to represent the life instincts or the desire to live, including basic survival needs, self-preservation, and sexual drives.

Escape conditioning A type of learning that occurs when an organism discovers that a particular voluntary behavior will result in the removal of an unwanted or aversive stimulus. Also called escape behavior.

Ethnocentrism A specific type of prejudice in which an individual favors their own culture or ethnic group's values, attitudes, and actions over other cultural groups.

Eugenics A form of genetic engineering that suggests that specific individuals should be selected for reproduction. The term was coined by Galton and is really an expression of the belief that individuals should be selected for breeding purposes in order to enhance certain characteristics.

Eustress The positive stress resulting from accepting challenges and pursuing goals.

Evolutionary perspective The psychological perspective that focuses on how social behaviors and mental processes are the product of natural selection and human adaptation to the environment over the course of evolution. The evolutionary perspective is heavily influenced by the seminal writings of Charles Darwin.

Excitatory postsynaptic potential (EPSP) A depolarizing potential in a postsynaptic neuron that makes the receiving neuron more likely to fire an action potential.

Experimental group A group of participants in an experiment that receive the independent variable (treatment). Also called the experimental condition.

Experimental method A carefully controlled scientific procedure involving the manipulation of variables to determine cause and effect.

Experimenter bias The tendency for researchers to unknowingly influence the results in an experiment. Also called researcher bias.

Explicit memory The information that can be consciously recalled when requested and sometimes becomes disrupted because of age or amnesia. This type of memory includes conversations, facts and events, and everything we normally think of as memory. Explicit memory includes both semantic and episodic memory. Also called declarative memory.

External locus of control According to Rotter, the belief that some individuals hold, that is what happens to them may be largely determined by fate, luck, or the actions of others.

Extinction (1) a phenomenon in classical conditioning that involves the elimination or weakening of a conditioned behavior when the conditioned stimulus (CS) is repeatedly presented without the unconditioned stimulus (UCS); (2) a phenomenon in operant conditioning that involves the elimination or weakening of a voluntary response due to the reinforcement no longer being provided after the behavior.

Extrasensory perception (ESP) The idea that perception can occur without sensation; not supported by scientific research. Extrasensory perception includes controversial claims such as telepathy (mind reading), precognition (predicting the future), clairvoyance (the awareness of remote events), and psychokinesis (moving objects with the mind).

Extrinsic motivation The performance of a behavior in order to obtain a reward or avoid punishment.

Extroversion A Big Five personality trait that is expressed in individuals who are confident, social, and externally focused.

Face validity The extent to which the material on a test appears on the surface to accurately measure what it intends to measure. Face validity is determined either by a nonexpert or by an expert that only gives a quick evaluation of the test.

Factor analysis A statistical procedure that reduces the number of variables by placing them in clusters of related items.

False consensus effect The tendency for individuals to overestimate how many others share their opinions or behave the same way that they do.

Family therapy A form of treatment in which all the members of the family are treated together. This approach is based on the theory that the individual is a product of his or her environment and that to produce change within the individual, the environment must be altered.

Feature detectors According to Hubel and Wiesel, the specialized neurons in the brain that are responsive to particular elements of an image including straight lines, edges, curves, angles, or direction.

Fetal stage The third and final stage in prenatal development that lasts from week nine until birth. This stage involves a rapid period of organ and body growth during which bodily systems reach maturity in order to ensure survival outside of the womb.

Fight or flight reaction An automatic physiological and emotional response to a stressor that involves the activation of the sympathetic nervous system to prepare the body to attack or flee.

Figure-ground A Gestalt principle in which an individual views an object in the visual field as two separate components. The object (figure) is separate and more important than the area surrounding it (ground) or the background.

Fixation (1) according to psychoanalytic theory, the failure of psychosexual development to proceed normally from one stage to the next, results in an individual engaging in activities associated with the stage that has the unresolved

conflict; (2) in problem solving the inability to see a problem from a new perspective.

Fixed-interval schedule A reinforcement schedule in operant conditioning in which the reinforcement is given for the first correct response after a set period has occurred.

Fixed-ratio schedule A reinforcement schedule in operant conditioning in which the reinforcement is given after a set number of correct behaviors have occurred.

Flashbulb memory A specific type of episodic memory that involves an especially detailed remembrance of an event that is highly personal and intensely emotional.

Flat affect A condition in which virtually no stimulus can produce an emotional response. Flat affect is an example of a negative symptom of schizophrenia.

Flight of ideas The rapid shift in conversation from one subject to another, based on superficial associations, which sometimes occurs during mania or schizophrenia.

Flooding A type of behavioral implosion therapy, which involves having the patient immediately confront the most anxiety-producing situation related to their fear in a manner that is harmless, but also does not allow for the opportunity to escape.

Fluid intelligence The type of intelligence that involves the rapid processing of information and memory span, needed to solve new types of problems, which decreases in late adulthood; considered flexible, or adaptive thinking.

Flynn effect A recently discovered phenomenon that demonstrates that the average IQ has been rising dramatically over successive generations.

Foot-in-the-door technique A persuasion method that involves having someone comply with a small request first in order to increase the likelihood that they will agree to a second larger request later.

Forebrain The sophisticated part of the human brain that includes the cerebral cortex and the subcortical structures of the cerebrum including the limbic system. It is the well-developed forebrain that allows for the complex thoughts and behaviors unique to humans.

Formal operational stage The fourth and final stage of Piaget's cognitive development theory that is characterized by the ability to think abstractly, imagine hypothetical situations, and apply logical rules to envision objects and ideas that they have never seen. This stage begins at approximately age twelve.

Fovea A small central region of the retina where cones are concentrated and visual acuity is the sharpest.

Framing effect The way a problem is worded influences the conclusions that are made.

Fraternal twins See *dizygotic twins*.

Free association A psychoanalytic method in which the patient is instructed to say anything that comes to mind, no matter how trivial or unimportant it may seem.

Frequency The number of complete wavelengths that pass a specific point within a second.

Frequency distribution A table that contains data about how often certain scores occur or how many subjects fit into each category that is often used for nominal data.

Frequency histogram A specialized type of bar graph that displays data from a frequency distribution.

Frequency polygon A specialized type of line graph that displays data from a frequency distribution.

Frequency theory A theory for pitch that suggests that the basilar membrane vibrates at the same frequency as the sound wave. The frequency theory best explains low-pitched sounds.

Frontal lobes The area of the cerebral cortex located behind the forehead responsible for higher-level thinking, reasoning, planning, judgment, and impulse control.

Frustration–aggression hypothesis The theory that aggression is caused by stress (frustration), which results when an individual is prevented from reaching a goal.

Functional fixedness In problem solving, a tendency or mental set in which one considers only the common uses of objects rather than the possibilities for novel or unusual functions.

Functional magnetic resonance imaging (fMRI) The brain imaging technique that uses magnetic fields to produce images of the brain and tracks brain activity in real time by measuring blood flow carrying oxygen to active brain tissues.

Functionalism An early theoretical perspective in psychology used by William James, which emphasized how conscious behavior helps one adapt to the environment. This perspective of thought held that the mind should be studied in terms of its usefulness to the organism in adapting to its environment.

Fundamental attribution error (FAE) The tendency to use a dispositional (internal) explanation without considering the situational (external) factors that might be influencing the behavior of someone else.

g factor According to Spearman, the construct of a general intelligence factor that is responsible for a person's overall performance on tests of mental ability as opposed to specific abilities.

GABA The major inhibitory neurotransmitter involved in relaxation and sleep. Low levels of GABA are associated with anxiety disorders.

Ganglion cells The cells in the retina whose axons form the optic nerve. Also called retinal ganglion cells.

Gate control theory The theory that pain signals travel to the brain through the spinal cord and pass through a series of "invisible gates" that can be opened or closed.

Gender The cultural, psychological, and behavioral characteristics associated with being male or female.

Gender identity The internal recognition that an individual is male or female and the assimilation of this belief into one's self-concept.

Gender roles The expected appearance, personality traits, and behaviors connected to being male or female that mainly relate to environmental factors such as family and cultural interactions.

Gender schema theory The theory that emphasizes a cognitive component to explain how gender roles are learned in childhood. According to this theory, children develop a separate mental category (schema) for each gender and organize information about behavior and activities into these two specific gender categories.

Gender typing The acquisition of gender roles.

General adaptation syndrome (GAS) According to Selye, the reaction to chronic stress occurs in three stages: alarm, resistance, and exhaustion.

Generalization (1) a phenomenon in classical conditioning in which an organism learns to respond (CR) to stimuli that are *similar* to the conditioned stimulus (CS); (2) a phenomenon in operant conditioning in which an organism learns to voluntarily respond to stimuli that are similar to the original stimulus.

Generalized anxiety disorder (GAD) Axis I anxiety disorder characterized by chronic, widespread, and persistent anxiety. Because the source of the anxiety cannot be identified, this is sometimes called free floating.

Generativity versus stagnation According to Erikson, the seventh stage in psychosocial development that involves finding fulfillment and providing guidance for future generations that occurs during middle adulthood.

Genital stage The fifth and final stage in Freud's psychosexual development theory in which sexual impulses reappear at puberty. The libido is centered on the genitals during this stage, but is no longer directed toward the parent.

Genotype The genetic makeup for a trait in an individual, which may or may not be expressed.

Germinal stage The first stage in prenatal development that lasts from zero to two weeks. The stage involves the zygote traveling along the fallopian tube to the uterus where it will attach during implantation and form the placenta that provides oxygen and nutrients to the organism. Also called the zygotic stage.

Gestalt psychology The early perspective in psychology that involves the study of consciousness most frequently in the areas of perception, learning, and problem solving. Gestalt psychology emphasizes the idea that the whole is greater than the sum of its parts.

Gestalt therapy A form of treatment that helps clients to identify their current feelings, behaviors, and needs in order to confront their problems directly. According to Gestalt therapy, psychological illness and interpersonal problems result if a person has not assumed responsibility for their thoughts and emotions.

Gifted Individuals with an IQ over 130 or those who have special talents, creativity, or leadership ability.

Glial cells (glia) The cells that provide nourishment, protection, and insulation for neurons. These supportive brain cells also protect the brain from toxins and produce the myelin sheath.

Glucose The blood sugar that provides energy for bodily functions that is broken down by the body from foods that have recently been eaten.

Glutamate The major excitatory neurotransmitter associated with memory and learning. Excess levels are linked to migraines and seizures.

Gonads The endocrine glands consisting of the testes and ovaries that produce hormones needed for sexual reproduction.

Grammar The rules that define how a language is used so that people speaking the same language understand each other. The broad overall term grammar contains two separate parts: semantics and syntax.

Group polarization The tendency for groups of like-minded individuals who interact to make more extreme decisions after an issue is discussed.

Groupthink The tendency for a cohesive decision-making group to ignore or dismiss reasonable alternatives because of the desire for a unanimous decision.

Gustation A synonym for the sense of taste.

Habituation A type of conditioning in which organisms demonstrate weaker responses to a stimulus that has been presented repeatedly indicating that they have become used to or familiar with that particular stimulus.

Hallucination A false perceptual experience in which an individual sees, hears, smells, tastes, or feels something that is not actually present. Hallucinations are considered positive symptoms in schizophrenia.

Hallucinogens A category of psychotropic drugs that lead to hallucinations, delusions, or unusual perceptions. Also called psychedelic drugs.

Halo effect The tendency when rating an individual to use one particular characteristic as the basis for other aspects of their personality (e.g., physically attractive people are more likely to be judged as intelligent, friendly, and talented than unattractive people).

Hawthorne effect The effect on participants' performance attributable to their knowledge that they are being watched or participating in an experiment.

Heritability A mathematical measure that indicates the amount of variation among individuals that is related to genes, which is an estimate and only applies to the population and not individuals. Heritability is expressed as a numerical value ranging from 0 to 1.0 and can be translated into a percentage.

Heroin A powerfully addictive, illicit opiate drug.

Heuristic A problem-solving strategy that is likely to produce a solution quickly, but does not guarantee a correct answer.

Hierarchy of needs According to Maslow, the theory of motivation that arranges in order of importance a total of five needs including physiological, safety, belonging and love, esteem, and self-actualization. In this stage model of motivation, the needs at the bottom of the pyramid take precedence over the others.

Higher-order conditioning A form of classical conditioning in which the previously trained conditioned stimulus now functions as an unconditioned stimulus to train a new conditioned stimulus. Also called second-order conditioning.

Hindbrain The area often referred to as the "primitive" part of the brain that coordinates basic bodily functions and is composed of the cerebellum, pons, and medulla.

Hindsight bias The tendency for an individual to believe that he or she could have predicted the outcome of an event after it already happened.

Hippocampus A limbic system structure surrounding the thalamus responsible for explicit memory formation and learning.

Histrionic personality disorder Axis II personality disorder characterized by individuals whose behavior is highly emotional and dramatic. Histrionics are often conceited, self-centered, and shallow, yet constantly search for approval.

Homeostasis A balanced internal state or equilibrium that one's body attempts to achieve through the use of internal regulatory mechanisms in order to stay alive.

Hormones The endocrine system messengers that are transported by the bloodstream throughout the body, which are capable of influencing behavior over minutes, hours, or weeks.

Human factors psychology The specialty of psychology concerned with creating, designing, and producing machines and systems that are functional and easy to use by people. Simply stated, the study of human factors involves psychology plus engineering.

Humanist perspective A psychological perspective that focuses on the human capacity for goodness and creativity. Humanistic theories emphasize the importance of self-esteem, free will, and choice in human behavior. This perspective emerged from the pioneering work of Abraham Maslow and Carl Rogers.

Hypnosis A state of heightened suggestibility, deep relaxation, and intense focus considered by some psychologists to be an altered state of consciousness.

Hypnotic analgesia The reduction or elimination of pain through hypnosis.

Hypochondriasis Axis I somatoform disorder in which individuals are convinced that they have a very serious medical condition despite the fact that they remain in good health and medical tests come back negative. These individuals may dramatically misinterpret small physical changes as indicators of serious medical conditions and suffer from chronic fear and worry.

Hypothalamus A limbic system structure located below (hypo) the thalamus responsible for maintenance functions (eating, drinking, body temperature, and sex) and control of the autonomic nervous system. It also controls much of the endocrine system's activities through connections with the pituitary gland.

Hypothesis A testable and falsifiable prediction explaining the relationship between an independent and a dependent variable.

Iconic memory The storage of a very brief visual image for a fraction of a second. Also called visual sensory store.

Id According to Freud, the part of the personality that is completely unconscious. The id consists of innate sexual and aggressive instincts and drives. It operates on the pleasure principle, seeking to achieve immediate gratification and avoid discomfort.

Identification According to Freud, the resolution of the phallic stage conflict that results when an individual adopts the values, behaviors, and social roles of the same sex parent.

Identity A collection of many separate components, including career, culture, gender, political, religious, personality, and interests that will shape adult behavior.

Identity versus role confusion According to Erikson, the fifth stage in psychosocial development occurs during adolescence and involves achieving a sense of self.

Idiographic The approach to personality study that emphasizes the aspects of personality which are unique to each person.

Illusory correlation An incorrect perception that two variables are related, or an overestimation about the strength of the relationship.

Imaginary audience The tendency of adolescents to believe that other people are watching their every move and talking about them more than is actually happening. An aspect of adolescent egocentrism.

Implicit memory The information that is created automatically without conscious effort and can be tested through behavioral responses. The categories of implicit memory are debatable but often include priming, conditioned reflexes, and procedural memory. Also called nondeclarative memory.

Imprinting The phenomenon that occurs in some birds that are biologically programmed to form an attachment to and follow the first moving object they see. Imprinting was studied by Konrad Lorenz.

Inattentional blindness The failure to perceive a particular stimulus that is in the field of vision because attention is being focused somewhere else.

Incentive theory A motivation theory that recognizes that humans are not only pushed into action by internal drives, but they are also motivated by the pull of incentives or external stimuli.

Independent variable (IV) The event, treatment, or condition that is being manipulated or controlled by the experimenter. Only the experimental group is exposed to the independent variable during an experiment.

Individualistic culture A culture that emphasizes personal success and individual achievement. Examples include cultures found in the United States and Western Europe.

Inductive reasoning A cognitive process in which individuals make a conclusion about what is most likely true based on specific examples or determine general principles by analyzing examples.

Industrial-organizational psychology A specialty in psychology concerned with psychological issues related to the work environment: employee motivation and selection. There are multiple subfields of industrial-organizational psychology including human factors, personnel, and organizational.

Inferential statistics A group of statistical measurements that indicate whether or not results based on the sample are significant enough to be applied to the larger population, or if the results of the research were most likely caused by chance.

Inferiority complex According to Adler, a feeling of helplessness and insecurity that results from constant criticism and repeated failure.

Information processing How information travels through the nervous system including perception, memory creation, reasoning, and formulating responses.

Informational social influence The desire to conform to the behavior of others that occurs because an individual believes that the information presented is correct.

Information-processing model of memory According to Atkinson and Shiffrin, the theory that describes memory as a sequential process that moves through three distinct stages: sensory memory, short-term memory, and long-term memory.

Information-processing theory A cognitive approach that explains that dreams are methods that the mind uses to sort out the events of the day and place them into memory.

Informed consent The ethical requirement that participants must know that they are involved in research and participate voluntarily.

In-group Individuals that we view as being similar to ourselves.

In-group bias The natural tendency for people to notice negative characteristics in members of out-groups, and not in members of their own in-group.

Inhibitory postsynaptic potential (IPSP) A depolarizing potential in a postsynaptic neuron that makes the receiving neuron less likely to fire an action potential.

Insanity A legal definition that indicates if a particular individual can be held responsible for his or her actions in a court of law.

Insight A type of learning that involves a sudden flash of inspiration rather than a strategy that was researched by Kohler. The "Aha!" experience when a solution to a problem suddenly appears or becomes obvious.

Insomnia A sleep disorder characterized by the chronic inability to fall asleep or stay asleep.

Instinctive drift The tendency for animals to abandon learned behaviors and replace them with ones that are instinctive or innate.

Insulin A hormone produced in the pancreas that converts glucose to stored fat and removes it from the bloodstream. It is involved in the utilization of sugar and carbohydrates in the body. Also used in insulin-shock therapy.

Integrity versus despair According to Erikson, the eighth and final stage in psychosocial development that occurs in late adulthood and involves reflection and evaluation on whether or not life was meaningful.

Intelligence The capacity to acquire knowledge, reason effectively, and adapt to one's surroundings by utilizing a combination of inherited abilities (nature) and learned experiences (nurture).

Intelligence quotient (IQ) A specific score on an intelligence test that may or may not be an accurate measure of the cognitive capabilities of that particular individual. The original formula for IQ was created by William Stern to enable comparisons to be made between individuals of different ages. Stern's formula for IQ is mental age divided by chronological age multiplied by 100.

Intermittent reinforcement The rewarding of some, but not all, correct responses. It may vary according to ratio or interval. Also called a partial reinforcement schedule.

Internal locus of control According to Rotter, the belief that some individuals hold that what happens to them may be largely determined by hard work or effort.

Internalized speech According to Vygotsky, the speech that individuals rely on to learn about their world. As children mature, private speech becomes internalized.

Interneurons The neurons which are located in the brain and spinal cord that facilitate communication between afferent and efferent neurons. Also called association neurons.

Interpersonal psychotherapy (IPT) A form of psychodynamic treatment that involves assisting the client in developing skills to improve his or her relationships with family members, friends, and coworkers, as well as dealing with difficult changes in life.

Interposition A monocular depth cue in which one object appears closer to the viewer because it partially blocks the view of another object. Also called overlap.

Interpretation A method that psychoanalysts use to explain the hidden meanings of a patient's actions, thoughts, emotions, and dreams.

Interrater reliability A method used for determining if a test is reliable (repeatable) by comparing the scores given by two different examiners of the same individual test subject.

Intimacy versus isolation According to Erikson, the sixth stage in psychosocial development in young adulthood that involves developing relationships based on love and friendship.

Intrinsic motivation The performance of behavior out of genuine interest rather than any potential benefit associated with the activity.

Intrinsic reinforcements A form of reward that is the result of the activity itself because the activity is interesting, pleasurable, and rewarding.

Introspection An early research process used by structuralists like Wilhelm Wundt and Edward Titchener that involves having subjects report the contents of their own mind as objectively as possible, usually in relation to stimuli such as light, sound, or odors.

Introverted A personality trait that is expressed in individuals that are internally focused, more self-conscious, less social, and quiet.

Irreversibility The child's inability to mentally reverse a sequence of events or logical operations which is present during Piaget's preoperational stage.

James–Lange theory of emotion A theory of emotion that proposes that the subjective experience of emotion follows the physiological changes that occur in reaction to a stimulus. William James believed that if we find ourselves trembling, then we will feel the emotion of fear, and if we find ourselves crying, that will result in the emotion of sadness.

Just noticeable difference See the *difference threshold*.

Kinesthesis The sense that provides information about the location of body parts in relation to one another. The specialized receptor cells for kinesthesis are called proprioceptors and are located in the joints and muscles of the body.

Language A form of communication consisting of symbols that can be arranged to derive meaning.

Language acquisition device According to Chomsky, the built-in biological readiness to learn the grammatical rules for any language including syntax, semantics, and pronunciation.

Latency stage The fourth stage in Freud's psychosexual development theory in which sexual desires are dormant that occurs between the ages of 6 and 11. The libido remains hidden during this stage and the individual focuses on developing intellectual and social skills with members of the same sex. Children are interested in identifying with the same sex parent.

Latent content According to Freud, the unconscious desires are the cause of dreams. These latent (hidden) desires are usually related to sexual or aggressive drives. Latent content is determined by the analyst through interpretation.

Latent learning A type of learning that involves an organism mastering a new behavior without effort, awareness, or reinforcement, and this behavior is not demonstrated unless a need or reinforcement is presented. The word *latent* refers to something that is hidden, so in the case of latent learning, the behavior the organism has mastered remains hidden until there is a need to perform the learned response.

Lateral hypothalamus The region of the hypothalamus responsible for increasing hunger; stimulation of this region causes a well-fed animal to eat and damage to it will result in a starving animal refusing to eat.

Lateralization The specific functions controlled by each half of the cerebral cortex. Also called hemispheric specialization.

Law of effect According to Thorndike, the law that states that a voluntary behavior followed by a positive outcome will be repeated and a voluntary behavior followed by failure would not be repeated.

Learned helplessness According to Seligman, the loss of motivation and failure to attempt escape from unpleasant stimuli that occurs if the individual perceives that they are not able to exert control over his or her environment. Learned helplessness is sometimes used to explain that depression can result when individuals believe that they no longer have the ability to determine the course of their own lives due to repeated failures or negative consequences.

Learning The enduring or relatively permanent change in an organism caused by experience or influences in the environment.

Lens A transparent tissue that focuses the sensory information in the form of light waves on the retina.

Lesions The removal of a portion of an organism's brain which is most often used in humans to stop the spread of brain tumors. Research based on the evaluation of patients with lesions has helped scientists localize brain regions responsible for memory, learning, speech, and other functions. Lesioning in animal subjects has been used as a research method.

Levels-of-processing model According to Craik and Lockhart, the model of memory that states that the attention given to the process of encoding impacts future recall. Deeper levels of processing as opposed to shallow levels of processing create more durable memories that can be recalled easier.

Libido According to Freud, all of the life instincts, especially the sexual drive, and the energy associated with them.

Light adaptation The chemical changes in the rods and cones, and pupil constriction that allow for an increase in sensitivity to light during very bright conditions.

Limbic system A bagel-shaped group of structures between the brainstem and the cerebral cortex in charge of learning, memory, emotion, and basic drives. The main structures of the limbic system include the hippocampus, amygdala, and hypothalamus.

Linear perspective A monocular cue for depth in which objects appear closer to the viewer if they are located farther away from the point where two parallel lines converge (meet).

Linguistic determinism Whorf's original theory that a person's language determines how he or she thinks. Psychologists disagree with Whorf's hypothesis that language determines thought, but most agree that language does influence thought in what is now thought of as the linguistic relativity hypothesis.

Lithium A naturally occurring, metallic element that is found in the form of a salt which is used as a mood stabilizer medication and is effective in the treatment of the mania stage present in bipolar disorder.

Locus of control According to Rotter, the amount of confidence that one has regarding the level of influence (control) one believes one has over events in one's life. See also *external locus of control* and *internal locus of control*.

Longitudinal studies A research method that studies the same individual or group of individuals over a lengthy period to examine changes in the development of behaviors and attitudes related to growth and aging.

Long-term memory The third stage in the Atkinson and Shiffrin information-processing model of memory considered to be a generally permanent storage capable of containing a limitless amount of information.

Long-term potentiation The repeated stimulation of neural networks that strengthens the connections between neurons and results in the formation of new dendrites, leading to learning and memory creation.

Low-ball technique A compliance method that involves convincing someone to commit to an agreement, and then increasing the effort or cost required to fulfill the commitment. The low-ball technique is a two-step process. First, obtain a commitment, and second, increase the effort or cost required to fulfill that commitment by revealing hidden or additional costs.

Lucid dream A dream in which individuals realize they are dreaming, and can act to change and control the dream. Many cultures teach people to increase their rate of lucid dreaming; however, many psychologists find this concept controversial.

Magnetic resonance imaging (MRI) A brain imaging technique that utilizes strong magnetic fields that cause molecules to vibrate at different frequencies producing detailed images of slices of brain tissue.

Maintenance rehearsal A memory technique that involves repeating information.

Major depressive disorder An Axis I mood disorder characterized by one or more major depressive episodes lasting for longer than two weeks resulting in a significant impairment of physical, emotional, cognitive, and behavioral functioning. Suicidal risk is a significant concern associated with this diagnosis. Also called unipolar depression.

Mania A state that involves hyperactivity, euphoria, a decreased need for sleep, talkativeness, inflated self-esteem, and excessive involvement in activities without regard to their painful consequences (e.g., buying sprees, foolish business investments, sexual indiscretions, and reckless driving).

Manifest content According to Freud, the plot of the dream that the dreamer can remember and report afterward.

Marijuana A psychotropic drug derived from the cannabis plant that contains the active ingredient of THC (tetrahydrocannabinol). It is often characterized as a mild hallucinogen. Also called cannabis.

Matching hypothesis The theory that individuals pair up in relationships with those who are similar to themselves in terms of their level of physical attractiveness.

Maturation The biological growth processes that enable changes in behavior and are connected to an individual's genetic blueprint meaning that they are relatively uninfluenced by experience. Maturation relates to behaviors that are driven mainly by nature and less influenced by nurture.

Mean A measurement of central tendency determined by computing the sum of all the scores in a set and dividing the sum by the total number of scores in the distribution. Also called the arithmetic average.

Median A measure of central tendency that indicates the middle score of a distribution, or the one that divides a distribution in half.

Medical model A model of psychopathology that proposes that mental illness is the result of disease or injury. The medical model views mental illness as a disease that requires medical care.

Medulla The area of the hindbrain below the pons on the brainstem in charge of survival functions (heartbeat, breathing, and digestion), and reflexes (sneezing, coughing, vomiting, and swallowing). Also called the medulla oblongata.

Melatonin A hormone that results in drowsiness when released into the bloodstream by the pineal gland.

Menarche The first menstrual period.

Meninges The three connected layers of protective membrane that surround the central nervous system including the pia mater, arachnoid mater, and dura mater.

Menopause The period when a woman no longer has the ability to reproduce and is marked by the end of the menstrual cycle that occurs in middle adulthood.

Mental retardation See *cognitive disability*.

Mental set The tendency for people to cling to old methods of solving problems even when they are no longer working. Mental set sometimes facilitates performance and sometimes impairs it. An impairment resulting from mental set is referred to as functional fixedness.

Mere exposure effect An increase in liking for a stimulus due to repeated contact.

Meta-analysis A research method that involves combining data from numerous studies on the same topic to generate a hypothesis based on a large sample.

Metacognitive processing The deliberate and conscious process of talking oneself through a problem that contributes to problem solving.

Methamphetamine A stimulant and psychotropic drug commonly called crystal meth that results in long-lasting and intense feelings of euphoria. An extremely physically and psychologically addictive illicit drug.

Method of loci The mnemonic process that involves associating the information that needs to be memorized with a series of locations typically in a familiar place through the use of vivid imagery.

Midbrain The area located above the hindbrain that is very small in humans and coordinates simple movements with sensory information.

Minnesota Multiphasic Personality Inventory (MMPI-2) A widely used empirically derived assessment that measures differences in personality and identifies emotional and behavioral problems.

Mirror neurons The nerve cells that fire when performing a particular action and when an individual watches somebody else perform the same action. Research suggests mirror neurons are involved in empathy, observational learning, and reading emotions in others.

Misinformation effect According to Loftus, the tendency for individuals who have been provided with misleading information to alter their memories by adding the false information to their recollections.

Mnemonic strategy A memory technique that is usually effortful, although sometimes automatic and designed to assist in the process of memory. Often these strategies include elaboration by creating connections with other material.

Mode A measure of central tendency that identifies the most frequently occurring score in a distribution.

Modeling (1) In social learning theory, a form of learning in which the subject imitates the actions or reactions of another person. (2) In behavior modification or behavior therapy, a technique based on imitation and perceptual learning. Modeling therapy has been successful in the treatment of a variety of mental disorders, especially phobias.

Monism The theory that the mind cannot be separated from the body because they are different aspects of the same thing.

Monoamine oxidase inhibitor (MAOI) A type of antidepressant medication that works by blocking the enzyme monoamine oxidase which leads to increased levels of the neurotransmitters norepinephrine and serotonin.

Monocular cue A perceptual cue for distance and how objects are positioned in the environment that involves only one eye.

Monozygotic twins Twins who share one hundred percent of the same genes, because they developed from a single fertilized egg. Also called identical twins.

Mood disorders A category of Axis I disorders that involve disturbances or extremes in emotion and vary in terms of their duration and severity.

Mood-congruent The retrieval process is aided if the individual is in the same emotional state (mood) when they are trying to remember something as when they first encoded the information. Also called mood-dependent memory.

Moro reflex An automatic response shown by newborns when startled that involves extending their limbs outward and then bringing them back in potentially to grab on to something or brace themselves. This reflex disappears after approximately seven months.

Morpheme The smallest unit of meaning in a language that results from combinations of phonemes.

Motion parallax A monocular cue in which an object appears closer to the viewer because it is moving in the opposite direction as the observer and appears to be moving faster.

Motor homunculus The symbolic representation of the motor cortex in the form of a distorted figure that represents the proportion of brain area dedicated to each body part in relationship to movement.

Multiple approach-avoidance conflict A situation where an individual must choose between two different options, both of which have positive and negative parts.

Multiple intelligences theory According to Gardner, the theory that there are various types of intelligence including verbal-linguistic, logical-mathematical, spatial, musical, bodily-kinesthetic, interpersonal, intrapersonal, and naturalist with the possibility of more to come.

Myelin sheath The insulating layer of fat cells surrounding the axon of the neuron that increases the speed of the electrical message (action potential). Myelin is produced by glial cells. Deterioration of the myelin sheath leads to the loss of muscle control associated with the disease multiple sclerosis (MS).

Narcissistic personality disorder Axis II personality disorder characterized by a grandiose sense of self-importance, fantasies of unlimited success, a need for excessive admiration, and a willingness to exploit others to achieve personal goals. Narcissists feel that they are entitled to special treatment and may use others in order to get what they want. They lack empathy for others and frequently believe others are envious of them.

Narcolepsy A rare sleep disorder characterized by chronic sleep attacks. An individual with narcolepsy may suddenly fall into REM sleep at any time, in any place, and often at inappropriate times.

Narcotics See *opiates*.

Nativist approach The theory that language development is the result of a genetically based ability.

Natural selection According to Darwin, traits and behaviors exist in humans because these attributes allowed our ancestors to adapt, survive, and reproduce.

Naturalistic observation The descriptive research method that involves carefully and systematically watching human or animal behavior as it occurs in the natural environment.

Nature In the nature versus nurture debate, this term refers to influences on behavior that are genetic or biological.

Nature versus nurture The ongoing debate in psychology regarding the relative contributions of genes (nature) and environment (nurture) in regard to particular behaviors.

Negative correlation A correlation that indicates that high scores on one variable will be paired with low scores on the other variable. Also called inverse correlation.

Negative punishment An operant conditioning technique that involves removing a desirable stimulus after the behavior to decrease the likelihood of the behavior occurring in the future.

Negative reinforcement An operant conditioning technique that involves removing an undesirable (aversive) stimulus after the behavior to increase the likelihood of the behavior happening again in the future.

Negative skewed distribution A distribution in which most of the scores will be high and the tail of the distribution will be pointing to the left or the negative side of the number line. The mean will be lower than the median in a negatively skewed distribution. Also called left skewed.

Negative symptoms The symptoms of schizophrenia that involve behaviors, thoughts, or emotions that are a normal part of functioning that are absent or dramatically decreased in the individual.

Nerve A bundle of axons from many neurons.

Nerve deafness See *sensorineural deafness*.

Nervous system The brain and spinal cord, plus all of the neurons traveling throughout the rest of the body.

Neural network A hypothetical model of an integrated system of communication consisting of groups of neurons that are connected with one another sending and receiving messages.

Neurogenesis The development of new neurons.

Neuroleptics Conventional antipsychotic medications that had movement side effects and worked as antagonists by blocking dopamine transmission.

Neuron A highly specialized nerve cell responsible for receiving and transmitting information in electrical and chemical forms. Neurons are the fundamental building blocks of the nervous system.

Neurotransmitters The chemical messengers that bind with the dendrites of the receiving neuron at specific receptor sites.

Neutral stimulus (NS) A factor in the environment that does not cause the reaction being studied before acquisition.

Night terrors A sleep disorder characterized by an individual who abruptly awakens during stage four sleep and experiences increased physiological responses, such as faster heart rate and rapid breathing. Also called sleep terrors.

Nightmare A dream occurring during REM sleep that is associated with fear or dread.

Node of Ranvier The regularly spaced gaps in the myelin sheath along the axon enabling the ion exchange which results in saltatory conduction.

Nomothetic personality studies The approach to personality study that emphasizes the use of large numbers of participants in order to generate basic principles of behavior that can be applied to all individuals.

Nondeclarative memories See *implicit memories.*

Nondirective According to Rogers, a type of therapy in which the client is at the center of the process; does the thinking, talking, and problem solving.

Norepinephrine A neurotransmitter associated with mood and sleep. Low levels are associated with depression.

Normal distribution A symmetrical bell curve that forms if the mean, median, and mode are all equal and located at the center of the distribution.

Normative social influence The desire to conform to the behavior of others that occurs because of the need to be accepted and liked.

Norm (1) The conditioned social rule that provides information on how to behave. (2) The typical score for a pretested group that allows for the comparison of an individual test subject with the larger group.

NREM The stages of sleep that do not include REM consisting of stages one to four. Also called non-REM sleep.

Nucleus accumbens A small region of the forebrain near the limbic system associated with the pleasure or reward circuit. An area rich in dopamine receptors that is involved in drug dependency.

Null hypothesis A prediction that the independent variable will have no effect on the dependent variable or that the findings resulted from chance. The goal of research is to reject the null hypothesis.

Nurture In the nature versus nurture debate, this term refers to the influence of environmental factors, such as family, nutrition, culture, interactions with others, education, and wealth, on behavior.

Obedience A change in behavior in response to a demand from an authority figure.

Object permanence According to Piaget, the awareness that items (objects) continue to exist even when they cannot be seen. The understanding of object permanence appears around nine months, halfway through Piaget's sensorimotor stage of cognitive development.

Objective personality test A questionnaire that asks individuals to indicate if specific statements about behaviors, symptoms, emotions, or thoughts relate to them personally. Also called self-report inventory.

Observational learning A type of learning that involves how organisms develop new skills, knowledge, and behaviors by watching other organisms perform and imitating these behaviors.

Obsession A persistent, irrational, and unwanted thought, which cannot be dismissed and results in high levels of anxiety characteristic of individuals with obsessive-compulsive disorder.

Obsessive-compulsive disorder (OCD) Axis I anxiety disorder is characterized by persistent, repetitive, and unwanted thoughts (obsessions) and behaviors (compulsions).

Obsessive-compulsive personality disorder Axis II personality disorder characterized by perfectionist behaviors and a preoccupation with doing things the correct way.

Occipital lobes An area of the cerebral cortex located at the back of the cortex responsible for visual processing.

Oedipus complex According to Freud, a boy's sexual attraction to the opposite sex parent (mother) and a desire to eliminate the parent of the same sex (father), who is seen as a rival. Also called Electra complex for girls.

Olfaction A synonym for the sense of smell.

One-word stage A stage in language development when infants communicate by using only single words, called holophrases, to express themselves that occurs between ten and eighteen months. Also called holophrastic stage.

Operant conditioning According to Skinner, a type of learning that involves voluntary, goal-directed behavior that is under the organism's control. Behavior is shaped and maintained by consequences (rewards or punishments) that follow a response.

Operational definition A variable that is stated as precisely as possible including how it will be measured in order for replication to occur.

Opiate A specific type of depressant that comes from an opium poppy plant that produces euphoria, pain reduction, and insensitivity to stimuli in the environment. Opiates are extremely physically and psychologically addictive. Also called narcotics.

Opponent-process theory (1) The theory of color vision that states that there are three pairs of opponent neurons that work together. One-half of the opponent pair is inhibited by the other half of the pair that is activated. The complementary pairs are red–green, blue–yellow, and white–black. (2) An emotion theory that states all emotions are accompanied by an opposite emotional reaction; for example, fear is followed by relief, sadness by happiness.

Optic chiasm The place in the brain where the optic nerve from each eye meets. Half of the optic fibers cross to the opposite hemisphere at the optic chiasm, thus providing information from both eyes to each hemisphere of the brain.

Optic disk The place on the retina where the optic nerve leaves the eye and there are no photoreceptors.

Optimistic explanatory style The tendency to explain negative events in terms that are external, unstable, and specific. These individuals are more resistant to depression.

Oral stage The first stage in Freud's psychosexual development theory in which the libido or sexual energy is located in the mouth and the infant derives pleasure from placing things in his or her mouth. This stage occurs from birth to approximately one year of age. Fixation can result in an oral personality.

Organ of Corti The lining on the basilar membrane of the inner ear that contains the hair cells which are the receptors for hearing.

Organizational psychology A subtype of industrial-organizational psychology that supports companies and organizations by creating more productive work climates in order to increase employee morale and productivity.

Ossicles The three tiny bones in the middle ear that transmit the sound vibrations from the eardrum to the cochlea. The ossicles consist of the malleus (hammer), incus (anvil), and stapes (stirrup).

Out-group homogeneity The ability to distinguish differences among members of one's in-groups more easily than among members of out-groups.

Out-group A group that is perceived as being different from the group one belongs to.

Overconfidence bias The tendency to overestimate how correct one's predictions and beliefs about ideas actually are.

Overextension An error in language when young children are too broad in their use of a particular word.

Overgeneralization (1) An error in language when young children apply rules about grammar to every example before they learn about exceptions. Also called overregularization. (2) A cognitive distortion consisting of a blanket and all-inclusive judgment an individual makes about who they are and their entire life based on only one specific incident.

Overjustification effect The unusual result that happens if a person is given an extrinsic reward for performance that causes his or her level of intrinsic motivation for the same task to decrease in the future.

Overlearning The continued rehearsal of material after one has mastered it. Overlearning has been shown to reduce the amount of forgetting and help individuals hold on to material over longer periods.

Pancreas The endocrine gland located close to the stomach that produces insulin and glucagon, which regulate sugar metabolism.

Panic disorder Axis I anxiety disorder characterized by recurrent unexpected panic attacks, followed by at least one month of persistent concern about having another panic attack.

Parallel distributed processing model The theory that suggests that encoding of memories happens through the building of connections and that retrieval occurs through the spreading of activation within this large network. Also called connectionist model.

Parallel processing The activity of a combination of many neurons firing in multiple brain regions at once, rather than individually in order for the brain to be faster and more efficient.

Paranoid personality disorder Axis II personality disorder that refers to an overall disposition that is extremely suspicious (paranoid), secretive, scheming, and argumentative.

Paranoid schizophrenia Axis I psychological disorder and subtype of schizophrenia that involves the presence of numerous and organized delusions, usually of persecution, but sometimes of grandeur or control. Auditory and visual hallucinations often accompany the delusions. Paranoid schizophrenics have lost touch with reality.

Parapsychology The study of extrasensory perceptions (ESP).

Parasympathetic nervous system The branch of the autonomic nervous system that acts to calm the body, maintain bodily functions, and conserve energy. When the parasympathetic nervous system is activated, the body is in a state of "rest and digest" as all the bodily systems slow down except for digestion. This is key to replenishment of bodily resources.

Parietal lobes The area of the cerebral cortex located directly behind the frontal lobes that are in charge of receiving sensory information about the somatic senses of touch, pain, and temperature. The somatosensory cortex is at the front of the parietal lobes.

Partial reinforcement schedule The operant conditioning technique reinforcing the desired behavior only some of the time. This technique creates behaviors that are less likely to become extinct. Also called intermittent reinforcement.

Peg-word mnemonic system A method that requires that the person first memorize a series of words (pegs) connected to numbers. In order to memorize a list each new term is associated with the peg-word through the use of imagery.

Penis envy According to Freud, the desire girls or women have to possess a male sex organ. This concept is rarely accepted by modern psychologists.

Percentile rank The percentage of scores equal to or below a specific score in a distribution.

Perception The interpretation of sensations in the brain. Perception includes the cognitive processes of receiving, encoding, storing, and organizing sensations.

Perceptual constancy The ability to hold onto the perception of an object despite continuous change.

Perceptual set The predisposition to interpret an event or stimulus in a particular way based on beliefs, emotions, or previous experiences.

Peripheral nervous system (PNS) The part of the nervous system that includes all the neural cells and nerves outside of the spinal cord and skull and carries information to and from the central nervous system through motor and sensory neurons.

Peripheral route of persuasion The basis for attitude change that focuses on positive or negative associations and emotional appeals.

Individuals are persuaded by surface or external factors and not the strength of the argument presented.

Permissive parenting According to Baumrind, the parenting style in which the parent provides few expectations and rules and allows the child to make their own decisions. There are high levels of communication as well as warmth and love.

Persona According to Jung, it is an archetype which is described as a mask that a person presents to other people, and this mask is shown to the outside world when an individual is acting out a role from the collective unconscious.

Personal constructs According to the personality theory of George Kelly, the concepts that individuals create to help them predict or explain their experiences.

Personal fable According to Elkind, a sense that one is completely unique and invincible that develops during adolescence. An aspect of adolescent egocentrism.

Personal unconscious According to Jung, the unconscious that contains an individual's painful or upsetting memories and information that has been repressed.

Personality disorders A category of Axis II disorders that are characterized by chronic and unchanging patterns of perception, behavior, emotion, or thinking that are substantially inconsistent with the expectations of one's culture. These patterns must be rigid, maladaptive, and result in personal distress and difficulty functioning. Personality disorders begin during adolescence and continue throughout adulthood.

Personality psychology A specialty of psychology that examines an individual's stable traits and factors that influence temperament. Personality psychologists develop methods of personality assessment.

Personnel psychology A subtype of industrial/organizational psychology that assists companies with the process of hiring and evaluating worker performance based on data from empirical research. Personnel psychologists may also be involved in administering tests and providing employee training.

Person–situation controversy The ongoing debate in psychology regarding whether or not traits (person) or the situation is more reliable in terms of predicting behavior.

Persuasion A type of social influence that involves various methods designed to change the behavior of others by convincing them to alter their beliefs or behaviors.

Pessimistic explanatory style The tendency to explain setbacks and failures in terms that are personal or internal, global, and stable. Associated with a higher risk for depression.

Phallic stage The third stage in Freud's psychosexual development in which the libido is focused on the genitals occurring from approximately three to six years of age. Children are attracted to their opposite sex parent and feel hostility toward the same sex parent in what is known as the Oedipus or Electra complex.

Phenotype The observable characteristics of genes.

Phenylketonuria (PKU) A condition caused by a recessive gene resulting in the inability to process a specific amino acid leading to a buildup of toxins in the nervous system that will result in brain damage and mental retardation if it is not detected early and treated with dietary restrictions.

Phi phenomenon An illusion of movement created when a group of stationary lights placed in a row turn on and off in rapid sequence. The result is the perception by the brain of a single light moving across space.

Phobia An Axis I anxiety disorder characterized by an intense, irrational, and persistent fear of a specific object or situation that poses no actual danger, which leads to avoidance and anxiety that disrupts normal life. The *DSM-IV-TR* divides phobias into separate categories of specific phobias, social phobias, and agoraphobia.

Phonemes The smallest units of sound in a language, including the first sounds infants make.

Photoreceptors The specialized receptor cells (rods and cones) responsible for sensing light waves and converting them into neural messages.

Phrenology The study of how bumps on an individual's head indicated personality traits, skills, and intelligence.

Physical dependence The presence of physiological withdrawal symptoms.

Pineal gland An endocrine gland that regulates sleep cycles by releasing the hormone melatonin.

Pitch The highness or lowness of a sound determined by the frequency of the sound wave.

Pituitary gland The gland that regulates various biological processes including growth, breast milk production, childbirth contractions, and bonding. The pituitary communicates to other glands to coordinate the release of hormones and is therefore sometimes called the master gland.

Place theory A theory for pitch that states that an individual perceives a range of pitches because sound waves activate hair cells in different locations (places) along the basilar membrane. Place theory explains the perception of high-pitched sounds well, but does not accurately represent low-pitched sounds.

Placebo A chemically inert material that has the same appearance as an active drug; allows psychologists to test the effects of the expectations of subjects who believe they are actually taking a drug. The placebo effect is any situation in which subjects believe they are experiencing a manipulation by the experimenter when in fact they are not.

Plasticity The ability of the brain to modify itself as an adaptation to experience or repair itself after damage. For example, if a particular area in the brain is damaged, nearby areas can learn to assume the functions of the regions that were destroyed by developing new connections between dendrites.

Pleasure principle According to Freud, the id's desire for immediate satisfaction and the avoidance of pain.

Polygraph An instrument used to record various physiological measures such as galvanic skin response, and heart rate. The validity of this device is controversial and the results of a polygraph test are not allowed into evidence in most American courts. Also called a "lie detector."

Pons The section of the hindbrain located above the medulla on the brainstem in charge of sleep, arousal, dreams, and facial expressions.

Population All the members of a group that could be selected for research and to whom the results apply.

Positive correlation A correlation that indicates that as one variable increases, so does the second variable or as one variable decreases, so does the other. In a positive correlation, both variables move in the same direction. Also called direct correlation.

Positive psychology The scientific study of human virtues such as wisdom, altruism, justice, and courage.

Positive punishment An operant conditioning technique that involves adding an undesirable (aversive) stimulus also called a punisher after the behavior to decrease the likelihood of the behavior occurring in the future.

Positive reinforcement An operant conditioning technique that involves the procedure of adding a desirable stimulus after the behavior to increase the likelihood of the behavior occurring in the future.

Positive symptoms The symptoms of schizophrenia that involve thoughts and behaviors that are unpleasant additions to the functioning of an individual. Examples of positive symptoms of schizophrenia include hallucinations, delusions, and disorganized thought.

Positively skewed A type of distribution in which most of the scores will be low and the tail of the distribution will be pointing toward the right, or positive side, of the number line. The mean will be higher than the median in a positively skewed distribution. Also called right skewed.

Positron emission tomography (PET) A brain imaging device that involves the injection of a small harmless amount of radioactive material such as glucose (sugar) into the bloodstream and indicates areas of the brain active during cognitive tasks by tracking the specific structures using the radioactive material as fuel resulting in a color-coded image.

Postconventional level According to Kohlberg, the third and final level of moral development in which decisions about morality are based on social contracts and universal ethics.

Posthypnotic amnesia The phenomenon in which individuals are not able to remember what transpired while they were hypnotized.

Posthypnotic suggestion The idea that statements made by a hypnotist, while a person is hypnotized, will be able to influence the person's behavior later.

Post-traumatic stress disorder (PTSD) Axis I anxiety disorder characterized by intense feelings of anxiety, horror, and helplessness after experiencing a traumatic event such as a violent crime, natural disaster, or military combat.

Power test An assessment that measures abilities under testing conditions involving little or no time pressure.

Preconscious According to Freud, the level of the mind that contains information an individual is aware of but not currently thinking about and is located between the unconscious and conscious.

Preconventional level According to Kohlberg, the first level of moral development in which decisions about morality are based on punishment and rewards.

Predictive validity The extent to which a score on a test forecasts (predicts) future behaviors or results.

Prefrontal cortex An area of the cerebral cortex made up of association areas that control conscious thoughts and actions, working memory, and short-term and long-term planning. The prefrontal cortex is the area at the very front of the frontal lobes. Also called prefrontal association area.

Prefrontal lobotomies A type of psychosurgery that includes the removal of certain areas of the prefrontal cortex of the brain or the severing of connections between the prefrontal cortex and the rest of the brain. This method is not used today.

Prejudice A negative attitude held regarding members of another group that is emotionally, rigidly, or inflexibly felt and acted on.

Premack principle The theory that states that the opportunity to engage in a preferred activity can be used to reinforce a less-preferred activity. Also called Premack's principle.

Preoperational stage According to Piaget's cognitive development theory, the second stage characterized by symbolic but prelogical thought and not merely sensory and motor experiences. This stage involves symbolic thought, language, pretend play, egocentrism, centration, animism, and irreversibility. It occurs between the ages of two and seven.

Primacy effect In verbal learning, the tendency to recall items at the beginning of the list better than items in the middle. There is little proactive interference at this point.

Primary auditory cortex An area of cortex located in the upper area of the temporal lobes that processes most auditory information.

Primary drive An innate bodily function. Examples of stimuli having a primary motivational effect are food, water, air, temperature, or an intense stimulus such as a loud noise or electric shock.

Primary emotions The emotions that are universally recognized across cultures. These emotions include fear, anger, joy, sadness, disgust, contempt, and surprise.

Primary motor cortex The strip of cortex at the rear of the frontal lobes, parallel to the sensory cortex that controls voluntary movement.

Primary reinforcer A stimulus that increases the likelihood that an organism will repeat a particular behavior because it fulfills a biological need.

Primary sexual characteristics The traits directly related to reproduction including the reproductive organs and external genitalia that develop during puberty, allowing individuals to become capable of producing viable sperm or eggs.

Primary somatosensory cortex The strip of cortex at the front of parietal lobes, parallel to the motor cortex in charge of receiving sensory input for touch and body position. Also called the sensory cortex.

Primary visual cortex The area of the cortex located in the occipital lobes that processes visual information.

Priming The retrieval process is aided for an individual if they have been exposed to a stimulus previously. This prior exposure or priming will make it more likely that they will recall that same or a similar stimulus later.

Prisoner's dilemma A social trap based on a scenario when two people are immediately separated after being arrested for a serious crime. Prisoners have the choice to cooperate with their partner or to compete by confessing. The best result would be for both partners to cooperate.

Proactive interference A memory problem that occurs when previously learned information interferes with the ability to recall a new memory.

For proactive interference, old information gets in the way of new information and prevents the recall of new information. Also called negative inhibition or negative transfer.

Procedural memory The most well-known category of implicit memory that consists of the long-term memory of skills, habits, and cognitive rules involved in particular tasks.

Projection A defense mechanism that involves unconsciously reducing anxiety by attributing one's own fears, feelings, faults, or unacceptable thoughts and behaviors to another person or group.

Projective test A personality assessment in which the participant is given an ambiguous stimulus and asked to respond to it. Projective tests are used in psychodynamic and psychoanalytic therapy. Common examples include the Rorschach Inkblot Test and the Thematic Apperception Test.

Prosocial behaviors The actions taken by an individual that are intended to help others.

Prototype The best example of a category.

Proximity A Gestalt principle that objects, events, or individuals that are physically close to each other are perceived as a group.

Psychiatric nurse A nurse that has an RN degree that specializes in treating individuals suffering from psychological illnesses. Psychiatric nurses dispense psychotropic medications and provide assistance and support to patients.

Psychiatrist A physician (MD) that works with the diagnosis and treatment of psychological illnesses. Psychiatrists are licensed to prescribe psychotropic medications as a part of treatment. In addition to biomedical treatment, many psychiatrists also utilize psychotherapy.

Psychoactive drug A substance that produces changes in consciousness effecting thought, mood, and perception. Also called psychotropic drugs.

Psychoanalysis A specific type of psychotherapy developed by Sigmund Freud designed to treat psychological illnesses by discovering the unconscious conflicts and motives responsible for the symptoms individuals are experiencing. Also called analysis.

Psychoanalyst A therapist that utilizes Freudian psychoanalysis in the diagnosis and treatment of psychological illnesses that is usually, although not always, a medical doctor or psychologist with a PhD or PsyD.

Psychoanalytic perspective A psychological perspective developed by Sigmund Freud that explains personality and human behavior as being the result of unresolved unconscious conflicts from childhood or unconscious sexual and aggressive instincts.

Psychodynamic perspective A psychological perspective that emerged from the pioneering work of Freud's psychoanalysis. This perspective continues to emphasize the importance of the unconscious and childhood experiences, but disagrees with Freud's emphasis on sexual drives in determining personality. These revisions include an increased focus on conscious influences, social interaction, and culture in the development of personality and how development continues across the lifespan.

Psychodynamic therapy A type of treatment that involves the various modern methods of psychotherapy that are based on the principles of psychoanalysis. Often these therapies are shorter in duration, identify specific goals, and involve the therapist taking a more active versus passive role in the process.

Psychological dependence The intense cravings created by the reinforcing properties of some psychotropic drugs.

Psychology The scientific study of the behavior and mental processes of human and nonhuman animals.

Psychometrics A specialty of psychology concerned with mathematical or numerical methods of measuring psychological variables by creating valid and reliable tests.

Psychopathology The scientific investigation of the cause (etiology), diagnosis, and treatment of mental illness. Also called abnormal psychology.

Psychopharmacology The scientific study of how drugs impact physical, cognitive, and behavioral functioning by interacting with the nervous system.

Psychophysics A specialty of psychology heavily influenced by German scientist Gustav Fechner who studies how physical stimuli (sensations) translate to psychological experiences (perceptions).

Psychosis A severe psychological disorder characterized by a loss of touch with reality and significant impairment in thought (delusions), perception (hallucinations), language, and emotion associated with severe mental illness.

Psychosocial development Erikson's developmental stage theory in which individuals pass through eight developmental stages, each involving a crisis that must be successfully resolved.

Psychosurgery The most drastic form of biomedical therapy involving the purposeful surgical removal or destruction of particular areas in the brain.

Psychotherapist A broad designation that includes a variety of professionals that have been specifically trained and granted a license to practice by a state board to provide therapy to individuals with psychological illnesses or adjustment problems.

Psychotherapy A variety of communication techniques and interventions designed to assist individuals suffering from psychological illnesses to identify and overcome difficulties they are experiencing. Also called therapy or talk therapy.

Public goods dilemma A social trap in which individuals must decide how much to contribute to a shared resource.

Punishment An operant conditioning technique designed to decrease a voluntary behavior.

Puzzle box A small cage with a lever that can be pressed to release a latch and free the animal. Edward Thorndike used puzzle boxes to study instrumental learning and the law of effect with cats.

p value An inferential statistic that indicates if the data from an experiment are statistically significant. In order for the results to be considered statistically significant, the p value must be =.05.

Quasi-experiment A type of experiment that does not include random assignment. In quasi-experiments, the difference between the experimental and the control groups has been previously determined because the variable being studied has already taken effect.

Random assignment An experimental method that ensures that each participant has an equal chance of being assigned to either the experimental or the control group. Random assignment is required in order to determine if there is a cause and effect relationship between the independent and the dependent variables.

Random sample A sample of cases drawn from the larger population in such a way that every member of the population has an equal chance of being drawn for the sample.

Random selection An experimental method that involves choosing a random sample in which each member of the population has an equal chance of being selected for the sample.

Range A measure of variance that describes the distance or spread between the highest and the lowest scores in the distribution.

Rational-emotive behavioral therapy (REBT) A type of psychotherapy developed by Albert Ellis that is designed to eliminate emotional problems through the rational examination of irrational beliefs.

Rationalization A defense mechanism that involves unconsciously reducing anxiety by creating logical excuses for unacceptable thoughts and behaviors.

Reaction formation A defense mechanism that involves unconsciously reducing anxiety by acting or saying the exact opposite of the morally or socially unacceptable beliefs held by an individual.

Reality principle According to Freud, the ego works according to the reality principle by balancing the impulses of the id with the constraints of reality and the superego's desire for perfection.

Recall The ability to retrieve information or experiences from memory consciously without clues such as an essay question.

Recency effect The ability to recall the items at the end of a list well.

Receptor site The area at the end of a dendrite on a postsynaptic neuron that receives neurotransmitters to initiate cell firing. The receptor sites of dendrites are specifically designed for particular neurotransmitters.

Reciprocal determinism According to Bandura, how people think, how people behave, and what their environment is like all interact to influence the consistency of behavior.

Recognition The ability to remember information consciously through the use of previously learned material such as a multiple-choice question.

Reference group A group with which an individual shares common aspects of social identity such as gender, interests, ethnicity, and occupation.

Reflex An automatic response to a stimulus dependent on unlearned neural connections; exhibiting reflexive behavior.

Refractory period The stage when repolarization is occurring and the neuron cannot fire because it is resetting itself to its original resting potential state.

Regression A defense mechanism that involves unconsciously reducing anxiety by reverting to thoughts and behaviors that would be more appropriate during an earlier period of development. Individuals may behave in a childlike manner to get what they want.

Regression to the mean The tendency for unusual or extreme events to move toward the average when remeasured, due to unreliability of measurement.

Reinforcement An operant conditioning technique designed to increase a voluntary behavior.

Reinforcer Any stimulus that increases the chance that a particular voluntary behavior will be repeated in the future.

Relative brightness A monocular cue in which an object appears closer to the viewer because it is bright and reflects a greater amount of light.

Relative clarity A monocular cue in which an object appears closer to the viewer because it is clear within the atmosphere. Atmospheric changes can include dust, fog, clouds, and precipitation.

Relative deprivation A phenomenon that occurs when we compare ourselves with our reference group and find that regardless of how much wealth, status, and appreciation we are receiving, it is less than what others who are similar to us have.

Relative height A monocular cue in which an object appears closer to the viewer because it is lower in the visual field.

Relative size A monocular cue in which an object appears closer to the viewer because it is larger in comparison with other objects in the visual field.

Reliability The consistency or repeatability of a particular assessment over repeated measurements.

REM sleep The stage of sleep during which rapid eye movements (REM) and dreams usually occur. This stage is often referred to as paradoxical sleep because it is simultaneously characterized by active eye movements and brain wave activity as well as the loss of muscle movement. Also called paradoxical sleep.

Replication The experimental method that involves repeating the exact procedures and obtaining the same results. In order to reduce the risk that the results occurred by chance all conclusions drawn from psychological research must be replicated.

Repolarization The stage when the sodium–potassium pump is returning the ions to their original positions either inside or outside of the axon reestablishing the resting potential.

Representative sample A sample that is similar to the population as a whole in regard to variables that might impact the results such as gender, religious affiliation, income, and ethnicity.

Representativeness A heuristic or shortcut that involves judging the likelihood of an event in terms of how well it seems to match a particular prototype, which can result in either a correct or incorrect analysis of the situation. Also called a representative heuristic.

Repression A defense mechanism that involves unconsciously reducing anxiety by blocking a painful incident or event from awareness. Anxiety-producing unacceptable wishes and thoughts are pushed into the unconscious.

Residual schizophrenia Axis I psychological disorder and subtype of schizophrenia characterized by at least one schizophrenic episode, but the absence of significant positive symptoms. The individual may experience some remnants (residual) symptoms such as social withdrawal, unusual beliefs, or peculiar behaviors.

Resistance According to Freud, a psychoanalytic method that includes the various methods that patients employ to avoid confronting the\painful, repressed memories, and conflicts that are the actual cause of their problems.

Resting potential The state while the neuron is waiting for a message, in which the fluid-filled interior of the axon has a negative charge and the fluid exterior has a positive charge. During the resting potential, the axon is said to be polarized and the sodium (Na^+) ions are on the outside and the potassium (K^+) ions are on the inside.

Reticular activating system (reticular formation and connections) The network of nerves running vertically through the brainstem and extending to the thalamus responsible for arousal to stimuli, sleep, attentiveness, and the filtering of incoming stimuli. Damage can result in coma or death.

Reticular formation See *reticular activating system*.

Retina A photosensitive layer of receptor cells located at the back of the eye where transduction for vision occurs.

Retinal disparity A binocular cue in which an object appears closer to the viewer because there is a larger difference between the separate images provided by each eye when viewing the object. Also called binocular disparity.

Retrieval The recovery of information from memory storage that can either occur rapidly with little or no effort or require attention and effort.

Retrieval cue A stimulus or aid that helps to elicit the recall of a memory by an individual.

Retrieval failure The forgetting or inability to retrieve information that has been successfully stored in long-term memory.

Retroactive interference A memory problem that happens when recently learned information prevents the recall of old memories. For retroactive interference, new information gets in the way of old information and prevents the recall of old information. Also called retroactive inhibition.

Retrograde amnesia The inability to remember events or information stored before the illness or injury that caused the amnesia.

Reuptake The process by which neurotransmitters are reabsorbed by the presynaptic neuron.

Reversibility The cognitive ability that develops during Piaget's concrete operational stage in which an individual can perform actions and mentally undo or reverse them.

Risky shift The tendency for individuals to make more extreme (risky) decisions after having a group discussion than they would have made individually.

Rods The photoreceptors that are very sensitive under low light conditions such as nighttime but do not provide as much acuity or detail and cannot see color. The rods are primarily responsible for peripheral vision and black-and-white vision.

Rooting reflex An automatic response shown by newborns when their cheek is touched that involves turning toward the source. This reflex gradually weakens during the first six months after birth.

Rorschach Inkblot Test A projective assessment that involves participants being presented with a series of cards that have blots of ink on them one at a time in a specific order. Participants must explain what they see and their response is interpreted by the test administrator.

Saltatory conduction The electrical message (action potential) jumping across gaps (nodes of Ranvier).

Sample A small subset of individuals chosen to represent the population in research; an attempt should be made to make the sample as representative of the population as possible.

Sampling bias A selection method resulting in a sample that is not representative of the population or that does not provide all of the members of a population an equal chance to be chosen for the study that can result in distorted findings.

Satiety The feeling of being full and not hungry that results in decreasing the likelihood that an individual will be motivated to eat.

Savant syndrome A rare condition marked by an island of brilliance in relation to limited cognitive abilities. A savant is someone who is diagnosed as cognitively disabled or with a developmental disorder such as autism but that also displays an exceptional skill in a limited domain such as music, art, math, or calculating dates.

Scaffolding The providing of just enough assistance to the learner in order for them to understand. Scaffolding is related to the zone of proximal development because the teacher continually adjusts how much support is needed as learning progresses.

Scapegoat theory The theory for prejudice that states that innocent out-group members are blamed by an individual or community for a negative experience.

Scatterplot A graph that illustrates the correlation between two or more variables. Positive correlations create scatterplots where the data forms a curve or line going up and negative correlations create curves on a scatterplot that go down. Also called a scattergram.

Schachter–Singer theory An emotion theory that states physical arousal and cognitive labeling of that arousal combine to produce the subjective experience of emotion. Also called two-factor theory of emotion.

Schema A mental framework that organizes past experiences in order to make faster or more accurate perceptions.

Schizoid personality disorder Axis II personality disorder characterized by individuals that are detached from and not interested in forming social relationships. These individuals have difficulty experiencing pleasure and display a very narrow range of emotional responses in social situations.

Schizophrenia A group of Axis I psychological disorders involving a breakdown of the thinking process, disengagement from reality, and flattened affect (emotion). Schizophrenia is characterized by significant disturbances in cognition, emotion, perceptions, behavior, and speech that dramatically impair functioning.

Schizotypal personality disorder Axis II personality disorder characterized by social isolation and the presence of odd beliefs and behaviors. This personality disorder is the one that is closest to schizophrenia.

School psychologist A psychologist who works directly with students who exhibit emotional or learning problems to overcome educational difficulties in a K-12 setting.

Scientific method The process of developing knowledge by creating a theory and a hypothesis, selecting a method and designing a study, collecting and analyzing the results, and finally publishing results.

Secondary disposition (trait) According to Allport, a personality trait that influences behavior to a much lesser extent and includes individual preferences in terms of food, music, fashion, and hobbies.

Secondary drives A source of motivation that is learned through experience. Examples include learned desires such as success, power, affection, money, appearance, or security. Some psychologists include fear, anxiety, and certain verbal cues as learned drives as well.

Secondary reinforcers Originally neutral stimuli that come to function as reinforcers as the result of their learned association with primary reinforcers.

Second-order conditioning See *higher-order conditioning*.

Secondary sex characteristics The characteristics that have no effect on physical reproduction, but also develop during puberty.

Secure attachment An emotional bond the child develops with a caregiver. The securely attached child uses the caregiver as a secure base to explore the environment and interact with strangers. In the context of the strange situation experiment, the child is visibly upset when the mother leaves, but calms down shortly after the mother returns.

Selective attention The process of making choices regarding which stimuli to focus on and which to ignore. Selective attention plays a significant role in determining what information is transferred from sensory memory to short-term memory or from short-term to long-term memory.

Selective serotonin reuptake inhibitor (SSRI) A category of antidepressant medications that reduce the reuptake of the neurotransmitter serotonin. Commonly prescribed SSRIs include Prozac (fluoxetine), Paxil (paroxetine), and Zoloft (sertraline).

Self-actualization According to Maslow, the motive that drives people to reach their greatest potential.

Self-concept The unique beliefs and personality characteristics one has about oneself.

Self-effacing bias The tendency to attribute our failures to dispositional factors and our successes to situational factors. This results in modesty by taking responsibility for one's failures and crediting the contributions of others for one's successes and is more common in collectivist cultures.

Self-efficacy According to Bandura, the level of confidence an individual has regarding his or her ability to perform particular tasks or skills. Individuals may have high or low self-efficacy.

Self-esteem The value judgment one makes about how worthy of a person one is based on comparisons with oneself in the past as well as how one measures up to others.

Self-fulfilling prophecy (1) A phenomenon that occurs when the expectations people have about themselves lead them to alter their behavior, causing their expectations to come true. (2) A phenomenon that occurs when your beliefs about another person or group lead you to act in a way that brings about the behaviors you expect from them and confirm your original impression.

Self-handicapping A strategy individuals use to create a convenient situational explanation for potential failures before they happen.

Self-reference effect The tendency for an individual to have improved recall for information that personally relates to their life.

Self-report inventories Questionnaires that ask people to judge their agreement with statements describing behavior that might be indicative of some particular trait.

Self-serving bias The tendency to attribute one's successes to dispositional factors and failures to situational factors. This is due to the desire to see oneself in a positive way and is more common in individualistic cultures.

Semantics In language, the part of grammar that involves the meaning of words and their combinations.

Semantic encoding The deep processing of meaning that provides the strongest results for memory retention. Also called semantic code.

Semantic memory An explicit memory of general knowledge material that is not specifically related to particular places, times, or events.

Sensation The experience of sensory stimuli and knowledge about the surrounding world based on information received via the sensory organs.

Sensorimotor stage According to Piaget's cognitive development theory, the first stage that occurs from birth to two years of age. Learning during this stage develops through sensory and motor experiences.

Sensorineural deafness Hearing loss that results from damage to the aspects of the auditory system related to the transduction of sound waves. Damage to the cochlea or cilia on the basilar membrane, or the auditory nerve can all result in sensorineural deafness. Severe sensorineural deafness may be treated with a cochlear implant. Also called nerve deafness.

Sensory adaptation The decline in sensitivity that is the result of exposure to a constant and unchanging stimulus.

Sensory homunculus A symbolic representation of the sensory cortex in the form of a distorted figure that represents the proportion of brain area dedicated to each body part in relationship to sensitivity of stimuli.

Sensory memory The first stage in the information-processing model of memory developed by Atkinson and Shiffrin that involves very short-lived recordings of sensory information that usually last for seconds or less. Sensory memory includes both echoic (very brief auditory memories) and iconic (very brief visual memories) that allow the brain to process the information before it fades from memory. Also called the sensory register.

Separation anxiety The normal distress experienced by a young child when a caregiver leaves. Separation anxiety is the strongest between the ages of ten months and six years.

Serial position effect The ability to remember the items at the beginning and the end of a list better than items presented in the middle of a list. Also called the primacy recency effect.

Serial processing Solving a problem one step at a time, a relatively slow process in comparison to parallel processing.

Serotonin A neurotransmitter involved in mood, sleep, and appetite. Low levels are associated with depression, eating disorders, sleep disturbances, and aggression.

Set point theory The theory that individuals have a genetically predetermined range of weight that is maintained by biological processes without effort.

Sex The biological definition of being male or female which is determined by specific anatomical differences.

Sexual-response cycle The four stages of sexual response for both males and females: excitement, plateau, orgasm, and resolution phases.

Shallow processing According to Craik and Lockhart, thinking and memory processes that involve concentrating on the surface characteristics of a concept. The result of shallow processing is often weak, temporary memories that are difficult to retrieve.

Shape constancy The tendency to perceive objects as being the same shape despite the fact that the image on the retina may involve a change in angle or orientation.

Shaping An operant conditioning technique of achieving a desired behavior by gradually reinforcing successively closer approximations of a behavior until the entire correct behavior is displayed.

Short-term memory The second stage in the Atkinson and Shiffrin information-processing model, which has a capacity for approximately seven plus or minus two pieces of information. Without rehearsal, information can be retained for approximately ten to thirty seconds.

Shuttle box A device used to study operant conditioning in animals that has two chambers connected by a doorway that can be opened or closed by the researcher.

Signal detection theory The theory used by psychologists to evaluate how accurately individuals notice faint stimuli under a variety of conditions. Whether or not an individual notices a faint stimulus depends on the stimulus itself, the background stimulation, and characteristics of the individual including their level of attention, motivation, and experience.

Similarity A Gestalt principle in which objects, events, or individuals that are alike in appearance are perceived to belong to the same group.

Simultaneous conditioning A classical conditioning procedure in which the conditioned stimulus (CS) and unconditioned stimulus (UCS) are introduced at the same time.

Single blind A procedure in which the participants are unaware of whether they are receiving the independent variable (drug) or the placebo.

Situational attribution An explanation for behavior based on factors outside the person (luck, social etiquette, and so on). Also called external attribution.

Size constancy The tendency to perceive objects as being the same size despite the fact that the image on the retina may increase or decrease.

Skinner box A small apparatus that studies operant behavior in animals by providing a controlled environment. Also called an operant chamber.

Sleep A state of consciousness during which the brain passes through a series of distinct stages.

Sleep apnea A sleep disorder in which the individual suffers from momentary cessations of breathing that last about ten seconds, until the person briefly wakes up, begins breathing, and falls back asleep.

Sleepwalking A sleep disorder characterized by walking during stage four of sleep. Also called somnambulism.

Social cognitive theory of personality The theory of how personal characteristics, social interactions, and cognitive evaluations are involved in developing an individual's personality.

Social desirability bias The tendency for participants to not answer personal questions honestly in order to depict themselves in a positive way. Also called social desirability response set.

Social dilemma A situation in which individuals must choose whether to cooperate or compete with others. Also called a social trap.

Social exchange theory The theory that individuals balance the costs and rewards of helping and are more likely to assist others if the potential for reward is high and potential costs are low.

Social facilitation The tendency for the presence of others, such as an audience or coworkers, to increase individual performance on easy or well-rehearsed tasks.

Social influence The study of how other individuals' thoughts and actions shape one's own beliefs, feelings, and behaviors.

Social interference The tendency for an individual's performance to decline when complex or poorly learned tasks are performed in the presence of others.

Social learning theory The theory that gender roles may be acquired through the observation of models and operant conditioning.

Social loafing The phenomenon of people contributing less when working with others in a group than when performing the same task alone due to the lessoning of personal accountability.

Social phenomenon theory A theory for hypnosis that states that individuals who are hypnotized are simply playing a role that they have become caught up in, and the behavior they demonstrate is a result of doing what is expected of them in their role.

Social phobia An Axis I anxiety disorder in which the irrational fear an individual has regarding social situations or performing in public prevents him or her from taking part in normal interactions because of the potential threat of embarrassment. Also called social anxiety disorder.

Social psychology A specialty of psychology that focuses on the individual in relation to society and emphasizes how we think about, shape, and connect with one another.

Social striving The increased effort of some individuals when working as part of a group which is more common in collectivist cultures.

Social worker An individual with a master's degree in social work (MSW) who provides treatment for psychological illnesses. Social workers assist clients by coordinating access to support for occupational training, housing, and financial assistance. They

focus more on how environmental factors impact functioning.

Socio-cultural perspective A psychological perspective that focuses on the contribution of diversity and culture to human behavior and mental processes.

Soma The center of the neuron that contains the nucleus and produces energy for the neuron. Also called the cell body.

Somatic nervous system The branch of the peripheral nervous system that consists of the nerves that carry information from the sensory receptors to the central nervous system and the nerves that send information from the central nervous system to regulate voluntary control of skeletal muscles.

Somatization disorder Axis I somatoform disorder in which individuals suffer from a large number of vague and long-lasting physical complaints that do not have an identifiable physical cause.

Somatoform disorders A category of Axis I disorders characterized by physical complaints about conditions that are caused by psychological factors.

Somnambulism See *sleepwalking*.

Sound localization The interpretation by the brain of sound waves entering both ears in order to determine the direction the noise is coming from.

Source amnesia The inability to recall the origin (source) of where a particular memory was acquired despite having a strong recollection of the actual detail about the memory itself.

Source traits According to Cattell, the personality characteristics that underlie the causes of behaviors. Source traits are not easily put into categories and may not have common names.

Spaced practice A procedure in which study time is broken up over several days resulting in increased retention as compared to massed practice. Also called distributed practice.

Specific phobia An Axis I anxiety disorder in which the individual has an irrational fear of objects and situations such as heights, closed spaces, snakes, and spiders that do not pose any actual threat, which prevents them from normal functioning.

Speed test An assessment that determines an examinee's score based in part on how quickly they solve the problems presented.

Spinal reflex The unlearned response to stimuli that happens without instruction from the brain including the knee-jerk and withdrawal reflexes.

Split-half reliability A method used for determining if a test is repeatable (reliable) by comparing the scores on one-half of the test to the scores on the other half of the test.

Spontaneous recovery In classical conditioning, the reoccurrence of an extinguished response following a rest period between extinction and retesting, and with no retraining.

Stability versus change The debate regarding the degree to which as we age our personalities stay the same (stability) or transform (change), resulting in new traits and behaviors.

Standard deviation (SD) A mathematical representation of how far on average each of the individual scores in a data set varies from the mean. In other words, the standard deviation is the average distance of each score from the mean.

Standardization (1) The requirement that the procedures of test administration are kept the same. (2) The establishment of norms or standards for scoring, and interpreting a psychological test. It usually involves administering the test to a large group of people representative of those for whom the test is intended.

State-dependent memory The retrieval process is aided if the individual is in the same physical and mental state that they were in when the information was encoded.

Statistical model The theory that abnormality is defined as behavior that is rare and unusual.

Statistically significant The likelihood that the results of an experiment are not due to chance. Statistical significance does not refer to how important the results are.

Stereotype threat A phenomenon that occurs when an individual's belief that negative stereotypes will be used by others to rate his or her performance results in the individual experiencing anxiety, which leads to lower performance.

Stereotypes The cognitive component of prejudice consisting of schemas for entire groups that assume that all or most of the members share the same negative traits.

Stimulant A category of psychotropic drugs that leads to increased physiological activity and alertness. Such drugs counteract fatigue and produce mood upswings.

Strange situation An experimental method used by Ainsworth that involves a series of orchestrated scenarios with a baby, a caregiver, and a stranger designed to assess the type of attachment bond present between the child and caregiver.

Stranger anxiety The distress and fear experienced when infants or small children are around individuals who are unfamiliar to them.

Stratified sample The process of dividing the population into subgroups (strata) to create a sample that contains members of each subgroup in the same proportion that exists in the larger population. For example, if the population being studied is forty percent Danish and sixty percent Swedish, the stratified sample would also be forty percent Danish and sixty percent Swedish.

Stress An emotional response to demands that are perceived as threatening or exceeding a person's resources or ability to cope.

Stressor The stimulus or event in the environment resulting in psychological tension and threats to internal homeostasis.

Striving for superiority According to Adler, finding personal fulfillment and overcoming challenges.

Stroboscopic effect The perception of movement by the brain when a series of images that change slightly are presented in rapid sequence. Also called the stroboscopic illusion.

Structuralism An early theoretical perspective in psychology founded by Edward Titchener which emphasized examining consciousness by breaking it down into its basic components or structures including sensations, images, and feelings.

Sublimation A defense mechanism that involves unconsciously reducing anxiety by directing aggression toward a more socially acceptable outlet, such as exercise, hard work, sports, or hobbies. Sublimation is a healthier version of displacement.

Subliminal perception The interpretation of very weak or quick stimuli below one's level of consciousness.

Subliminal stimulus A weak stimulus presented below threshold that cannot be consciously registered.

Substance abuse A diagnosis that involves individuals continuing to use a drug despite negative physical or social consequences.

Substance dependence A diagnosis that involves continued drug use despite significant negative physical and social consequences that is also characterized by physical and psychological dependence. Also called addiction.

Subtractive color mixing The removal of wavelengths through absorption. When all of the subtractive primary colors of paint (red, blue, and yellow) are mixed together, the resulting color is black or a lack of any reflected light.

Superego According to Freud, the part of the personality that reminds individuals what ideal behavior consists of and begins developing during childhood. The superego operates on a morality principle, seeking to enforce ethical conduct.

Superordinate goal An obstacle that requires cooperation to ensure success.

Suppression According to Freud, a conscious effort on the part of an individual to block painful memories or unacceptable wishes. Suppression, unlike defense mechanisms, is a conscious process.

Suprachiasmatic nucleus (SCN) A small region within the hypothalamus involved in the regulation of the sleep cycle by controlling the release of melatonin by the pineal gland.

Surface traits According to Cattell, clusters of highly related behaviors.

Survey A descriptive research method in which individuals are asked to reply to a series of questions or to rate their agreement with various statements. Surveys are designed to discover the beliefs, opinions, and attitudes of a sample to draw conclusions about the population.

Sympathetic nervous system The branch of the autonomic nervous system that is active during emergencies. The fight-or-flight response in which all of the bodily systems are aroused except for digestion.

Synapse The extremely narrow space between the terminal button of the sending neuron and the receptor site of the receiving dendrite, which is the location of neurotransmission. Also called the synaptic cleft or gap.

Synaptic vesicles The tiny sacs located in the terminal buttons that are responsible for storing neurotransmitters.

Synesthesia A phenomenon occurring in some individuals in which stimulation of one sensory system generates unexplained sensations in another sensory system.

Syntax The part of grammar that refers to the system of rules within a language regarding the order of how words can be arranged.

Systematic desensitization Wolpe's behavioral therapy method that involves the use of a gradual process of extinguishing a learned phobia by working through a hierarchy of fear-evoking stimuli while staying deeply relaxed.

Tardive dyskinesia The often permanent involuntary movements of the face or tongue that result from extended use of conventional antipsychotics in some individuals. Tardive dyskinesia can also lead to uncontrollable twitching and jerking motions of the arms and legs.

Taste aversions The classically conditioned avoidance of a particular food item or liquid after it becomes associated with nausea.

Telegraphic speech A type of speech that contains only the words essential to meaning, typically nouns and verbs, and lacks other parts of speech typical of children between the ages of 18 and 30 months. Telegraphic speech begins in the two-word stage of language acquisition.

Temperament The biologically influenced activity level, behaviors, and emotional responses typically demonstrated by individuals that is a part of personality.

Temporal comparison The process of comparing our current abilities and traits with our past performance that can lead to either an increase or decrease in self-esteem.

Temporal lobes An area of the cerebral cortex located above the ears responsible for auditory processing (hearing), olfaction (smell), and the recognition of faces.

Teratogens Any chemical, virus, or other agent that reaches the fetus and that can result in harm or a birth defect. Of particular risk is the consumption of alcohol during pregnancy which may lead to fetal alcohol syndrome.

Terminal buttons The small knoblike structures at the end of an axon that contain neurotransmitters in vesicles (sacs) to be released across the synapse. Also called terminal buds or axon terminal.

Testosterone The male sex hormones.

Test-retest reliability A method used for determining if a test is repeatable (reliable) by comparing the scores of the same individuals who take the very same test on two different occasions. Since the test is unchanged, differences from test to retest reflect either change or inconsistency of the individual from one occasion to another.

Texture gradient A monocular cue in which an object appears closer to the viewer because it has a more detailed, distinct texture.

Thalamus A forebrain area consisting of two connected egg-shaped structures located at the top of the brainstem that filters and relays sensory information except for smell to the appropriate parts of the cerebral cortex.

Thanatos According to Freud, the Greek word for death that represents the dark side of human nature including aggressive urges and self-destructive behaviors.

Thematic apperception test (TAT) A projective test consisting of a series of cards that each has a different picture. Participants create a story about the picture and what the person chooses to discuss is considered important. The TAT is used to measure both achievement and affiliation motivations or as a starting point for conversations between clients and psychologists.

Theory An organized explanation for data gained through empirical processes.

Theory of mind The ability to understand the thoughts and intentions of others and predict their behavior that develops in people around the age of four.

Third-variable problem A problem with correlational research because even if two variables are strongly correlated, it is still possible that a third and possibly unknown variable is the reason for the correlation that has been discovered. One of the reasons that correlation does not prove causation.

Threshold The minimum amount of excitatory neurotransmitters that must be received in order for a neuron to fire. If a neuron's threshold is met, the cell fires, but if the minimum threshold is not reached the cell does not fire.

Tip-of-the-tongue phenomenon The retrieval failure that happens when an individual cannot locate the desired word in their memory even though they are sure they know it.

Token economy A reward system with objects or points that can then be traded in for primary reinforcers. Token economies have been successful at changing behaviors in institutional settings including schools, prisons, and mental hospitals.

Tolerance A condition in which an individual will need to take greater amounts or stronger versions of a drug in order to achieve the same psychotropic effect.

Top-down processing The formation of a perception that occurs by utilizing one's memories, expectations, and experiences.

Touch receptor cells The cells responsible for different functions, such as pressure, cold, warmth, and pain.

Trace conditioning A type of forward conditioning in which the conditioned stimulus (CS) is introduced and stopped before the unconditioned (UCS) is introduced. The presentation of the two stimuli is divided by an interval of time.

Trait An enduring and stable personality characteristic that influences a person to act in a consistent way and serves to distinguish one person from another.

Transduction The transformation of energy received from environmental stimuli by specialized receptor cells in sensory organs into neural messages.

Transference According to psychoanalytic theory, the tendency to react to the therapist emotionally in the same way that the patient did toward his or her parents or other important figures during childhood.

Trial and error The problem-solving technique in which individuals attack a problem by making random guesses using little reasoning or analysis.

Trichromatic theory of color vision The theory of color vision that states that there are three types of color photoreceptors (cones) in the retina of each eye that are either most sensitive to red, green, or blue wavelengths. All of the colors of the visible spectrum can be perceived by combining these three reflected wavelengths. Also called the Young–Helmholtz trichromatic theory of color vision.

Tricyclic antidepressant A category of antidepressant medications that inhibit reuptake of the neurotransmitters serotonin and norepinephrine.

Trust versus mistrust According to Erikson, the first stage in psychosocial development, which involves developing a sense that the world is supportive and safe. This stage occurs between birth and approximately 18 months.

Tympanic membrane A membrane that vibrates in response to the funneled sound waves. Also called the eardrum.

Type A personality A personality pattern characterized by individuals that are usually in a rush and respond to increased stress by working more, competing harder, or with aggression. Type A's have a higher incidence of heart attacks, ulcers, and other stress-related diseases.

Type B personality A personality pattern characterized by individuals who are more relaxed and patient. They allow stress to "roll off their backs" and are generally less driven.

Unconditional positive regard The acceptance and appreciation of an individual, faults and all. Unconditional positive regard was proposed by humanist Carl Rogers and is a critical component of client-centered therapy.

Unconditioned response (UCR) In classical conditioning, an unlearned reaction caused by an unconditioned stimulus.

Unconditioned Stimulus (UCS) In classical conditioning, something in the environment that causes an unlearned reaction including physiological reflexes.

Unconscious According to Freud, the level of the mind that contains hidden thoughts, wishes, memories, and feelings that an individual cannot bring into conscious awareness. The unconscious is mainly filled with unacceptable sexual or aggressive thoughts and wishes and unresolved conflicts from childhood that could result in personality difficulties for individuals.

Unconsciousness The state in which an individual has no sense of who they are and are not experiencing thought or responding to the environment. Individuals in a coma or under the influence of anesthesia are in a state of unconsciousness.

Undifferentiated schizophrenia Axis I psychological disorder and subtype of schizophrenia characterized by those who do not exhibit a pattern of symptoms that fits any of the subtypes of schizophrenia. A patient may have highly organized delusions or motor disorders, but not to the extent that he or she is considered either a paranoid or a catatonic schizophrenic.

Universal grammar The commonalities in basic underlying structure of all human languages proposed by linguist Noam Chomsky.

Validity The ability of a test to measure what it is designed to measure or, in other words, accuracy.

Variable-interval A reinforcement schedule in operant conditioning in which reinforcement is given for the first correct response after a changing period of time has occurred.

Variable-ratio A reinforcement schedule in operant conditioning in which reinforcement is given after a changing number of correct behaviors have occurred.

Ventromedial hypothalamus The region of the hypothalamus responsible for stopping hunger; stimulation of this region in animals will depress hunger and destruction of this region in animal's brain results in overeating behavior.

Vestibular sense The sense that helps one keep his or her balance by providing information about changes in body position in relation to gravity. Also called equilibrium.

Virtual reality therapy The use of three-dimensional computer programs to assist patients in treatment.

Visual acuity The ability to notice fine details in images or clarity of vision.

Visual capture The tendency to focus primarily on information from the sense of vision if conflicting information from other senses is being received.

Visual cliff An apparatus designed to examine if depth perception exists in newborn animals and infants who have just learned to crawl. The visual cliff consists of a glass-topped table that creates the illusion of a drop-off on one side.

Volley theory The theory that the perception of high-pitch sounds requires the activity of multiple neurons working together.

Wavelength The distance between the peak of one wave and the peak of the next wave.

Weber's law The formula for determining the just noticeable difference that states that the minimum amount of change needed to create a just noticeable difference is a constant percentage of the original stimulus. Larger stimuli require greater increases in intensity for a difference to be noticed.

Weber's law is effective for predicting the JND for most senses over a wide range of intensities, but it does not work as well for extremes.

Wernicke's aphasia A neurological condition that occurs as a result of damage to Wernicke's area in the left temporal lobe. Individuals have problems understanding language in others and/or producing meaningful speech.

Withdrawal The unpleasant physical symptoms that result if the addict stops taking the drug associated with substance dependence. Withdrawal symptoms vary depending on the drug and often include cold sweats, vomiting, convulsions, hallucinations, depressed mood, and anxiety.

Womb envy According to Horney, the unconscious desire by some men to be able to have the ability to give birth.

Word salad A type of thought disturbance associated with schizophrenia involving speech in which the words that are selected have little or no meaning or connection to each other, making it impossible to understand the individual.

Working memory model According to Baddeley, the theory that there is a central executive that controls and directs attention through a visuospatial sketchpad (visual picture) and phonological loop (verbal rehearsal).

Yerkes–Dodson law The theory that an optimal level of psychological arousal helps performance. On simple tasks, performance is better if arousal levels are somewhat higher and on difficult tasks performance is best if arousal levels are slightly lower. People are thus motivated to seek a moderate level of stimulation that is neither too easy nor too hard.

Young–Helmholtz trichromatic theory of color vision See *trichromatic theory of color vision.*

Zone of proximal development According to Vygotsky, the difference between what children are capable of learning and doing without assistance, and what they can accomplish with the extra help provided by others.

Zygote A single-celled organism containing the genetic information contributed by each parent.

Index

NOTES

NOTES